MARITIME HISTORY SERIES

Series Editor

John B. Hattendorf, *Naval War College*

Volumes Published in this Series

Pietro Martire d'Anghiera, et al.
The history of travayle in the West and East Indies (1577)
Introduction by Thomas R. Adams,
John Carter Brown Library

Alvise Cà da Mosto
Questa e una opera necessaria a tutti li naviga[n]ti (1490)
bound with:
Pietro Martire d'Anghiera
Libretto de tutta la navigatione de Re de Spagna (1504)
Introduction by Felipe Fernández-Armesto,
Oxford University

Martín Cortés
The arte of navigation (1561)
Introduction by D. W. Waters,
National Maritime Museum, Greenwich

John Davis
The seamans secrets (1633)
Introduction by A. N. Ryan, University of Liverpool

Francisco Faleiro
Tratado del esphera y del arte del marear (1535)
Introduction by Onesimo Almeida, Brown University

Gemma, Frisius
De principiis astronomiae & cosmographiae (1553)
Introduction by C. A. Davids, University of Leiden

Tobias Gentleman
Englands way to win wealth, and to employ ships and marriners (1614)
bound with:
Robert Kayll
The trades increase (1615)
and
Dudley Digges
The defence of trade (1615)
and
Edward Sharpe
Britaines busse (1615)
Introduction by John B. Hattendorf, Naval War College

Pedro de Medina
L'art de naviguer (1554)
Introduction by Carla Rahn Phillips, University of Minnesota

Jean Taisnier
A very necessarie and profitable booke concerning navigation (1585?)
Introduction by Uwe Schnall,
Deutsches Schiffahrtsmuseum, Bremerhaven

Lodovico de Varthema
Die ritterlich un[d] lobwirdig Rayss (1515)
Introduction by George Winius, University of Leiden

Gerrit de Veer
The true and perfect description of three voyages (1609)
Introduction by Stuart M. Frank, Kendall Whaling Museum

The true and perfect description of three voyages

(1609)

Gerrit de Veer

A Facsimile Reproduction
With an Introduction by

STUART M. FRANK

Published for the
JOHN CARTER BROWN LIBRARY
by
SCHOLARS' FACSIMILES & REPRINTS
DELMAR, NEW YORK
1993

SCHOLARS' FACSIMILES & REPRINTS
ISSN 0161-7729
SERIES ESTABLISHED 1936
VOLUME 478

New matter in this edition
© 1993 Academic Resources Corporation
All rights reserved

Printed and made in the United States of America

The publication of this work was assisted by a grant from the
National Endowment for the Humanities,
an agency of the Federal government

The first work in this volume
is reproduced from a copy in,
and with the permission of,
the John Carter Brown Library
at Brown University

The second work in this volume
was originally issued by the
Hakluyt Society in London, 1876,
and is reproduced here with
permission of the Society

Library of Congress Cataloging-in-Publication Data

Veer, Gerrit de.

[Waarachtige beschrijving . . . . English]
A true and perfect description of three voyages /
Gerrit de Veer ;
a facsimile reproduction with an introduction
by Stuart M. Frank.
p.   cm. —
(Scholars' Facsimiles & Reprints, ISSN 0161-7729 ; v. 478)
Originally published: London : T. Pauier, 1609.
Includes bibliographical references.
ISBN 0-8201-1478-2
1. Northeast Passage.
2. Barentsz, Willem, ca. 1550-1597.
3. Heemskerk, Jacob van, 1567-1607.
I. Title.
G690   1564.V3913   1993
910'.916324—dc20   93-7016
CIP

VEER, GERRIT DE.

The true and perfect description of three voyages, so strange and woonderfull, that the like hath neuer been heard of before: done and performed three yeares, one after the other, by the ships of Holland and Zeland, on the north sides of Norway, Muscouia and Tartaria, towards the kingdomes of Cathaia & China; shewing the discouerie of the straights of Weigates, Noua Zembla, and the countrie lying vnder 80. degrees; which is thought to be Greenland ...

Imprinted at London for T. Pauier. 1609.

Collation: 18 cm. (4to): A^{2}B-X^4 (X4 blank). [164] p.

Notes: Translation, by William Phillip, of: Waerachtighe beschrijvinghe van drie seylangien. Author's name taken from title of 1st edition.

References: JCB Lib. cat., pre-1675, II, p. 67; Alden, J.E. *European Americana*, 609/127.

JCB Library copy: Acq: 07330. Acquired before 1874. This copy lacks last leaf (blank). Call number: F609 V419t [R].

Tracings: 1. Arctic regions. 2. Northeast Passage. 3. Voyages and travels. 4. Barentsz, Willem, d. ca. 1550-1597. 5. Heemskerk, Jacob van, 1567-1607. I. Phillip, William, fl. 1600. II. Title.

Introduction

Of all the explorers and adventurers to navigate high latitudes under the Dutch tricolor, Willem Barents[1] is the one most closely associated with the blossoming of Dutch commerce and culture in the seventeenth-century Golden Age. Henry Hudson's name is better known; but Hudson's greatest discoveries were made in the service of England and had the ultimate effect of perpetuating the futile, centuries-long British romance with conquest of the Northwest Passage. Jan Huyghens van Linschoten's name also figures prominently in the annals of Dutch Arctic exploration, as it was he who trumpeted with boosterist fervor—in flowery, pious prose that was translated into a half-dozen languages—the cheerful prospects for an Arctic route to China that never materialized. But thanks to the modest chronicle written by Gerrit de Veer, the Arctic voyages in which Barents, Linschoten, and De Veer participated in the 1590s had a different effect in Holland, curtailing any potential fixation on northern passages to the Orient and directing Dutch economic and maritime prowess into more practical and more fruitful channels.

The analogies are many between Barents's three voyages and the voyage of Christopher Columbus a century earlier. Like their Spanish precursors, the Dutch intended to establish a viable route to China; and like Columbus, the Dutch failed in their primary objective, in three attempts coming no closer to the Orient than the day they sailed. However, like the Columbus voyages, the Dutch experience in the Arctic resulted in unprecedented discoveries and in unanticipated consequences affecting the course of commerce and the course of empire for centuries afterward; and, as with the Columbus voyages, these secondary successes were largely credited to the dedication, stamina, and personal resourcefulness of a single, larger-than-life individual whose leadership posthumously achieved the stature of paradigm.

INTRODUCTION

The Arctic expeditions came at a propitious moment for Holland. Less than two decades earlier, in 1576, the conclusion of a bitter religious Reformation had solidified Dutch intellectual and spiritual independence from Spain; and scarcely six years had passed since the defeat of the Armada demonstrated the ultimate vulnerability of Spanish suzerainty over the United Provinces. Now, in 1594, poised on the brink of a magnificent cultural and commercial florescence, Holland was engaged in a protracted struggle for social, political, and economic independence. While political independence would only be achieved in stages, culminating in 1648, the struggle itself was premised on the commercial viability of the seaborne economy from which Dutch wealth and self-sufficiency increasingly derived.

One venue of Dutch ascendency on the high seas was to be the East Indies trade; the other would be the northern fisheries, and it is here that the significance of Barents's voyages resides. For by 1594, the allure of the Orient was already strong in the Netherlands. Ten years before, the Brussels entrepreneur Olivier Brunel had made a foray into the White Sea; and while he failed to discover a Northeast Passage to China, his voyage had fueled the now-flourishing Russian trade.

It was to reach the Orient that the Dutch merchants proposed to carry through Brunel's plan. But when the Barents voyages made it apparent that the search for a Northeast Passage was doomed to failure, they were able to make something profitable out of what Barents did find. For he had made meticulous observations, charting new islands and seas, reporting the presence and specific location of whales and walruses, and even testing the mettle of his crew through the ravages of an Arctic winter ashore. When the great Hudson retraced the route to Nova Zemlya a decade later, he confirmed the accuracy of Barents's findings and ratified Barents's reputation as a visionary navigator and dauntless champion. By the time it was over, the Dutch had become experts at navigating northern waters, had trained a generation of ice-pilots, and had secured for themselves an option on a frozen empire that they were uniquely able to exploit. It may be said of the northern fisheries, as it has of the Dutch reclamation of land from the sea, that

INTRODUCTION

few societies and few epochs in history have been able to make so much of so little, or been so ready to capitalize upon whatever opportunities might fortuitously present themselves.

On the surface it may seem remarkable that it was Barents—rather than any of the greater luminaries that were involved—whose name is principally attached to these Arctic voyages. Contrary to nearly universal popular belief, Barents had nothing to do with conceiving the project and was not himself in actual charge of any of the expeditions.[2] He was not a prominent merchant nor even (until the three Arctic voyages) a mariner of any particular distinction. He was neither one of the project organizers nor one of its spokesmen at court. He wrote no book or journal recounting his experiences; in fact, writings attributed to him are scarce and of controversial authenticity.[3] He came from humble parentage on the remote West Frisian island of Terschelling, and he was almost the only one among a distinguished roster of captains, pilots, and supercargoes who did not come from the clubby seafaring aristocracy of Enkhuizen. Even chronicler Gerrit de Veer, a mere subaltern on the second and third voyages, had family connections at court and a brother who was a city councilor of Amsterdam and minister plenipotentiary to King James I of England.

However, as it turned out, Barents was the only one of the principals to participate in all three voyages; it was his incisive observations and relentlessly accurate recording of topographical and navigational details that resulted in highly developed maps and greatly improved practical knowledge of the Arctic region;[4] and it was his persistence, tenacity, and skill that came to epitomize the heroic ordeals of the third voyage with its forced wintering-over on Nova Zemlya. Barents's martyrdom at the moment of triumph seems to have elevated him in the public imagination—as more violent circumstances did Magellan, Hudson, Cook, and Franklin—to the level of the near-legendary, a figure of tragic dimensions who, nevertheless, remains untainted by the kind of culpability for their own tragic fates with which those others have been indicted.

Ironically, Barents's participation in the Arctic voyages was something of an afterthought. The idea for the first expedition

INTRODUCTION

originated with a group of merchants in Middelburg, in the southerly province of Zeeland, and their counterparts in Enkhuizen, on the Zuider Zee, where North Holland meets Friesland. In the wake of Brunel, they proposed to find and traverse the elusive Northeast Passage by sailing north from Holland, then northeast and east around Nova Zemlya, and through uncharted seas adjacent to what is now known to be the Siberian Arctic. Two ships of about 100 tons each were fitted out, one representing each of the parties. The Middelburg vessel was *the Swane* ("Swan"), from the nearby port of Veere, commanded by Cornelis Cornelisz Nay (or Nai) of Enkhuizen. The other was the *Mercurius* ("Mercury") of Enkhuizen, commanded by Brant Ysbrantsz Tetgales of Enkhuizen. Only after the plan was fully hatched were they joined in this ambitious venture by merchants of Amsterdam, who were evidently loath to be left out of what they saw as an opportunity to improve trade with the Russian North while opening a route to the riches of the Orient. Accordingly, a third vessel was added, also named *Mercurius*[5] and also measuring about 100 tons, representing Amsterdam. This second *Mercurius* was given to the command of Willem Barents, late of Friesland. Cornelis Cornelisz Nay was designated commander-in-chief or "admiral" of the expedition as a whole, making Barents on all counts third in the pecking order.

Assigned to each of the Zeeland and Enkhuizen ships were also two classes of wardroom officers who exercised considerable authority in all substantive matters pertaining to the voyage: a pilot, entrusted with the fine points of navigation and seamanship, thereby precluding any necessary expertise on the part of the captain (as the third voyage would reveal); and a supercargo, the commercial agent of the merchant-owners charged with protecting and promoting their interests. Both of the pilots were professional seamen from Enkhuizen, Pieter Dircksz Stickbolle on the *Swane* and Claes Cornelisz on the *Mercurius* of Enkhuizen. François de la Dale represented the Zeeland merchants as supercargo aboard the *Swane,* while the supercargo on the *Mercurius* was Jan Huygens Linschoten, whose responsibilities included keeping a journal of the voyage. No supercargo was assigned to the *Mercurius* of Amsterdam, and Barents also served as his own pilot and navigator, which testifies to the confidence the Amsterdam

INTRODUCTION

owners must have had in his ability despite his having "never commanded an expedition, and this was the only occasion when he sailed to the Arctic as a captain."[6]

It was on this first voyage that the first monumental discovery was made. Its significance seems to have been intuited by De Veer,[7] but, as it had little relevance to the stated objective of discovering an Arctic route to China, it could not have been fully appreciated by the merchants and supercargoes at the time. On 7 July 1594 at Willems Island, in 75° 55′ North latitude on the northwest coast of Nova Zemlya, "they found great store of driff-wood [sic], and many sea-horses [walruses], being a kinde of fish [sic] that keepeth in the sea, having very great teeth, which at this day are vsed insteed of iuorie or elephants teeth."[8] About three weeks later, around 77° North in the pack ice at the northeast extremity of Nova Zemlya, they encountered great numbers of walrus; and De Veer adopts the occasion to expound rapturously upon the creatures themselves and their potential value on the Russian market:

> . . . Vpon the 31 of July got to the Islands of Orange. And there went to one of those islands, where they found about 200 walrushen or sea-horses, lying upon the shoare to baste [bask] themselues in the sunne. The sea-horse is a wonderfull strong monster of the sea, much bigger than an oxe, which keepes continually in the seas, halling a skinne like a sea-calfe or seale, with very short hair, mouthed like a lyon, and many times they lye vpon the ice; they are hardly killed vnlesse you strike them iust vpon the forehead; it hath foure feet, but no eares, and commonly it hath one or two young ones at a time. And when the fisher-men chance to find them vpon a flake of ice with their yong ones, shee casteth her yong ones before her into the water, and then takes them in her armes, and so plungeth vp and downe with them, and when shee will reuenge herselfs vpon the boats, or make resistance against them, then she casts her yong ones from her agains, and with all her force goeth towards the boate: whereby our men were once in no small danger, for that the seahorse had almost striken her teeth into the steme of their boate, thinking to ouerthrowe it; but by means of the great cry the men made, shee was afraid, and swomme away agains, and tooke her yong ones agains in her armes. They haue

INTRODUCTION

two teeth sticking out of their mouthes, on each side one, each beeing aboute halfe an elle long, and are esteemed to bee as good as any iuorie or elophants teeth, specially in Muscouia, Tartaria, and there abouts where they are knowne, for they are as white, hard, and euen as iuory.[9]

It was only later, in retrospect, after Hudson had corroborated Barents's observations and the quest for a Northeast Passage was finally abandoned, that Dutch merchants came to recognize the opportunities implicit in De Veer's chronicle. It was for oil rather than ivory that Holland would mount annual forays into the Arctic to harvest the bountiful supply of walruses and whales that Barents and Hudson had inadvertently discovered. And within its first decade, by 1620, this so-called "little fishery" (*kleine visscherij*)—along with the "great fishery" (*groote visscherij*), the herring fishery—would become a cornerstone of Dutch activity in northern waters. There, well-seasoned Dutch navigators and pilots, familiar with the territory and confident of their capabilities, for a century and a half outshone all other contenders.

The first voyage was also distinguished by the fleet's initial penetration of waters east of Nova Zemlya, a necessary prerequisite to the projected sea-route to the Orient, but little else of consequence resulted beyond the promise and expectation of better things to come. The inevitable forebodings of disaster had been set to rest and practical knowledge of the region improved, but no remarkable discoveries of open water were made, no trade relations with Russia strengthened, and no Northeast Passage to China revealed. While in other circumstances the entire enterprise might have been judged a failure and scrapped, Linschoten's over-optimistic report, based on his journal, was evidently sufficient to garner the support of Prince Mauritz and the States General of the United Provinces to mount a second expedition in larger ships in the spring of the following year.

Accordingly, in June 1595 six ships sailed in company on the same mission, two from each of the three provinces. A seventh vessel, an anonymous 40-ton yacht of Rotterdam, was also sent along for the purpose of carrying home the good news once the fleet had successfully navigated the Northeast Passage. The flotilla was again

INTRODUCTION

placed in charge of Cornelis Cornelisz Nay, this time sailing for Zeeland in the *Griffoen* ("Griffon"), about 200 tons. The other Zeeland ship was the *Swane* of Veere (which had been Nay's command on the previous outing) under Captain Lambert Gerritsz Oom of Enkhuizen. Brant Ysbrantsz Tetgales, who on the first expedition had skippered the 100-ton *Mercurius,* was now given the *Hoope* ("Hope") of Enkhuizen, 200 tons, and was designated vice admiral. The *Mercurius,* now commanded by Thomas Willemsz, was the other Enkhuizen ship. The Amsterdam contingent was led by Willem Barents in the *Winthont* (literally, *wind-hound,* "Greyhound"), 200 tons; Cornelis Jacobsz served as his sub-captain and De Veer was one of his officers. Barents was also designated Chief Pilot of the expedition, again making him third in the hierarchy. His former command on the previous voyage, the *Mercurius* of Amsterdam, was now consigned to Harman Jansz. Hendrik Hartman, skipper of the nameless Rotterdam yacht, completed the roster of captains.

With Chief Pilot Barents in general charge of navigation, the owners evidently found it unnecessary to bestow much individual authority upon the pilots assigned to the other vessels, but supercargoes were much in evidence. François de la Dale represented the Zeeland merchants for the second time, along with one N. Buys. In addition to Linschoten, the veteran of the previous expedition who played such an important part in promoting this second voyage, the supercargoes for Holland and Friesland were Jacob van Heemskerck and Jan Cornelisz Rijp, both of them distinguished scions of the merchant aristocracy.

The results of the second voyage were disappointing, and this time the failure was evidently sufficient to cool Linschoten's ardor and discourage the States General from further direct participation. But while the government declined to subsidize outright a third campaign, partly owing to the favorable recommendation of Petrus Plancius[10] they "encouraged" the merchants to mount their own privately-financed venture by posting a prize for its successful completion.

As long as they were financing the trip without government support, the owners were determined to have their interests protected. The influence of supercargoes had increased over the previous two

INTRODUCTION

outings, but on the third voyage they were actually put in charge. The surviving records consequently reflect a certain deficiency in the kinds of nautical detail that one would ordinarily expect to find indelibly attached to a serious expedition of seaborne discovery—at the very least providing the names and tonnage of the ships, and the names, ranks, and ratings of the participants. This time there were only two vessels, and the names and tonnages are not recorded. Both were placed under the command of men who had served on the previous voyage as supercargoes, Jacob van Heemskerck and Jan Cornelisz Rijp, each of whom was given the titles Master and Supercargo. Neither was a seaman by profession and neither was really qualified to undertake so dangerous a voyage in uncharted waters. Barents was placed aboard Heemskerck's lead vessel with the title Master Pilot, again relegating him to third rank among the principals; De Veer was evidently second mate in the same ship. Fortunately, Heemskerck turned out to be a capable manager aware of Barents's superior qualifications and experience and seems regularly to have deferred to Barents's judgment.

The two ships set sail in the spring of 1596 on what would turn out to be the most productive and, for one of them, the most harrowing of the three voyages. Almost from the start disputes arose between the pilots as to what course to follow and what strategy to adopt. Heemskerck evidently sided with Barents, and Rijp with his own pilot, with the result that the schism between the ships deepened. They arrived in company at Bear Island in latitude 74° 30′ North on 9 June, and were still together when eleven days later they made the most significant discovery of the three voyages, sighting the "very great" land that Barents himself is credited with naming Spitsbergen ("pointy mountains"),[11] where they landed on 21 June. The archipelago is but sketchily drawn on Barents's map, where it is labeled merely "the New Land" *(Het nieuwe land)*. For many years it was thought by mariners and cartographers to be an extension of Greenland.[12]

Unable to agree on the further disposition of the voyage, on the first of July[13] the vessels parted company and sailed their separate ways. Rijp and his pilot wandered around the ice for the remainder of

INTRODUCTION

the season and, failing in any attempt to rejoin Heemskerck, returned home with little to show for their maverick tour of the Arctic.[14]

On the other hand, the fate of Heemskerck's vessel is celebrated in legend and lore. They reached the northeastern extremity of Nova Zemlya but were unable to forge an easterly path through the pack-ice, even when open water was actually in sight. The decision to return to Holland came too late. Trapped in the ice at the end of August, the party involuntarily became the first Europeans to winter in 76° North. De Veer relates in deceptively dispassionate prose the anguished details of nine dreadful months of cold and deprivation ashore on Nova Zemlya—the depredations of a sunless winter, the crew's petitions to Heemskerck that he allow them to prepare an escape come spring, and their eventual flight in open boats—which is justly referred to in superlative terms as "one of the most remarkable achievements in polar annals."[15] The voyagers scratched their way southward along the primeval coast sustained by food obtained from Russian fishermen. Finally, on 21 September 1597, they reached Kola, where they were greeted by Jan Rijp, who had set out from Holland with a rescue party the previous spring. Heemskerck and the other survivors arrived back in Holland at the end of October; but Willem Barents, the architect of their escape and savior of the expedition, had perished in the ice the previous June, exactly one year after the discovery of Spitsbergen.

On three occasions in successive years, little flotillas had ventured out from the secure harbors and quiet canals of the Dutch provinces, navigating flimsy ships into a howling wilderness. Their purpose had been to pioneer a route to the Orient through uncharted waters, thereby circumventing restrictions that had been imposed on their trade by Spain and England, and securing their own manifest destiny through maritime prowess. When it was over, they had failed to find China but had secured an Arctic empire of oil and fish which alone would have been sufficient to sustain their livelihood indefinitely. In tandem with the brilliant successes of the East India trade and lesser enterprises in the West Indies, South America, and Africa, the northern fisheries—the true heir and most tangible result of the Barents voyages—created wealth and stability on a scale

INTRODUCTION

comparable to Renaissance Venice, with a kindred burgeoning of the arts, architecture, science, and learning. This Golden Age would last as long as the northern fisheries could be made profitable, more than a century and a half; and in this nation of mariners, Willem Barents would ever be counted among its most venerated heroes.[16]

A Note on the Illustrations

The original Amsterdam edition of de Veer, printed by C. Claeszoon in 1598, and its 1599 re-issue also printed by C. Claeszoon, included superbly engraved illustrations. The early editions in other Continental languages generally used re-engraved plates of reduced size and/or degraded quality, and the first English edition of 1609, which is reproduced in this volume, was issued with no illustrations at all.

As a helpful supplement to the English edition, which we have reprinted in facsimile here, we have added, immediately following this introduction, reproductions of all 32 of the fascinating illustrations found in the sixteenth-century Dutch editions, in this case taken from the John Carter Brown Library copy of the Amsterdam 1599 edition.

The Hakluyt Society reprint of 1876, also reproduced in this facsimile volume, contained only a sampling of the complete set of illustrations that appeared in the Amsterdam editions of 1598 and 1599.

Further Reading

The introductory essays by Charles T. Beke and Lieutenant Koolemans Beynen in the 1876 Hakluyt Society edition of Gerrit de Veer's narrative remain, even after almost a century and a half, the most comprehensive and authoritative treatments of the literary and historical circumstances surrounding the Barents voyage.

Apart from the Hakluyt Society productions, the literature in English on the search for a Northeast passage is spotty. A great deal has been written about Frobisher and Hudson, for example, but I am

INTRODUCTION

particularly fond of a rather scholarly and beautifully literate popular history by Ernest S. Dodge, late director of the Peabody Museum of Salem, Massachusetts. Entitled *Northwest by Sea* (New York: Oxford University Press, 1961), it examines the Frobisher and Barents voyages in the larger context of Arctic exploration, and provides a concise introduction to the more protracted search for a route to the Pacific through Arctic Canada.

Still, by far the most compelling and revealing treatise on high-latitude exploration is a masterpiece by the distinguished Canadian historian and social theorist Pierre Berton, *The Arctic Grail: The Quest for the North West Passage and the North Pole, 1818-1909* (New York: Viking, 1988). While its specific relation to Barents and the Northeast Passage is only tangential, *The Arctic Grail* subtly discerns the quintessentially irrational impulses that drove the Arctic conquistadors and their sponsors, and exposes the bureaucratic obstacles, militaristic foibles, and ethnocentric conceits by which such expeditions have ever been plagued.

Finally, David Roberts's *Great Exploration Hoaxes* (San Francisco: Sierra Club, 1982), which has nothing whatever directly to do with Barents or the Northeast Passage, is a perfect complement to *The Arctic Grail*, imparting an appropriate caveat about the illusory nature of the goals for which men strive and the often fraudulent nature of the men who have striven.

STUART M. FRANK
Kendall Whaling Museum

INTRODUCTION

NOTES

1. The surname, which is spelled in various ways, is actually the patronymic Barentszoon or Barendtszoon and has been rendered in such English and Scandinavian forms as Barentson, Berendsen, etc. There is generally great variation in the spelling of seventeenth-century Dutch and Flemish personal and place names and usage is irregular even within the essays in the Hakluyt editions of De Veer's narrative. An attempt has been made here to render names consistently, wherever possible avoiding judgments on orthographic propriety. However, the choice of the English and modern Dutch form *Barents* over the older Dutch forms *Barendsz* and *Barentsz* is clearly one of convention over philology.

2. Even the article on Willem Barents in the classic eleventh edition of the *Encyclopedia Britannica* (3:397), which was published long after the Hakluyt Society's reprints of the De Veer narrative (see below) and which cites De Veer as the authoritative source on the Barents voyages, fails to recognize that Barents was not actually in charge of any of the expeditions. The author fails to mention Cornelis Nay or Jacob van Heemskerck at all, and falls into the popular trap of blithely assuming that Barents was the commander of all three voyages.

3. See relevant listings under Barents in the Index of Charles T. Beke and Lt. Koolemans Beynen, eds., *The Three Voyages of William Barents to the Arctic Regions (1594, 1595, and 1596)*, 2d ed. (London: Hakluyt Society, [1853] 1876) (cited hereafter as Hakluyt).

4. The Arctic map is presumed to have been drawn by Barents at his winter quarters on Nova Zemlya and carried back by Heemskerck. The Nova Zemlya map was drawn or redrawn by De Veer based on Willem Barents's observations. Both were engraved by Baptists van Doetechum [Baptista à Doetechum] (fl. 1588-1633) as illustrations for the first edition of De Veer's chronicle (1598).

5. Also known as the *Messenger* (see Hakluyt, p. *cv*, fn. 1), which Dodge insists is incorrect (Ernest S. Dodge, *Northwest by Sea* [New York: Oxford University Press, 1961], p. vii).

6. Dodge, p. 47.

7. De Veer did not go on the first voyage, but presents detailed particulars gathered after the fact, from eyewitnesses and from his own experience on subsequent voyages.

8. De Veer, First Voyage, 7 July 1594 (Hakluyt, p. 14).

9. De Veer, First Voyage, 31 July 1594 (Hakluyt, p. 25).

INTRODUCTION

10. Petrus Plancius (1552-1622), a celebrated Flemish theologian, cartographer, and mapmaker for the Dutch East India Company, was an adherent of the theory advocating an open polar sea and thus a proponent of the possibility of navigating across the northern perimeter of Asia to China. He prepared the maps for Linschoten's narrative, published in 1596. Baptista van Doetechum, who engraved Barents's maps for the De Veer narrative in 1598, and other members of the Doetechum family of engravers were sometime employees and associates of Plancius.

11. Hakluyt, p. xx.

12. The speculation that Barents may even have circumnavigated Spitsbergen or perhaps one of the larger islands in the archipelago (Hakluyt, p. cxxx) seems unlikely given De Veer's silence in that quarter and Barents's topographically equivocal representation of "*Het nieuwe land*" on his Arctic map.

13. Not "the 1st of June," as erroneously stated in Hakluyt, p. cxxxi.

14. Hakluyt, pp. cxxxi-cxxxii.

15. Hugh Robert Mill, "Geography," *Encyclopedia Britannica*, 11th ed., 21:626.

16. Barents's name is memorialized in the expansive branch of the Arctic Ocean that Barents first charted and in a half-dozen other geographical features of the Barents Sea region. *Willem Barents* was also the name of the research schooner that revisited the Arctic seven times for scientific purposes during 1878-84 (see W. F. J. Mörzer Bruyns, ed., *De eerste tocht van de Willem Barents naar de Noordelijke IJszee, 1878* [2 vols., Zutphen: De Walburg, 1985]) and both of the Netherlands's floating-factory whaleships, which were placed in service in 1946 and 1955, respectively, to prosecute whaling in the polar seas around Antarctica. In a similar spirit, the modern research vessel that carried teams of archaeologists and historians on several forays to Spitsbergen and Jan Mayen Island in the 1980s was named *Plancius*.

Waerachtighe Beschrijvinghe

Van drie seylagien / ter werelt noyt soo vreemt ghehoort/

die jaeren achter malcanderen deur de Hollandtsche ende Zeelandtsche schepen by noorden Noorweghen/Moscovia ende Tartaria/na de Coninckrijcken van Catthai ende China, soo mede van de vermaninghe van de Weygats, Nova Sembla, en van 't Landt op de 80. graden/ dat men acht Groenlandt te zijn/ daer noyt mensch ghewest is/ ende bande selle verschrickende Beyren ende ander Zee-monsters ende ondjachtsische houde/ ende hoe op de laerste reyse t'schip int ys beset is/ ende tvolck op rieyne schuyten over ende langs der Zee ghevaren. Alles met seer grooten perijckel/ moeyten ende ongeloosselijcke swaricheyt. Ghedaen deur Gerrit de Veer van Amstelredam.

NAVARCHVS HOLLANDVS

SAMI VTA

Ghedruckt t'Amstelredam, by Cornelis Claesz, op 't Water, in 't Schrijf-boeck, A°. 1599.

Dese Caerte bewijst de seylagie van Kildupn totte Eylant van Orangien/soo verde Willem Barentsz. oon de eerste reyse gheseylt heeft tot zijn wederkeer/daer in de Haven van Lom bs bay leyt/die zyn naem vande vogels heeft die daer op in menichte houden/groot van lichaem/cleyn van vleughels/ also dat te verwonderen is dat de cleyne vleughels dat swaer lichaem draghen connen. Sy hebben haer nesten op steyle berghen/om vande vossen beschermt te zijn. Broeden maer een Ey teffens. Door de menschen waren se niet verschrickt/al greepmen se op haer nest: so vloghen d'ander daer ontrent effenwel niet wech.

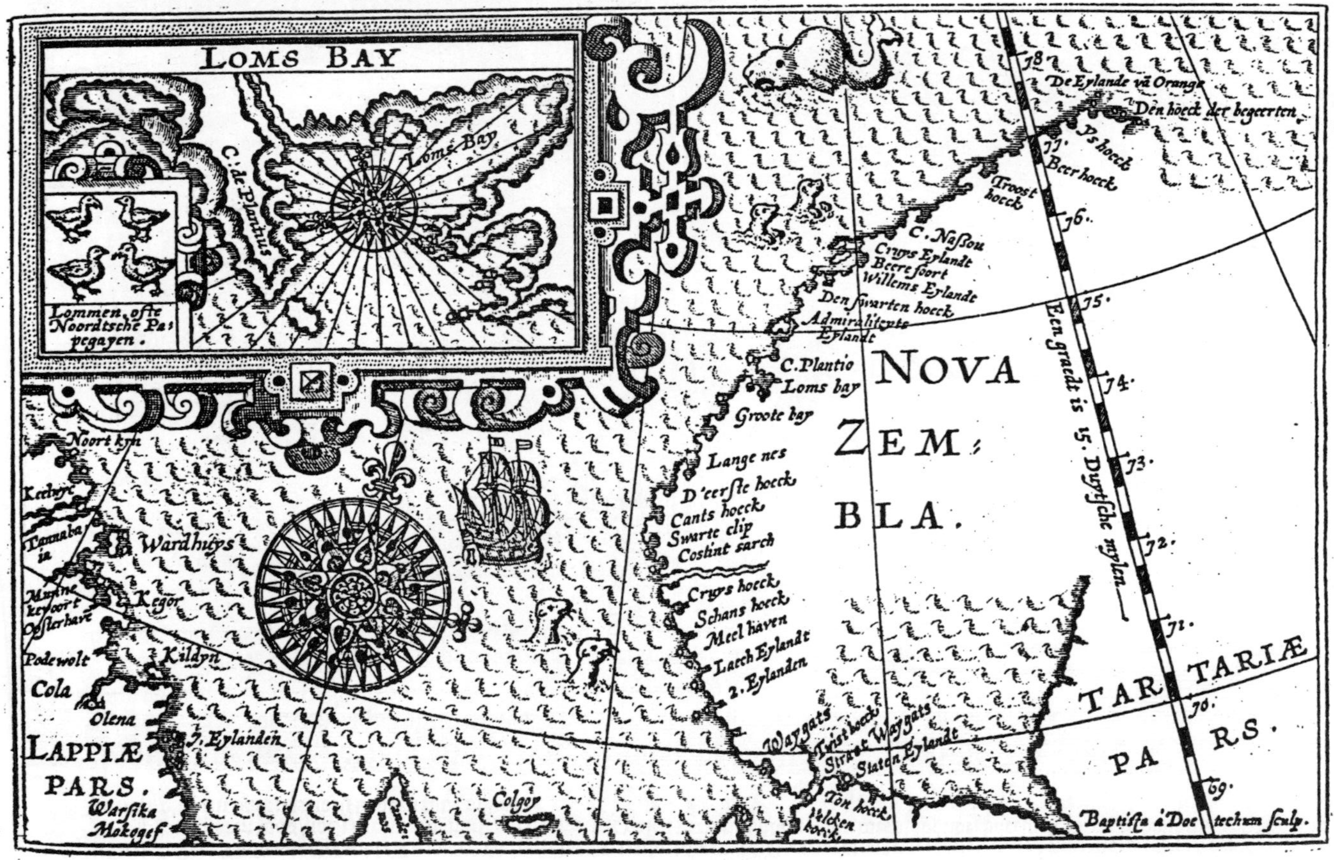

Afbeeldinghe van Willems Eylandt/ Cruys Eylandt ende Beeren fort/ daer een Beer een wonderbaerlijck cracht ende moed ghetoont hadde/ Hoe wel hy gheschoten was/ noch evenwel by naest een boot met volck vernielt hadde/ naer werdt wonderbaerlijck werrghehouden/ ende t'volck verlost/ die ham nae noch booden ende pilden.

Voor dat de dier schepen wederom ontrent de Weegaets by malcanderen quamen/ Willem Barentsz. met sijn schip ende Jacht van benoorden Nova Zembla/ende de Zeelander met de Enckhuyser met de Weegats/ende haer toets wederom na huys namen/also sy maer uytghesonden waren om de gheleghentheyt/streckinghe ende coursen van de lande van Tartarien ende de Tartarische Zee te vernemen.

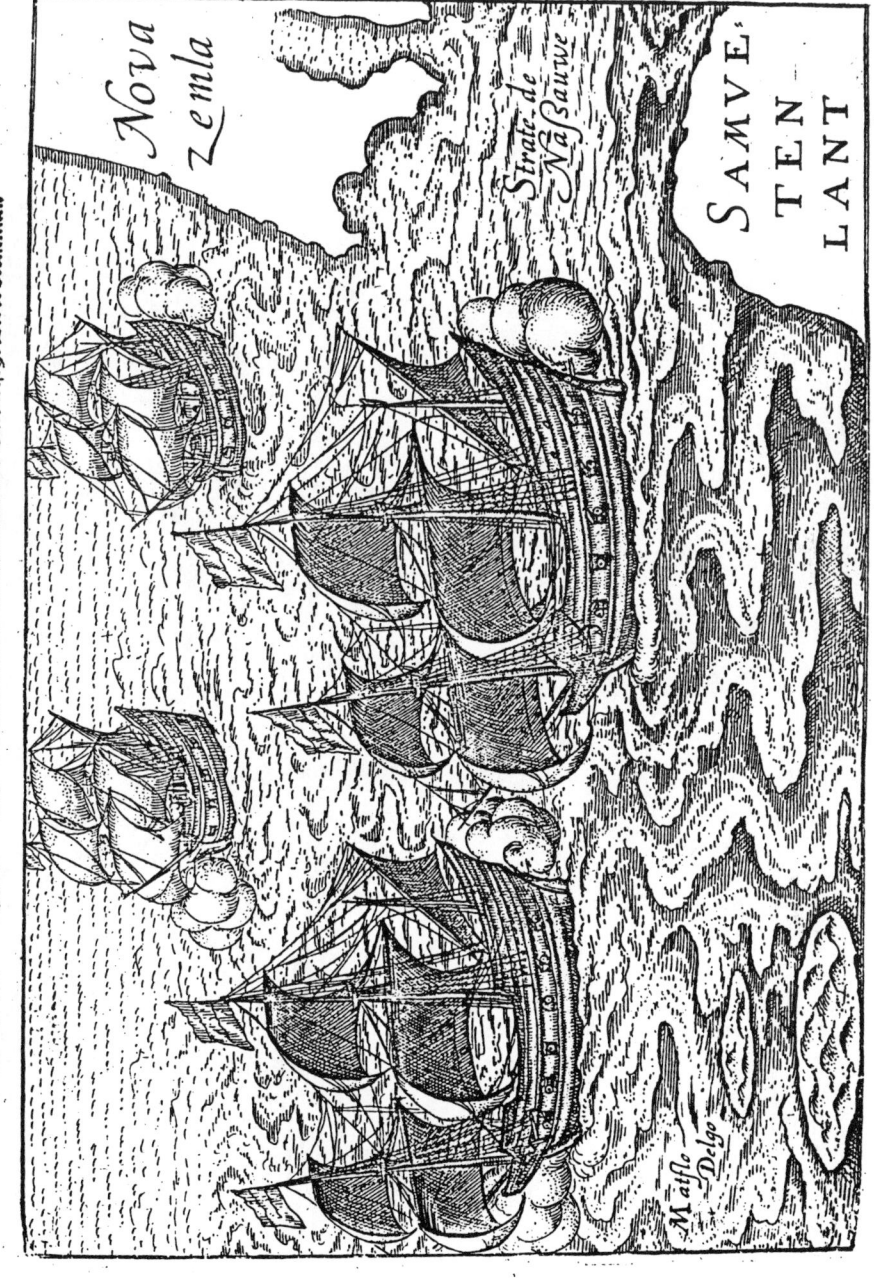

Caerte vande Tartiten ende haer Coninck, van haer ghelegentheyt, cleedinghe ende wesen, ende van haer seden, ende eenen baren der selver, met de wijse van dese boogt trecken, ende hoe ons volck munnicich met haer ghespolien, ende daer nae seer bjienbelijck vanden anderen ghescheyden zijn.

¶ Hier blijcket van de heerlijcke moort, die wt eñ weder, officieljcken, bes[ch]ictelijcken, beestlinden inden Bosch, hoe sijn thien van ons volck seer beestijck verscheurde ende hoe wp rot twee mael met gantsscher gewelt met twee en dertigh sser van boorden, ende seer langhe bombe waren doorsten, ende seer langhe bombe waren eenen sin boven conden, ende dat sp sae langhe sp lesde, hoe wel sp gewont, gequetst, ende gheslaghen was, offen wel sijn aes niet verlaten wilde.

Afbeeldinghe van een wonderlijcken Hemel/ghesien den 4. Junij/ anno 1596. den stille zyde hander Sonne schen ooch een Son/ ende daer tegen twee Reghen-boghen door alle de 3. Sonnen heuren/ ende daer nae noch twee Reghen-boghen/d'een wijt rondtomme der Sonnen/ ende d'ander dwerrs door de groote ronde/ ende sijt groote ronde stont be onderste kant verheven boven den Horizont 28. graden.

Afbeeldinghe van een wonderlijcst ghebeert/ die wy hadden tresfare een wijreden/ sellen Wey/ daer wy rwe te ropden inde Zee/ wernnde hem een strick om den hals te werpen/ maer hp sachet/ soo hresschet upt dat hy up wederom tsscherp borent/ ende haesden meer geweer/ ende bedochten hem langen tijdt met twee schuyten volcks/ ende sworden in fluchten eer wy han bemuessteren conden/ ende hier neur werdt dit Eplant daer natrent dit gheschiede/ het Beyren Eplandt ghenaemt.

Afbeeldinghe hoe dat wy ontrent de Eylanden van Spitsbergen int ys bleef sitten/ ende in groot perijckel quamen/ daer wy met naeuwer noot het schip redden/ ende hoe dat een yffelijcken Berp achter een schots passigghende/ deur ons ghetrocken waeser worden/ ende tegghens ons aen quam/ also dat wy ons wreck moesten op schorten/ ende tegghens hom te weer stellen/ ende hoe hy met grooter moeyte van ons ouerwonnen ende gheoot werde.

Afbeeldinghe hoe dat wy ontrent de ijshaven int ijs beset werden dat wy nerghens heen mochten/ende dat al onsen arbeyt te vergheefs was die wy deden om het ijs van ons te setten/om eenighe openinghe te ghecrijghen/ende hoe wy by naest drie mannen (doent ijs drijvende werdt) verloren hadden/ten ware datse met een slingher slach int drijven voorby het schip/de sintte/schoot/ende bras die uyt schip hinghen/niet ghesprongen hadden deur haer rasicheyt/ende alsoo int schip quamen/ twelck ijselijck om sien was.

J

Beteyckeninghe hoe dat tsp nae langhe moepelijck om swerven int ys vast raeckten/ dat soo ghewelvich opt schip quam dat dit dist
ghem/ dat te schem al te bersten en de in dzsen batter een ende ontrent was/ maer tees noch onderstens op/ daer deur Willem Barrents. ende sijn mact in
ghem clepn petsichel waren/ die vooz aent schip opt ps laghen om te waten hoe hoogh het schip vooz gheresen was/ waent het sat vooz gantsch om hoogh/
ende achter schzant schier inden grondt te leggghen/ ende derzijt in dat ghewoel sterrue de back up/ ende sieppen de schuyt naer 't Landt met sommighe van
ten bzoodts.

Afbeeldinghe van die Beyren die ontrent het schip quamen/ daer van de eene achter een schots ys bleef legghen/ ende d'ander twee met schip quamen/ d'eene nam een stuck ulees uit de tobben daert in te verderschen stont/ende werdt nievlercrijst ghescoten dat sy neer sloghe/ d'ander niet werrende wat sijn macker oberghecomen was/stont langhe stil ende roock hem aen/ ende liep ten lesten wech/. Daer nae quam sy weder teghen ons volcs aen/ ende rechte sich op sijn achterste poaten/om op ons aente ballen/ maer werdt middelercijst door ghescholten/ende wy rechten hem op sijn poaten/ en
hieten hem also bedrijesen.

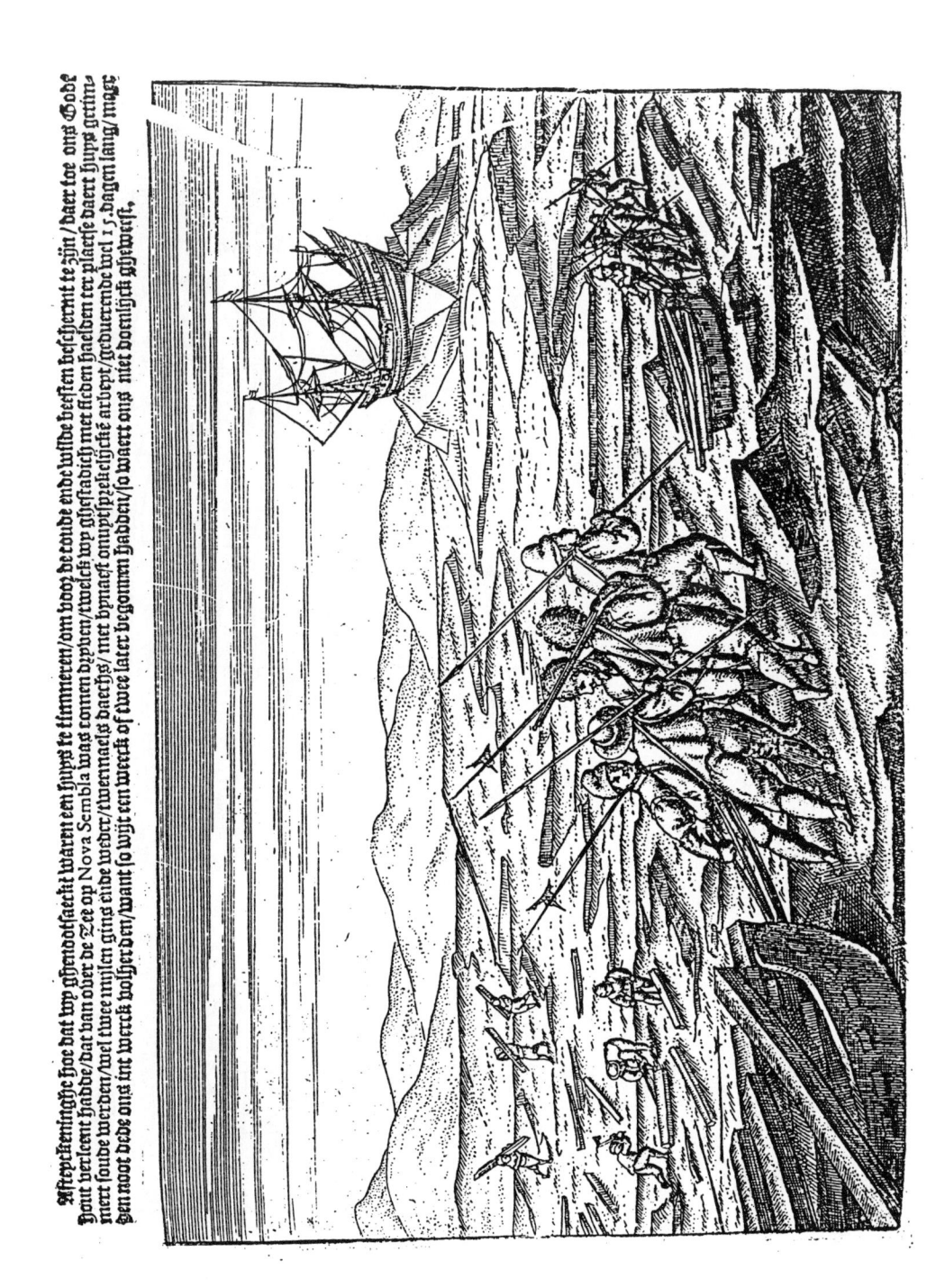

Asen vermaninghe hoe dat wy ghenoodtsaeckt waren een schips te timmeren/om voor de oude ende wilde beesten beschermt te zijn/daer toe ons God voort verleent hadde/dat van over de Zee op Nova Sembla was comen drijven/twelck wy gheschickt met sieben mesten ter plaetse daert schips ghetimmert soude werden/wel twee mijlen ginck ende weder/tweemaelts daechs/met bynaeft onuitspekelijcke arbeyt/gheduerende wel 15. dagen lang/mogen noot bede ons int werck volgherden/want so wijst een weeck of twee later begonnen hadden/so waert ons niet doenlijck gheweest.

¶ Sterckeninghe Hoe datse begonnen Het Huys te maecken/ ende thout daer toe tsamen sleepten/ ende thuys oprechtten/ daerse een schots
Peyboom op setten/ ende maecktent op de Moorsche wyse met balcken op malcanderen/ daer van sy de naden dicht bysten ofte calfaten/ om des sne=
eus ende des coudens wille/ boven meest viercant met deelen overgheleyt/ met een schoorsteen ende portael.

Afbeeldinghe Hoe dat wy inde selen stonden om de leste steede met groot uyterst schip naet thuys te bringhen/ ende datter die Beyren ontbersiens tot ons ten quamen/ daer van wy gantsch verschrickt verschickt upt de touwen sprongen/ een deel naet schip loopende / daer van de eene int wuich loopen tusschen een schots ys in viel tot sijn groot perijckel/ ende d'ander deel blijvende ontrent de Slede/hebbende maer twee hellebaerden/ die selben haer ter wer: maer hart dat de Beyren ons ander loopende holst naet schip nae liepen/soo werdt de gevallen man noch berijst/ ende quam noch met den goede hande Sle-den boven over schip noch daer in/ende de Beyren poorschen tegent schip op te coemen/ maer worpen deur werpen van brantstout en stercken hand hellebaerden affgeskaertt dat se int epnde werch liepen.

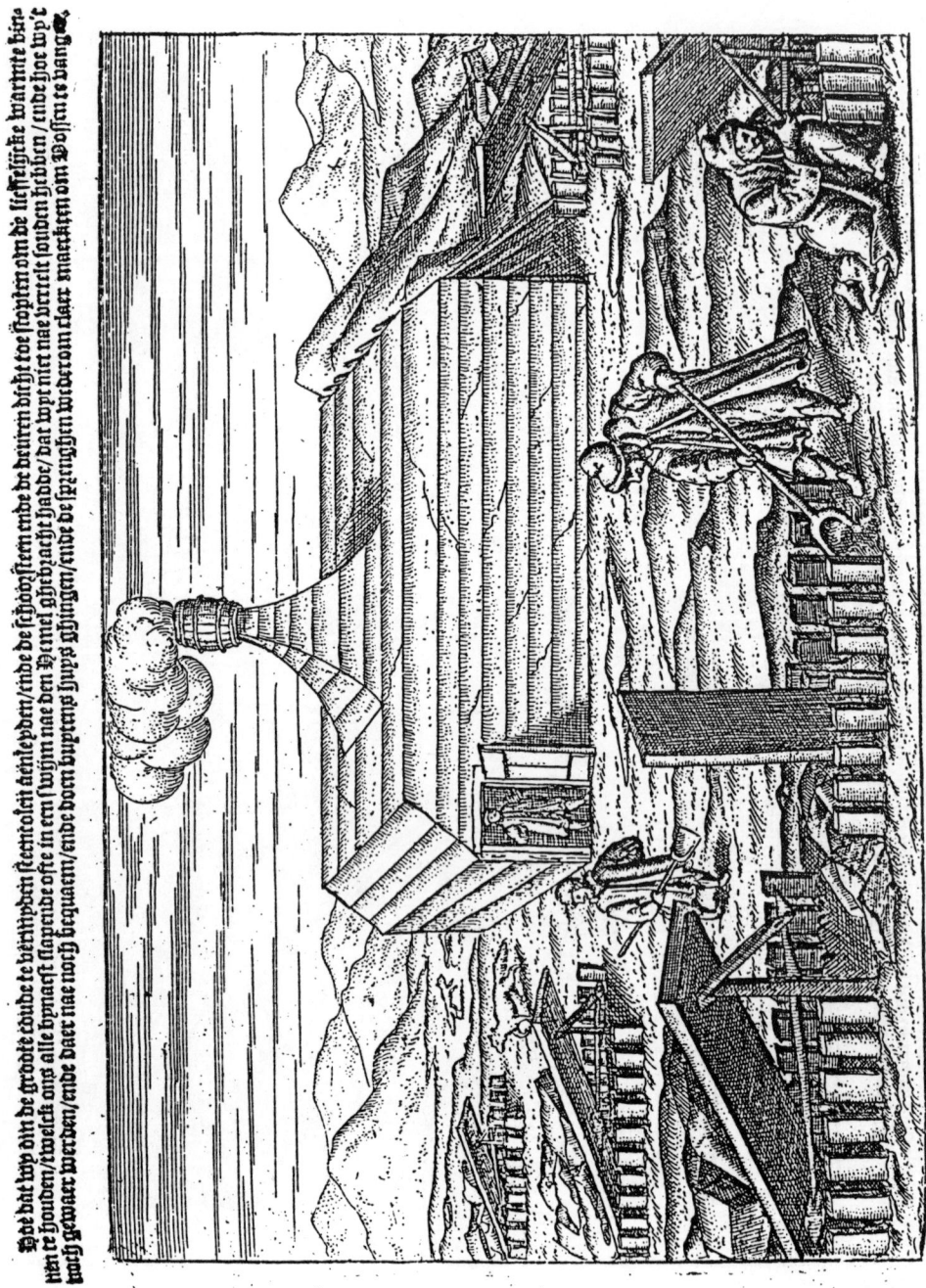

Tot dat wp om de groote toube te verttipben stertolett aenlepben/ende de buyten birb toe stopten om de lieffelijcke waermte binnen te houden/twelch ons alle bymatst slapende ofte in een suijm nae den vremel ghebzacht hadde/dat wp niet naebehzit souden hzijben/ende hoe wp't
wijs gewaer worden/ende daer nae noch frequent/ende doen buptens sups gstingen/ende de sprengben wederom daer maecktem om Boffus te bange.

¶ Hoeldincghe had een wreden Bey, die seer stout toffet hyofs amyttam, ende dyeff voor de deur dyeldhoden werde van een ham ons volck die inde deur stont, daernae wert sonderl ponit sneers upt hatte, twelck ons panisch dienstich was om inde Langen te handen, die wy voort haen dem ghezyect van smous seer spaertsch ghesonderken, ende doen ganssche naesten over handen.

Besluytinge hoe dat wy gereetschap begonden te maecken om de schuyt haerdich te maecken om na huys te varen / maer dat wy door de langhduerende koude ende ongemack / gantsch uytgheteert ende crachteloos waren / ende moesten uyter werck scheyden / want wy de schuyt niet conden weder crijgen nae het huys / om die albaer op te timmeren / daer deur wy den noot bynaest verloren gaven / duchtende dat wy nu de pericijlighe winter ouer was / efsomel daer souden moeten blijuen ende vergaen / deur dat wy te swack waren / den arbeyt te verdraghen.

Beschrijvinghe ende afteyckeninghe hoe dat wy teghent open water ons Bock ghereet maeckten ende op timmerden/ om bequamelijcker deur de Zee te gheraecken/ alsoo wy een verden wech wel van drie hondert mijlen langhs de Zee cust met de open schuyten moesten seylen / eer wy by'tnaeste landt quamen daer menschen woonden/ over de witte Zee in Rußlandt.

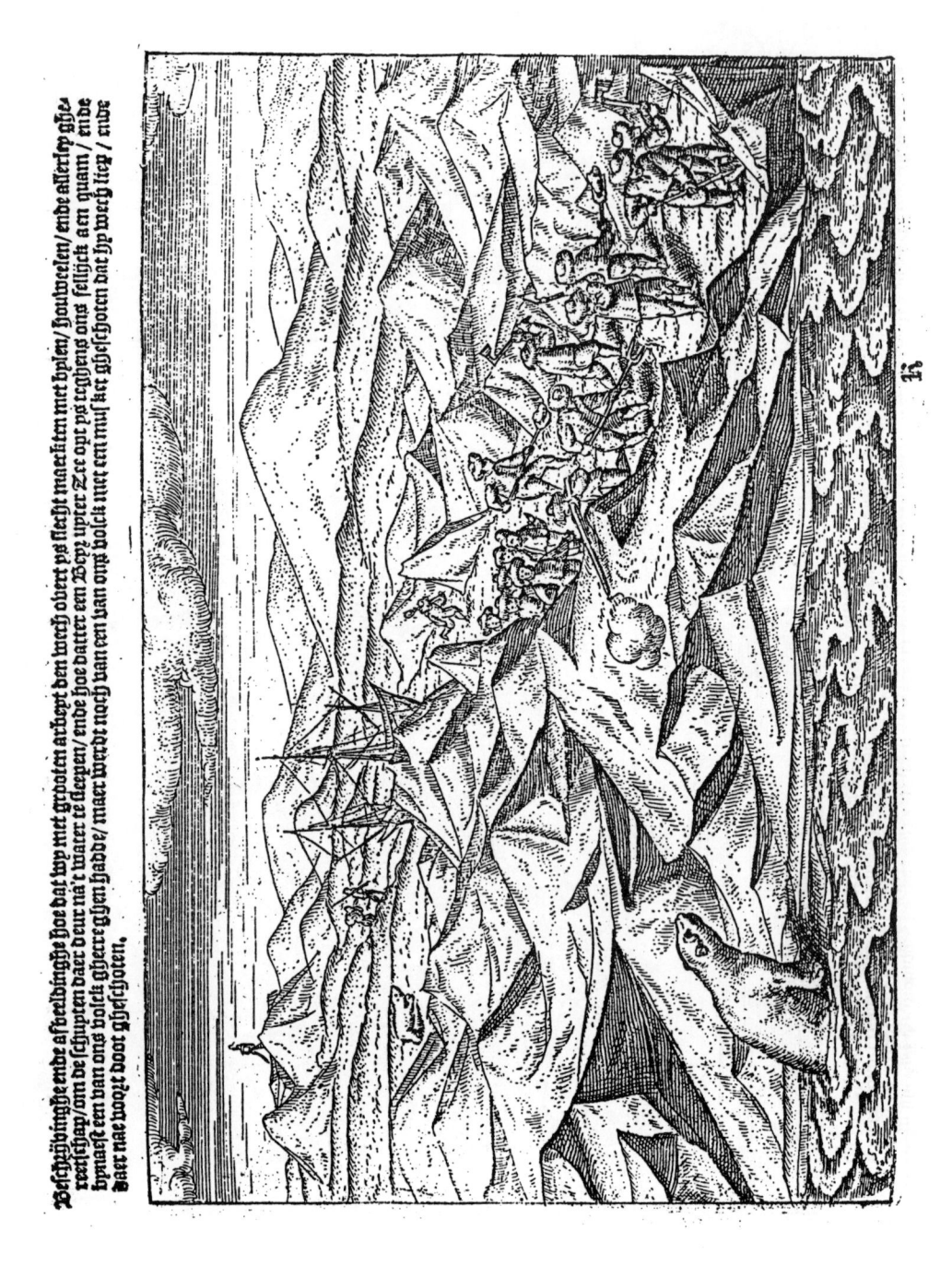

Beſchrijvinghe ende afbeeldinghe hoe dat wy met grooten arbeyt den wech overt ys ſlecht maeckten met bylen / houweelen / ende allerley gheretſchap / om de ſchuyten daer deur na't water te ſlepen / ende hoe datter een Beyr opter Zee opt ys tegghens ons ſeltſjck aen quam / ende hynaeſſe een van ons bolck gheereghen hadde / maer wecht noch van een van ons bolck met een muſkaer ghescoten dat hy wech liep / ende daer nae woort gheſchoten.

Alle dinghe ende beschrijvinghe hoe dat wy de schuyten int water sleypten/ ende diversche sieben met Godt upket schip daer in brochten/ soo vit-ruilde ende Coopmans goet/ als anders/ soo mede Willem Barentsz. ende Claes Andriesz. die beyde sieck waren/ oock na de schuyten sleypten/ ende ons onder malcanderen verdeelden/ in elcke schuyt meest eten deel/ ende begaven ons also op Gods ghenade ter zee/ met groot verlan-ghen nae thuys/ God danckende dat de ure ghecomen was dat wy van dat wilde/ woeste/ stille/ koude Landt gaerkten.

Afbeeldinge ende betekeninghe hoe dat daer de drijvende semperschijse dant ys/beyde de schuyten by nacht in sulcken ghedzeden waren/ daer se in groot perijckel van bleven met naumer noodt noch een tros aent landt creghen/daer deur sy de schuyten uyt het dzif ys aent vaste Landt creghen/ende hen stacken met alle t'goet daer uyt losten/ ende de schuyt weder om becrimmer den met grooten arbeyt/ waer ten ende gevaerlijckheyt/op welcke plaetse Willem Barentsz. ende Claes Andriesz. zijn naer/beyde op een uere s'daechs daer nae stozven.

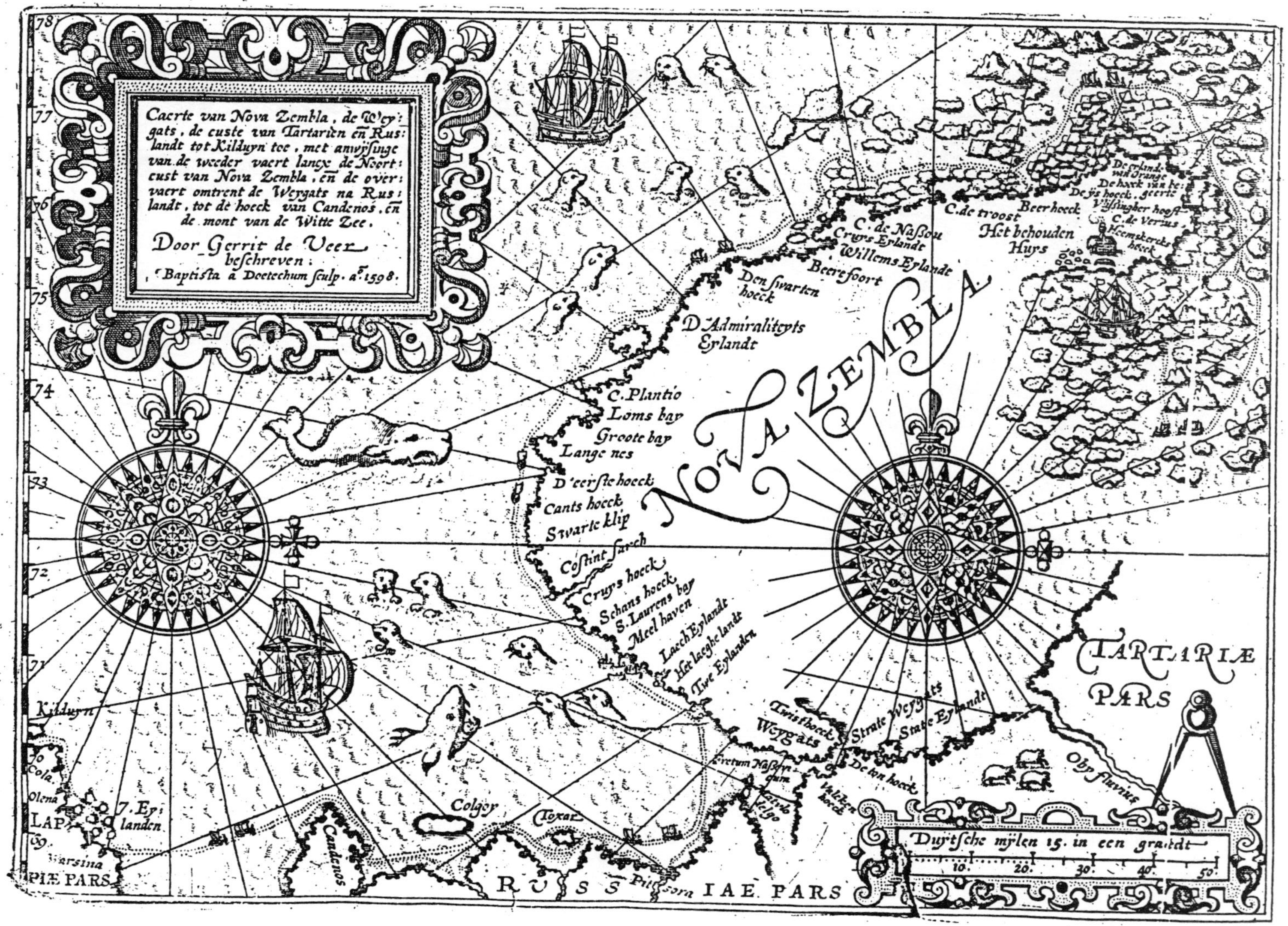

Caerte van Nova Zembla, de Weygats, de custe van Tartarien en Ruslandt tot Kilduyn toe, met anwysinge van de weeder vaert lancx de Noort-cust van Nova Zembla, en de overvaert omtrent de Weygats na Ruslandt, tot de hoeck van Candenos, en de mont van de Witte Zee.
Door Gerrit de Veer beschreven:
Baptista à Doetechum sculp. a° 1598.
NOVA ZEMBLA
TARTARIÆ PARS
RUSSIAE PARS
C. de Nassou
Cruys Eylandt
Willems Eylandt
C. de troost
Beer hoeck
Het behouden Huys
C. de Verzus
Heemskercks hoeck
Beerefoort
Den swarten hoeck
D'Admiraliteyts Eylandt
C. Plantio
Loms bay
Groote bay
Lange nes
D'eerste hoeck
Cants hoeck
Swarte klip
Costint sarch
Cruys hoeck
Schans hoeck
S. Laurens bay
Meel haven
Laech Eylandt
Het laeghe landt
Twe Eylanden
Twist hoeck
Weygats
Strate Weygats
State Eylandt
De ton hoeck
Valcken hoeck
Fretum Nassovium
Oby fluvius
Colgoy
Toxar
Candenos
Pitzora
Kilduyn
7. Eylanden
Cola
Olena
LAPPIÆ PARS
Warsina
Duytsche mylen 15. in een graedt
10. 20. 30. 40. 50.
78
77
76
75
74
73
72
71
70
69

Afbeeldinghe hoe dat wy deur deur grooten noodt hant bydendē pt afte tgoet wt ons schuyten opt ys darsten/ende beschutten mede/ daer ober wy ent tente opsloeghen/om ons daer onder wat te rusten/stellende een man opte schiltwacht/ende hoe datter ter middernacht drie Beyrē tot ons quamen/daer van wy den eenen schoten/ende d'ander siepen woort/die des anderen daeghs wederom quamen/ende den booden Beyr een groot stuck breets sleypten/ende daer van atē/maer werde van ons daer naer noch werch gheboien.

Afsteekentrage ende betrijsghe dat wy hant ys gheschoven worden/ ende soo ghewelich aenghepartst/ dat wy in duysent perijckelen waren/ want de schuyt schoof suf stucken/ ende wy verloren veel goets/als wy naet eene grepen/so ontsanck ons het ander/ wanteer ys wack ons onder de boeten bichwils weth/ ende schoof dan weder om int ons allen om hooch tegent yast: ys aen/dat dan deur self de ghewelt in stucken brack/ ons tot groot perijckel/ dat wy de breuen in stucken gheschoven worden/oft ganch ont den hals sonne.

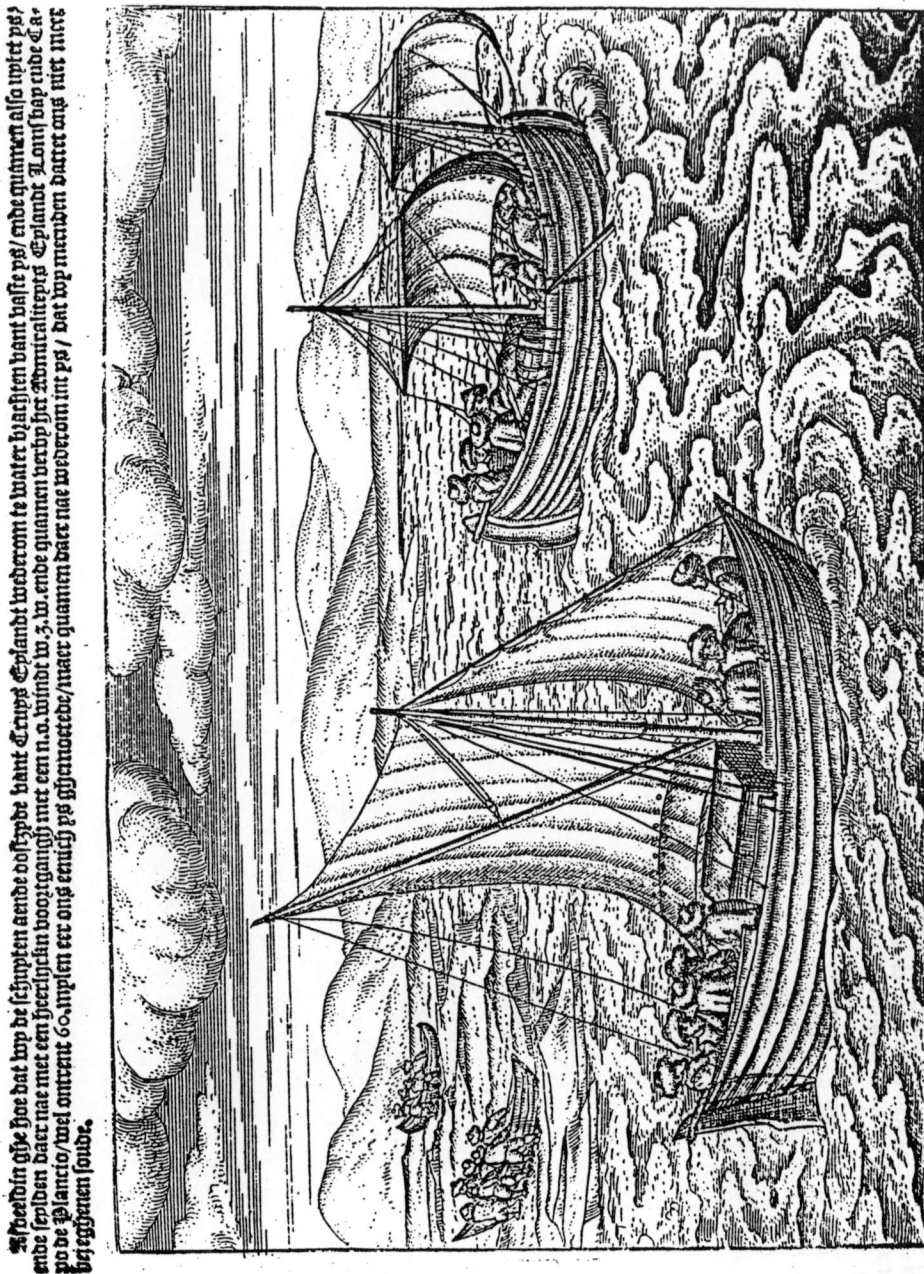

¶ Hoe dat wy de schepen aende oostzyde vant Cruys Eylandt wederom te water brachten vant vaste ys/ ende quamen also weder bys/
ende feylden daer nae met een heerlijcken voortganghe met een n.o. windt in z. w. ende quamen verby het Admiraliteyts Eylandt Loms bay ende Capo de Plancio/ wel omtrent 60.mylen ter ons eenich ys ghemoete/ maer quamen daer nae wederom int ys/ dat wy meriken datter ons niet mee-
brenghen soude.

Afbeeldinghe hoe dat wy nae langh verdrietich ommswerven by twee Russche Lodgien quamen/daer volck in waren/ by ons schip waers te voren inde Wergats gheweest hadden/ ende hoe wy malcanderen vast berijst aensaghen/ maer conden niet veel spreken/ mars de Russen betuesen ons groote vriendtschap/ ende waren met ons te vreden/ ende wy waren seer verblijdt/ ende danckten Godt dat wy nu weder by luyden ghecomen waren/ die wy in vertschen maenden niet ghesien hadden.

Afbeeldinge hoe dat wy aen een Russische Lodgien quamen/ als wy meenden dat wy al over de witte Zee waren/ ende datse ons onderrechten dat wy noch mit om den hoeck van Candinas waren/en hoe datse ons veel vriendtschap deden/en victualie vercochten/ als Speck/Meel/Boter ende Honich/ welck ons een goede moet maeckte/dat wy soo ontset werden/ende den rechten cours aengheweesen was/maer meest bekommert zijnde met ons andere maets/die van ons berdwaelt ende noch zewaert in waren.

Afbeeldinghe hoe dat wy na langhe ontswerven aende westsyde aende witte Zee quamen/daer wy ten suysten Lodgie vonden met 13. suyssichen/die ons groote vriendschap deden/ende ons in haer hutten namen en spysden/daer wy oock twee Lappen met haer wyven en kinderen/die in sulcken staet waren/gaer cleedinge en wesen/en hoe dat wy en onse ander maets die van ons versselt waren/daer ontvesiinghs by malkanderen quamen.

¶ Afteykeninghe van Kilduyn/ende hoe dat wy by bye daussen quamen/die in een cleyn Jnstjien woonden/ ende daer vernamen dat wy niet verre van
Cola waren/ende vertvillichden haer daer se een van haer met een handen ontten nae Cola sonden/om te vernemen oft daer eenighe schepen waren die nae
Hollandt souden varen/en hoe dat Jan Cornelis. de slaers te hoyen in onse compaignie gheturest was/daer met zijn schip lach/en tot ons quam met al-
lederlep spijse ende voopraecht van Wijn/Bier/Broodt/Botter/Suycker/en anders meer/om ons te verversschen/en hoe wy met hem tot Cola quammen/ en
hoe de stadt en 's Coopmans huys gelegen is/en hoe de duyssen haer schuyten opten hals dragen alsse vande eene riviere nae d'ander willen.

THE
True and perfect Description of three Voyages,

so strange and woonderfull,
that the like hath neuer been
heard of before:
Done and performed three yeares, one after the other, by the Ships of
Holland and *Zeland*, on the North sides of *Norway*, *Muscouia* and
Tartaria, towards the Kingdomes of *Cathaia* & *China*, shewing
the discouerie of the Straights of *Weigates*, *Noua Zembla*,
and the Countrie lying vnder 80. degrees; which is
thought to be *Greenland*: where neuer any man had
bin before: with the cruell Beares, and other
Monsters of the Sea, and the vnsupportable and extreame cold
that is found to be in
those places.
And how that in the last Voyage, the Shippe was so inclosed by the
Ice, that it was left there, whereby the men were forced to build a
house in the cold and desart Countrie of *Noua Zembla* wherin
they continued 10. monthes togeather, and neuer saw nor
heard of any man, in most great cold and extreame
miserie; and how after that, to saue their liues, they
were constrained to sayle aboue 350. Duch
miles, which is aboue 1000. miles English,
in litle open Boates, along and ouer the
maine Seas, in most great daunger,
and with extreame labour, vnspeakable troubles, and
great hunger.

Imprinted at London for *T. Pauier.*
1609.

TO THE RIGHT WOR-
shipfull, Sir *Thomas Smith* Knight, Gouernour of the *Muscouy* Company, &c.

RIGHT WORSHIPFVLL,

BEing intreated by some of my Friends, and principally by M. Richard Hakluyt (a diligent obseruer of all Proceedings in this nature) to Translate and publish these three yeares Trauelles and Discoueries, of the Hollanders to the North-easts I could not deuise how to consecrate my Labours so properly to any, as to your selfe, considering not onely the generall good affection the whole Kingdome takes notice, that you beare to all Honorable actions of this kinde, be they for Discouerie, Traffique, or Plantation; but also in respect of that particular charge, most worthily recommended to your care, ouer the Trade of the English *in those* North-east Partes.

Many attempts and proffers (I confesse) there haue bin to find a passage by those poorest parts, to the richest; by those barbarous, to the most ciuile; those vnpeopled, to the most popular; these Desarts, to the most fertile Conntries of the World: and of them all, none (I dare say) vndertaken with greater iudgement, with more obdurate Patience, euen aduersus Elementa, aduersus ipsam in illis locis rerum naturam, then these three by the Hollanders.

If any of our Nation be employed that way in time to come, here they haue a great part of their Voiage layd open, and the example of

A ij.   that

The Epistle Dedicatorie.

that industrious people (first excited to this and other famous Voyages, by imitation of some of ours) for the conquering of all difficulties and dangers; those people (I say) that of all Christians, and for ought I know, of all Adams Posteritie, haue first nauigated to 81. Degrees of Northerly Latitude, and wintered in 76. where they had no Inhabitants, but Foxes, Beares, and Deare, to keepe them company.

And were it for nothing else, but to register the miraculous prouidence of the Creator, and his admirable and vnspeakeable workes in these congealed Climats, vnknowen vtterly to the Ancients, and to demostrate how much we are obliged to his omnipotent fauour, for planting vs in so temperate, so ciuill, and so Religious a part of the World, as this blessed Island; I thinke omission in this kinde were little lesse then Sacriledge.

As it is, I humbly desire you to vouch-safe it your protection, and to esteeme mee,

Alwayes deuoted to your seruice,

WILLIAM PHILLIP.

The

The fyrst part of the Nauigation into the North Seas.

It is a most certaine and an assured assertion, that nothing doth more benefit and further the Common-wealth (specially these Countries) then the art and knowledge of Nauigation, in regard that such Countries and Nations as are strong and mightie at Sea, haue the meanes and ready way to draw, fetch, and bring vnto them for their maintenaunce, all the principalest commodities and fruites of the earth, for that thereby they are inabled to bring all necessary things for the nourishment and sustentation of man from the vttermost partes of the world, and to carry and conuay such wares and Marchandizes, (whereof they haue great store and aboundance) vnto the same places, which by reason of the art of Nauigation, and the commodities of the Sea, is easily to be effected and brought to passe. Which Nauigation as it dayly more & more increaseth (to the great woonder and admiration of those, that compare the Sea-faring & Nauigation vsed in our forefathers times, yea & that also that hath beene practised in our age, with that which now at this present is daily furthered & sought out) so there are continually new voiages made, & strange Coasts discouered; the which although they be not done by the first, second, or third voiage, but after, by tract of time, first brought to their full effect, and desired commoditie, and the fruits thereof, by continuance of time reaped. Yet we must not be abasht, nor dismayed, at the labour, toile, trauaile, and dangers sustayned in such voiages, to that end made, although as I said before the benefit thereof be not had nor seene in the first, second, third, or more voiages, for what labour is more profitable, & worthier praise and commendation, then that which tendeth vnto the common good and benefit of all men? Although such as are vnskilfull, contemners, & deriders of mens diligence and proceedings therein, at the first esteeme it

As the art of Nauigation more increaseth, so there are daily more new countries found out.

Diligence and continuance, effect that which is sought.

We must not leaue of by some mens dislike or dispraise in our proceedings.

B.

The Nauigation into the North-seas.

an vnprofitable and needlesse thing, when as the end prooueth beneficiall & commodious. If the famous Nauigators Cortesius Nonius, and Megalanes, & others, that in their times, sought out and discouered the Kingdomes, Countries, and Ilands farre distant from vs, in the extreamest parts of the world; for the first, second, or third voyage, that had succeeded vnfortunately with them: had left off and giuen ouer their nauigatiō; they had not afterward reaped nor enioyed the fruites, benefites, and commodities thereof. Alexander magnus (after he had woone all Grecia, and from thence entred into little & great Asia; and comming to the farthest parts of India, there found some difficultie to passe) sayd, If we had not gone forward, and persisted in our intent, which other men esteemed and held to be impossible, we had still remayned and stayed in the entry of Cicilia, where as now we haue ouerrunne & past through all those large and spacious Countries: for nothing is found and effected all at one time, neither is any thing that is put in practise, presently brought to an end. To the which end, Cicero wisely saith; God hath giuen vs some things, & not all things, that our successours also might haue somewhat to doe. Therefore we must not leaue off, nor stay our pretence in the middle of our proceedinges, as long as there is any commoditie to be hoped, & in time to be obtayned: for that the greatest and richest treasures are hardliest to be found. But to make no long digression from our matter, concerning the dayly furtheraunce of the most necessarie and profitable art of Nauigation, that hath been brought to full effect, not without great charges, labour, and paines; ouerslipping and not shewing with how long and troublesome labour and toyle, continually had, the passages to the East and West *Indies*, America, Brasilia, and other places, through the straight of Magellanes, in the South sea, twise or thrise passing vnder the Line, and by those meanes other Countries & Ilands, were first found out and discouered.

A thing not continued can not be effected.

All things are effected in conuenient time.

Let vs looke into the White Seas, that are now so commonly sayled (on the north side of Muscouia) with what cumbersome labour and toyle, they were first discouered: What hath now made this Voyage so common and easie? is it not the same, and as long a voyage as it was, before it was fully knowne and found out? I but the right courses, which at the first were to be sought, by crossing the Seas from one Land to another, & are now to be held aloofe into the Seas, and directly sayled; hath of difficult and toylesome, made them easie and

That which in the beginning is hard, by continuance of time is made easie and light.

The Nauigation into the North-seas.

and ready voyages.

This small Discourse I thought good to set downe, for an introduction vnto the Reader, in regard that I haue vndertaken to describe the Three Voyages made into the North Seas, in three yeares, one after the other; behind Norway, and along and about Muscouia, towardes the Kingdome of Cathaia and China: whereof, the two last, I my selfe holpe to effect; and yet brought them not to the desired end that we well hoped.

First, to shew our diligent, and most toylesome labour and paynes taken, to find out the right course; which we could not bring to passe, as we well hoped, wished, and desired, and possible might haue found it, by crossing the Seas, if we had taken the right course; if the Ice and the shortnesse of time, and bad crosses had not hindered vs: And also to stoppe their mouthes, that report and say, that our proceeding therein, was wholly vnprofitable and fruitelesse; which perauenture in time to come, may turne vnto our great profite and commoditie. For he which proceedeth and continueth in a thing that seemeth to be impossible, is not to be discommended: but hee, that in regarde that the thing seemeth to be impossible, doth not proceed therein, but by his faint heartednesse and sloath, wholly leaueth it off. *The first finding is hard, but the second attempt is easier.*

Wee haue assuredly found, that the onely and most hinderaunce to our voyage, was the Ice, that we found about Noua Zembla, vnder 73. 74. 75. and 76. degrees; and not so much vpon the Sea betweene both the Landes: whereby it appeareth, that not the nearenesse of the North pole, but the Ice that commeth in and out from the Tartarian Sea, about Noua Zembla, caused vs to feele the greatest cold. Therefore in regard that the nearenesse of the Pole was not the cause of the great cold that we felt, if we had had the meanes to haue held our appoynted and intended course into the North-east, we had perauenture found some enteraunce: which course we could not hold from Noua Zembla, because that there we entred amongst great store of Ice; and how it was about Noua Zembla, we could not tell, before we had sought it; and when we had sought it, we could not then alter our course, although also it is vncertaine, what we should haue done, if we had continued in our North-east course, because it is not yet found out. But it is true, that in the Countrie lying vnder 80. degrees, (which we esteeme to be Greenland) there is both Leaues and Grasse to be seene: Wherein, such Beastes as feed of Leaues and Grasse, (as *Not the nearenes of the North pole, but the Ice in the Tartarian sea, causeth the greatest cold.*

B 2. Hartes,

The Nauigation into the North-seas.

Harts, Hindes, and such like beastes liue, whereas to the contrary In noua Zembla, there groweth nether leaues nor grasse, and there are no beasts therein but such as eate flesh, as Beares, & Foxes, &c. Although Noua Zembla, lyeth 4. 5. and 6. degrees more Southerly from the pole, then the other land aforesaid. It is also manifest, that vpon the South and North side of the line of the sunne on both sides, between both the Tropicos, vnder 23. degrees and a halfe, it is as hot, as it is right vnder the Line. What wonder then should it be, that about the North Pole also, and as many degrees on both sides, it should not bee colder then right vnder the Pole? I will not affirme this to bee true, because that the colde on both sides of the North Pole hath not as yet beene discouered and sought out, as the heat on the North and South side of the line hath beene. Onely thus much I will say, that although we held not our direct pretended course to the North-east, that therefore it is to be iudged, that the cold would haue let our passage through that way, for it was not the Sea, nor the neerenesse vnto the Pole, but the Ice about the land, that let & hindered vs (as I sayd before) for that as soone as we made from the land, & put more into the sea, although it was much further Northward, presently we felt more warmth, and in ye opinion our Pilote William Barents dyed, who notwithstanding the feareful and intollerable cold that he indured, yet he was not discouraged, but offered to lay wagers with diuers of vs, that by Gods helpe, he would bring that pretended voiage to an end, if he held his course North-east from the North Cape. But I will leaue that, and shewe you, of the three Voyages aforesaid, begun and set forth by the permission and furtherance of the generall States of the vnited Prouinces, and of Prince Maurice, as Admirall of the Sea, and the rich Towne of Amsterdam. Whereby the Reader may iudge and conceaue what is to bee done, for the most profite and aduantage, and what is to be left.

A comparison of the heate vnder the line, with the cold vnder the North Pole.

The resolute intent and opinions of William Barents.

First you must vnderstand, that in Anno 1594. there was 4. ships set foorth out of the vnited Prouinces, whereof two were of Amsterdam; one of Zelandt, and one of Enckhuysen, that were appointed to saile into the North Seas, to discouer the Kingdomes of Cathaia, and China; North-ward from Norway, Muscouia, and about Tartaria, whereof William Barents, a notable skilfull and wise Pilote, was Commander ouer the Ships of Amsterdam, and with them vpon Whit-sunday departed from Amsterdam and went to the Texel.

Upon

The Nauigation into the North-seas.

Vpon the fifth of Iune they sailed out of the Texel, and hauing a good wind and faire weather, vpon the 23. of Iune, they arriued at Kilduin in Muscouia, which for that it is a place well knowen and a common Voyage, I will make no further discription thereof.

The 29. of Iune, at foure of the clocke in the after noone, they set saile out of Kilduin, and so 13. or 14. miles out-right, sailed North-east, with a north north-west wind, and close weather.

The 30. of Iune they sayled East North-east 7. miles, till the Sunne was East South-east, with an North wind, with 2. Schower sailes, there they cast out their lead, at 100. fadome deepth, but found no ground.

From whence the same day they sailed East north-east 5. miles, till the Sunne was full South, hauing the wind North with 2. Schower sailes, where once againe they cast out the lead 100. fadome deepe, but found no ground, and then from noone to night the same day, they sailed East, & East and by North 13. miles, till the Sunne was North-west, and there casting out their lead, they had ground at 120. fadome, the ground being oasie, and blacke durt.

The 1. of Iuly, after they had sailed one quarter 4. miles East, and East and by North, early in the morning they cast out the lead, & found ground at 60. fadome, where they had an oasie small sandy ground, and within an houre after they cast out the lead againe, and had ground at 52. fadome, being white sand mixed with blacke, and some-what oasie: after that they sailed 3. miles East and by North, where they had ground at 40. fadome, being gray sand mixed with white. From thence they sailed 2. miles East-ward, with a North north-east winde, there they had ground at 38. fadome, being red sand mixed with black, the Sunne being South-east and by east. From thence they sailed 3. miles, East and by South, & East South-east til noone, where they had the Sunne at 70. degrees and ½. there they cast out the lead againe, and had ground at 39. fadome, being small gray sand, mixed with blacke stippelen and peeces of Shels.

Then againe they sailed 2. miles South-east, and then woond North-ward with an East north-east wind, and after sailed 6. miles North-east all that day, with a South-east wind, till the Sunne was North North-west, the weather being cold, and the lead being cast foorth they found ground at 60. fadome, being small gray oasie sand, mixed with a little blacke, and great whole shels: after that the same Euening to the

B 3. first

The Nauigation into the North-seas.

first quarter, they sailed 5. miles, East north-east, and North-east and by East, and after that East north-east, and North-east and by East 5. miles, vntill the second of July in the Morning, and there they had 65. fadome deepe, the ground oasie with blacke slime or durt.

The same day from Morning to Noone, they sailed 3. or 4. miles East north-east, the wind blowing stiffe South-east, whereby at Noone they were forced to table in the fore-saile, and driue with a Schower saile, in mistie weather, for the space of 3. or 4. miles, vntill Euening, holding East, and East and by South, after that the winde blew South-west, and about 5. of the clocke in the after-noone, they cast out the lead, but had no ground at 120. fadome. That Euening the weather cleared vp againe, and they sailed about 5. miles before the wind East north-east, for the space of 3. houres, and then againe it began to be mistie, so that they durst not saile forward, but lay hulling in the wind, where vpon Sunday morning being the 3. of July, when the Sunne was North-east, they cast out the lead and found ground at 125. fadome, being blacke durt or slime.

From thence they sailed 8. Miles East North-east, till the Sunne was South-east, and casting out the lead, found ground at 140. fadom, being blacke slimie durt, at which time they tooke the high of the Sun and found it to be 73. degrees and 6. minutes, & presently againe they cast out the lead, and had 130. fadome deepth, the ground being blacke slime. After that they sayled 6. or 7 miles further East north-east, till the Sunne was North-west.

On Sunday in the Morning being the 3. of July, it was very faire and cleare weather, the wind blowing South-west, at which time William Barents found out the right Meridien, taking the high of the Sunne with his Crosse-staffe when it was South-east, and found it to be eleuated in the South-east 28. degrees and a halfe, and when it had past ouer West & by North, it was but 28. degrees & a half aboue the Horizon, so that it differed 5. points and a half, which being deuided there rested 2. points and ½. so that their compasse was altered 2. points. and ½. as it appeared the same day, when the sunne was in her higth betweene South south-west, and south-west and by south, for the Sun was south-west and by south, and yet was not declined, and they had 73. degrees and 6. minutes.

The 4. of July in the morning, they sailed 4. Miles east and by north, and casting out the lead found ground at 125 fadome being slimie.

The Nauigation into the North-seas.

mie. That night the weather was mistie againe, and in the Morning the winde was east, then they sailed 4. miles South-east and by south, till the Sunne was east, and then againe they cast out the lead, & found ground at 108. fadome, blacke durt, then they wound north-ward, & sailed 6. Miles, north north-east, and north-east and by north, vntill the Sunne was south south-west, and then they saw the Land of Noua Zembla, lying South-east and by East 6. or 7. miles from them, where they had blacke durty ground at 105. fadome. Then they woond south-ward againe, and sailed 6. Miles, south and by West, till the Sunne was West north-west, there they had 68. Fadome deepe, with durtie ground as before the wind being south-east.

Then they woond East-ward & sailed 6. Miles east and by south, at which time, William Barents tooke the heigth of the Sunne with his Crosse-staffe, when it was at the lowest, that is between north north-east, and east and by north, and found it to bee eleuated aboue the Horizon 6. degrees & ⅓. part, his declination being 12. degrees & 55. minuts, from whence substracting the aforesaid heigth, there resteth 16. degrees and 35. minutes, which being substracted from 90. degrees, there resteth 73. degrees and 25. minutes which was, when they were about 5. or 6. miles from the Land of Noua Zembla.

Then they woond east-ward and sailed 5. miles, east & by south, and east South-east, and past by a long point of Land that lay out into the sea, which they named Langenes, and hard by that point East-ward, there was a great Bay, where they went a land with their boate, but found no people.

Three or foure Miles from Langenes east north-east, there lay a long point, and a Mile east-ward from the said point there was a great Bay, and vpon the east-side of the said Bay, there lay a Rock not very high aboue the water, and on the West-side of the Bay, there stood a sharpe little hill, easie to be knowne, before the Bay, it was 20. fadome deepth, the ground small blacke stones, like pease: from Langenes to Cape Bapo East north-east it is 4. miles.

From Cape Bapo to the West point of Lombsbay north-east and by north are 5. miles, and betweene them both there are 2. Creekes. Lombsbay is a great wide Bay, on the West-side thereof hauing a faire Hauen 6. 7. or 8. fadome deepe, blacke sand, there they went on shore with their boate, & vpon the shore placed a beacon, made of an old Mast which they found there; calling the Bay Lombsbay, because of

a cera certaine kind of Beares so called, which they found there in great abounbance.

The East point of Lombsbay, is a long narrow point, & by it there lyeth an Island, and from that long point to Sea-ward in, there is a great Creeke. This Lombsbay lyeth vnder 74. Degrees and part. From Lombsbay to the point of the Admirals Island, they sailed 6. or 7. Miles, North-east and by North. The Admirals Island is not very faire one the East-side, but a farre off very flat, so that you must shunne it long before you come at it, it is also very vneuen, for at one casting off the lead they had 10. fadome deepe, and presently at another casting of the lead they had but 6. fadome, and presently after that againe 10. 11. and 12. fadome, the streame running hard against the flats.

From the East-end of the Admirals Island, to Cape Negro, that is the Blacke point, they sailed about 5. or 6. Miles, East North-east, and a Mile without the Black point it is 70. fadome deepe, the ground slimie, as vpon Pamphius, right East-ward of the Blacke point, there are 2. sharpe pointed hilles in the Creeke, that are easie to be knowen.

The 6. of July, the Sunne being North, they came right before the Blacke point with faire weather, this Blacke point lyeth vnder 75. Degrees and 20. minutes. From the Blacke point to Williams Island, they sailed 7. or 8. Miles, East North-east, and between them both about halfe a Mile, there lay a small Island.

The 7. of July they sailed from Williams Island, and then William Barents tooke the height of the Sunne, with his Crosse-staffe, and found it to be eleuated aboue the Horizon in the south-west and by south 53. Degrees and 6. minutes, his declination being 22. Degrees and 49. minutes, which being added to 53. Degrees and 6. minutes, make 75. Degrees and 55. minutes. This is the right height of the Pole of the said Island. In this Island they found great store of Driff-wood, & many Sea-horses being a kinde of fish that keepeth in the Sea, hauing very great teeth, which at this day are vsed insteed of Iuorie or Elophants teeth, there also is a good road for ships, at 12. & 13. fadome deepe against all winds, except it be West south-west, and West winds, and there they found a piece of a Russia ship, and that day they had the wind East North-east, mistie weather.

The 9. of July they entered into Beeren-fort, vpon the road vnder Williams Island, and there they found a white Beare, which they
per-

The Nauigation into the North-seas.

perceiuing, presently entered into their Boate, and shot her into the body with a musket, but the Beare shewed most wonderfull strength, which almost is not to be found in any beast, for no man euer heard the like to be done by any Lyon or cruel beast whatsoeuer; for notwithstanding that she was shot into the bodie, yet she leapt vp, & swamme in the water, the men that were in the boate rowing after her, cast a rope about her necke, and by that meanes drew her at the sterne of the boat, for that not hauing seene the like Beare before, they thought to haue carryed her aliue in the shippe, and to haue shewed her for a strange wonder in Holland; but she vsed such force, that they were glad that they were rid of her, and contented themselues with her skin only, for she made such a noyse, and stroue in such sort, that it was admirable, wherewith they let her rest and gaue her more scope, with the rope that they held her by, and so drew her in that sort after them, by that meanes to wearie her: meane time, William Barents made neerer to her, but the Beare swome to the boate, and with her fore-feet got hold of the sterne thereof, which William Barents perceiuing, said, she will there rest her selfe, but she had another meaning, for she vsed such force, that at last she had gotten half her body into the boat, wherewith the men were so abashed, that they run into ye further end of the boate, and thought verily to haue been spoiled by her, but by a strange means they were deliuered from her, for that the rope that was about her necke, caught hold vpon the hooke of the Ruther, whereby the Beare could get no further, but so was held backe, and hanging in that manner, one of the men boldly stept foorth from the end of the Scute, and thrust her into the bodie with a Halfe-pike; & therewith she fell downe into the water, and so they rowed forward with her to the ship, drawing her after them, till shee was in a manner dead, wherewith they killed her out-right, and hauing fleaed her, brought the skinne to Amsterdam.

The 20. of July. they sailed out of Beren-fort fro Williams Island, & the same day in the morning got to the Island of Crosses, and there went on land with their Pinnace, and found the Iland to bee barren, and full of Cliffes and Rocks, in it there was a small Hauen, whereinto they rowed with their boat. This Island is about halfe a Mile long, and reacheth East and West; on the West end it hath a Banke, about a third part of a Mile long, and at the East end also another Banke, vpon this Island there standeth 2. great Crosses, the Iland

C lyeth

The Nauigation into the North-seas.

lyeth about 2. long Miles from the firme land, and vnder the East-end thereof there is good road, at 26. fadome soft ground; and somewhat closer to the Island on the Strand, at 9. fadome sandy ground.

From the Island of Crosses to the point of Cape Nassawe, they sailed east, and east and by north about 8. miles: it is a long flat point which you must bee carefull to shunne, for thereabouts at 7. fadome there were flats or sholes, very farre from the Land; It lyeth almost vnder 76. Degrees and a halfe. From the West-end of Williams Island, to the Island with the Crosses is 3. miles, the course North.

From Nassaw point they sailed East and by South, and east south-east 5. miles, & then they thought that they saw land in North-east and by East, & sailed towards it 5. miles North-east to descrie it, thinking it to be another land, that lay north-ward from Noua Zembla, but it began to blow so hard out of the West, that they were forced to take in their Marsaile, & yet the wind rose in such manner, that they were forced to take in all their sailes, and the sea went so hollow, that they were constrained to driue 16. houres together without saile 8. or 9. Miles East north-east.

The 11. of July their boat was by a great waue of the sea sunke to the ground, and by that meanes they lost it, and after that they draue without sailes 5. miles, East and by South; at last the Sunne being almost South-east, the wind came about to the North-west, and then the weather began somewhat to cleare vp, but yet it was very mistie. Then they hoysed vp their sailes againe and sailed 4. Miles till night, that the Sunne was North and by East, and there they had 60. fadome depth, muddie ground, and then they saw certaine flakes of Ice, at which time vpon the 12. of July they woond west, and held North-west, and sailed about a mile with mistie weather, and a north-west wind, and sailed vp & downe west south-west 3. or 4. Miles to see if they could find their boat againe: after that they wound againe with the wind, and sayled 4. miles south-east, till the sunne was south-west, and then they were close by the Land of Noua Zembla, that lay East and by North, and West & by south; from thence they wound ouer againe till noone and sayled 3. Miles, North and by West, and then till the Sunne was North-west, they held North-west and by North 3. Miles, then they wound East-ward and sailed 4. or 5. Miles north-east, and by east.

The 13. of July at night, they found great store of Ice, as much as

the

The Nauigation into the North-seas.

they could descrie out of the top, that lay as if it had been a plaine field of Ice, then they wound West-ward ouer from the Ice, and sailed about 4. miles West south-west, till the Sunne was east and by north, and that they saw the Land of Noua Zembla, lying South south-east from them.

Then they wound North-ward againe and sailed 2. Miles, till the Sunne was East south-east, and then againe found great store of Ice, and after that sailed South-west and by south 3. miles.

The 14. of July, they wound North-ward againe, & sayled with 2. Schower sailes North and by East, and North north-east 5. or 6. Miles, to the height of 77. Degrees and ½ part, and entred againe amongst the Ice, being so broad that they could not see ouer it, there they had no ground at 100. fadome, and then it blew hard West north-west.

From thence they wound South-ward, and sailed South south-west 7. or 8. miles, & came againe by the land that shewed to be 4. or 5. high hilles. Then they wound Northward, and till Euening sayled North 6. Miles, but there againe they found Ice.

From thence they wound South-ward and sailed South and by west 6. miles, and then againe entred into Ice.

The 15. of July, they wound South-ward againe, sayling South and by west 6. miles, and in the Morning, were by the land of Noua Zembla againe, the Sunne being about North-east.

From thence they wound North-ward againe, ant sayled North and by east 7. miles, and entred againe into the Ice. Then they wound South-ward againe, the Sunne being west and sailed South south-west, and south-west and by south 8. or 9. miles, vpon the 16. of July.

From thence they wound North-ward, and sailed north and by east 4. miles, after that againe they wound west-ward and sailed West and by south 4. miles, and then they sailed north north-west 4. miles, and then the wind blew north north-east, and it froze hard; this was vpon the 17. of July.

Then they wound East-ward, and sailed East till noone, 3. Miles, and after that east and by south 3. Miles; from thence about Euening they wound northward & sailed north and by east 5. miles, till the 18. of July in the morning: then they sailed north & by west 4. miles, & there entred againe amongst a great many flakes of Ice, from whence they wound southward, & close by the Ice they had no grosd at 150. fadom.

The Nauigation into the North-seas.

Then they sayled about 2. houres South-east, and East south-east, with mystie weather, & came to a flake of Ice, which was so broad that they could not see ouer it, it being faire still weather, and yet it froze, and so sailed along by the Ice 2. houres; after that it was so mistie, that they could see nothing round about them, and sailed South-west two Miles.

The same day William Barents tooke the height of the Sun, with his Astrolabium, and then they were vnder 77. degrees and a ½ of the Pole, and sailed South-ward 6. Miles, and perceiued the firme land, lying South from them.

Then they sailed till the 19. of July in the Morning, West south-west, 6. or 7. miles, with a North-west wind, and mistie weather, & after that South-west and south-west and by west 7. miles, the Sunne being 77. degrees 5. minutes lesse. Then they sailed 2. miles South-west, & were close by the land of Noua Zembla, about Cape Nassaue.

From thence they wound north-ward, & sailed north 8. miles, with a West north-west wind, and a mist, and till the 20. of July in the Morning North-east and by north 3. or 4. miles, and when the Sunne was east they wound West, and till Euening sailed South-west 5. or 6. miles, with mistie weather, and then south-west and by south 7. miles, till the 21. of July in the Morning.

Then they wound North-ward againe, and from Morning till euening sailed North-west and by west 9. Miles, with mistie weather, and againe north-west and by west 3. miles, and then wound South-ward, and till the 22. of July in the Morning sailed South South-west 3. Miles, with mistie weather, and till euening South and by West, 9. Miles, all mistie weather.

After that they wound North-ward againe, and sailed North-west and by North 3. Miles, and then 2. Miles north-west, and in the morning being the 23. of July the wind blew North-west, and then they cast out the lead, and had 48. fadome muddie ground.

Then they sailed 2. Miles North north-east and North & by East, and 2. Miles North-east, at 46. fadome deepe, after that they wound West-ward, and sailed west and by north 6. miles, there it was 60. fadome deepe, muddy ground.

Then they wound Eastward and sailed 3. miles East and by north, then againe 9. or 10. miles east and east & by South, and after that 5. or 6. miles East and east and by south, & after that 5. or 6. miles more, east and

The Nauigation into the North-seas.

and by south till euening, being the 24. of July; then againe 4. Miles South-east and by east, the wind being east North-east.

Then they wound North-ward, and till the 25. of July in the Morning sailed North and north and by West 4. miles, there they had 130. fadome deepe muddie ground; then they sailed north-ward where they had 100. fadome deepe, and there they saw the Ice in the North-east, and then againe they sailed 2. miles, North and by West.

Then they woand South-ward, towards the Ice, and sailed south-east one mile; after that they wound North-ward againe, and sailed North 6. Miles, and were so inclosed about with flakes of Ice, that out of the top they could not discerne any thing beyond it, and sought to get through the Ice, but they could not passe beyond it, and therefore in the euening they wound south-ward againe, and sailed along by the Ice, south & by west 5. miles, & after that south south-east 3. miles.

The 25. of July at night, they tooke the heigth of the Sunne, when it was at the lowest between North and north-east, and north-east and by north, it being eleuated aboue the Horizon 6. degrees, and ½ his declinatiō being 19. degrees 50. minutes, now take 6. degrees ½ from. 19. degrees and 50. minuts, and there resteth 13. degrees 5. minutes, which substracted from 90. there resteth 77. degrees lesse 5. minutes.

The 26. of July, in the Morning they sailed 6. miles South south-east, till the Sunne was South-west, & then South-east 6. miles, and were within a mile of the land of Noua Zembla, & then wound north-ward from the land and sailed 5. miles North-west with an east wind, but in the Euening they wound South-ward againe, and sailed south-south-east 7. Miles, and were close by the Land.

Then they wound north-ward againe, and sailed North north-east 2. or 3. Miles: from thence they wound South-ward, and sailed South south-east 2. or 3. Miles, and came againe to Cape Trust.

Then they wound againe from the Land, North-east, about halfe a mile, and were ouer against the sandes of 4. fadome deepe, betweene the rocke and the land, and there the sands were 10. fadome deepe, the ground being small blacke stones; then they sailed North-west a little while, till they had 43. fadome deepe soft ground.

From thence they sailed North-east 4. Miles, vpon the 27. of July, with an East south-east wind, and wound South-ward againe, Where they found 70. fadome deepe, clay ground, and sayled south, and South and by East 4. miles, and came to a great Creek; & a Mile

C 3 and

The Nauigation into the North-seas.

and a halfe, from thence there lay a banke of sand of 18. fadome deepe, clay sandy ground, and betweene that sand or banke & the land, it was 60. and 50. fadome deepe, the coast reaching east and west by the Compasse.

In the euening they wound stife North-ward, and sailed 3. Miles North north-east; that day it was mistie, and in the night cleare, and William Barents tooke the height of the sunne with his Crosse-staffe, and found it to be eleuated aboue the Horizon 5. degrees 40. minutes, his declination being 19. degrees 25. minutes, from whence substracting 5. Degrees 40. minutes, there resteth 13 Degrees 45. minutes, which substracted from 90. rested 76. Degrees 31. minutes, for the height of the Pole.

Vpon the 28. of July, they sailed 3. miles North north-east, and after that wound South-ward, and sailed 6. miles South south-east, and yet were then 3. or 4. miles from the land.

The 28. of July, the height of the sun being taken at noone, with the Astrolabiū, it was found to be eleuated aboue the Horizon 57 degrees & 6. minutes, her declination being 19. degrees & 18 minutes, which in all is 76. degrees and 24. minutes, they being then about 4. miles from the land of Noua Zembla, that lay all couered ouer with Snow, the weather being cleare, and the wind East.

Then againe (the Sunne being about South-west) they wound North-ward and sailed one mile North North-east, and then wound againe, and sailed another mile South-east, then they wound Northward againe, and sailed 4. miles North-east and North-east and by North.

The same day the height of the sunne being taken it was found to be 76. Degrees and 24. minutes, & then they sailed North-east 3. Miles, & after that North-east and by east 4. miles, and vpon the 29. of July came into the Ice againe.

The 29. of July the height of the Sunne being taken with the Crosse-Staffe, Astrolabium, and Quadrant, they found it to bee eleuated aboue the Horizon 32. degrees, her declination being 19. Degrees, which substracted from 32. there resteth 13. Degrees of the Equator, which being substracted from 90. there rested 77. Degrees, and then the neerest north point of Noua Zembla, called the ice point, lay right East from them.

Then

The Nauigation into the North-seas.

There they found certaine Stones that glistered like gold, which for that cause they named gold-Stones, and there also they had a faire Bay with sandy ground.

Upon the same day they wound South-ward againe, and sailed South-east 2. miles betweene the Land and the Ice, and after that from the Ice point East, and to the South-ward 6. Miles to the Islands of Orange; and there they laboured forward betweene the Land and the Ice, with faire still weather, and vpon the 31. of July got to the Islands of Orange. And there went to one of those Islands, where they found about 200. Walrushen or Sea-horses, lying vpon the shoare to baske themselues in the sunne. This Sea-horse is a wonderfull strong monster of the sea, much bigger then an Oxe, which keepes continually in the seas, hauing a skinne like a Sea-calfe or Seale, with very short haire, mouthed like a Lyon, and many times they lie vpon the Ice; they are hardly killed vnlesse you strike them iust vpon the fore-head, it hath foure feet, but no eares, and commonly it hath one or two yong ones at a time. And when the Fisher-men chance to finde them vpon a flake of Ice with their yong ones, shee casteth her yong ones before her into the water, and then takes them in her armes and so plungeth vp and downe with them, and when shee will reuenge her selfe vpon the boats, or make resistance against them, then she casts her yong ones from her againe, & with all her force goeth towards the Boate, (whereby our men were once in no small danger, for that the Sea-horse had almost stricken her teeth into the sterne of their Boate) thinking to ouerthrowe it, but by meanes of the great cry that the men made, shee was afraid, and swomme away againe, and tooke her yong ones againe in her armes. They haue two teeth sticking out of their mouthes on each side one, each beeing about halfe an Elle long, and are esteemed to bee as good as any Iuorie or Elophants teeth, specially in Muscouia, Tartaria, and thereabouts where they are knowne, for they are as white, hard, and euen as Iuory.

Those Sea-horses that lay bathing themselues vpon the Land, our men supposing that they could not defend themselues beeing out of the water, went on shoare to assaile them, and fought with the, to get their teeth that are so rich, but they brake all their Hatchets, Curtle-axes, and Pikes in pieces, and could not kill one of them, but strucke some of their teeth out of their mouthes, which they tooke with them: and when they could get nothing against them by fighting, they

agreed

The Nauigation into the North-seas.

agreed to goe aboard the ship, to fetch some of their great Ordinance, to shoot at them therewith; but it began to blow so hard, that it rent the Ice into great peices, so that they were forced not to do it, & therewith they found a great white Beare that slept, which they shot into the body, but she ranne away, and entred into the water; the men following her with their boat, and kil'd her out-right, and then drew her vpon the Ice, and so sticking a halfe pike vp-right, bound her fast vnto it, thinking to fetch her when they came backe againe, to shoot at the Seahorses with their Ordinance, but for that it began more and more to blow, and the Ice therewith brake in peeces, they did nothing at all.

After that W. Barents had begun this voyage vpon the fifth of June, 1594. and at that time (as I sayd before) set saile out of the Texell, the 23. of the same month arriuing at Kilduin in Muscouia, and from thence tooke his course on the North side of Noua Zembla, wherein he continued till the first of August, with such aduentures as are before declared, till he came to the Island of Orange: after he had taken all that paine, and finding that he could hardly get through, to accomplish and ende his pretended Voyage, his men also beginning to bee weary and would saile no further, they all together agreed to returne back againe, to meet with the other ships that had taken their course to the Weygates, or the Straights of Nassawe, to know what discoueries they had made there.

There returne backe againe.

The first of August they turned their course to saile backe againe from the Islands of Orange, and sailed west and west by south 6. miles to the Ice point.

From the Ice point to the Cape of Comfort, they sailed West and somewhat South 30. Miles, betweene them both there lyeth very high Land, but the Cape of Comfort is very low flat land, and on the west end thereof there standeth foure or fiue blacke houels or little hilles like country houses.

Vpon the 3. of August, from the Cape of Comfort they wound North-ward, and sailed 8. Miles north-west, and by north, and North north-west, and about Noone they wound South-ward, till euening, and sailed south and by west, & south-south-west 7. Miles, & then came to a long narrow point of land one Cape Nassaw.

In the Euening they wound North-ward againe, and sailed north and by east 2. Miles, then the winde came North, and therefore they wound West-ward againe, & sailed North north-west one Mile, then

The Nauigation into the North-feas.

wind turned east, and with that they sailed from the 4. of August in the Morning till Noone West and by north 5. or 6. Miles, after that they sailed till Euening South-west 5. Miles, and after that South-west 2. Miles more, and fell vpon a low flat land which on the east-end had a white patche or peece of ground.

After that they sailed till Morning, being the 5. of August, West south-west, 5. miles, then south-west, 14. Miles, and then West 3. miles till the 6. of August.

The 6. of August they sailed West south-west, 2. or 3. Miles, then South-west, and south-west, and by South 4. or 5. miles, then south-west and by west 3. miles, and then South-west and by West 3. miles, and after that west south-west and South-west and by south 3. miles, till the 7. of August.

The 7. of August till Noone they sailed 3. miles west south-west, then 3. Miles west, and then they wound South-ward till Euening, and sailed 3. miles South-east and South-east and by east, then againe west south-west, 2. Miles, after that they sailed South 3. Miles, till the 8. of August in the Morning, with a West South-west winde.

The 8. of August they sailed South-east and by South 10. Miles, and then South-east and by East vntill Euening 5. Miles, and then came to a low flat land, that lay south-west and by South, and North-east and by North, and so sailed 5 Miles more, and there they had 36. fadome deepe, 2. Miles from the land, the ground blacke sand; There they sailed towards the land, till they were at 12. fadome, and halfe a Mile from the land it was Stony ground.

From thence the land reacheth south-ward for 3. miles, to the other low point that had a blacke Rocke lying close by it, and from thence the land reacheth South south-east 3. miles, to another point; and there lay a little low Island from the point, and within halfe a mile of the land it was flat ground, at 8. 9. and 10. fadome deepe, which they called the black Island, because it shewed blacke aboue, then it was very mistie, so that they lay in the wind, and sailed 3. Miles West North-west, but when it cleared vp, they wound towards the land againe, and the Sunne being South, they came right against the Blacke Island, and had held their course East South-east.

There W. Barents tooke the height of the sunne it being vnder 71. degrees and $\frac{1}{3}$, and there they found a great Creeke, which William Barents iudged to be the place where Oliuer Brunel had beene before, called

The Nauigation into the North-seas.

called Costincsarth.

From the Blacke Island, they sailed South, and South and by east to another small point 3. miles, on which point there stood a Crosse, and therefore they called it the Crosse-point, there also there was a flat Bay, and low water, 5. 6. or 7. fadome deep, soft ground.

From Crosse-point they sailed along by the land South South-east 4. Miles, and then came to another small point, which behinde it had a great Creeke, that reached East-ward: This point they called the fifth-point or S. Laurence point. From the fifth point they sailed to the Sconce point 3. Miles, South south-east, and there lay a long blacke Rocke close by the land, whereon there stood a Crosse; then they entered into the Ice againe, and put inward to the Sea because of the Ice. Their intent was to saile along the coast of Noua Zembla to the Wey-gates, but by reason that the Ice met them, they wound West-ward, and from the 9. of August in the Euening, till the 10. of August in the Morning, sayled West and by North 11. Miles, and after that 4. miles west north-west, and North-west and by west, the winde being North; in the Morning they wound East-ward againe and sailed vntill Euening 10. Miles East and east and by south; after that east and east and by north 4. Miles, and there they saw land, and were right against a great Creeke, where with their boat they went on land, and there found a faire Hauen 5. fadome deepe, sandy ground. This Creeke on the North-side hath 3. blacke points, and about the 3. points lyeth the road, but you must keepe somewhat from the 3. point, for it is stonie, and betweene the 2. and 3. point there is another faire Bay, for North-west, North; and North-east winds, blacke sandy ground. This Bay they called S. Laurence Bay, and there they tooke the height of the Sunne, which was 70. degrees and ½.

From S. Laurence Bay, south south-east 2. miles to Sconce point, there lay a long blacke rocke, close by the land, whereon there stood a Crosse, there they went on land with their boat, & perceiued that some men had bin there, and that they were fled to saue themselues, for there they found 6. Sacks with Ric-meale buried in the ground, and a heap of stones by the Crosse, and a bullet for a great piece, and there abouts also there stood another Crosse, with 3. houses made of wood, after the North-countrey manner: and in the houses they found many barrels of Pike-staues, whereby they coniectured, that there they vsed to take Salmons, and by them stood 5. or 6. Coffins, by graues, with dead
mens

The Nauigation into the North-seas.

mens bones, the Coffins standing vpon the ground all filled vp with stones; there also lay a broken Russia ship, the Keele thereof being 44. foot long, but they could see no man on the land: it is a faire Hauen for all winds, which they called the Meale-hauen, because of the Meale that they found there.

From the blacke Rocke or Cliffe with the Crosse, 2. Miles South south-east there lay a low Island, a little into the Sea; from whence they sailed 9. or 10. Miles South south-east, there the height of the Sunne was 70. degrees and 50. minutes, when it was South southwest.

From that Island they sailed along by the land 4. miles South-east and by South, there they came to 2. Islands, whereof the vttermost lay a mile from the land: these Islands they called S. Clara.

Then they entered into the Ice againe, and wound inward to sea, in the wind, and sailed from the Island vntill Euening West South-west 4. Miles, the wind being North-west; that Euening it was very mistie, and then they had 80. fadom deepe.

Then againe they sailed South-west and by West, and West South-west, 3. Miles, there they had 70. fadome deepe, and so sayled till the thirteenth of August in the Morning, South West and by West foure Miles, two houres before they had ground at fiftie sixe Fadome, and in the Morning at fortie fiue fadome, soft muddy ground.

Then they sayled till Noone sixe Miles South-west, and had twentie foure Fadome deepe, blacke sandie ground, and within one houre after, they had two and twentie Fadome deepe, browne reddish sands then they sailed sixe Miles South-west, with fifteene fadome deepe, red sand: after that two Miles South-west, and there it was fifteene Fadome deepe, red sand, and there they sawe land and sayled forward South-west vntill Euening, till wee were within halfe a mile of the land, and there it was seuen fadome deepe, sandy ground, the land, being low flat Downes reaching East and West.

Then they wound from the land, and sailed North, and North and by East 4. miles, from thence they wound to land againe, and sayled til the 14. of August 5. or 6. miles south-west, sailing close by the land, which (as they gesse) was the Island of Colgoyen, there they sailed by the lād east-ward 4. miles; after that 3. miles east, & east & by south,

D 2   then

The Nauigation into the North-seas.

then the weather became mistie, whereby they could not see the land, and had shallow flat water at 7. or 8. fadome; then they tooke in the Marsaile and lay in the wind, till it was cleare weather againe, and then the Sunne was South south-west, yet they could not see the land: there they had 100. fadome deepe, sandy ground, then they sailed East 7. miles; after that againe 2. miles East south-east, and South-east and by east, & againe till the 15. of August in the morning, 9. miles East south-east, then from morning till noone they sailed 4. Miles east south-east, and sailed ouer a flat or land, of 9. or 10. fadome deepe, sandy ground, but could see no land, and about an houre before noone it began to waxe deeper, for then wee had 12. and 13. fadome water, and then wee sayled East south-east 3. miles, till the Sunne was South-west.

The same day the sunne being south-west, William Barents tooke the height thereof, and found it to be eleuated aboue the Horizon 35. degrees, his declination being 14. degrees and $\frac{1}{4}$ so y as there wanted 55. degrees of 90. which 55. and 14. Degrees and $\frac{1}{4}$ being both added together, made 69. degrees 15. minutes, which was the height of the Pole in that place, the winde being North-west, then they sailed 2. Miles more East-ward, and came to the Islands called Matsloe and Delgoy, and there in the morning they meet with the other shippes of their company, being of Zelandt and Enck-huysen, that came out of Wey-gates the same day, there they shewed each other where they had bin, and how farre each of them had sailed, and discouered.

The ship of Enck-huysen had past the Staights of Wey-gates, and said, that at the end of Wey-gates he had found a large sea, and that they had sailed 50. or 60. Miles further East-ward, and were of opinion that they had been about the riuer of Obi, that commeth out of Tartaria, & that the land of Tartaria reacheth north-east-ward againe from thence, whereby they thought that they were not far from Cape Tabin, which is y point of Tartaria, that reacheth towards the king-dom of Chathai, North-east and then south-ward, and so thinking that they had discouered inough for that time, & that it was too late in the yeare to saile any further, as also that their Commission was to discouer the scituation, and to come home againe before winter, they turned againe towards the Wei-gates, and came to an Island about 5. Miles great, lying south-east from Wei-gates on the Tartarian side, and called it the States Island, there they found many Stones, that

were

The Nauigation into the North-seas.

were of a Cristale Mountaine being a kind of Diamont.

When they were met together as I sayd before, they made signes of ioy, discharging some of their ordinance, and were merry, the other shippes thinking that William Barents had sailed round about Noua Zembla, & had come backe againe through the Wei-gates: & after they had shewed each other what they had done, and made signes of ioy for their meeting, they set their course to turne backe againe for Holland, and vpon the 16. of August they went vnder the Islands of Matsloe and Delgoy, and put into the road, because the wind was north-west, and lay there till the 18. of August.

The 18. of August they set saile, and went forward West northwest, and almost West and by North, and so sailed 12. miles, and then west and by south 6. Miles, and came to a sand of scarce 5. fadome deepe, with a north-west wind, and in the euening they wound northward and sailed East north-east 7. or 8. miles, the wind being northerly, & then they wound West-ward & sailed till the 19. of August in the morning west 2. miles, then 2. miles south-west, and after that 2. miles south-east: there they wound West-ward againe, and sailed till Euening with a calme, and after that had an East winde, and at first sailed West north-west, and North-west and by west 6. or 7. Miles, and had ground at 12. fadome: then till the 20. of August in the morning, they sailed West north-west, and north-west and by West, 7. miles with an Easterly wind, & then againe sailed West north-west, and North-west and by West 7. miles, then West north-west 4. Miles, and draue forward till euening with a calme: after that they sailed West north-west and North-west and by west 7. Miles, and in the night time came to a sand of 3. fadome deepe right against the land, and so sailed along by it, first one mile North, then 3. Miles North north-west, and it was sandy hilly land, and many points: and then sailed on forward with 9. or 10. fadome deepe, along by the land, till noone, being the 21. of August, North-west 5 Miles; and the West point of the land, called Candinaes, lay north-west from them 4. Miles.

From thence they sailed 4. Miles North north-west, and then north-west and by North 4. Miles, and 3. Miles more North-west, and north-west & by North, and then North-west 4. Miles, til the 22. of August in the Morning: and that morning they sailed North-west 7. miles, & so till euening, west north-west & north-west & by west 15. miles, the wind being north, after that 8. miles more west north-west,

The Nauigation into the North-seas.

and then till the 23. of August at Noone, West north-west 11. miles, the same day at noone the Sunne was cituated aboue the Horizon 31. Degrees and ⅓ part, his declination was 11. Degrees and ⅓ partes; so that it wanted 58. Degrees and ⅓ of 90. Degrees, and adding the declination being 11. Degrees ⅔ to 58. Degrees, and ⅓ partes, then the height of the Pole was 70. Degrees and ⅓ part: then they sailed North-west, and north-west and by west, till Euening 8. miles, and then North-west and by west, and West north-west 5. Miles, and then vntill the 24. of August in the Morning, North-west, and by west 6. miles, after that West, and West south-west, 3. Miles, and then past close by the Island of Ware-huysen in the roade. From Ware-huysen hither-ward because the way is well knowne, I neede not to write thereof, but that from thence they sailed altogether homeward, and kept company together till they came to the Texel, where the ship of Zelandt past by, and William Barents with his Pinnace, came vpon a faire day, being the 16. of September before Amsterdam, and the ship of Enck-huysen, to Enck-huysen, from whence they were set foorth. William Barents men brought a Sea-horse to Amsterdam, being of a wonderfull greatnesse, which they tooke vpon a flake of Ice, and killed it.

The end of this Voiage.

A

A Briefe Declaration of

a Second Nauigation made in Anno 1595. Behinde *Norway*, *Muscouia*, and *Tartaria*, towards the Kingdoms of *Cathaia* and *China*.

The 4. ships aforesaid being returned home about Haruest-time, in Anno 1594. they were in good hope that the Voiage aforesaid would be done, by passing along through the Straights of Weygates, and specially by the report made by the 2. ships of Zelandt, and Enck-huysen, wherein Iohn Huyghen of Linschoten was committed, who declared the manner of their trauell in such sort, that the Generall States and Prince Maurice resolued, in the beginning of the next yeare to prepare certaine ships, not only (as they went before) to discouer the passage, but to send certaine wares and Merchandises thither, wherein the Marchants might lade what wares they would, with certaine Factors to sell the saide wares, in such places as they should arriue, neither paying straight nor custome. Peter Plantius a learned Cosmographer being a great furtherer and setter forward of this Voiage, and was their chiefe instructer therein, setting downe the scituation of the Coasts of Tartaria, Cathaia, and China; but how they lye, it is not yet sufficiently discouered, for that the courses and rules by him set downe, were not fully effected, by meanes of some inconueniences that fell out, which by reason of the shortnesse of time could not be holpen. The reasons that some men (not greatly affected to this Voyage) vse to propound, to affirme it not possible to be done, are taken (as they say) out of some old & auncient Writers: which is, ÿ 350. miles at the least of the North Pole on both sides are not to be

sailed

The Nauigation into the North-seas.

sailed, which appeareth not to be true, for that the white Sea, and farther North-ward, is now sayled & daily fisht in, cleane contrary to the writings and opinions of auncient Writers; yea, & how many places hath bin discouered that were not knowne in times past: It is also no marueile (as in the beginning of the first description of this Voyage I haue sayd) that vnder the North Pole for 23. degrees, it is as cold on both sides, one as the other, although it hath not beene fully discouered. Who would beleeue that in the Periudan Mountaines, and the Alpes that lye betweene Spaine, Italie, Germanie, and France, there is so great cold, that the Snow thereon neuer melteth, and yet lye a great deale neerer the Sunne, then the Countries lying on the North-Seas doe, being low Countries; by what meanes then is it so cold in those Hilles: onely by meanes of the deepe Vallies wherein the Snow lyes so deepe, that the Sunne cannot shine vpon the ground, by reason that the high Hilles keepe the Sunne from shining on them. So it is (as I iudge) with the Ice in the Tartarian seas, which is also called the Ice-sea, about Noua Zembla, where the Ice that commeth into those seas out of the Riuers that are in Tartaria and Cathaia, can not melt, by reason of the great quantitie thereof, and for that the sun sheweth not high aboue those places, & therefore casteth not so great a heat, as it can easily melt: which is the cause that the Ice lyeth there still, as the Snowe doth in the Hilles of Spaine aforesayd, and that the sayd Ice maketh it farre colder there, then it is a great deale neerer the Pole in the large seas, and although those places that are not discouered, cannot bee so well described, as if they were discouered: yet I thought good to say thus much for a memoriall; and now I will proceed to the declaration of the second Voyage made into the North-seas.

In Anno 1595. The generall States of the vnited Prouinces, and Prince Maurice, caused seuen shippes to bee prepared to sayle through the Wey-gates or the Staights of Nassaue, to the Kingdome of Cathaia and China: Two out of Amsterdam, two out of Zelandt, two out of Enck-huysen, and one out of Roterdam: sixe of them laden with diuers kindes of Wares, Marchandizes, and with Money, and Factors to sell the said wares; the seuenth beeing a Pinace, that had Commission, when the other shippes were past about the Cape de Tabin (which is the furthest point of Tartaria) or so farre that they might saile foorth South-

ward

The Nauigation into the North-feas.

ward, without any let or hinderance of the Ice, to turne backe againe, and to bring Newes thereof: and I being in William Barents ship, that was our chiefe Pilote, and Iames Heinſ-kerke chiefe Factor, thought good to write downe the same in order, as it is here after declared, as I did the first Voyage, according to the course and stretching of the land as it lyeth.

First, after we had been muſtered at Amſterdam, and every man taken an oath, that was then purpoſely miniſtered vnto vs; vpon the 18. of June wee ſailed to the Texel, from thence to put to ſea with other ſhips that were appointed to meet vs at a certaine day; & so to begin our Voiage in the Name of God.

The 2. of July wee set saile out of the Texel, in the Morning at breake of day, holding our courſe North weſt and by North, and ſayled about ſixe miles.

After that wee ſailed North north-weſt 18. miles, till the 3. of July in the Morning, being then as wee eſteemed vnder 55. Degrees, then the wind being North-weſt, and North north-weſt, calme weather, wee ſailed Weſt, and Weſt and by South 4. Miles, till the 4. of July in the Morning: after that the winde being North northweſt, and rather more Northerly, wee ſayled Weſt, and weſt and by North 15. Miles, till the 5. of July in the Morning, and after that 8. Miles more till the Sunne was weſt.

Then we wound about and ſailed 10. Miles North-eaſt, till the 6. of July in the Morning, and so held on our courſe for the space of 24. miles till the 7. of July, the Sunne being South, and held the ſame courſe for 8. Miles, till mid-night.

Then wee wound about and ſailed Weſt ſouth-weſt fourteene Miles, till the ninth of July in the Morning, and then againe wee wound North Eaſt-ward, till Euening and so ſayled about tenne Miles.

And then eighteene Miles more eaſt-ward, till the tenth of July in the Euening; then we wound about againe and ſailed South-weſt, eight Miles, till the 11. of July, the Sunne then being South-Eaſt.

Then wee wound North, and North and by Eaſt, about ſixteene Miles, till the twelue of July, and then North and by Weſt tu. miles.

The 13. of July wee wound about againe, and ſailed South-
weſt

The Nauigation into the North-seas.

west, and West South-west 10. Miles, till about three houres before Euening: then wee wound againe, and sailed North north-east 10. Miles, till the 14. of July, the Sunne being South South-east, and then North and by East, and North north-east 18. Miles, till the 15. of July in the Morning: after that North and by East 12. miles, vntill Euening, then wee saw Norway: and then wee sayled North and by East 18. Miles, till the 16. of July in the Euening; at the time the Sunne being North-west, and vpon the 17. of July, North-east, and North-east and by North, 24. Miles, till the sunne was in the West.

Then againe we sayled north-east 20. miles, till the 18. of July, the Sunne being North-west, from thence wee sayled North-west, and by North 18. Miles, till the 19. of July, when the Sunne was west.

From thence againe we wound about, North-east and by North and North-east till the 20. of July, while sixe Glasses were run out, in the first quarter, and then stayed for our Pinnace, that could not follow vs, because the wind blew so stiffe: that quarter being out, we saw our company lying to Lee-ward, to stay for vs, and when we were gotten to them, wee helde our course (as before) till Euening, and sailed about 30. Miles.

Then we sayled South-east and by East 26. Miles, till the 21. of July in the Euening, when wee let our watch, and held on the same course for 10. miles till the 22. of July, the sun being South south-east, the same euening the sun being south south-west we saw a great Whale, right before our bough, that lay and slept, which by the rushing of the ship that made towards it, and the noyse of our men awaked, and swamme away, or els wee must haue sailed full vpon her, and so wee sayled eight Miles, till the Sunne was North North-west.

The thirteenth of July wee sayled South-east and by South fifteene Miles, till the sunne was South South-west, and saw land about foure Miles from vs, Then wee wound of from the Land, when the Sunne was about South South-west, and sayled twentie foure Miles till Euening, that the Sunne was North-west.

After that we sayled North-ward tenne Miles, till the fifteenth of July, at Noone, and then North North-west eight Miles till Mid-night, then wee wound about againe, and sayled East South-east, and South-east and by South, till the twentie sixe of July, the
Sunne

The Nauigation into the North-seas.

Sunne being South, and had the Sunne at seauentie one Degrees and ¼.

The Sunne beeing South South-west, wee wounde about againe, and sayled North-east and by North, till the Seauen and twentie of July, the Sunne being South; being vnder 72. degrees and ¼. partes.

After that, wee sayled full North-east 16. Myles, till the 28. of July, the Sunne being East. Then we wound about againe South and by East, till the Sunne was North-west, and sayled 8. Miles. After that, South-east and by South 18. Miles, till the 29. of July at midnight.

After that, we wound about againe, East and by North, and sayled eight miles, till the 30. of July, when the Sunne was North: then we wound South south-east, with calme weather, till the 31. of July, that the Sunne was North-west, and sayled sixe Miles.

From thence wee sayled East-ward 8. Myles, till the first of August about midnight, in calme faire weather, and saw Trumpsand South-east from vs, the Sunne being North: and wee being tenne Miles from the land, and so sayled till the Sunne was East, with a litle cold gale out of the East North-east, and after that, South-east 9. Myles and a halfe, till the Sunne was North-west.

Then we wound about againe, being halfe a Mile from the land, and sayled East and by North three miles, till the 3. of August, the Sunne South-west: and then along by the land about 5. Miles.

Then we wound about againe, because there lay a Rocke or Sand, that reached about a mile and a halfe out from the land into the Sea, whereon Isbrant the Vize-admirall stroke with his Shippe: but the weather being faire and good, he got off againe. When he stroke vpon it, he was a litle before vs; and when we heard him cry out, and saw his Shippe in danger, wee in all haste wound about, & the Wind being North-east and by East, and South-east and South-east and by South, wee sayled 5 or 6. Myles along by the land, till the Sunne was South, vpon the 4. of August.

Then we tooke the height of the Sunne, and found it to be Seauentie and one degrees and ¼. At which time till noone, wee had calme weather: and hauing the Wind Southerly wee sayled East and by North, till the fifth of August, the Sunne being South-east,

the

The Nauigation into the North-seas.

the North Cape lying about two miles, East from vs, and when the Sunne was North-west, the mother and her daughters lay Southward from vs foure miles, and in that time we sailed about fourteene miles.

Then we sailed East north-east, till the 6. of August, when wee had the Sunne West north-west, and then If-brandt the Uize-admirall, came to vs with his ship, and so bating some of our sayles, wee sayled about 10. miles.

Then we hoysed vp our sailes againe, till the Sunne was Northwest, and after that halde vp againe with an East, and East-northeast wind, and sailed south and by west with a stiffe gale, till the 7. of August, that the Sunne was south-east, then their came a ship of Enckhuysen out of the white sea, and then we esteemed that wee had sailed about 8. Miles.

The Sunne being south, the North Cape lay south-west and by south from vs, about a mile and a halfe, and the mother and her daughters south-west from vs, about 3. miles, then hauing an East and by north wind we wound about, and held our course North and by east, and sailed 14. miles till the 8. of August, when the Sunne was southwest; then we wound south and by east, aud so held her course till the 9. of August, that the sunne was south; and then we saw a high point of land south-east from vs, and another high point of land south-ward, about 4. miles from vs, as we gest, and so we sailed about 14. miles: and then againe we wound North-east, & by North, till the 10. of August, the sun being east, and sailed about 8. miles; after that we wound south-ward againe, till the sunne was North-west, and sailed (as we gest) 10. miles.

Then wee wound about againe, when the North Cape lay West and by south from vs about 9. Miles, the North-kyen being South and by West from vs, about 3. Miles, and sailed North north-east till the 11. of August, in very mistie weather 10. miles, till the sunne was south.

From thence wee wound about againe, with an East North-east wind, and sailed south-east and by south 8. Miles, till the sunne was south-west, vpon the 12. of August, then the North-kyen lying southwest and by south from vs about 8. miles, we lay and draue at sea, in calme weather, till the 13. of August, when the sunne was south southwest, and in that time sailed about 4. miles.

The

The Nauigation into the North-seas.

Then we sailed south-east and by east, about 4. Glasses, and then the Iron-hogge, with her companie (being Marchants) tooke their course south-ward, and wee sailed till the 14. of August (when the sunne was south) about 18. miles, and from thence for the most part, held one course till the 15. of August, the sunne being East, and there we cast out the lead and found 70. fadome deepe, and sailed 38. Miles till the sunne was south.

The sunne being south and the height thereof being taken, it was found to be 70. Degrees and 47. minutes, then in the night time wee cast out the lead, & found ground at 40. fadome, it being a bancke, the sunne being North-west, we cast out the lead againe and had ground at 64. fadome, and so wee went on East south east till the 16. of August, the sunne being North-east, & there the line being out, we found no ground at 80. fadome, and after that we sailed East and east, and by south, and in that time wee cast the lead often times out, and found ground at 60. and 70. Fadome either more or lesse, and so sailed 36. Miles, till the sunne was south.

Then we sailed East, and so continued till the 17. of August, the sunne being east, and cast out our lead, and found 60. Fadome deepe, clay ground, and then taking the height of the sunne, when it was south-west and by south, we found it to be 69. Degrees and 54. Minutes, and there we saw great store of Ice, all along the coast of Noua Zembla, and casting out the lead had 75. fadome soft ground, and so sayled about 24. miles.

After that we held diuers courses because of the Ice, and sayled south-east and by east, and south south-east, for the space of 18. miles, till the 18. of August, when the Sunne was East, and then wee cast out the lead againe, and found 30. fadome soft ground, and within 2. houres after that 25. fadome, red sand, with small shels: Three glasses after that we had ground at 20. fadome, red sand, with blacke shels, as before: then we saw 2. Islands, which they of Enck-huysen gaue the names of Prince Maurice and his brother, which lay from vs south-east 3. miles, being low land, and then we sailed 8. miles, till the Sunne was South.

Then we sailed East, and oftentimes casting out the lead we found 20. 19. 18. and 17. fadome deepe, good ground mixed with blacke shels, and saw the Wey-gates (the Sunne being west) which lay east north-east from vs about 5. miles, and after that we sailed about 8. miles.

Then

The Nauigation into the North-seas.

Then we sailed vnder 70. Degrees, vntill we came to the Wey-gates, most part through broken Ice, and when we got to Wey-gates, we cast out our lead, and for a long time found 13. and 14. fadom, soft ground, mixed with blacke shels, not long after that wee cast out the lead and found 10. fadome deepe, the wind being North, and wee forced to hold stifly aloofe, in regard of the great quantitie of Ice, till about midnight, then we were forced to wind North-ward, because of certaine rocks that lay on the South-side of Wey-gates, right before vs, about a mile and a halfe, hauing ten fadome deepe: then wee changed our course, and sailed West North-west for the space of 4. Glasses, after that we wound about againe East, and East and by South, and so entred into Wey-gates, and as wee went in, we cast out the lead, and found 7. fadome deepe little more or lesse, till the 19. of August, and then the sunne being South-east, we entered into the Wey-gates, in the road, the Wind being North.

The right Chanell betweene the Image point and the Samuter land was full of Ice, so that it was not well to be past through, and so we went into the road (which wee called the Trayen Bay, because we found store of Trayen-oyle there, this is a good bay for the course of the Ice, and good almost for all Windes, and we may saile so farre into it as we will, at 4. 5. & 3. fadome, good anchor-ground, on the East side it is deepe water.

The 20. of August, the height of the Sunne being taken with the Crosse-staffe, wee found that it was eleuated aboue the Horizon 69. Degrees 21. minuts, when it was South-west and by South, being at the highest, or before it began to descend.

The 21 of August we went on land with in the Wey-gates with foure and fiftie men, to see the scituation of the Countrey, and being 2. miles within the land, we found many Vel-werck, Trayen, and such like wares, and diuers foot-steps of men, and Deere; whereby wee perceiued that some men dwelt thereabouts, or else vsed to come thither.

And to assure vs the more therrof, wee might perceiue it by the great number of Images, which wee found there vpon the Image or Beelthoocke (so called by vs) in great abourndance, whereof ten dayes after we were better informed by the Samuters and the Russians, when we spake with them.

The Nauigation into the North-seas.

And when wee entered further into the Land, wee vsed all the meanes we could, to see if we could find any houses, or men, by whom wee might bee informed of the scituation of the Sea there abouts, whereof afterward wee had better intelligence by the Samuters, that tolde vs, that there are certaine men dwelling on the Wey-gates, and vpon Noua Zembla, but wee could neither finde men, houses, nor any other things, so that to haue better information, we went with some of our men further South-east into the land, towards the Sea side; and as we went, we found a path-way made with mens feete in the Mosse or Marsh-ground, about halfe knee deepe, for that going so deepe wee felt hard ground vnder our feete, which at the deepest was no higher then our shoes, and as wee went forward to the Sea Coast, wee were exceeding glad, thinking that wee had seene a passage open, where wee might get through, because we saw so little Ice there: and in the Euening entering into our ship againe, wee shewed them that newes. Meane time our Maister had sent out a boat to see if the Tartarian Sea was open, but it could not get into the Sea because of the Ice, yet they rowed to the Crosse-point, and there let the Boate lye, and went ouer the Land to the West point, and there perceiued that the Ice in the Tartarian Sea, lay full vpon the Russian Coastes, and in the mouth of Wey-gates.

The twentie three of August wee found a Lodgie, or Boate of Pitzore, which was sowed together with bast or ropes, that had beene North-ward to seeke for some Sea-horses teeth, Trayen, and Geese, which they fetcht with their Boat, to lade in certaine shippes that were to come out of Russia, through Wey-gates.

Which shippes they sayd (when they spake with vs) were to saile into the Tartarian Sea, by the Riuer of Oby to a place called Vgolita in Tartaria, there to stay all Winter, as they vsed to doe euery yeere: and told vs that it would yet bee nine or tenne Weekes ere it began to Freeze in that place, and that when it once began to freeze, it would freeze so hard, that as then men might goe ouer the Sea into Tartaria, (along vpon the Ice) which they called Mermare.

The 24. of August in the Morning betimes, we went on board of the Lodgie, to haue further information and instruction of the Sea, on the East side of Wey-gates, and they gaue vs good instruction, such as you haue heard.

The 25. of August we went againe to the Lodgie, and in friendly maner spake with them, we for our parts offering them friendship; and then they gaue vs 8. fat Geese, that lay in the bottome of their Boat: we desired that one or two of them would goe with vs on board our ship, and they willingly went with vs to the number of seuen; and being in our ship they wondered much at the greatnesse, and furniture of our ship: and after they had seene and looked into it in euery place, we set Fish, Butter, and Cheese before them to eat, but they refused it, saying, that that day was a fasting day with them, but at last when they saw some of our pickled-Herrings, they eat them both heads, tayles, skin, and guts, and hauing eaten thereof, we gaue them a small firkin of Herrings, for the which they gaue vs great thankes, knowing not what friendship they should doe vs to requite our courtesie, and wee brought them with our Pinnace into the Traen Bay.

About Noone wee hoysed vp our anchors with a West north-west winde; the course or stretching of Wey-gates, is east to the Cruis point, and then North-east to the Twist point, & somewhat more Easterly. From thence the land of Wey-gates reacheth North north-east, and North and by East, and then North, and somewhat westerly, we sayled North-east and East-ward 2. miles, by the Twist point, but then we were compelled to saile backe againe, because of the great store of Ice, and tooke our course to our road aforesaid: and sayling backe againe wee found a good place by the Crosse point to anchor in, that night.

The 26. of August in the Morning we hoysed anchor, and put out our fork-saile, and so sailed to our old road, there to stay for a more conuenient time.

The 28. 29. and 30. of August till the 31. the winde for the most part was South-west, and William Barents our Captaine, sayled to the Southside of Wey-gates, and there went on land, where wee found certaine Wilde men (called Samuters) and yet not altogether wilde, for they being 20. in number stayd & spake with our men, being but 9. together, about a mile within the land, our men not thinking to find any men there (for that we had at other times beene on land in the Wey-gates, and saw none) at last it being mistie weather, they perceiued men, fiue and fiue in a company, and wee were hard by them

before

The Nauigation into the North-Seas.

Wey-gates, and saw none) at last, it being mistie weather, they perceiued men 5. and 5. in a company, and wee were hard by them before we knew it: then our Interpretor went alone towardes them to speake with them; which they perceiuing, sent one towardes vs, who comming almost to our men, tooke an Arrow out of his quiuer, offering to shoote at him; wherewith our Interpretor, being without Armes, was afraide, and cryed vnto him, saying (in Russian speach;) Shoote not, we are friends: which the other hearing, cast his Bow and Arrowes to the ground, therewith giuing him to vnderstand that he was well content to speake with our man: which done, our man called to him once againe, and sayd: Wee are friendes: whereunto he made answere & sayd; then you are welcome: and saluting one the other, bended both their heades downe towardes the ground, after the Russian manner: this done, our Interpretor questioned with him, about the scituation & stretching of the Sea eastward through the Straightes of Wey-gates; whereof he gaue vs good instruction, saying: that when they should haue past a poynt of Land about 5. dayes sayling from thence, shewing North-eastward;) that after that, there is a great Sea (shewing towardes the South-east vpward,) saying, that hee knew it very well, for that one had been there that was sent thither by their King with certaine Souldiers, whereof he had been Captaine.

The maner of their Apparell is, like as we vse to paint Wild men, but they are not wilde; for they are of reasonable iudgement: they are apparelled in Hartes skins from the head to the feete, vnlesse it be the principallest of them, which are apparelled, whether they bee men or women, like vnto the rest, as aforesayd, vnlesse it bee on their heads, which they couer with certaine coloured Cloth lyned with Furre: the rest weare Cappes of Hartes or Buckes skinnes, the rough side outwardes, which stand close to their heades, and are very fitte. They weare long Hayre, which they plaite and fold, and let it hang downe vpon their backes. They are (for the most part all) short and low of stature, with broad flat faces, small eyes, short legges, their knees standing outwards; and are very quicke to goe and leape. They trust not Strangers; for although that wee shewed them all the courtesie and friendship that wee could, yet they trusted vs not much: which we perceiued hereby, that as vpon the first of September we went againe on land to them, and that one of our men desired

The Nauigation into the North-seas.

to see one of their Bowes: they refused it, making a signe that they would not doe it. Hee that they called their King, had Centinels standing abroad, to see what was done in the Countrie, and what was bought and sould: At last, one of our men went neerer to one of the Centinels, to speake with him, and offered him great friendship, according to their accustomed manner, withall giuing him a Bisket; which he with great thankes tooke, and presently eate it; and while he eate it, hee still lookt diligently about him on all sides what was done.

Their Sleades stood alwayes ready with one or two Hartes in them, that runne so swiftly with one or two men in them, that our Horses are not able to follow them. One of our men shot a Musket towards the Sea, wherewith they were in so great feare, that they ranne and leapt like mad men: yet at last, they satisfied themselues, when they perceiued that it was not maliciously done to hurt them, and we told them by our Interpretor, that wee vsed our Peeces in stead of Bowes; whereat they wondered, because of the great blow and noyse that it gaue and made: and to shew them what we could doe therewith, one of our men tooke a flatte Stone about halfe a handfull broad, and set it vpon a Hill a good way off from him: which they perceiuing, and thinking that wee meant some-what thereby, 50. or 60. of them gathered round about vs; and yet some-what farre off, wherewith hee that had the Peece, shotte it off, and with the Bullet smote the Stone in sunder: whereat they woondred much more then before.

After that, we tooke our leaues one of the other, with great friendship on both sides; and when we were in our Penace, we al put off our Hattes, and bowed our Heades vnto them, sounding our Trumpets: They (in their manner) saluting vs also, & then went to their Sleades againe.

And after they were gone from vs, and were some-what within the Land, one of them came ryding to the shore, to fetch a rough heawed Image, that our men had taken off the shore, & caryed into the Boate: And when he was in our Boate, and perceiued the Image, hee made vs a signe that wee had not done well to take away the Image: Which wee beholding, gaue it to him againe: Which when he had receiued, he placed it vpon a hill right by the sea side, and tooke

The Nauigation into the North-seas.

it not with him, but sent a Slead to fetch it from thence: and as farre as wee could perceiue, they esteemed that Image to be their God; for that right ouer against that place in the Wey-gates, which wee called Beelthooke, wee found certaine hundreds of such carued Images, all rough about the Heads, being somewhat round, and in the middle hauing a litle hill in stead of a Nose; and about the Nose two cuttes, in place of Eyes; and vnder the Nose a cutte, in place of a Mouth. Before the Images, wee found great store of Ashes, and Bones of Hartes: whereby it is to be supposed, that there they offered vnto them.

Hauing left the Samuters, the Sunne being South-ward, William Barents our Captaine, spake to the Admirall to will him to set sayle, that they might goe forward: but they had not so many wordes togeather, as was betweene them the day before; for that when the Admirall and Vize-admirall had spoken with him, the Admirall seeming to be well contented therewith, said vnto him: Captaine, What thinke you were best for vs to doe? He made answere. I thinke wee should doe well to set sayle, and goe forward on our Voyage, that wee may accomplish it. Whereunto the Admirall answeared him, and sayd. Looke well what you doe Captaine: at which time, the Sunne was North-west.

The 2. of September a litle before Sunne rising, wee put foorth our Anckor to get out, for that the Winde as then blew South southwest; it being good weather to get out, and ill weather to lie still: for we lay vnder a low Bancke. The Admirall and Vize-admirall, seeing vs making out, began also to hoyse their Anckors, and to set sayle.

When wee put out our Focke-sayle, the Sunne was East and by South: and then we sayled to the Crosse-poynt, and there wee cast Anckor to stay for the Vize-admirals Pinnace; which with much labour and paines, in time got out of the Ice, by often casting out of their Anckor: and in the euening shee got to vs: in the morning about 2. houres before Sunne rising, we set sayle, and by Sunne rising, we got within a mile East-ward of the Twist-poynt, and sayled North-ward 6. miles, till the Sunne was South. Then wee were forced to wind about, because of the great quantitie of Ice, and the Mist that then fell, at which time the Winde blew so vncertaine, that

that we could hold no course, but were forced continually to winde and turne about, by reason of the Ice, and the vnconstantnesse of the wind, together with the mist, so that our course was vncertaine, and we supposed that we had sailed south-ward vp towardes the Samuters countrey, and then held our course south-west, till the watchers were north-west from vs; then we came to the point of the States Island, lying East-ward about a musket shot from the land, hauing 13. fadome deepe.

The 4. of September, we hoysed anchor, because of the Ice, and sailed betweene the firme land and the States Island, where wee lay close by the States Island at 4. and 5. fadome deepe, and made our shippe fast with a cable cast on the shoare, & there we were safe from the course of the Ice, and diuers time went on land, to get Hares whereof there were many in that Island.

The 6. of September, some of our men went on shore vpon the firme land to seeke for stones, which are a kinde of Diamont, whereof there are many also in the States Island: & while they were seeking ye stones, 2. of our men lying together in one place, a great leane white beare came sodainly stealing out, and caught one of them fast by the necke, who not knowing what it was that tooke him by the necke, cried out and said; Who is that that pulles me so by the necke? wherewith the other that lay not farre from him, lifted vp his head to see who it was, and perceiuing it to be a monsterous beare, cryed and sayd, Oh Mate it is a Beare, and therewith presently rose vp and ran away.

The Beare at the first faling vpon the man, bit his head in sunder, and suckt out his blood, werewith the rest of the men that were on land, being about 20. in number, ran presently thither, either to saue the man, or else to driue the beare from the dead body: and hauing charged their peeces and bent their pikes set vpon her, that still was deuouring the man, but perceiuing them to come towardes her, fiercely and cruelly ran at them, and gat another of them out from the companie which she tare in peeces, wherewith all the rest ran away.

We perceiuing out of our ship and Pinace that our men ran to the sea-side to saue themselues, with all speed entered into our Boates, and rowed as fast as we could to the shoare to relieue our men. When being on land, we beheld the cruell spectacle of our two dead men, that had beene so cruelly killed and torne in peeces by the Beare, wee seeing that

The Nauigation into the North-seas.

that incouraged our men to goe backe againe with vs, and with peeces, curtelaxes, and halfe-pikes to set vpon the Beare, but they would not all agree thereunto: some of them saying, our men are already dead, and we shall get the Beare well enough, though wee oppose not our selues into so open danger, if wee might saue our fellowes liues, then we would make haste, but now wee neede not make such speede, but take her at an aduantage, with most securitie for our selues, for we haue to doe with a cruell fierce and rauenous beast. Whereupon three of our men went forward, the Beare still deuouring her prey, not once fearing the number of our men, and yet they were thirtie at the least: the three that went forward in that sort, were Cornelius Iacobson, Maister of William Barents shippe, William Gysen, Pilote of the Pinace, and Hans van Nufflen, William Barents Purser: and after that the sayd Maister and Pilote had shot three times, and mist, the Purser stepping somewhat further forward, and seeing the Beare to be within the length of a shot, presently leauelled his peece, and discharging it at the Beare, shot her into the head, betweene both the eyes, and yet shee held the man still fast by the necke, and lifted vp her head, with the man in her mouth, but shee beganne somewhat to stagger, wherewith the Purser and a Scotishman, drew out their courtlaxes, and stroke at her so hard, that their Courtlaxes burst, and yet she would not leaue the man, at last William Geysen went to them, and with all his might stroke the Beare vpon the snowt with his peece, at which time the Beare fell to the ground, making a great noyse, and William Geyson leaping vpon her cut her throat. The seuenth of September wee buryed the dead bodyes of our men in the States Island, and hauing fleaed the Beare, carryed her skinne to Amsterdam.

The ninth of September, wee set saile from the States Island, but the Ice came in so thicke and with such force, that wee could not get through, so that at Euening wee came backe againe to the States Island, the winde being Westerly. There the Admirale and the Pinace of Roterdam, fell on ground by certaine rockes, but gote off againe without any hurt.

The tenth of September, wee sayled againe from the States Island, towards the Weygates, and sent two Boates into the Sea, to certifie vs what store of Ice was abroad: and that Euening we came

The Nauigation into the North-seas.

all together into Wey-gates, and anckored by the Twist point.

The 11. of September in the Morning, we sailed againe into the Tartarian sea, but we fell into great store of Ice, so that wee sailed backe againe to the Wey-gates, & anckored by the Crosse point, and about mid-night we saw a Russian Lodgie, that sailed from the Beeli point towardes the Samuters Land. The 13. of September, the Sunne being South, there beganne a great storme to blowe out of the South South-west, the weather being mistie, melancholly, and snowie, and the storme increasing more and more we draue through.

The 14. of September the weather beganne to bee somewhat clearer, the winde being North-west, and the Storme blowing still out of the Tartarian Sea, but at Euening it was faire weather, and then the winde blewe North-east, the same day our men went on the other side of Wey-gates, on the firme land, to take the depth of the channell, and entered into the bough behinde the Islands, where there stood a little howse made of wood, and a great sail of water to the land. The same Morning wee hoysed vp our anchor, thinking once againe to try what we could doe to further our Uoyage, but our Admirall being of another minde, lay still till the fifteene of September.

The same day in the Morning, the winde draue in from the East end of the Wey-gates, whereby wee were forced presently to hoyse anchors, and the same day sailed out from the West end of the Wey-gates, with all our Fleete, and made home-wardes againe, and that day past by the Islands called Matfloe and Delgoy, and that Night wee sayled twelue Miles, North-west and by West, till Saterday in the Morning, and then the winde fell North-east, and it began to snow.

The 16. of September, from Morning to Euening, wee sayled West North-west 18. Miles, at 42. Fadome deepe, in the night it snowed & there blew very much winde out of the North-east: the first quarter wee had 40. Fadome deepe, but in the Morning we saw not any of our ships.

After that wee sailed all the night againe, till the 17 of September in the Morning, with two schower sailes, North-west and by West, and West North-west 10. Miles, the same day in the second quarter we had 50. Fadome deepe, and in the Morning 38.

Fadome

The Nauigation into the North-seas.

fadome deepe, sandy ground with blacke shels.

Sunday in the Morning wee had the winde North, and North North-west with a great gale, and then the Admirals Pinnace kept vs company, and sailed by vs with one saile from Morning to Euening, South South-west, and South-west and by South, for the space of 6. Miles.

Then wee saw the point of Candynaes, lying South-east from vs, and then wee had 27. Fadome deepe, redde sand with blacke shels. Sunday at night wee put out our focke saple, and wound North-ward ouer, and sayled all that night till Sunday in the Morning, 7. or 8. Miles North-east, and North-east and by East.

The 18. of September in the Morning, wee lost the sight of the Pinnace that followed vs, and till Noone sought after her, but wee could not finde her, and sailed East-ward 3. Miles, and from Noone till Night, wee sailed North and by East foure Miles. And from Sunday at night, till Tuesday in the Morning, North-east and by North, seuen Miles, and from Morning till Noone, North-east and by North 4. Miles; and from Noone till night, North-east 5. or 6. Miles at 55. Fadome deepe; the same Euening wee woond South-ward and sailed so till Morning.

The 20. of September, wee sayled South and by West, and South South-west 7. or 8. Miles, at 80. fadome deepe, blacke slimie ground; from Morning till Noone, wee sailed with both our Marsh sailes, South west, and by West 5. Miles, and from Noone to night, West and by South 5. Miles.

The 21. of September from night, till thursday in the morning, wee sayled one quarter West, and so till day still West 7. miles at 64. fadome deepe, oasie ground.

From Morning till noone south-west 5. Miles at 65. fadome deepe. Oasie ground: at noone wee wound North-ward againe, and for three houres, sayled North-east two Myles: then we wound West-ward againe, and sayled till night, while halfe our second quarter was out, with two Schoure sayles south south-west, and southwest and by south sixe myles. After that, in the second quarter, wee wound North-ward, and sayled so till Fryday in the morning.

The 22. of September, wee sayled North and by East, and North North-

The Nauigation into the North-seas.

North-east 4. miles, and from morning till noone, North-east 4. Myles. Then we wound West-ward againe, and sayled North-west and by West, and North-west three Miles: After that, the first quarter North-west and by West fiue miles: The second quarter, West and by North foure miles, and till Saterday in the morning, being the 23. of September, West South-west, and South-west and by West foure miles: From Saterday in the morning till euening, we sayles with two Schoure sailes South-west and South-west and by West 7. or 8. miles, the Winde being North North-west. In the Euening we wound North-ward, and sayled till Sunday in the morning, being the 24. of September, with two Schoure sayles, too neare East, with a stiffe North North-west Wind 8. miles; and from morning till noone East and by South three miles, with a North Winde: Then we wound West-ward, and till euening sayled West South-west three miles; and all that night, till Monday in the morning: The 25. of September, West and by South sixe miles, the Winde being North. In the morning the Winde fell North-east, and we sailed from morning till euening West, and West & by North 10. miles hauing 63. Fadome deepe sandy ground.

From Euening till Tuesday in the Morning, being the 26. of September, we sailed West 10. Miles, and then in the Morning we were hard by the land, about 3. Miles East-ward from Kildwin, and then we wound off from the land, and so held off for 3. houres together, after that we wound towards the land againe, and thought to goe into Kilduin, but we were too low, so that after-noone we wound off from the land againe, and till Euening sailed East North-east 5. Miles. and from Euening til two houres before Wednesday in the Morning, being the 27. of September, we sailed East 6. Miles, then we wound West-ward, and till Euening sailed West and by North 8. Miles, and in the Euening came againe before Kilduin, then wee wound farre off from the land, and sailed 2. quarters North-east and by East, and East North-east 6. Miles, and about Friday in the Morning, being the 28. of September wee wound about againe, and sayled with diuers variable Windes, sometimes one way, then another way till Euening, then wee gest that Kilduin lay West from vs foure Miles, and at that time wee had an East North-east Winde,

and

The Nauigation into the North-seas.

and sayled North North-West, and North-West and by North, till Satterday in the Morning 12. or 13. Miles.

The nine and twenteeth of September in the Morning, wee sayled North-West, and by West foure Miles, and all that day till Euening it was faire, still, pleasant, and Sunne-shine Weather. In the Euening wee went West South-West, and then wee were about sixe Miles from the land, and sayled till Sunday in the Morning, beeing the 30. of September, North North-West eight Miles, then wee wound towardes the Land, and the same day in the Euening entered into Ward-house, and there wee stayed till the tenth of October. And that day wee set sayle out of Ward-house, and vpon the eighteene of Nouember, wee arriued in the Maes.

The course or Miles from Ward-house into Holland, I haue not here set downe, as being needlesse, because it is a continuall Voiage knowne to most men.

The end of the second Voyage.

The third Voyage Northward to the Kingdomes of *Cathaia*, and *China*, in Anno 1596.

AFTER that the seuen Shippes (as I saide before) were returned backe againe from their North Voiage, with lesse benefit then was expected, the Generall States of the vnited Prouinces consulted together, to send certaine ships thither againe a third time, to see if they might bring the sayd Voyage to a good end, if it were possible to bee done: but after much consultation had, they could not agree thereon, yet they were content to cause a Proclamation to be made, that if any either Townes or Marchants, were disposed to venture to make further search that way, at their owne charges, if the Voyage were accomplished, and that thereby it might bee made apparant, that the sayd passage was to be sayled, they were content to giue them a good reward, in the Countryes behalfe, naming a certaine summe of money. Whereupon in the beginning of this yeare, there was two ships rigged, and set foorth by the Towne of Amsterdam, to sayl that Voyage, the men therein being taken vp vpon two conditions: viz. What they should haue if the Voyage were not accomplished, and what they should haue if they got through, and brought the Voiage to an end, promising them a good reward if they could effect it, thereby to incourage the men, taking vp as many vnmarryed men as they could, that they might not bee disswaded by meanes of their wiues and children, to leaue off the Voyage. Vpon these conditions, those two shippes were ready to set saile in the beginning of May.

The Nauigation into the North-seas.

In the one, Iacob Heemskerke Hendrickson, was Master and Factor for the Wares and Marchandises; and William Barents chiefe Pilote. In the other Iohn Cornelison Rijp, was both Master and Factor for the goods that the Marchants had laden in her.

The 5. of May all the men in both the shippes were mustered, and vpon the tenth of May they sayled from Amsterdam, and the 13. of May got to the Vlie. The sixteenth wee set saile out of the Vlie, but the tyde being all most spent, and the winde North-east, we were compelled to put in againe; at which time, Iohn Cornelisons ship fell on ground, but got off againe, and wee anchored at the East ende of the Vlie. The 18. of May wee put out of the Vlie againe, with a North-east winde, and sayled North North-west. The 22. of May wee saw the Ilands of Hitland, and Feyeril-land, the winde beeing North-east. The 24. of May, wee had a good winde, and sayled North-east, till the 29. of May: then the Winde was against vs, and blewe North-east in our Top-sayle. The 30. of May we had a good Winde, and sailed North-east, and we tooke the heigth of the sunne with our Crosse-staffe, and found that it was eleuated aboue the Horizon 47. Degrees and 42. Minutes, his declination was 21. Degrees and 42. Minutes. so that the height of the Pole was 69. Degrees and twentie foure Minutes.

The first of June wee had no night, and the second of June wee had the Winde contrary, but vpon the fourth of June, wee had a good winde, out of the West North-west, and sayled North-east.

And when the Sunne was about South South-east, wee saw a strange sight in the Element: for on each side of the Sunne there was another Sunne, and two Raine-bowes that past cleane through the three Sunnes, and then two Raine-bowes more, the one compassing round about the Sunnes, and the other crosse through the great rundle; the great rundle standing with the vttermost point, eleuated aboue the Horizon 28. Degrees: at Noone the Sunne beeing at the highest, the height thereof was measured, and wee found by the Astrolabium, that it was eleuated aboue the Horizon 48. Degrees, and 43. Minutes, his declination was 22. Degrees and 17. Minutes, the which beeing added to 48. Degrees 43. Minutes, it was found that wee were vnder 71. Degrees of the heigth of the Pole.

Iohn

The Nauigation into the North-seas.

Iohn Cornelis shippe held aloofe from vs, and would not keepe with vs, but wee made towardes him, and sayled North-east, biting a point of our Compasse, for wee thought that wee were too farre West-ward, as after it appeared, otherwise wee should haue held our course North-east. And in the Euening when wee were together, wee tolde him that wee were best to keepe more Easterly, because wee were too farre West-ward, but his Pilote made answere, that they desired not to goe into the Straights of Weygates. There course was North-east and by North, and wee were about 60. Miles to Sea-warde in from the Land, and were to sayle North-east, when wee had the North Cape in sight, and therefore wee should rather haue sailed East North-east, and not North North-east, because wee were so farre West-ward, to put our selues in our right course againe: and there wee tolde them, that wee should rather haue sayled East-ward, at the least for certaine Miles, vntill wee had gotten into our right course againe, which by meanes of the contrary Winde wee had lost; as also because it was North-east: but whatsoeuer wee sayde, and sought to councell them for the best, they would holde no course but North North-east, for they alleaged, that if wee went any more Easterly, that then wee should enter into the Wey-gates, but wee being not able to perswade them, altered our course one point of the Compasse, to meete them, and sayled North-east and by North, and should otherwise haue sayled northeast, and somewhat more East.

The fifth of June wee sawe the first Ice, which wee wondered at, at the first, thinking that it had beene white Swannes, for one of our men walking in the Fore-decke, on a suddaine beganne to cry out with a loude voyce, and sayd; that hee sawe white Swans: which wee that were vnder Hatches hearing, presently came vp, and perceiued that it was Ice, that came driuing from the great heape, showing like Swannes, it being then about Euening, at mid-night, wee sailed through it, and the Sunne was about a Degree eleuated aboue the Horizon in the North.

The sixth of June, about foure of the Clocke in the afternoone, wee entred againe into the Ice, which was so strong that wee could not passe through it, and sayled South-west, and by West, till eight Glasses were runne out, after that wee kept on our course North,
North-

The Nauigation into the North-seas.

North-east, and sayled along by the Ice.

The seuenth of Iune wee tooke the height of the Sunne, and found that it was eleuated aboue the Horizon thirtie eight Degrees and thirtie eight Minutes, his declination beeing twentie ~ : Degrees thirtie eight Minutes; which beeing taken from thirtie eight Degrees thirtie eight Minutes, wee found the Pole to bee seuentie foure Degrees; there wee found so great store of Ice, that it was admirable: and wee sayled along through it, as if wee had past betweene two Lands. The water being as greene as grasse, and wee supposed that we were not farre from Greene-land, and the longer wee sayled the more and thicker Ice we found.

The eight of Iune, wee came to so great a heape of Ice, that wee could not saile through it, because it was so thicke, and therefore wee wound about South-west and by West, till two Glasses were runne out, and after that three Glasses more South South-west, and then South three Glasses, to sayle to the Island that wee saw, as also to shunne the Ice.

The ninth of Iune wee found the Islande, that lay vnder 74. Degrees and 30. Minutes, and as wee gest, it was about fiue miles long.

The tenth of Iune wee put out our Boate, and therewith eight of our men went on Land, and as wee past by Iohn Cornelisons shippe, eight of his men also, came into our Boate, whereof one was the Pilote. Then William Barents asked him, whether wee were not too much West-ward, but hee would not acknowledge it: whereupon there passed many wordes betweene them, for William Barents sayde hee would prooue it to bee so, as in trueth it was.

The eleuenth of Iune going on Land, wee found great store of Sea-Mewes Egges vpon the shoare, and in that Island, wee were in great danger of our liues: for that going vp a great Hill of Snowe, when we should come downe againe, wee thought wee should all haue broken our neckes, it was so slipperie, but wee sate vpon the Snowe, and slidde downe, which was very dangerous for vs, to breake both our armes and legges, for that at the foote of the Hill there was many Rockes, which wee were likely to haue fallen vpon, yet by Gods help wee got safely downe againe.

The Nauigation into the North-seas.

Meane time William Barents sate in the Boate, and sawe vs slide downe, and was in greater feare then wee, to behold vs in that danger. In the sayd Island wee found the varying of our Compasse, which was 13. Degrees, so that it differed a whole point at the least: after that wee rowed aboard Iohn Cornelisons shippe, and there wee eate our Eggs.

The 12. of June in the morning, wee saw a white Beare, which wee rowed after with our Boate, thinking to cast a Roape about her necke; but when we were neere her, shee was so great, that wee durst not doe it, but rowed backe againe to our Shippe to fetch more men and our Armes, and so made to her againe with Muskets, Hargubushes, Halbertes, and Hatchets. Iohn Cornelysons men comming also with their Boate to helpe vs: and so beeing well furnished of Men and Weapons, wee rowed with both our Boates vnto the Beare, and fought with her while foure Glasses were runne out, for our Weapons could doe her litle hurt: and amongst the rest of the blowes that wee gaue her, one of our men stroke her into the backe with an Axe, which stucke fast in her backe, and yet she swomme away with it; but wee rowed after her, and at last wee cut her head in sunder with an Axe, wherewith she dyed: and then wee brought her into Iohn Cornelysons Shippe, where wee fleaed her, and found her Skinne to bee twelue foote long: which done, wee eate some of her flesh; but wee brookt it not well. This Island wee called the Beare-Island.

The 13. of June, we left the Island, and sayled North, and somewhat Easterly, the Winde being West and South-west, and made good way: so that when the Sunne was North, wee gest that wee had sayled 16. miles North-ward from that Island.

The 14. of June, when the Sunne was North, wee cast out our Lead 113. Fadome deepe, but found no ground, and so sayled forward till the 15. of June, when the Sunne was South-east, with mistie and mistling weather, and sayled North and North and by East: about Euening it cleared vp, and then wee saw a great thing driuing in the Sea, which wee thought had been a Shippe: but passing along by it, wee perceiued it to be a dead Whale, that stouncke monsterously; and on it there sate a great number of Sea-meawes: At that time, we had sayled 20. miles.

The

The Nauigation into the North-seas.

The 16. of June, with the like speede wee sayled North and by East, with mistie weather; and as we sayled, wee heard the Ice before wee saw it: but after, when it cleared vp, wee saw it, and then wound off from it, when as wee guest wee had sayled 30. miles.

The 17. and 18. of June, wee saw great store of Ice, and sayled along vp it, vntill wee came to the poynt, which we could not reach, for that the Winde was South-east, which was right against vs, and the poynt of Ice lay South-ward from vs: yet we laueared a great while to get beyond it, but we could not do it.

The 19. of June we saw Land againe, then wee tooke the height of the Sunne, and found that it was eleuated aboue the Horizon 33. degrees and 37. minutes: her declination being 23. degrees and 26. minutes; which taken from the sayd 33. degrees and 37. minutes, we found that we were vnder 80. degrees and 11. minutes: which was the height of the Pole there.

This Land was very great, and we sayled West-ward along by it, till wee were vnder 79. degrees and a halfe, where we found a good road, and could not get neere to the Land, because the Winde blew North-east, which was right off from the Land: the Bay reacht right North and South, into the Sea.

The 21. of June we cast out our Anchor, at 18. Fadome before the Land; and then wee, and Iohn Cornelysons men, rowed on the West side of the Land, and there fetcht Balast: and when wee got on Board againe with our Balast, wee saw a white Beare that swamme towardes our Shippe; wherevpon we left off our worke, and entering into the Boate with Iohn Cornelisons men, rowed after her, and crossing her in the way, droue her from the Land, where-with shee swamme further into the Sea, and wee followed her; and for that our Boate could not make good way after her, we manned out our Scute also, the better to follow her: but shee swamme a mile into the Sea; yet wee follewed her with the most part of all our men of both shippes in three Boates, and stroke often times at her, cutting and heawing her, so that all our Armes were most broken in peeces. During our fight with her, shee stroke her Clowes so hard in our Boate, that the signes thereof were seene in it; but as hap was, it was in the forehead of our Boate: for if it had been in the middle thereof, shee had (peraduenture) ouer-throwne it, they haue such force in their Clawes:

At

The Nauigation into the North-seas.

At laſt, after we had fought long with her, and made her wearie with our three Boates that kept about her, wee ouercame her, and killed her: which done, we brought her into our ſhippe, and fleaed her: her ſkinne being 13. foote long.

After that, we rowed with our Scute, about a mile inward to the Land, where there was a good Hauen, and good Anchor ground, the Eaſt-ſide being ſandie, there wee caſt out our Leade, and found 16. Fadome deepe, and after that 10. and 12. Fadom, and rowing further, we found that on the Eaſt-ſide there was two Iſlands, that reached Eaſt-ward into the Sea: on the Weſt-ſide alſo there was a great Crecke or Riuer, which ſhewed alſo like an Iſland. Then we rowed to the Iſland that lay in the middle, and there we found many red Geeſe-Egges, which we ſaw ſitting vpon their Neſts, and draue them from them, and they flying away, cryed, red, red, red: and as they ſate wee killed one Gooſe dead with a ſtone, which we dreſt and eate, and at leaſt 60. Egges, that we tooke with vs aboard the ſhippe, and vpon the 22. of June, wee went aboard our ſhippe againe.

Thoſe Geeſe were of a perfit red coulor, ſuch as come into Holland about Weiringen, and euery yeere are there taken in aboundance, but till this time it was neuer knowne where they hatcht their Egges, ſo that ſome men haue taken vpon them to write, that they ſit vpon trees in Scotland, that hang ouer the Water, and ſuch Egges as fall from them downe into the Water, become yong Geeſe, and ſwimme then out of the Water; but thoſe that fall vpon the Land burſt in ſunder, and are loſt: but this is now found to be contrary, and it is not to be wondered at, that no man could tell where they breed their Egges, for that no man that euer we knew, had euer beene vnder 80. degrees, nor that Land vnder 80. Degrees, was neuer ſet downe in any Cart, much leſſe the red Geeſe that breed therein.

Red Geeſe breed their yong Geeſe, vnder 80. Degrees in Green-land.

Note.

It is here alſo to be noted, that although that in this land which we eſteeme to be Greene-land, lying vnder 80. Degrees, and more, then groweth leaues and graſſe, and that there are ſuch beaſts therein as eate graſſe, as Harts, Buckes and ſuch like Beaſtes as liue thereon, yet in Noua Zembla, vnder 76. Degrees, there groweth neither leaues nor graſſe, nor any beaſts that eate graſſe or leaues, liue therein; but ſuch beaſts as eate fleſh, as Beares and Foxes: and yet this Land lyeth full 4. Degrees from the North-pole, as Greene-land aforeſaid doth.

The Nauigation into the North-seas.

The 23. of June we hoysted Anchor againe, and sayled North-west-ward into the sea; but could get no further, by reason of the Ice; and so wee came to the same place againe where wee had laine, and cast Anchor at 18. Fadome: and at Euening being at Anchor, the Sunne being North-east, and somewhat more East-warde, wee tooke the height thereof, and found it to be eleuated aboue the Horizon 13. degrees and 10. minutes; his declination being 23. degrees and 28. minutes: which substracted from the height aforesaid, resteth 10. degrees and 18. minutes, which being substracted from 90. degrees, then the height of the Pole there was 79. degrees and 42. minutes.

After that, wee hoysted Anchor againe, and sayled along by the West side of the Land, and then our men went on Land, to see how much the needle of the Compasse varyed : Meane time, there came a great white Beare swimming towardes the Shippe, and would haue climbed vp into it, if we had not made a noyse; and with that we shot at her with a Peece, but she left the Shippe, and swam to the Land, where our men were : which wee perceiuing, sayled with our Shippe towardes the Land, and gaue a great shoute; wherewith our men thought that wee had fallen on a Rocke with our Shippe, which made them much abashed; and therewith the beare also being afraide, swam off againe from the Land, and left our men, which made vs gladde: for our men had no Weapons about them.

Touching the varying of the Compasse, for the which cause our men went on Land, to try the certaintie thereof: it was found to differ 16. degrees.

The 24. of June we had a South-west Winde, and could not get aboue the Island, and therefore wee sayled backe againe, and found a Hauen that lay foure Myles from the other Hauen, on the West side of the great Hauen, and there cast Anchor at twelue Fadome deepe: there wee rowed a great way in, and went on Land; and there wee founde two Sea-horses Teeth that waighed sixe Pound: Wee also found many small Teeth, and so rowed on board againe.

The 25. of June wee hoysted Anchor againe, and sayled along by the Land, and went South, and South South-west, with a
North

The Nauigation into the North-seas.

North North-east Winde, vnder 79. Degrees. There we found a great Creeke or Riuer, whereinto we sailed ten miles at the least, holding our course South-ward; but we perceiued that there wee could not get through: there wee cast out our Leade, and for the most part found ten fadome deepe, but wee were constrained to lauere out againe, for the Winde was Northerly, and almost full North, and wee perceiued that it reached to the firme Land, which we supposed to be Low-land, for that wee could not see it any thing farre, and therefore wee sailed so neere vnto it, till that wee might see it, and then we were forced to lauere, and vpon the 27. of June we got out againe.

The twenty eight of June, wee gate beyonde the point that lay on the west-side, where there was so great a number of Birds, that they flew against our sailes, and we sailed 10. Miles South-ward, and after that West, to shun the Ice.

The twenty nine of June, wee sayled South-East and somewhat more Easterly, along by the land, till wee were vnder 76. degrees and 50. Minutes, for wee were forced to put off from the land, because of the Ice.

The thirteeth of June, we sayled South, and somewhat east, and then we tooke the height of the Sunne, and found that it was eleuated aboue the Horizon 38. Degrees and 20. Minutes, his declination was 23. Degrees and 20. Minutes, which being taken from the former height, it was found that wee were vnder 75. Degrees.

The first of July, wee saw the Beare-Island againe, and then Iohn Cornelison and his Officers came aboard our ship, to speake with vs about altering of our course, but wee being of a contrary opinion, it was agreed that wee should follow on our course, and hee his: which was, that hee (according to his desire) should saile vnto 80. Degrees againe: for hee was of opinion, that then hee should finde a passage through, on the East-side of the Land, that lay vnder 80. Degrees. And vpon that agreement wee left each other, they sayling North-ward, and wee South-ward, because of the Ice, the Winde being East South-east.

The second of July, wee sailed East-ward, and were vnder 74. Degrees, hauing the Winde North North-West, and then we
wound

The Nauigation into the North-seas.

wound ouer another Bough, with an East North-east Winde, and sayled North-ward. In the Euening the Sunne beeing about North-West, and by North, wee wound about againe, (because of the Ice) with an East Winde, and sailed South Southeast, and about East South-east, and then we wound about againe (because of the Ice) and the Sunne being South south-West, we wound about againe, and sailed North-east.

The third of July, wee were vnder 74. Degrees, hauing a South-east and by East Wind, and sailed north-east and by north: after that we wound about againe with a South Wind, and sayled East South-east, till the sunne was North-West, then the Wind began to be somewhat larger.

The fourth of July, wee sailed East and by North, and found no Ice, which wee wondered at, because wee sailed so high, but when the Sunne was almost South, we were forced to winde about againe, by reason of the Ice, and sailed West-ward, with a North Wind, after that the Sunne beeing North, wee sailed East South-east, with a North-east Wind.

The fifth of July, wee sailed North North-east, till the Sunne was South: then wee wound about, and went East South-east, with a North-east Winde. Then wee tooke the height of the Sunne, and found it to bee eleuated aboue the Horizon 39. Degrees 27. Minutes, his declination beeing 22. Degrees and 53. Minutes, which taken from the high aforesaid, we found that wee were vnder the height of the Poole seuentie three Degrees and 20. Minutes.

The seuenth of July, wee cast out our whole Lead-lyne, but found no ground, and sayled East and by South, the Wind being North-east and by East, and were vnder 72. Degrees and 12. Minutes.

The eight of July, we had a good North-west Wind, and sailed East and by North, with an indifferent cold gale of Wind, and got vnder 72. Degrees and 15. Minutes. The ninth of July, we went East and by North, the Wind being West. The tenth of July, the Sunne being South south-West, we cast out our Lead, and had ground at 160. Fadome, the Winde being North-east, and by North, and we sailed East and by South, vnder 72. Degres.

H 2 The

The Nauigation into the North-seas.

The 11. of July, we found 70. Fadome deepe, and saw no Ice, then we gest that we were right South, and North from Dandinaes, that is the East-point of the White-Sea, that lay Southward from vs, and had sandy ground, and the Bancke stretched North-ward into the Sea, so that wee were out of doubt that we were vpon the Bancke of the White Sea, for wee had found no sandy ground all the Coast along, but onely that Bancke. Then the winde being East and by South, we sayled South, and South and by East, vnder 72. Degrees, and after that, we had a South South-East Winde, and sayled North-East to get ouer the Bancke.

In the Morning wee draue forward with a calme, and found that wee were vnder 72. Degrees, and then againe wee had an East South-east Winde, the Sunne beeing about South-west, and sayled North-east, and casting out our Lead found 150. Fadome deepe clay ground; and then we were ouer the Bancke, which was very narrow, for wee sailed but 14. Glasses, and gate ouer it, when the sunne was about North North-east.

The twelfth of July, wee sayled North and by East, the Winde beeing East, and at Euening the Sunne being North North-east, we wound about againe, hauing the Winde North North-east, and sayled East and by South, till our first quarter was out.

The thirteenth of July, wee sayled East, with a North North-east Winde: then wee tooke the height of the Sunne, and found it to bee eleuated aboue the Horizon 54. Degrees and 38. Minutes, his declination was 21. Degrees and 54. Minutes, which taken from the height aforesaid, the height of the Pole was found to be 73. Degrees, and then againe wee found Ice, but not very much, and wee were of opinion that wee were by Willoughbies-land.

The fourteenth of July wee sayled North-east, the Winde being North North-west, and in that sort sayled about a dinner time, along through the Ice, and in the middle thereof wee cast out our leade, and had 90. Fadome deepe, in the next quarter wee cast out the Leade againe, and had 100. Fadome deepe, and we sayled so farre into the Ice, that wee could goe no surther: for wee
could

could see no place where it opened, but were forced (with great labour and paine) to lauere out of it againe, the Winde blowing West, and wee were then vnder seuentie foure Degrees and tenne Minutes.

The fifteenth of July wee draue through the middle of the Ice with a calme, and casting out our Leade had 100. Fadome deepe, at which time the Winde being East, wee sayled West.

The sixteenth of July wee got out of the Ice, and sawe a great Beare lying vpon it, that leaped into the Water when shee saw vs: Wee made towards her with our shippe, which shee perceiuing gotte vp vpon the Ice againe, wherewith wee shot once at her.

Then we sailed East South-east, and saw no Ice, gessing that wee were not farre from Noua Zembla, because wee saw the Beare there vpon the Ice, at which time we cast out the Lead and found 100. fadome deepe.

The seuenteenth of July, wee tooke the height of the sunne, and it was eleuated aboue the Horizon 37. Degrees, and 55. Minutes, his declination was 21. Degrees and 15. Minutes, which taken from the height aforesaid, the heigh of the Pole was 74. Degrees and 40. Minutes: and when the Sunne was in the South, wee saw the Land of Noua Zembla, which was about Lomsbay: I was the first that espied it. Then wee altered our course, and sayled North-east and by North, and hoysed vp all our sailes, except the Fore-saile and the Lesien.

The eighteenth of July wee saw the Land againe, beeing vnder 75. Degrees, and sayled North-east and by North, with an North-west Winde, and wee gate aboue the point of the Admirals Island, and sailed East North-east, with a West Winde, the Land reaching North-east, and by North.

The ninteenth of July wee came to the Crosse-Island, and could then get no further, by reason of the Ice, for there the Ice lay still close vpon the Land, at which time the Winde was West, and blewe right vpon the Land, and it lay vnder 76. Degrees and 20. Minutes. There stood 2. Crosses vpon the Land, whereof it had the Name.

The twenteeth of July wee anchored vnder the Island, for wee

The Nauigation into the North-seas.

wee could get no further for the Ice. There wee put out our Boate, and with eight men rowed on Land, and went to one of the Crosses, where we rested vs awhile, to goe to the next Crosse, but beeing in the way we saw two Beares by the other Crosse, at which time wee had no weapons at all about vs. The Beares rose vp vpon their hinder feete to see vs (for they smell further then they see) and for that they smelt vs: therefore they rose vpright, and came towards vs, wherewith we were not a little abashed, in such sort that wee had little lust to laugh, and in all haste went to our Boate againe, still looking behinde vs, to see if they followed vs, thinking to get into the Boate, and so put off from the land, but the Master stayed vs, saying, hee that first beginnes to runne away, I will thrust this Hake-staffe (which hee then held in his hand) into his Ribs, for it is better for vs (sayd hee) to stay altogether, and see if we can make them afraid with whooping and hallowing, and so wee went softly towardes the Boate, and gote away glad that wee had escaped there clawes, and that wee had the leysure to tell our fellowes thereof.

The one and twenteeth of July, wee tooke the height of the Sunne, and found that it was eleuated aboue the Horizon thirtie fiue Degrees and fifteene Minutes, his declination was one and twentie Degrees, which being taken from the height aforesaide, there rested fourteene Degrees, which substracted from ninetie Degrees, then the heigh of the Pole was found to bee seuentie six Degrees and fifteene Minutes, then wee found the variation of the Compasse to be iust twentie sixe Degrees. The same day two of our men went againe to the Crosse, and found no Beares to trouble vs, and wee followed them with our Armes, fearing least wee might meet any by chance, and when we came to the second Crosse, wee found the foote-steps of 2. Beares, and saw how long they had followed vs, which was an hundreth foote-steps at the least, that way that wee had beene the day before.

The two and twentie of July, being Munday, wee set vp another Crosse, and made our Marke thereon: and lay there before the Crosse Iland, till the fourth of August, meane time we washt and whited our linnen on the shoare.

The thirtie of July, the Sunne being North, there came a
Beare

The Nauigation into the North-seas.

Beare so neere to our shippe, that wee might hit her with a stone, and wee shot her into the foote with a Peece, wherewith shee ranne halting away.

The one and thirteeth of July, the Sunne being East North-east, seuen of our men killed a beare, and sleaed her, and cast her body into the Sea. The same day at Noone (by our Instrument) wee found the variation of the nedle of the Compasse to be 17. Degrees.

The first of August, wee saw a white Beare, but shee ranne away from vs.

The fourth of August wee got out of the Ice, to the other side of the Island, and anchored there: where, with great labour and much paine, wee fetched a Boate full of stones from the land.

The fifth of August wee set saile againe towardes Ice-point, with an East Wind, and sailed South south-east, and then North North-east, and saw no Ice by the land, by the which wee lauered.

The sixth of August, wee gate about the point of Nassawe, and sayled forward East, and East and by South, along by the land.

The seuenth of August, wee had a West South-west Wind, and sayled along by the Land, South-east, and South-east and by East, and sawe but a little Ice, and then past by the Trust-point, which we had much longed for: at Euening we had an East Wind, with mistie Weather, so that wee were forced to make our ship fast to a peece of Ice, that was at least 36. fadome deepe, vnder the water, and more then 16. fadome aboue the water: which in all was 52. fadome thick, for it lay fast vpon ground the which was 36. fadome deepe. The eight of August in the Morning, wee had an East wind, with mistie Weather.

The 9. of August, lying still fast to the great peece of Ice, it snowed hard, & it was misty weather, and when the sunne was south, we went vpon the Hatches (for we alwayes held watch) whereas the Master walked along the ship, he heard a beast snuffe with his nose, and looking ouer-bord, he saw a great beare hard by the ship, where with he cryed out, a Beare, a beare; and with that all our men came by from vnder hatches, and saw a great beare hard by our boat, seeking to get into it, but we giuing a great shoute shee was afrayd, and
swamme

The Nauigation into the North-Seas.

swamme away, but presently came backe againe, and went behinde a great peece of Ice, whereunto wee had made our Shippe fast, and climbed vpon it, and bouldly came towardes our Shippe to enter into it: but wee had torne our Scute sayle in the Shippe, and lay with foure Peeces before at the Bootespritt, and shotte her into the body: and with that, shee ranne away; but it snowed so fast, that wee could not see whither shee went: but wee guest that she lay behinde a high Hoouell; whereof there was many vpon the peece of Ice.

The Tenth of August, being Saterday, the Ice began mightily to breake, and then wee first perceiued that the great peece of Ice whereunto wee had made our Shippe fast, lay on the ground, for the rest of the Ice draue along by it, wherewith wee were in great feare that wee should be compassed about with the Ice, and therefore wee vsed all the diligence and meanes that wee could, to get from thence, for wee were in great doubt: and being vnder sayle, wee sayled vpon the Ice, because it was all broken vnder it, and got to an other peece of Ice; whereunto wee made our Shippe fast againe with our Sheate Anchor, which wee made fast vpon it; and there wee lay till Euening: and when wee had supped, in the first quarter, the sayd peece of Ice began on a sodaine to burst and rende in peeces, so fearefully that it was admirable; for with a great cracke it burst into foure hundred peeces at the least: but lying fast to it, weied our Cable, & got off from it, vnder the water it was ten Fadome deepe, and lay vpon the ground, and two fadome aboue the Water; and it made a fearefull noyse both vnder and aboue the Water when it burst, and spread it selfe abroad on all sides.

And being with great feare, gotten from that peece of Ice, wee came to an other peece, that was sixe Fadome deepe vnder the Water: to the which we made a Rope fast on both sides.

Then wee saw an other great peece of Ice, not farre from vs, lying fast in the Sea, that was as sharpe aboue, as it had been a Tower; whereunto wee rowed: and casting out our Lead, wee found that it lay 20. Fadome deepe, fast on the ground vnder the Water, and 12. Fadome aboue the Water.

The Nauigation into the North-seas.

The 11 of August being sunday, wée rowed to another péece of Ice, & cast out our lead, and found that it lay 18 fadom déepe fast to the ground vnder the water, and 10 fadome aboue the water. The 12 of August, we sailed néere vnder the land, ý better to shun ý Ice, for ý the great flakes that draue in the sea, were many fadome déepe vnder the water, and we were better defended from them being at 4. and 5 fadome water, and there ran a great current of water from the hill. There we made our ship fast againe to a péece of Ice, and called that point, the small Ice point.

The 13 of August in the morning, there came a Beare from the east point of the land, close to our ship, and one of our men with a péece, shot at her, and brake one of her legs, but she crept vp the hill with her thrée féet, and wée following her, killed her, and hauing flead her, brought the skinne aboard the ship. From thence we set saile, with a little gale of winde, and were forced to lauere, but after, that it began to blow more out of the South and South-South-East.

The 15 of August, we came to the Iland of Orange, where we were inclosed with the Ice, hard by a great péece of Ice where we were in great danger to lose our ship, but with great labour and much paine we got to the Iland, the winde being South-East, whereby we were constrained to turne our ship, and while we were busied thereabouts, and made much noise, a Beare that lay there and slept, awaked, and came towards vs to the ship, so that we were forced to leaue our worke about turning of the ship, and to defend our selues against the Beare, and shot her into the body, wherewith she ran away to the other side of the Iland, and swam into the water, and got vp vpon a péece of Ice, where shée lay still, but we comming after her to the péece of Ice where shée lay, when she saw vs, she leapt into the water, and swam to the land, but we got betwéene her and the land, and stroke her on the head with a hatchet, but as often as we stroke at her with the hatchet, she duckt vnder the water, whereby we had much to do before we could kill her: after she was dead we flead her on the land, and toke the skin on board with vs, and after that, turned our ship to a great péece of Ice, and made it fast therevnto.

The 16 of August, ten of our men entring into one boat, rowed to the firme land of Noua Zembla, and drew the boate vp

A   vpon

The Nauigation into the North-seas.

vpon the Ice, which done, we went vp a high hill, to see the situation of the land and found that it reached South East, & South South East, and then againe South, which we disliked, for that it lay so much Southward: but when we saw open water, South East, and East South East, we were much comforted againe, thinking ỹ we had won our voyage, & knew not how wee should get some inough on boord, to certifie VVilliam Barents thereof.

The 18. of August we made preparation to set saile, but it was all in vaine: for we had almost lost our sheat Anchor, and two new ropes, and with much lost labour got to the place againe from whence we came: for the streame ran with a mighty currant, and the Ice draue very strongly vpon the cables, along by the shippe, so that we were in feare that we should loose all the cable that was without the ship, which was 200. fadome at the least, but God prouided well for vs, so that in the end, wee got to the place againe from whence we put out.

The 19. of August it was indifferent good weather, the winde blowing South west, the Ice still driuing, and we set saile with an indifferent gale of wind, and past by ỹ point of Desire, whereby we were once againe in good hope, and when we had gotten aboue the point, we sailed South-east into the sea-ward, 4. miles, but then againe we entred into more Ice, whereby we were constrained to turn back againe, & sailed North-west vntil we came to ỹ land againe, which reacheth frō the point of Desire, to the head point, south and by west 6. miles: from the head point to Flushingers head, it reacheth South west, which are 3. miles one from the other: from the Flushingars head, it reacheth into the sea, east south east, and from Flushingers head to the point of the Iland, it reacheth south west, and by south, and South west 3. miles: from the Island point, to the point of the Ice hauen, the land reacheth West South west 4. miles: from the Ice hauens point to the fall of water, or the streame bay, and the Low land it reacheth West & by South, and East and by North 7. miles: from thence the land reacheth East and West.

The 21 of August we sailed a great way into the Ice hauen, and that night ankored therein: next day the streame going extreame hard Eastward, we haled out againe from thence, and sailed againe to the Island point, but for that it was mistie weather,

The Nauigation into the North-seas.

comming to a peece of Ice, we made the ship fast thereunto because the winde began to blow hard South west and South South West. There we went vp vpon the Ice, and wondred much thereat, it was such manner of Ice: For on the top it was ful of earth, and there we found aboue 40. Egges, and it was not like other Ice, for it was of a perfect azure coloure, like to the skies, whereby there grew great contentiō in words amongst our men, some saying that it was Ice, others that it was frozen land: for it lay vnreasonable high aboue the water, it was at least 18. fadome vnder the water close to the ground, and 10. fadome aboue the water. there we stayed all that storme, the wind being Southwest and by West.

The 23. of August we sailed againe from the Ice, south east ward into the sea, but entred presently into it againe, & wound about to the Ice hauen. The next day it blew hard North North west, and the Ice came mightily driuing in, whereby we were in a manner compassed about therewith, and withall the winde began more and more to rise. and the Ice still draue harder and harder, so that the pin of the rother and the rother were shorne in peeces and our boate was shorne in peeces betwéene the ship and the Ice, we expecting nothing else, but that the ship also would be prest and crusht in peeces with the Ice.

The 25. of August the weather began to be better, and we toke great paines, and bestowed much labour to get the Ice, wherewith we were so inclosed, to go from vs, but what meanes soeuer we vsed it was all in baine, but when the sun was South-west, the Ice began to driue out againe with the streame, & we thought to saile southward about Noua Zembla, to the straites of Wergates, for that seeing we could there find no passage. We hauing past Noua Zembla, were of opinion that our labour was all in baine, and that we could not get through, and so agreed to go that way home againe; but comming to the streame Bay, we were forced to go back againe, because of the Ice which lay so fast thereabouts, and the same night also it froze, that we could hardly get through there, with the little wind that we had, the winde then being North.

The 26. of August there blew a reasonable gale of winde at which time we determined to saile back to the point of Desire, &

I 2

The Nauigation into the North-seas.

so home againe, seeing ẏ we could not get through ẏ Wergats, although we vsed al the meanes & industry we could to get forward, but whē we had past by ẏ Ice hauen, ẏ Ice began to driue w such force, ẏ we were inclosed round about therwith, & yet we sought al the meanes we could to get out, but it was all in vaine: and at that time we had like to haue lost thrée men that were vpon the Ice to make way for the ship, if the Ice had held ẏ course it went, but as we draue back againe, & that the Ice also wheron our men stood, in like sort draue, they being nimble, as ẏ ship draue by the, one of them caught hould of the beake head, another vpon the shroudes, and the third vpon the great brase that hung out behind, and so by great aduenture by the hold that they tooke, they got safe into the shippe againe, for which they thanked GOD with all their hearts: for it was much liklier that they should rather haue béene carried away with the Ice, but God, by the nimblenes of their hands, deliuered them out of that danger which was a pittifull thing to behold, although it fell out for the best, for if they had not béene nimble, they had surely dyed for it.

The same day in the euening, we got to the West side of the Ice hauen, where we were forced in great cold, pouerty, misery, and griefe, to stay all that Winter, the winde then being East-North-east.

The 27 of August the Ice draue round about the ship, and yet it was good wether, at which time we went on land, and being there it began to blow South-east, with a reasonable gale. and then the Ice came with great force before the bough, and draue the ship vp foure foote high before, and behind it séemed as if the kœle lay on the ground, so that it séemed that the ship would bee verthrowne in the place, whereupon they that were in the ship, put out the boate, therewith to saue their liues, and withall put out a flagge to make a signe to vs, to come on board: which we perceiuing, and beholding the ship to be lifted vp in that sort, made all the haste we could to get on board, thinking that the ship was burst in péeces, but comming vnto it, we found it to be in better case then we thought it had béene.

The 28 of August, wée gat some of the Ice from it, and the ship began to sit vpright againe, but before it was fully vpright, as William Barents and the other pilot went forward to the bough to sée how the ship lay, and how much it was risen; and while they were busie vpon their knées and elbowes to measure how much it was, the ship burst out of the Ice with such a noyse and so great a crack, that they thought verely that they were all cast away, knowing not how to saue them selues.

The 29 of August, the ship lying vpright againe, we vsed all the meanes we could, with yron hookes, & other instruments, to breake the flakes of Ice that lay one heap'd vpō the other, but al in vaine; so that we determined to commit our selues to the mercie of God, and to attend ayde from him, for that the Ice draue not away in any such sort that it could helpe vs.

The 30 of August, the Ice began to driue together one vpon the other with greater force then before, and bare against the ship is a boystrous south-west wind, and a great snowe, so that all the whole ship was borne vp and inclosed, whereby all that was both about it and in it, began to crack, so that it seemed to burst in a 100 péeces, which was most fearfull both to sée and heare and made all y haire of our heads to rise vpright with feare: & after y, the ship (by the Ice on both sides that ioyned and got vnder the same) was driuen so vpright, in such sort, as if it had bin lifted vp with a wrench or vice.

The 31 of August, by the force of the Ice, the ship was driuen vp 4 or 5 foote high at the beake head, and the hinder part thereof lay in a clift of Ice, whereby we thought that the ruther would be fréed from the force of the flakes of Ice, but notwithstanding, it brake in péeces staffe and all: and if that the hinder part of the ship had bin in the Ice that draue, as well as the fore part was then all the ship would haue bin driuen wholly vpon the Ice, or possibly haue ran on groūd, and for that cause wée were in great feare, and set our Scutes and our boate out vpon the Ice, if néede were, to saue our selues, but within 4 houres after, the Ice draue away of it selfe, wherewith we were excéeding glad, as if we had saued our liues, for that the ship was then on float againe, and vpon that we made a new ruther and a staffe, and hung the ruther out vpon the hooks, that if we chanced to be born vpon the Ice againe, as we had bin, it might so be fréed from it.

The 1. of September being Sunday, while we were at praier, the Ice began to gather together againe, so that the ship was lifted up

The Nauigation into the North-seas.

vp two foote at the least, but the Ice brake not. The same euening the Ice continued in ý sort stil driuing and gathering together, so that we made preparation to draw our Scute and the boate ouer the Ice vpon the land, the wind then blowing South-east.

The 2. of September, it snowed hard with a North-east wind, & the ship began to rise vp higher vpõ the Ice, at which time the Ice burst and crakt, with great force, so that we were of opinion to cary our Scute on land in that fowle weather with 13. barrels of bread, & two hogsheds of wine to sustaine our selues if need were.

The 3 of Septéber it blew hard but snowed not so much, ý wind being North Northeast, at which time we began to be loose from the Ice, whereunto we lay fast, so that the Scheck, broke from the Steuen, but the planks wherewith the ship was lyned, held the Scheck fast and made it hang on, but the boutlose and a new tail if we had fallen vpon the Ice) brake by the forcible pressing of the Ice, but held fast againe in the Ice, and yet the ship was staunch, which was wonder, in regard ý the Ice draue so hard, and in great heapes, as big as the salt hils that are in Spaine, and within a harquebus shot of the ship, betwéene the which we lay in great feare and anguishe.

The 4. of September, the weather began to cleare vp, and we sawe the Sunne, but it was very cold the wind being North, we being forced to lye still.

The 5. of September, it was faire sunshine weather and very calme, and at euening when we had supt the Ice compassed about vs againe, and we were hard inclosed therewith, the ship beginning to lye vpon the one side, and leakt sore, but by Gods grace, it became staunch againe, wherewith we were wholly in feare to lose the ship, it was in so great danger: at which time we tooke counsell together & caried our old sock saile, with pouder, lead, péeces mus-kets & other furniture on land, to make a tent about our Scute, & we had drawn vpon the land & at that time we carried some bread and wine on land also, with some timber, therewith to mend our boate, that it might serue vs in time of néede.

The 6. of September, it was indifferent faire sea-wether & sun-shine, the wind being West, whereby we were somewhat comforted, hoping that the Ice would driue away, and that we might get from thence againe.

The Nauigation into the North-seas.

The 7. of September it was indifferent wether againe, but we perceiued no opening of the water, but to the contrary it lay hard inclosed with Ice, & no water at all about the ship, no not so much as a bucket full. The same day 5 of our men went on land, but 2 of them came backe againe, the other three went forward about 2 miles into the land & there found a riuer of Sweet water, where also they found great store of wood, that had bin driuen thither, and there they found the foote-steps of harts and hinds, as they thought, for they were clouen footed, some greater footed then others, which made them Iudge them to be so.

The 8. of September, it blew hard East North-east, which was a right contrary wind to doe vs any good touching the carrying away of the Ice, so that we were still faster in the Ice, which put vs in no small discomfort.

The 9. of September, it blew North-east, with a little snowe, whereby our ship was wholy inclosed with Ice for ye wind draue the Ice hard against it, so that we lay 3. or 4. foote deepe in the Ice, and our Sheck in the after steuer, brake in peeces, and the ship began to be somewhat loose before, but yet it was not much hurt.

In the night time two beares came close to our ship side, but we sounded our trumpet, and shot at them, but hit them not, because it was darke, and they ran away.

The 10. of September, the wether was somwhat better because the wind blew not so hard, and yet all one wind.

The 11. of September it was calme wether, & 8. of vs went on land, euery man armed, to see if that were true as our other three companions had said, that there lay wood about the riuer, for that seeing we had so long wound and turned about, sometime in the Ice & then againe got out, & thereby were compelled to alter our course, and at last sawe that we could not get out of the Ice but rather became faster, and cou'd not loose our ship, as at other times we had done, as also that it began to be winter, we tooke counsell together what we were best to doe, according to the time, that we might winter there, and attend such aduenture, as God would send vs: and after we had debated vpon the matter (to keepe and defend our selues both from the cold and the wild beasts) we determined to build a house vpon the land, to keepe vs therein as well

as

The Nauigation into the North Seas.

as we could, and so to commit our selues vnto the tuition of God, and to that end we went farther into the land, to find out the conuenientest place in our opinions, to raise our house vpon, and yet we had not much stuffe to make it withall, in regard that there grew no trees nor any other thing in that country conuenient to build it withall: but we leauing no occasion vnsought, as our men went abroad to view the country, and to see what good fortune might happen vnto vs, at last we found an vnexpected comfort in our need, which was, that we found certaine trees roots and all, (as our three companions had said before) which had bin driuen vpon the shoare, either from Tartaria, Muscouia, or els where; for there was none growing vpon that land, wherewith (as if God had purposely sent them vnto vs) we were much comforted, being in good hope, that God would shew vs some further fauour; for that wood serued vs not onely to build our house, but also to burne and serue vs all the winter long, otherwise without all doubt, we had died there miserably with extreame cold.

How God in our extremest need, when we were forced to lye all the winter vpon the land sent vs wood to make vs a house, and to serue vs to burne in the cold winter.

The 12 of September it was calme wether, and then our men went vnto the other side of the land, to see if they could finde any wood neerer vnto vs, but there was none.

The 13 of September, it was calme but very misty wether, that we could doe nothing, because it was dangerous for vs to goe into the land, in regard that we could not see the wild beares, and yet they could smell vs, for they smell better then they see.

The 14 of September it was cleere sunshine wether, but very cold, and then we went into the land, and laid the wood in heapes one vpon the other, that it might not be couered ouer with the snow, and from thence ment to carry it to the place where we intended to builde our house.

The 15 of september, in the morning, as one of our men held watche, wee saw three beares, whereof the one lay still behind a peece of Ice, the other two came close to the ship; which we perceiuing, made our peeces ready to shoote at them, at which time there stood a tub full of beefe, vpon the Ice, which lay in the water to be seasoned, for that close by the ship there was no water: one of the Beares went vnto it, and put in his head to take out a peece of the beefe, but she fared therewith as the dog did with the pudding, for as she was snatching at the beefe, she was shot into the

The Nauigation into the North-seas.

the head wherewith she fell downe dead, and neuer stir'd: the other beare stood still, and lokt vpon her fellow, and when she had stood a good while, she smelt her fellow, and perceiuing that she was dead, she ran away, but we tooke halberts and other armes with vs and followed her, and at last she came againe towards vs, and we prepared our selues to withstand her, wherewith she rose vp vpon her hinder feet, thinking to rampe at vs but while she reared her selfe vp, one of our men shot her into the belly, and with that she fell vpon her fore-feet againe, and roaring as loud as she could, ran away. Then we tooke the dead beare, and ript her belly open; and taking out her guts, we set her vpon her fore feet, that so she might freese as she stood, intending to carry her w vs into Holland, if we might get our ship loose, & when we had set ye beare vpon her foure feet, we began to make a slead, thereon to drawe the wood to the place where we went to build our house, at that time it froze two fingers thicke in the salt water, and it was exceeding cold, the wind blowing North-east.

The 16. of September, the sunne shone, but towards the euening it was misty, the wind being easterly, at which time we went to fetch wood with our sleads, & then we drew foure beames aboue a mile vpon the Ice and the snow, that night againe it frose aboue two fingers thicke.

The 17. of September thirteene of vs went where the wood lay, with our sleads, and so drew fiue and fiue in a slead, and the other three helped to lift the wood behind, to make vs draw the better, and with more ease and in that manner we drew wood twice a day, and laid it on a heape by the place where we ment to build our house.

The 18. of September the wind blew west, but it snowed hard, and we went on land againe to continue our labour, to draw wood to our place appointed, and after dinner the sun shone and it was calme wether.

The 19. of September, it was calme sunshine wether, and we drew two sleads full of wood fiue thousand paces long, and that we did twice a day.

The 21 of September, it was misty wether, but towards euening it cleared vp, and the Ice still draue in the sea, but not so strangly as it did before, but yet it was very cold.

The Nauigation into the North-Seas.

The 22 of September, it was faire still weather, but very cold, the wind being west.

The 23 of september, we fetcht more wood to build our house, which we did twice a day, but it grew to be misty and still weather againe, the wind blowing East, and East-north-East, that day our Carpentur being of purme caet dyed, as we came aboord about euening.

The 24 of September, we buryed him, vnder the seiges, in the clift of a hill, hard by the water, for we could not dig vp the earth, by reason of the great frost and cold, and that day we went twise with our sleads to fetch wood.

The 25 of September, it was darke weather, the wind blowing West and West-south-west, and south-west, and the Ice began somewhat to open, and driue away; but it continued not long, so that hauing driuen about the length of the shot of a great péece, it lay thrée fadoms déepe vpon the ground, and where we lay, the Ice draue not, for we lay in the middle of the Ice, but if we had layn in the maine sea, we would haue hoysed sayle, although it was so late in the yeare. The same day we raised vp the principles of the house, and began to worke hard thereon, but if the ship had bin we would haue left our building, and haue made our after [part] of our ship, that we might haue bin ready to saile away if it had bin possible, for that it grieued vs much to lye there all that winter, which we knew would fall out to be extreame bitter, but being bereaued of all hope, we were compelled to make necessitie vertue, and with patience to attend what issue God would send vs.

The 26 of September, we had a west wind and an open sea, but our ship lay fast, wherewith we were not a little grieued, but it was Gods will, which we most patiently bare, and we began to make vp our house, part of our men fetchd wood to burne, the rest played the Carpenters: and were busie about the house, & then we were sixtéene men in all, for our Carpenter was dead, and of our sixtéene men there was still one or other sicke.

The 27 of September it blew hard north-east, and it froze so hard, that as we put a nayle into our mouthes, (as when men worke Carpenters worke they vse to doe) there would Ice hang thereon when wee tooke it out againe, and make the blood follow,

The Nauigation into the North-seas.

low: the same day there came an old Beare and a yong one towards vs, as we were going to our house, bæing altogether (for we durst not go alone) which we thought to shoot at, but she ran away, at which time the Ice came forcibly driuing in, and it was faire sunshine weather but so extreame cold, that we could hardly worke, but extremity forced vs thereunto.

The 28 of September, it was faire weather, and the sun shon, the wind being west and very calme, the sea as then being open, but our ship lay fast in the Ice and stirred not, the same day there came a beare to the ship, but when she espied vs, she ran away and we made as much hast as we could to build our house.

The 29. of September in the morning, the wind was West, and afternoone it blew Northly, and then we saw three Beares betweene vs and the house, an old one and two yong, but we notwithstanding drew our goods from the ship to the house, and so got before ye Beares & yet they followed vs: neuertheles we would not shun the way for them, but hollowed out as loud as we could, thinking that they would haue gone away, but they would not once go out of their foote-path, but got before vs, wherewith we, and they that were at the house, made a great noise, which made the Beares runne away, and wee were not a little glad thereof.

The 30. of September the winde was East, & East-south-east, and all that night and the next day it snowed so fast, that our men could fetch no wood it lay so close and high one vpon the other: then we made a great fire without the house, therewith to thaw the ground, that so we might lay it about the house, that it might be the closer; but it was all lost labour, for the earth was so hard, and frozen so deep into the ground, that we could not thaw it, and it would haue cost vs too much wood, and therefore we were forced to leaue off that labour.

The first of October the winde blew stiffe, North-east, & afternoone it blew North, with a great storme, & drift of snow, whereby we could hardly go in the winde, and a man could hardly draw his breath, the snow draue so hard in our faces, at which time wee could not see two ships length from vs.

The 2. of October before noone, the sun shone, and after noone it was cloudy againe, and it snew, but the weather was still, the

The Nauigation into the North seas.

winde being North, and then south, and we set vp our house, and vpon it we placed a May-pole made of frozen snowe.

The 3. of October before noone, it was calme Son-shine weather, but so cold, that it was hard to be indured, and after noone it blew hard out of the West, with so great and extreame cold, that if it had continued, we should haue béene forced to leaue our worke.

The fourth of October, the winde was West, and after noone North, with great store of snow, whereby we could not worke: at that time we brought our Ankor vpon the Ice to lye the faster, when we lay but an arrow shot from the water, the Ice was so much driuen away.

The 5. of October, it blew hard North-west, and the Sea was very open and without Ice, as farre as we could discerne, but we lay still frozen as we did before, and our ship lay two or thrée foote déepe in the Ice, and we could not perceiue otherwise, but that we lay fast vpon the ground, and then it was thrée fadome and a halfe déepe. The same day we brake vp the lower deck of the fore-part of our ship, and with those deales we couered our houses, and made it slope ouer head, that the water might run off, at which time it was very cold.

The 6. of October it blew hard West South-west, but towards euening, West North-west, with a great snow, that we could hardly thrust our heads out of the dore, by reason of ỹ great cold.

The 7. of October it was indifferent good wether, but yet very cold, and we calk't our house, and brake the ground about it at the foote thereof: that day the winde went round about the compasse.

The 8. of October, all the night before, it blew so hard, and the same day also, and snowed so fast, that we should haue smothered, if we had gone out into the aire: and to speake truth, it had not béene possible for any man to haue gone one ships length, though his life had laine thereon: for it was not possible for vs to goe out of the house or ship.

The 9. of October the winde still continued North, and blew and snowed hard, all that day the wind as then blowing from the land, so that all that day we were forced to stay in the ship the wether

The Nauigation into the North-seas.

ther was so foule.

The 10. of October the weather was somewhat fairer, and the winde calmer, and blew South-west, and West, and South-west, and that time the water flowed two fote higher then ordinary, which wee gest to proceede from the first North wind, which as then had blowne. The same day the wether began to bee somewhat better, so that we began to go out of our ship againe; and as one of our men went out, he chaunced to meete a Beare, and was almost at him before he knew it, but presently he ranne backe againe towards the ship, and the Beare after him; but the Beare comming to the place where before that we killed another Beare, and set her vpright, and there let her freeze, which after was couered ouer with Ice, and yet one of her pawes reached aboue it, shee stood still, whereby our man got before her, and clome vp into the ship, in great feare crying, A beare, a beare, which we hearing, came aboue hatches to looke on her, & to shoote at her, but we could not see her, by meanes of the exceeding great smoake, that had so sore tormented (vs while we lay vnder hatches) in the foule wether, which we would not haue indured for any money, but by reason of the cold and snowy wether, we were constrained to do it, if we would saue our liues, for aloft in the ship we must vndoubtedly haue dyed: the beare staied not long there, but run away, the wind then being North-east.

The same day about euening, it was faire wether, and we went out of our ship to the house, and carryed the greatest part of our bread thither.

The 11. of October it was calme wether, the wind being south, and somewhat warme, and then we carryed our wine and other viduals on land: & as we were hoysing the wine ouer-boord, there came a beare towards our ship, that had laine behinde a peece of Ice, and it seemed that we had waked her with the noise we made; for we had seene her lye there, but we thought her to be a peece of Ice; but as she came neere vs, we shot at her, and shee ran away, so we proceeded in our worke.

The 12. of October it blew North, and somewhat westerly, and then halfe of our men kept in the house, and that was the first time that we lay in it, but we indured great cold, because our cabins were not made; & besides that we had not clothes inough, &

we could kéepe no fire because our chimney was not made, where by it smoaked exceedingly.

The 13. of October the winde was North and North-west, it began againe to blow hard, and then thrée of vs went aboord the ship, and laded a sleade with béere, but when we had laden it, thinking to go to our house with it, sodainly there rose such a wind, so great a storme and cold, that we were forced to go into the ship againe, because we were not able to stay without, and we could not get the béere into the ship againe, but were forced to let it stand without vpon the sleade; being in the ship, we indured extreame cold, because we had but a few clothes in it.

The 14. of October, as we came out of the ship, we found the barrell of béere standing vpon the sleade, but it was fast frozen at the heads, yet by reason of the great cold, the béere that purged out, froze as hard vpon the side of the barrel as if it had bin glewed thereon, and in that sort we drew it to our house, and set the barrell an end, and dranke it first vp, but we were forced to melt the béere, for there was scant any vnfrozen béere in the barrell, but that thicke yeast that was vnfrozen lay the strength of the béere, so that it was to strong to drinke alone, and that which was frozen tasted like water, and being melted we mixt one with the other and so dranke it, but it had neither strength nor tast.

The 15 of October the wind blew North and east, & East South east, that day we mad place to set vp our dore, and shouled the snowe away.

The 16 of October, the wind blew South east and by South east, with faire calme weather: the same night there had bin a Beare in our ship, but in the morning she went out againe, when she saw our men: at the same time we brake vp another péece of our ship, to vse the deales about the portall, which as then we began to make.

The 17 of October, the wind was South and South-east, calme weather, but very cold, and that day we were busied about our portaile.

The 18 of October, the wind blew hard East South-east, and then we fetched our bread out of the Scute which we had drawne vp vpon the land, and the wine also which as then was not much frozen, and yet it had layne sixe wéeks therein, and not withstanding

The Nauigation into the North-seas.

ding that it had often times frozen very hard. The same day we saw an other beare, and then the sea was so couered ouer with Ice that we could see no open water.

The 19 of October ye wind blew North-east, & then there was but two men & a boy in the ship, at which time there came a Beare that sought forcibly to get into the ship, although the two men shot at her with peeces of wood, and yet she ventured vpon them, whereby they were in an extreame feare, each of them seeking to saue themselues, the two men leapt into the balust, and the boy clomed into the fore mast top, to saue their liues, meane time some of our men, shot at her with a musket, and then shee ran away.

The 20 of October it was calme sunshine weather, and then againe we saw the sea open, at which time we went on bord to fetch the rest of our beere out of the ship, where we found some of the barrels frozen in peeces, and the Iron heapes that were vpon the Iosam barrels were also frozen in peeces.

The 21 of October, it was calme sunshine wether, and then we had almost fetched all our victuals out of the ship.

The 22 of October, the wind blew coldly, and very stiff North-east, with so great a snow, that we could not get out of our dors.

The 23 of October, it was calme weather, and the wind blew North-east, then we went abord our ship, to see if the rest of our men would come home to the house; but wee feared yt it would blow hard againe, and therefore durst not stirre with the sicke man, but let him ly still that day, for he was very weake.

The 24. of October, the rest of our men being 8. persons, came to the house, and drew the sicke man vpon a slead, and then with great labour and paine, we drew our beate home to our house, and turned the bottome thereof vpwards, that when time serued vs (if God saued our liues in the Winter time) wee might vse it: and after that, perceiuing that the ship lay fast, and that there was nothing lesse to be expected then the opening of the water, wee put our Anchor into the ship againe, because it should not be couered ouer and lost in the snow, that in the spring time wee might vse it : for wee alwaies trusted in GOD that hee

would

The Nauigation into the North-seas.

would deliuer vs from thence towards Sommer time, either one way or other.

Things standing at this point with vs, as the sunne, when we might see it best and highest, began to be very low, we vsed all the speede we could to fetch all things with sleades out of our ship into our house, not onely meate and drinke, but all other necessaries, at which time the winde was North.

The 2 5. of October, we fetcht all things that were necessary for the furnishing of our Scute and our Boate: and when we had laden the last stead, and stood ready to draw it to the house, our master looked about him and saw three Beares behind the ship that were comming towards vs, whereupon he cryed out aloud to feare them away, & we presently leaped forth to defend our selues as well as we could: and, as good fortune was, there lay two halberds vpon the slead, whereof the master tooke one, and I the other, and made resistance against them, as well as we could; but the rest of our men ran to saue themselues in the ship, and as they ran, one of them fell into a clift of Ice, which grieued vs much: for we thought verily that the beares would haue ran vnto him, to deuoure him, but God defended him: for the Beares still made towards the ship after the men y ran thither to saue themselues. Meane time, we and the man that fel into the clift of Ice, tooke our aduantage, and got into the ship on the other side, which the Beares perceiuing, they came fiercely towards vs, that had no other armes to defend vs withall, but onely the two halberds, which wee doubting would not be sufficient, wee still gaue them worke to do by throwing billets and other things at them, and euery time we threw, they ran after them as a dogge vseth to do at a stone that is cast at him. Meane time we sent a man downe vnder hatches to strike fire, and another to fetch pikes, but we could get no fire, and so we had no meanes to shoote: at the last the Beares came fiercely vpon vs, we stroke one of them with a halberd vpon the snoute, wherewith she gaue back, when she felt her selfe hurt, and went away, which the other two y were not so great as she perceiuing, ran away: and we thanked God that wee were so well deliuered from them, & so drew our slead quietly to our house, and there shewed our men what had happened vnto vs.

The Nauigation into the North-seas.

The 26. of October the wind was North, and North-North-West, with indifferent faire wether: then we saw open water hard by the land, but we perceiued the Ice to driue in the sea, still towards the ship.

The 27. of October, the wind blew North-east, and it snowed so fast, that we could not worke without the doore. That day our men kil'd a white Fox, which they flead: and after they had rosted it, ate thereof, which tasted like Connies flesh: the same day we set vp our diall, and made the clock strike, and we hung vp a lamp to burne in the night time, wherein we vsed the fat of the beare, which we molt and burnt in the lampe.

The 28. of October, wee had the wind North-east, and then our men went out to fetch wood, but there fell so stormy wether, and so great a snow, that they were forced to come home againe: about euening the wether began to breake vp, at which time three of our men wen to the place where we had set the beare vpright, and there stood frozen thinking to pull out her teeth, but it was cleane couered ouer with snow: and while they were there, it began to snow so fast againe, that they were glad to come home, as fast as they could; but the snow beat so sore vpon them, that they could hardly see their way, & had almost lost their right way, whereby they had like to haue laine all that night out of the house.

The 29. of October the wind still blew North-east, & then we fetch'd segges from the Sea side, & laid them vpon the saile, that was spread vpon our house that it might be so much the closer & warmer: for the deales were not driuen close together, and the foule wether would not permit vs to do it.

The 30. of October, the wind yet continued North-east, and then the Sunne was full aboue the earth, a little aboue the Horison.

The 31. of October, the wind still blew North-east, wth great store of snow, whereby we durst not looke out of doores.

The first of Nouember the wind still continued North-east, & then we saw the moone rise in the East when it began to be darke, and the Sunne was no higher aboue the Horizon than wee could well see it, and yet that day we saw it not, because of the close wether and the great snow that fell, and it was extreame cold, so that we

L

we could not go out of the house.

The 2. of Nouember, the Wind blew West, and somewhat South, but in the euening it blew North, with calme wether, and that day we saw the Sunne rise South, South-east, and it went downe South South-West, but it was not full aboue the earth, but passed in the Horizon along by the earth: and the same day one of our men killed a Fox with a hatchet, which was flead, rosted and eaten: before the Sunne began to decline, wee saw no Foxes, and then the Beares vsed to go from vs.

The 3. of Nouember the Wind blew North-West w calme wether, and the Sunne rose South and by East, and somewhat more southerly, and went downe South and by West, and somewhat more Southerly; and then we could see nothing but the vpper part of the Sun aboue the Horizon, and yet the land where we were, was as high as the mast of our ship, then we toke the height of the Sunne, it being in the eleuenth degree and 48. minutes of Scorpio, his declination being 15. degrees and 24. minutes on the South side of the Equinoctiall line.

The 4. of Nouember it was calme wether, but then we saw the Sunne no more, for it was no longer aboue the Horizon, then our Chirurgion made a bath (to bathe vs in) of a Winepipe, wherein we entred one after the other, and it did vs much good, and was a great meanes of our health. The same day wee toke a white Fox, that often times came abroad, not as they vsed at other times: for that when the Beares left vs at the setting of the Sunne, and came not againe before it rose, the Fox to the contrary came abroad when they were gone.

The 5. of Nouember the wind was North, & somewhat West, and then we saw open water vpon the Sea, but our ship lay still fast in the Ice, and when the Sunne had left vs, we saw ye Mone continually both day and night, and neuer went downe when it as in the highest degree.

The 6. of Nouember the wind was North-West, still wether, and then our men fetcht a slead full of fire-wood, but by reason that the Son was not seene, it was very dark wether.

The 7. of Nouember it was darke wether, and very still, the wind West at which time we could hardly discerne the day from the night, specially because at that time our clock stod still, and

and by that meanes we knew not when it was day, although it was day, and our men rose not out of their Cabens all that day, but onely to make water, and therefore they knew not whether the light they saw, was the light of the day or of the Moone, whereupon they were of seuerall opinions, some saying it was the light of the day, the others of the night: but as we toke good regard thereunto, we found it to be the light of the day, about twelue of the clock at noone.

The 8. of Nouember, it was still wether, the wind blowing South, and South-West. The same day our men fetcht another sled of firewood, and then also we toke a white Fox, and saw open water in the Sea. The same day we shared our bread amongst vs, each man hauing foure pound and ten ounces, for his allowance in eight daies, so that then we were eight daies eating a barrell of bread, whereas before we ate it vp in fiue or sixe daies: we had no need to share our flesh and fish, for we had more store thereof, but our drinke failed vs, and therefore we were forced to share that also: but our best beere was for the most part wholly without any strength, so that it had no sauour at all: and besides all this, there was a great deale of it spilt.

The 9. of Nouember the wind blew North-east, and somewhat more Northerly, and then we had not much day-light, but it was altogether darke.

The 10 of Nouember, it was calme wether, the wind North-West, and then our men went into the ship to see how it lay, and we saw that there was a great deale of water in it, so that the balast was couered ouer with water, but that it was frozen, and so might not be pump't out.

The 11. of Nouember it was indifferent wether, the wind North-west: the same day we made a round thing of cable yearn, & like to a net, to catch Foxes withall, that we might get them into the house, & it was made like a trap, which fell vpon the Foxes as they came vnder it, and that day we caught one.

The 12. of Nouember the wind blew East, with a little light: that day we began to share our wine, euery man had two glasses a day, but commonly our drinke was water, which we molt out of snow which we gathered without the house.

The 13. of Nouember it was foule wether, with great snow,

The Nauigation into the North-seas.

the wind East.

The 14. of Nouember it was faire cleare wether, with a cleare sky, full of starres, and an East-wind.

The 15. of Nouember it was darke wether, the wind North-east, with a vading light.

The 16. of Nouember it was wether with a temperate aire, and an East-wind.

The 17. of Nouember it was darke wether, and a close aire, the wind East.

The 18. of Nouember it was foule wether, the wind South-east: then the maister cut vp a packe of course clothes, and diuided it amongst our men that needed it, therewith to defend vs better from the cold.

The 19. of Nouember, it was foule weather, with an East wind, and then the chest with linnin was opened, and deuided a-mongst the men for shift, for they had need of them, for then our onely care was to find all the means we could to defend our body from the cold.

The 20. of Nouember, it was faire stil weather, the wind Easterly, then we washt our sheets, but it was so cold, that when we had washt and wrong them, they presently froze so stiffe, that although we lay'd them by a great fire, the side that lay next the fire thawed, but the other side was hard frozen, so that we should sooner haue torne them in sunder then haue opened them, whereby we were forced to put them into the seething water againe to thaw them, it was so exceeding cold.

The 21. of Nouember, it was indifferent wether with a North-east wind, then wee agreed that euery man should take his turne to cleaue wood, thereby to ease our cooke, that had more then worke inough to doe twice a day to dresse meat, & to melt snowe for our drinke, but our Master & the Pilot, were exempted from ye worke.

The 22. of Nouember, the wind was south-east, it was faire wether, then we had but seuenteene cheeses, whereof one we ate amongst vs, and the rest were deuided to euery man one, for his portion, which they might eate when he list.

The 23. of Nouember, it was indifferent good weather, the wind South-east, and as we perceiued that the Fox vsed to come oftner, and more then they were woont, to take them the better,

we

The Nauigation into the North-seas.

we made certaine traps of thicke planckes, wheron we laid stones, & round about them placed peeces of shards fast in the ground, that they might not dig vnder them, and so got some of the foxes.

The 24. of Nouember, it was foule weather, & the winde North-east, & then we prepared our selues to go into the bath, for some of vs were not very well at ease, and so soure of vs went into it, and when we came out, our Surgion gaue vs a purgation, which did vs much good, and that day we tooke foure Foxes.

The 25. of Nouember, it was faire cleare weather, the winde West; and that day we tooke two foxes, with a springs that we had purposely set vp.

The 26. of Nouember, it was foule weather, and a great storme with a South-west wind, and great store of snowe, whereby we were so closed vp in the house, that we could not goe out, but were forced to ease our selues within the house.

The 27. of Nouember, it was faire cleare weather, the wind South-west, and then we made more Springes to get Fox, for it stood vs vpon to doe it, because they serued vs for meat, as if God had sent them purposely for vs, for wee had not much meate.

The 28. of Nouember, it was foule stormie weather, and the wind blew hard out of the North, and it snew hard, whereby we were shut vp againe in our house, the snow lay so closed before the dores.

The 29. of Nouember, it was faire cleare wether, & a good aire: the wind Northerly, and we sound meanes to open our dore, by shoueling away the snowe, whereby we got one of our dores open, and going out, we found al our Traps and Springes cleane couered ouer with snow, which we made cleane, and set them vp again to take Foxes: and that day we tooke one, which as then serued vs not onely for meat, but of the skins we made Caps to were vpon our heads, therewith to keepe them warme from the extreame cold.

The 30. of Nouember, it was faire cleare weather, the wind West, and fiue of vs went to the ship, all wel prouided of arms to see how it lay: and when we went vnder the fore decke, we tooke a Fore aliue in the ship.

The 1. of December, it was foule weather with a South-west wind

L 3

The Nauigation into the North-seas.

wind, and great stoare of snow, whereby we were once againe stopt vp in the house, & by that meanes there was so great a smoke in the house, that we could hardly make fire, and so were forced to lye all day in our cabens, but the Cooke was forced to make fire to dresse our meat.

The 2. of December, it was still foule weather, whereby we were forced to kéep stil in the house, & yet we could hardly sit by the fire, because of the smoake, and therefore stayd still in our cabens, and then we heated stones, which we put into our Cabens to warm our féet, for that both the cold and the smoke were vnsupportable.

The 3. of December we had the like weather, at which time as we lay in our Cabans, we might heare the Ire crack in the sea, and yet it was at the least halfe a mile from vs, which made a huge noyse, and we were of oppinion, that as then the great hils of Ice which we had séene in the sea, in summer time, brake one from the other, & for that during those 2. or 3. dayes, because of the extreame smoake, we made not so much fire as we commonly vsed to doe, it froze so sore within the house, that the wals and the roofe thereof were frozen two fingers thick with Ice, and also in our Cabens where we lay all those thrée daies, while we could not goe out by reason of the foule weather, we set vp the glas of 12. houres, & til it was run out, we set it vp againe, stil watching it lest we should misse our time. For the cold was so great, that our Clock was frozen, and might not goe, although we hung more waight on it then before.

The 4. of December, it was faire cleare weather, the wind Northeast, and then we began euery man by turne to dig open our dores that were closed vp with snow, for we saw that it would be often to doe, and therefore we agréed to work by turns, no man excepted but the Maister and the Pilot.

The 5. of December, it was faire weather, with an East-wind and then we made our Springes cleane againe to take Foxes.

The 6 of December, it was foule weather againe, with an Easterly wind, and extreame cold, almost not to be indured, whereupon we lookt pittifully one vpon the other, being in great feare, that if the extremity of ye cold grew to be more & more, we should all die there with cold, for that what fire soeuer we made, it would

not

The Nauigation into the North-seas.

not warme vs, yea and our sack which is so hotte, was frozen very hard, so that when we were euery man to haue his part, we were forced to melt it in the fire, which we shared euery second day about halfe a pint for a man, wherewith we were forced to sustain our selues, and at other times we dranke water, which agreed not well with the cold, and we needed not to coole it with snowe or Ice, but we were forced to melt it out of the snow.

The 7. of December, it was still foule weather, and we had a great storme, with a North-east-wind, which brought an extreame cold with it, at which time we knew not what to do, & while we sate consulting together, what were best for vs to do, one of our companions gaue vs counsell to burne some of the sea-coles that we had brought out of the ship, which would cast a great heat and continue long, and so at euening we made a great fire thereof, which cast a great heat: at which time we were very carefull to keepe it in: for that the heat being so great a comfort vnto vs, we tooke care how to make it continue long: whereupon wee agreed to stop vp all the doores and the chimney, thereby to keepe in the heate, and so went into our cabans to sleepe, well comforted with the heat, and so lay a great while talking together; but at last we were taken with a great swounding and daseling in our heads, yet some more then other some, which we first perceiued by a sick man, and therefore the lesse able to beare it, & found our selues to be very ill at ease, so that some of vs that were strongest, start out of their cabans, and first opened the chimney, and then the doores, but he that opened the doore fell downe in a swound vpon the snow, which I hearing, as lying in my Caban next to the doore, start vp and casting vinegar in his face, recouered him againe, and so he rose vp: and when the doores were open, we all recouered our healthes againe, by reason of the cold aire, and so the cold which before had beene so great an enemy vnto vs, was then the onely reliefe that we had, otherwise without doubt, we had died in a sodaine swound, after the Master, when we were come to our selues againe, gaue euery one of vs a little wine to comfort our hearts.

The 8. of December, it was foule weather, the wind Northerly, very sharpe and cold, but we durst lay no more coles on, as we did the day before, for that our misfortune had taught vs, that to

shun

than one danger we should not run into an other.

The 9. of December, it was faire cleare weather, the skie full of Starres, then we set our doore wide open, which before was fast closed vp with snowe, and made our Springes ready to take Foxes.

The 10. of December it was still faire Star-light weather, the wind North-east: then we tooke two Foxes, which were good meate for vs, for as then our victuals began to be scant, and the cold still increased, whereunto their skins serued vs for a good defence.

The 11. of December, it was faire weather, and a cleare aire, but very cold, which he that felt not would not beléeue, for our shoes froze as hard as hornes vpon our féet, and within, they were white frozen, so that we could not weare our shoes, but were forced to make great pattens, y upper part being ship skins, which we put one ouer thrée or foure paire of socks, and so went in them to kéepe our féet warme.

The 12. of December, it was faire cleare weather, with a North-west wind, but extreame cold, so that our house walles and Cabans where frozen a finger thicke, yea and the clothes vpon our backs were white ouer with frost, and although some of vs were of opinion that we should lay more coles vpon the fire to warme vs, and that we should let the chimney stand open, yet we durst not do it, fearing the like danger we had escaped.

The 13. of December it was faire cleare wether, with an East wind: then we tooke another Fox, and tooke great paines about preparing and dressing of our springes, with no small trouble, for that if we staied too long without the doores, there arose blisters vpon our faces and our eares.

The 14. of December it was faire wether, the wind North-east, and the sky full of starres, then we tooke the height of y right shoulder of the Rens. When it was South South-west, & somewhat more Westerly (and then it was, at the highest in our compas) and it was eleuated aboue the Horison twenty degrées and twenty eight minutes, his declination being sixe degrées, and eightéene minuts on the North side of the lyne, which declination being taken out of the height aforesaid there rested fourtéene degrées, which being takē out of 90. degrées, then the height of y pole was seuenty

The Nauigation into the North-seas.

sire degrées.

The 15 of December it was still faire weather, the wind East: that day we tooke two Foxes, and saw the Moone rise East-south-east, when it was twenty sixe daies old, in the signe of Scorpio.

The 16. of December, it was faire cleare weather, the wind East: at that time we had no more wood in the house, but had burnt it all: but round about our house there lay some couered ouer with snow, which with great paine and labour we were forced to digge out and so shouell away the snow, and so brought it into the house, which we did by turns, two and two together, wherin we were forced to vse great spéede, for we could not long endure without the house, because of the extreame cold, although we ware the Foxes skinnes about our heads, and double apparell vpon our backs.

The 17. of December, the wind still held North east, with faire weather, and so great frosts, that we were of opinion, that if there stood a barrell full of water without the doore, it would in one night firze from the top to the bottome.

The 18. of December, the wind still held North-east, with faire wether: then seuen of vs went out vnto the ship, to sée how it lay, and being vnder the decke, thinking to find a Fox there, we sought all the holes, but we found none; but when we entred into the Caben, and had stricken fire to sée in what case the ship was, and whether the water rose higher in it, there wée found a Fox, which we tooke, and carried it home, and ate it, and then we found that in eightéene dayes absence (for it was so long since we had béene there) the water was risen about a finger high, but yet it was all Ice, for it froze as fast as it came in, and the vessels which we had brought with vs full of fresh water out of Holland, were frozen to the ground.

The 19. of December it was faire wether, the wind being South: then we put each other in good comfort, that the sun was then a'most halfe ouer, and ready to come to vs againe, which we sorelonged for, it being a weary time for vs to be without the Sunne, and to want the greatest comfort that God sendeth vnto man here vpon the earth, and that wherein reioiceth euery liuing thing.

The 20. of Dece. before noone it was faire cleare wether, and then we we had taken a Fox but towards euening there rose such a storm in the South-west, with so great a snow that all the house was inclosed therewith.

The 21. of December it was faire cléere wether, with a North-east wind, then we made our doore cleane againe, and made a way to go out, and clensed our traps for the Foxes, which did vs great pleasure when we tooke them, for they seemed as dainty as Venison vnto vs.

The 22. of December it was foule wether, with great store of snow, the wind South-west, which stopt vp our doore againe, and we were forced to dig it open againe, which was almost euery day to do.

The 23. of December it was foule wether, the wind South-west, with great store of snow, but we were in good comfort that the Sunne would come againe to vs, for as we gest, that day he was in Tropicus Capricorni, which is the furthest signe that the sunne passeth on the South side of the line, and from thence it turneth North-ward againe. This Tropicus Capricorni lyeth on the South side of the Equinoctiall line, in twenty thrée degrées and eightéene minutes.

The 24. of December being Christmas Euen, it was faire wether, then we opened our doore againe, and saw much open water in the sea: for we had heard the Ice crack and driue: although it was not day, yet we could sée so farre: towards euening it blew hard out of the North-east, with great store of snow, so that all the passage that wee had made open before, was stopt vp againe.

The 25. of December being Christmas day, it was foule wether, with a North-west-wind, and yet though it was foule wether, we hard the Foxes run ouer our house, wherewith some of our men said it was an ill signe; and while we sate disputing why it should be an ill signe, some of our men made answere, that it was an ill signe because we could not take them, to put them into the pot to rost them, for that had béene a very good signe for vs.

The 26. of December it was foule wether, the wind North-west, and it was so cold that we could not warme vs, although we vsed all the meanes we could with great fires, good store of clothes, and with hot stones, and billets laid vpon our féete and
vpon

vpon our bodies, as we lay in our Cabens, but notwithstanding all this, in the morning our Cabens were frozen, which made vs behold one the other with sad countenance, but yet we comforted our selues againe as well as we could, that the Sunne was then as low as it could goe, and that it now began to come to vs againe, and we found it to be true: for that the daies beginning to lengthen, the cold began to strengthen, but hope put vs in good comfort, and eased our paine.

The 27. of December it was still foule wether, with a North-west wind so that as then we had not béene out in thrée daies together, nor durst not thrust our heads out of doores, and within the house it was so extreme cold, that as we sate before a great fire, and séemed to burne on the fore side, we froze behinde at our backs, and were al white as the country men vse to be when they come in at the gates of the towne in Holland with their sleds and haue gone all night.

The 28. of December it was still foule wether with a West wind, but about euening it began to cleare vp, at which time one of our men made a hole open at one of our doores, and went out to sée what news abroad, but found it so hard wether that he stayed not long, and told vs that it had snowed so much that the Snow lay higher then our house, and that if he had stayed out longer, his eares would vndoubtedly haue béene frozen off.

The 29. of December it was calme wether, and a pleasant aire the wind being Southward: that day, he, whose turne it was, opened the doore, and dig'd a hole through the snow, where wee went out of the house vpon steps, as if it had bin out of a Seller, at least seuen or eight steps high, each step a foote from the other, and then we made cleane our springes for the Foxes, whereof for certaine daies we had not taken any: and as we made them cleane, one of our men found a dead Fox in one of them, that was frozen as hard as a stone, which he brought into the house, and thawed it before the fire, and after, fleaing it, some of our men ate it.

The 30. of December it was foule wether againe, with a storme out of the West, and great store of snow, so that all the labour and paine that we had taken the day before to make steps to go out of our house, and to clense our springes, was al in vaine, for it was al couered ouer with snow againe, higher then it was before.

The 31. of December it was still foule wether, with a storme out of the North-west, whereby we were so fast shut vp into the house, as if we had béene prisoners, and it was so extreame cold, that the fire almost cast no heate: for as we put our féete to the fire, we burnt our hose before we could féele the heate, so that we had worke inough to do to patch our hose: and which is more if we had not sooner smelt, then felt them, we should haue burnt them ere we had knowne it.

After that with great cold, danger, & disease, we had brought this yeare vnto an end, we entred into ẏ yeare of our Lord God 1597. ẏ beginning whereof, was in ẏ same maner as ẏ end of Anno 1596. had béen, for the wether continued as cold, foule, & snowy as it was before, so that vpon the first of Ianuary we were inclosed in the house ẏ wind then being West: at the same time we agréed to share our wine euery man a small measure full, and that but once in two daies: and as we were in great care and feare that it would be long before we should get out from thence, (& we hauing but smal hope therin) some of vs spared to drink wine as long as wée could, that if we should stay long there, we might drinke it at our néed.

The 2. of Ianuary, it blew hard, with a West wind, and a great storme, with both snow and frost, so that in four or fiue daies we durst not put our heads out of ẏ doores, & as then by reason of the great cold, we had almost burnt all our wood, notwithstanding we durst not goe out to fetch more wood, because it froze so hard, & there was no being without the doore, but séeking about we found some péeces of wood, that lay ouer the doore, which we cloue, and withall cloue the blocks whereon we vsed to beate our stock-fish, and so holp our selues so well as we could.

The 3. of Ianuary, it was all one weather, and we had little wood to burne.

The 4. of Ianuary, it was still foule stormie weather, with much snow and great cold, the wind South-west, and we were forced to kéepe in the house: and to know where the wind blew, we thrust a halfe pike out at ẏ chimney, w a little cloth, or fether vpon it, but as soone as we thrust it out, it was presently frozen as hard as a péece of wood, and could not go about nor stirre with the wind.

The 5. of Ianuary, it was somewhat still and calme weather: then

then we digd our dore open againe, that we might goe out, and carry out all the filth that had bin made during the time of our being shut in the house; and made every thing handsome, and fetched in wood, which we cleft, and it was all our dayes worke to further our selues as much as we could, fearing lest we should be shut vp againe: and as there were three dores in our portall, and for y our house lay couered ouer in snow, we tooke y middle dore thereof away, and digged a great hole in the snow, that laie without the house, like to a side of a vault, wherein we might go to ease ourselues, and cast other filth into it: and when we had taken paines al day, we remembred our selues that it was Twelf Euen, then we prayed our Maister that we might be merry that night, and said that we were content to spend some of the wine that night which we had spared, and which was our share euery second day, and whereof for certaine daies we had not drunke, and so that night we made merry, and drunke to the three Kings, and therewith we had two pound of meale, whereof we made pancakes with oyle, and euery man a white bisket, which we sopt in wine: and so supposing that we were in our owne country, and amongst our frends, it comforted vs as well as if we had made a great banket in our owne house: and we also made tickets, and our Gunner was king of Noua Zembla, which is at least two hundred miles long, and lyeth betwéene two seas.

The 6 of January, it was faire weather, the wind north-east, then we went out and clensed our Traps to take Foxes, which were our Venison, and we digd a great hole in the snow, where our fire-wood lay, and left it close aboue like a vault; & from thence fetcht out our wood as we néeded it.

The 7. of January, it was foule weather againe, with a North west wind, and some snow, and very cold, which put vs in great feare to be shut vp in the house againe.

The 8. of January, it was faire weather againe, the wind North: then we made our Springes ready to get more Veneson: which we longed for, and then we might sée and marke day-light, which then began to increase, that the Sunne as then began to come towards vs againe, which put vs in no litle comfort.

The 9. of January, it was foule wether, with a North-west wind, but not so hard wether as it had bin before, so y we might go out

out of the dore, to make cleane our Springes, but it was no néed to bid vs goe home againe for the cold taught vs by experience not to stay long out, for it was not so warm to get any good by staying in the aire.

The 10. of January, it was faire weather, with a North-wind: then seuen of vs went to our ship, well armed, which we found in the same state we left it in, and it we saw many footesteps of Beares, both great and small, whereby it séemed that there had bin more then one or two Beares therein; and as we went vnder hatches, we stroke fire, and lighted a candle, and found that the water was rysen a foote higher in the ship.

The 11. of January, it was faire weather, the wind North-east, and the cold began to be somewhat lesse, so that as then we were bold to goe out of the dores, and went about a quarter of a mile to a hill, from whence we fetched certaine stones, which we layd in the fire, therewith to warme vs in our Cabans.

The 12. of January, it was faire cleare weather, the wind North-west: that euening it was very cleare, and the skie full of Stars, then we tooke the height of Occulus Tauri, which is a bright and well knowne Star, & we found it to be eleuated aboue ý Horison twenty nine degrées and fifty foure minuts, her declination being fiftéene degrées, fifty foure minutes on the North side of the lyne. This declination being subtracted from the height aforesaid, then there rested fourtéene degrées, which subtracted from ninety degrées, then the height of the pole was seuenty sire degrées, and so by measuring the height of that starre, and some others we gest that ý Sun was in the like height, and that we were there vnder seuenty sire degrées, and rather higher then lower.

The 13. of January, it was faire still weather, the wind westerlie, and then we perceaued that day-light began more and more to increase, and wee went out and cast bullets at the bale of ý flag staffe, which before we could not sée when it turnd about.

The 14. of January, it was faire weather, and a cleare light, the wind Westerlie, and that day we tooke a Fox.

The 15. of January, it was faire cleare weather, with a West wind, and sir of vs went abord the ship, where we found, the bolck-hanger, (which the last time that we were in the ship, we stucke in a hole in the fore decke, to take Foxes) puld out of the hole, and lay

in

The Nauigation into the North-seas.

in the middle of the ship, and al torne in péeces by the Beares as we perceiued by their foote-steps.

The 16. of Ianuary, it was faire weather, the wind Northerly, and then we went now & then out of the house to strech out our ioynts and our limes with going and running, that we might not become lame, & about noone time we saw a certaine rednes in the skie as a shew or missenger of the Sunne that began to come towards vs.

The 17. of Ianuary, it was cleare weather, with a North wind, and then still more and more wée perceiued that the Sun began to come neerer vnto vs, for the day was somewhat warmer, so that when wee had a good fire, there fell great péeces of Ice downe from the walles of our house, and the Ice melted in our cabins, and the water dropt downe, which was not so before, how great soeuer our fire was, but that night it was cold againe.

The 18. of Ianuary, it was faire cleare weather, with a southeast wind, then our wood began to consume, & so we agréed to burne some of our sea-coles, and not to stop vp the chimney, and then wée should not néede to feare any hurt, which wée did, and found no disease thereby, but we thought it better for vs to képe the coles, and to burne our wood more sparingly, for that the coles would serue vs better when we should saile home in our open Scute.

The 19. of Ianuary, it was faire weather, with a North wind, and then our bread began to diminish, for that some of our barels were not full waight, & so the diuision was lesse, and we were forced to mak our allowance bigger with that which we had spared before: and then some of vs went abord the ship, wherein there was halfe a barrell of bread, which we thought to spare till the last, and there secretly each of them tooke a bisket or two out of it.

The 20. of Ianuary, the ayre was cleare, and the wind southwest, that day we staied in the house, and cloue wood to burne, and brake some of our emptie barrels, and cast the Iron hoopes vpon the top of the house.

The 21. of Ianuary, it was faire weather, with a West wind: at that time taking of Foxes began to faile vs, which was a signe that the Beares would soone come againe, as not long after we

found

The Nauigation into the North-seas.

found it to be true, for as long as the Beares stay away, the Fores came abroad, and not much before the Beares come abroad, the Fores were but little seene.

The 22. of January, it was faire wether with a West wind: then we went out againe to cast the bullet, and perceiued that day light began to appeare, whereby some of vs said, that the Sun would soone appeare vnto vs, but William Barents to the contrary said, that it was yet two weeks to soone.

The 23. of January, it was faire calme weather, with a South-west-wind: then foure of vs went to the ship, and comforted each other, giuing God thankes, that the hardest time of the winter was past, being in good hope that we should liue to talke of those things at home in our owne country: and when we were in the ship, we found that the water rose higher and higher in it, and so each of vs taking a bisket or two with vs, we went home againe.

The 24. of January, it was faire cleare weather, with a West wind: then I, and Jacob Heinskecke, and another with vs went to the sea side, on the South side of Noua Zembla, where contrary to our expectation, I first saw the edge of the Sun, when with we went speedily home againe, to tell Willam Barents and the rest of our companions that ioyfull newes: but William Barents being a wise and well experienced pilot, would not beléeue it, esteeming it to be about fourteene daies to soone, for the Sunne to shin in that part of the world, but we earnestly affirmed the contrary, and said that we had seene the Sunne.

The 25. & 26. of January it was misty, and close weather, so y we could not see anything: then they that layd y contrary wager with vs, thought that they had woon, but vpon the twenty seuen day it was cleare weather, and then we saw the Sunne in his full roundnesse aboue the Horizon, whereby it manifestly appeared that we had seene it vpon the twenty foure day of January. And as we were of diuers opinions touching the same, and that we said it was cleane contrary to the opinions of all olde and newe writers, yea and contrary to the nature and roundnesse both of Heauen and Earth; some of vs said, that seeing in long time there had béen no day, that it might be that we had ouerslept our selues, whereof we were better assured: but concerning the thing in it selfe,

How the Sun which they had lost the 4. of Nouember did appere to them again vpon the

The Nauigation into the North-seas.

selfe, seeing God is wonderfull in all his workes, we will referre that to his almightie power, and leaue it vnto others to dispute of, but for that no man shall thinke vs to be in doubt thereof, if we should let this passe without discoursing vpon it, therefore we will make some declaration thereof, whereby we may assure our selues that we kept good reckening.

24. of Ianuary which was very strange, and cōtrary to al learned mens opinions.

You must vnderstand, that when we first saw the Sunne, it was in the fift degrée and 25. minutes of Aquarius, and it should haue staied according to our first gessing, till it had entred into the sixtéenth degrée and 27. minutes of Aquarius, before he should haue shewed there vnto vs, in the higth of 76. degrées.

Which we striuing and contending about it, amongst our selues, we could not be satisfied, but wondred thereat, and amongst vs were of opinion, that we had mistaken our selues, which neuerthelesse, we could be perswaded vnto, for that euery day, without faile we noted what had past, and also had vsed our clocke continually, and when that was frosen, we vsed our houreglasse of 12. houres long, whereupon we argued with our selues, in diuers wise, to know how we should finde out that difference, and leaue the truth of the time, which to trie we agréed to looke into the Ephemerides made by Iosephus Schala, printed in Venice, for the yéeres of our Lord 1589. till a 1600. and we found therein, that vpon the 24. day of Ianuary, (when the Sunne first appeared vnto vs) that at Venice the clocke being one in the night time, the Moone and Iupiter were in coniunction, whereupon we sought to knowe when the same coniunction should be ouer or about the house where we then were, and at last we found, ý the 24. day of Ianuary was the same day, whereon the coniunctiō aforesaid happened in Venice, at one of the clocke in the night, & with vs in the morning, when ý Sun was in the east: for we saw manifestly, that the two Planets afore said, approached néere vnto each other, vntill such time as the Moone & Iupiter stood one iust ouer the other, both in the signe of Taurus, and that was at six of the clocke in the morning, at which time the Moone and Iupiter were found by our Compas to be in coniunction, ouer our house, in the North and by east point, & the South part of the Compas was south-south-west, and there we had it right south, the Moone being eight daies old, whereby it appeareth, that the

Sunne

The Nauigation into the North-seas.

Sunne and the Moone were eight points different, and this was about fixe of the clocke in the morning: this place differeth from Venice fiue houres in longitude, whereby we maye gesse how much we were nearer east then the Citie of Venice, which was fiue houres, each houre being 15. degrees, which is in all 75. degrees, that we were more easterly then Venice, by all which it is manifestly to be seene, that we had not failed in our account, and that also we had found our right longitude, by the two Planets aforesaid, for the towne of Venice lieth vnder 37. degrees and 25. minutes in longitude, and her declination is 46. degrees and 5. minutes, whereby it followeth that our place of Noua Zembla lieth vnder 112. degrees and 25. minutes in longitude, and the high of the Pole 76. degrees, and so you haue the right longitude & latitude, but from the vttermost point of Noua Zembla, to the point of Cape de Tabin, the vttermost point of Tartaria, where it windeth southward: The longitude differeth 60. degrees, but you must vnderstand, that the degrees are not so great, as they are vnder the Equinoxial line, for right vnder the line a degree is sixteene miles, but when you leaue the line, either northward or southward, then the degrees in longitude do lessen, so that the neerer that a man is to the North or South Pole, so much the degrees are lesse: so that vnder the 76. degrees northward, where wee wintered, the degrees are but 3. miles, and ⅔ parts, whereby it is to be marked, that we had but 60. degrees to saile to the said Cape de Tabin, which is 220. miles, so the said Cape lieth in 172. degrees in longitude as it is thought: and being about it, it seemeth that we should be in the straight of Anian, where we may saile bouldlie into the South, as the land reacheth: Now what further instructions are to be had to know where we lost the sun vnder the said 76. degrees vpon the fourth of Nouember, I saw it againe vpon the 24. of Ianuary: I leaue that to be described, by such as make profession thereof, it sufficeth vs to haue shewed, that it failed vs not to appeare at the ordinary time.

The 25. of Ianuary, it was darke clowdy weather, the wind westerlie, so that the seeing of the Sunne the day before, was againe doubted of, and then many wagers were laid, and we still lokt out to see if the Sunne appeared, the same day we sawe a Beare, (which as long as the Sunne appeared not vnto vs we sawe

The Nauigation into the North seas

(is not) comming out of the south west towards our house, but when we shouted at her she came no néerer, but went away againe.

The 26. of Janurie, it was faire cléere weather, but in the Horrison there hung a white or darke cloude, whereby we could not sée the Sun, whereupon the rest of our companions, thought that we had mistuken our selues vpon the 24. day, and that the Sunne appeared not vnto vs, and mocked vs, but we were resolute in our former affirmation, that we had séene the Sunne, but not in the full roundnesse: That euening the sicke man that was amongst vs, was very weake, and felt him selfe to be extreame sicke, for he had laine long time, and we comforted him as well as we might, & gaue him the best admonition y we could, but he died not long after midnight.

The 27. of Januarie it was faire cléere weather, with a south-east winde, then in the morning we digd a hole in the snowe, hard by the house, but it was still so extreame cold, that we could not stay long at worke, and so we digd by turnes euery man a little while, and then went to the fire, and an other went and supplyed his place, till at last we digd seauen foote depth, wherewe went to burie the dead man, after that when we had read certaine chaptets and sung some Psalmes, we all went out and buried the man, which done we went in and brake our fasts, and while we were at meate, and discoursed amongst our selues, touching the great quantitie of snowe that continually fell in that place, wee said that if it fell out, that our house should be closed vp againe with snowe, we would find the meanes to climbe out at the chimney, whereupon our master went to trie if he could clime vp through the chimney, and so get out, and while he was climbing one of our men went forth of the dore, to sée if the master were out or not, who standing vpon the snowe, saw the Sunne, and called vs all out, wherewith we all went forth and saw the Sunne in his full roundnesse, alitle aboue the horrison, and then it was without all doubt, that we had séene the Sunne vpon the 24. of Januarie, which made vs all glad, and we gaue God hearty thankes, for his grace shewed vnto vs, that that glorious light appeared vnto vs againe.

The 28. of January, it was faire weather, with a west wind, then

The Nauigation into the North-seas.

then we went out many tymes to exercise our selues, by going, running, casting of the ball, (for then we might see a good way from vs) and to refresh our ioynts, for we had long time sitten dull, whereby many of vs were very loase.

The 29 of Ianuary, it was foule weather with great store of snow, the wind North-west, whereby the house was closed vp againe with snow.

The 30. of Ianuary, it was darke weather, with an East-wind, and we made a hole through the dore, but we shoueled not the, snow very farre from the portaile, for that as sone as we saw what weather it was, we had no desire to goe abroad.

The 31. of Ianuary, it was faire calme weather, with an East-wind, then we made the dore cleane, and shoueled away the snow, and threw it vpon the house, and went out, and we saw not the Sun shine cleare, which comforted vs, meane time we saw a Beare, that came towards our house, but we went softly in, and watcht for her till she came neerer, and as sone she was hard by we shot at her, but she ran away againe.

The 1. of February, being Candlemas eue, it was boisterous weather, with a great storme and good store of snow, whereby the house was closed vp againe with snow, and we were constrained to stay within dores, the wind then being North-west.

The 2. of February, it was foule weather, and as then the Sun had not rid vs of all the foule weather, whereby we were somewhat discomforted, for that being in good hope of better weather we had not made so great prouision of wood as wee did before.

The 3. of February, it was faire weather, with an Eastwinde, but very misty, whereby we could not see the Sun, which made vs somewhat melancholy, to see so great a miste, and rather more then we had had in the winter time, and then we digd our dore, open againe, and fetcht the wood that lay without about the dore into the house, which we were forced with great paine and labour to dig out of the snow.

The 4. of February, it was foule weather, with great store of snow, the wind being South-west, and then we were close vp againe with snow, but then we toke not so much paines as we did before, to dig open the dore, but when we had occasion or goe out we

The Nauigation into the North-seas.

we clomb out at the chimney, and eased our selues, and went in gaine the same way.

The 5. of February it was still foule weather, the wind being East, with great store of snow, whereby we were shut vp againe into the house, and had no other way to get out but by the chimney, and those that could not climb out, were faine to helpe themselues within as well as they could.

The 6. of February it was still foule stormie weather, with store of snow, and we still went out at the chimney, (and troubled not our selues with the doore,) for some of vs made it an easie matter to clime out at the chimney.

The 7. of February, it was stil foule weather, with much snow and a South-west wind, and we thereby forced to keepe the house, which grieued vs more then when the Sun shined not, for that hauing seen it and felt the heat thereof, yet we were forced not to inioy it.

The 8. of February, it began to be fairer weather, the wind being South-west, then we saw the Sun rise South South-east, and went downe South, South-west, by ye compas that we had made of lead, and placed according to the right meridian of that place, but by our common compas, it differed. tw o points.

The 9. of February, it was faire cleare weather, the wind South-west, but as then we could not see the Sunne, because it was close weather in the South, where the Sunne should goe downe.

The 10. of February, it was faire cleare weather, so that we could not tell where the wind blew, and then we began to feele some heat of the Sunne, but in the euening it began to blow some what cold out of the west.

The 11. of February, it was faire weather, the wind South, ye day about noone, there came a Beare towards our house, and we watcht her with our Muskets, but she came not so neere that wee could reach her, the same night we heard some Foxes stirring, which since the beares began to come abroad againe, we had much seen.

The 12. of February, it was cleare weather and very calme, the wind South-west, then we made our traps cleane againe, meane time there came a great Beare towards our house, which

N 3 made

The Nauigation into the North-seas.

made vs all goe, in and we leauelled at her with our muskets, and as she came right before our dore, we shot her into the breast, cleane through the heart, the bullet passing through her body and went out againe at her tayle, and was as flat as a counter, the Beare feeling the blow, lept backwards and ran twenty or thirty fote from the house, and there lay downe, wherewith we lept all out of the house and ran to her, and found her stil aliue, and when she saw vs, she reard vp her head, as if she would gladly haue done vs some mischefe, but we trusted her not, for that we had tryed her strength sufficiently before, and therefore we shot their twice into the body againe, and therewith she dyed, then we ript vp her belly, and taking out her guts drew her home to the house, where we flead her, and toke at least one hundred pound of fat out of her belly, which we molt, and burnt in our Lampe. This grease did vs great good seruice, for by that meanes we stil kept a Lampe burning all night long, which before we could not doe, for want of grease, and euery man had meanes to burne a Lamp in his Caban, for such necessaries as he had to doe. The Beares skin was nine fote long, and 7 fote bread.

The 13 of February, it was faire cleare weather with a hard West wind, at which time we had more light in our house by burning of Lamps, whereby we had meanes to passe the time away, by reading and other exercises, which before (when we could not extinguish day from night, by reason of the darknesse, and had not Lamps continually burning) we could not doe.

The 14. of February it was faire cleere weather, with a hard West wind before noone, but afternoone, it was still weather, then fiue of vs went to the ship, to see how it laie, and found the water to encrease in it, but not much.

The 15. of February, it was foule weather, with a great storme out of the south-west, with great store of snowe, whereby the house was closed vp againe, that night the Foxes came to deuoure the dead body of the Beare, whereby we were in great feare, that all the Beares thereabouts, would come theather, and therefore we agreed, as soone as we could to get out of the house to bury the dead Beare deepe vnder the snowe.

The 16. of February, it was still foule weather with great store of snowe, & a south-west wind, that day was Shroue-twes-
day

day, then wee made our selues some what merry in our great griefe and trouble, and euery one of vs dranke a draught of wine in remembrance that winter began to weare away, and faire weather to aproache.

The 17. of February, it was still foule weather and a darke sky, the wind South, then we opened our dore againe, and swept away the snow, and then we thrue the dead Beare into the hoale where we had digd out some wood, and stopt it vp, that the Beares by smelling it, should not come thither to trouble vs, and we set vp our springs againe to take Foxes, and the same day fiue of vs went to the ship, to see how it laie, which we found all after one sort, there we found foote-steps of many Beares, as though they had taken it vp for their lodging, when we had forsaken it.

The 18. of February, it was foule weather with much snow and very cold, the wind being south-west, and in the night time we burnt lampes, and some of our men laie awake, we heard a fox runne vpon the roofe of our house, which by reason of the snow, made the noise of their feete sound more then otherwise it would haue done, the snow was so hard, whereby we thought they had béene Beares, but when it was day, we sawe no footing but of Foxes, and we thought they had béene Beares, for the Fox which of it selfe is solitarie and fearefull, made that which was doubtfull to be more doubtfull and worse feared.

The 19. of February it was faire cleere weather, with a south-east wind, then we tooke the hight of the Sunne, which in long time before we could not doe, because the Horizon was not cleere and also for that it mounted not so high, nor gaue not so much shewe, as we were to haue in our Astrolabium, and therefore we made an instrument, that was halfe round, at the one end hauing 90. degrées marked thereon, whereon we hung a thrid with a Plumet of lead, as the water compasses haue, and therewith we tooke the hight of the Sunne, when it was at the highest, and found that it was thrée degrées eleuated aboue the Horizon, his declination eleuenth degrées and sixtéene minutes, which béeing added to the hight aforesaid made, 14. degrées & 16. minutes, which substracted from 90. degrées, there rested 75. degrées and 44. minutes for the higth of the Pole, but the aforesaid thrée degrées of higth, being taken at the lowest side of the Sunne, the

16.

The Nauigation into the North-seas.

16. minutes might well be added to the higth of the Pole, and so it was iust 76. degrees, as we had measured it before.

The 20. of February, it was foule weather with great store of snow, the wind south-west, whereby we were shut vp againe in the house, as we had béene often times before.

The 21. of February, it was still foule weather, the wind north-west, and great store of snow, which made vs grieue more then it did before, for we had no more wood, & so were forced to breake of some péeces of wood in the house, and to gather vp some that lay troden vnder féet, which had not bin cast out of the way, whereby for that day and the next night we holp our selues indifferent well.

The 22 of February it was clere faire weather, with a South-west wind, then we made ready a slead to fetch more wood, for néed compelled vs thereunto, for as they say hunger driueth the Wolfe out of his den, and eleuen of vs went together, all well appointed with our armes, but coming to the place where wee should haue the wood, we could not come by it, by reason it laie so déepe vnder the snow, whereby of necessitie we were compelled to goe further, where with great labour and trouble we got some: but as we returned backe againe therewith, it was so sore labour vnto vs that we wers almost out of comfort, for that by reason of the long cold and trouble that we had indured, we were become so weake & féeble, that we had litle strength, & we began to be indoubt, that we should not recouer our strengths againe, and should not be able to fetch any more wood, and so we should haue died with cold, but the present necessitie, and the hope we had of better weather, increased our forces, and made vs doe more then our strengthes afforded, and when we came néere to our house, we saw much open water in the Sea, which in long time we had not séene, which also put vs in good comfort, that things would be better.

The 23. of February, it was calme and faire weather, with a good aire, the wind south-west, and then we tooke two Foxes, that were as good to vs as venison.

The 24. of February, it was still weather, and a close aire, the wind south-west, then we drest our springes in good sort, for the Foxes, but tooke none.

The 25. of February, it was foule weather againe, and much
snow

The Nauigation into the North-seas.

with a North wind, whereby we were closed vp with snow againe, and could not get out of our house.

The 26. of February, it was darke weather, with a south-west wind, but very calme, and then we opened our doze againe, and exercised our selues with going and running, and to make our ioints supple, which were almost clinged together.

The 27. of February, it was calme weather, with a South wind, but very cold, then our wood began to lessen, which put vs in no small discomfort, to remember what trouble we had to draw the last stead-full home, and we must doe the like againe, if we would not die with cold.

The 28. of February, it was still weather with a south-west wind, then ten of vs went and fetcht and other stead-full of wood, with no lesse paine and labor then we did before, for one of our companions could not helpe vs, because that the first ioint of one of his great toes was frozen of, and so he could doe nothing.

The first of March, it was faire still weather, the wind west, but very cold, and we were forced to spare our wood, because it was so great labor for vs to fetch it, so that when it was day, we exercised our selues as much as we might, with running, going, and leaping, and to them that laie in their Cabins, we gaue hote stones to warme them, and towards night we made a good fire, which we were forced to indure.

The 2. of Marche, it was cold cleere weather, with a West wind, the same day we tooke the higth of the Sunne, and found that it was eleuated aboue the Horizon sixe degrees and 48. minutes, and his declination was 7. degrees and 12. minutes, which subtracted from 90. degrees, resteth 76. degrees for the higth of the Pole.

The 3. of March, it was faire weather with a West wind, at which time our sickemen were somewhat better, and sat vpright in their Cabins, to doe some thing to passe the time awaie, but after they found that they were too ready to stirre before their times.

The 4. of March, it was faire weather with a West wind, the same day there came a Beare to our house, whom we watcht with our peeces, as we did before, and shot at her & hit her, but she run away, at that time fiue of vs went to our ship, where we found that the Beares had made worke, & had opened our Cookes cub-

D   bert

The Nauigation into the North-seas.

berd, that was couered ouer with snow, thinking to finde some thing in it, and had drawne it out of the ship where we found it.

The 5. of March, it was foule weather againe, with a south-west wind, and as in the euening we had digd open our dore and went out, when the weather began to breake vp, we saw much open water in the Sea, more then before, which put vs in god comfort, that in the end we should get away from thence.

The 6. of March, it was foule weather, with a great storme out of the south-west, and much snow, the same day some of vs climbed out of the chimney and perceaued that in the Sea, and about the land there was much open water, but the ship lay fast still.

The 7. of March, it was still foule weather and as great a wind, so that we were shut vp in our house, and they that would goe out, must clime vp through the chimney, which was a common thing with vs, and still we sawe more open water in the Sea, and about the land, whereby we were in doubt that the ship in that foule weather and driuing of the Ice, would be loose (for as then the Ice draue) while we were shut vp in our house, and we should haue no meanes to helpe it.

The 8. of Marche, it was still foule weather, with a south-west stormie, and great store of snow, whereby we could see no Ice in the north-east, nor round about in the Sea, wereby we were of opinion that north-east from vs, there was a great Sea.

The 9. of March it was foule weather, but not so foule as the day before, and lesse snow, and then we could see further from vs, and perceiue that the water was open in the north-east, but not from vs towards Tartaria, for there we could still see Ice in the Tartarian Sea, otherwise called the Ice Sea, so that we were of opinion, that there it was not very wide, for when it was cleere weather, we thought many times that we saw the land, and showed it vnto our companions, south and south-east from our house, like a hilly land, as land commonly showeth it selfe, when we see it.

The 10 of March, it was cleere weather, the wind North, then we made our house cleane, and digd our selues out, and came forth, at which time we saw an open Sea, whereupon we said vnto each other, that if the ship were lose, we might venture to

saile

The Nauigation into the North-seas.

saile awaie, for we were not of opinion to doe it with our Scutes, considering the great cold that we found there: towards euening, nine of vs went to the ship with a slead to fetch wood, when al our wood was burnt, and found the ship in the same order that it laie and fast in the Ice.

The 11. of March, it was cold, but faire sunne-shine weather, the wind north-east, then we tooke the higth of the Sunne, with our Astrolabium, and found it to be eleuated aboue the Horizon ten degrees and 19. minutes, his declination was three degrees 41. minutes, which being added to the higth aforesaid, made 14. degrees, which substracted from 90. degrees, there resteth 76. degrees for the higth of the Pole: then twelue of vs went to the place where we vsed to goe, to fetch a slead of wood, but still we had more paine and labour therewith, because we were weaker, and when we came home with it and were very weary we prayd the master to giue either of vs a draught of wine, which he did, wherewith we were somewhat relieued, & comforted, and after that were the willinger to labour, which was vnsupportable for vs, if meere extremitie had not compelled vs thereunto, saying often times one vnto the other, that if the wood were to be bought for mony, we would giue all our earnings, or wages for it.

The 12 of March, it was foule weather, the wind north-east, then the Ice came mightily driuing in, which the south-west winde had bin driuen out, and it was then as could, as it had bin before in the coldest time of winter.

The 13. of March, it was still foule weather, with a storme out of the North-east, and great store of snow, and the Ice mightely driuing in with a great noyse, the flakes rustling against each other fearfull to heare.

The 14. of March, it was still foule weather with a great cast North-east wind, wherby the sea was as close as it had bin before, and it was extreame cold, whereby our sicke men were very ill, who when it was faire weather, were stirring too soone.

The 15. of march, it was faire weather, the wind North, that day we opened our dore to goe out, but the cold rather increased then diminished, and was bitterer then before it had bin.

The 16 of March, it was faire cleare weather, but extreame cold with a North wind, which put vs to great extremity, for that

The Nauigation into the North-seas.

we had almost taken our leaues of the cold, and then it began to come againe.

The 17 of March it was faire cleare weather, with a North winde, but stil very cold, wherby wee were wholy out of comfort, to see and feele so great cold, and knew not what to thinke, for it was extreame cold.

The 18. of March, it was foule cold weather, with good store of snow the wind North-east, which shut vs vp in our house, so that we could not get out.

The 19. of March, it was still foule and bitter cold weather, the wind North-east, the Ice in the sea cleauing faster and thicker together, with great cracking, and a hugh noyse, which we might easily heare in our house, but we delighted not much in hearing thereof.

The 20. of March, it was foule weather, bitter cold, and a North-east wind, then our wood began to consume, so that we were forced to take counsell together, for without wood we could not liue, and yet we began to be so weake, that we could hardly endure the labour to fetch it.

The 21. of March, it was faire weather, but still very cold, the wind North the same day the Sunne entred into Aries, in the equinoxciall lyne, and at noone we toke the hight of the Sunne, and found it to be eleuated 14. degrees aboue the Horizon, but for that the Sun was in the middle lyne, and of the like distance from both the tropiks, there was no declination, neither on the South nor north side, and so the 14. degrees aforesaid being substraded, from ninty degrees, there rested 76 degrees for the hight of the Pole. The same day, we made shoes of felt or rudg, which we drew vpon our feet, for we could not goe in our shoes, by reason of the great cold, for the shoes on our feet were as hard as hornes, and then we fetcht a sleadsful of wood home to our house, with sore and extreame labour, and with great extremity of cold which we endured, as if March went to bid vs farewell, for our hope and comfort was that the cold could not still continue in that force, but that at length the strength thereof would be broken.

The 22. of March, it was cleere still weather, the wind North-east, but very cold. whereupon some of vs were of aduice, seeing that the fetching of wood was so toylsome vnto vs, that euery day once

once we should make a fire of coales.

The 23. of March, it was very foule weather, with infernall bitter cold, the wind North-east, so that we were forced to make more fire, as we had bin at other times, for then it was as cold as euer it had bin, and it froze very hard in the flore and vpon the wales of our house.

The 24. of March, it was alike cold, with great store of snow, and a North wind, whereby we were once againe shut vp into the house, and then the coalls serued vs well, which before by reason of our bad vsing of them, we disliked of.

The 25. of March, it was still foule weather, the wind west, the cold still holding as strong as it was: which put vs in much discomfort.

The 26. of March, it was faire cleere weather, and very calme, then we digd our selues out of the house againe, and went out, & then we fetcht an other slead of wood, for the great cold had made vs burne vp all that we had.

The 27. of March, it was faire weather, the wind west and very calme, then the Ice began to driue away againe, but the ship lay fast and stird not.

The 28. of March it was faire weather the wind South-west, whereby the Ice draue away very fast. The same day sixe of vs went abord the ship, to see how it lay, and found it still in one sort, but we perceiued that the Beares had kept an euil fauoured house therein.

The 29. of March, it was faire cleere weather, with a Northeast wind, then the Ice came driuing in againe, the same day we fetcht another slead of wood, which we were euery day worse alike to doe, by reason of our weaknesse.

The 30. of March, it was faire cleere weather, with an East wind, wherwith the Ice came driuing in againe; after noone there came two Beares by our house, but they went along to the ship, and let vs alone.

The 31. of March, it was still faire weather, the wind Northeast, wherewith the Ice came still more and more driuing in, and made high hilles by sliding one vpon the other.

The 1. of Aprill, it blew stil out of the East, with faire weather

3 D   but

but very cold, and then we burnt some of our coales, for that our wood was too troublesome for vs to fetch.

The 2. of Aprill, it was faire weather, the wind north-east and very calme, then we tooke the higth of the Sunne and found it to be eleuated aboue the Horizon 18. degrees and 40. minutes, his declination being foure degrees and 40. minutes, which being substracted from the higth aforesaid, there rested 14. degrees, which taken from 90. degrees, the higth of the Pole was 76. degrees.

The 3. of Aprill it was faire cleere weather, with a north-east wind, and very calme, then we made a staffe to plaie at colfe, thereby to stretch our Iointes, which we sought by all the meanes we could to doe.

The 4. of Aprill, it was faire weather, the wind variable, that daie we went all to the ship and put out the cable that was made fast to the anchor, to the end that if the ship chanced to be loose, it might hold fast thereby.

The 5. of Aprill it was foule weather, with a hard north-east wind, wherewith the Ice came mightily in againe, and slid in great peeces one vpon the other, and then the ship laie faster then it did before.

The 6. of Aprill, it was still foule weather, with a stiffe north-west wind, that night there came a Beare to our house, and we did the best we could to shoot at her, but because it was moist weather, & the cocke foistie, our peece would not giue fire wherewith the Beare came bouldly toward the house, and came downe the staires close to the dore, seeking to breake in to the house but our master held the dore fast to, & being in great haste and feare, could not barre it with the peece of wood that we vsed thereunto, but the Beare seeing that the dore was shut, she went backe againe, and within two houres after she came againe, and went round about and vpon the top of the house, and made such a roaring, that it was fearefull to heare, and at last got to the chimney, and made such worke there, that we thought she would haue broken it downe, and tore the saile that was made fast about it in many peeces, with a great and fearefull noise, but for that it was night we made no resistance against her, because we could not see her, at last she went awaie and left vs.

The

The Nauigation into the North-seas.

The 7. of Aprill, it was foule weather, the wind south-west, then we made our muskets ready, thinking the Beare would haue come againe, but she came not, then we went vp vpon the house, where we saw what force the Beare had vsed, to teare away the saile, which was made so fast vnto the chimney.

The 8. of Aprill, it was still foule weather, the wind south-west, whereby the Ice draue away againe, and the Sea was open, which put vs in some comfort, that we should once get away out of that fearefull place.

The 9. of Aprill, it was faire cléere weather, but towards euening it was foule weather, the wind South-west, so that still y water became opener, whereat we much reioysed, and gaue God thanks that he had saued vs from the aforesaid cold, troublesome, hard, bitter, and vnsupportable Winter, hoping that time would giue vs a happy issue.

The 10. of Aprill it was foule weather, with a storme out of the North-east, with great store of snowe at which time the Ice, that draue away, came in againe, and couered all the sea ouer.

The 11. of Aprill, it was faire weather, with a great North-east wind, wherewith the Ice still draue one péece vpon another, and lay in high hilles.

The 21. of Aprill, it was faire cléere weather, but still it blew hard North-east, as it had done two dayes before, so that the Ice lay like hilles one vpon the other, and then was higher and harder then it had bin before.

The 13. of Aprill, it was faire cléere weather, with a North wind, the same day we fetcht a sled with wood, & euery man put on his shoes, that he had made of felt or rugg, which did vs great pleasure.

The 14. of Aprill, it was faire cleare weather, with a West wind, then we saw greater hilles of Ice round about the ship, then euer we had séene before, which was a fearefull thing to behold, and much to be wondred at, that the ship was not smitten in péeces.

The 15. of Aprill, it was faire calme weather with a North wind, then seauen of vs went aboard the ship, to sée in what case it was, and found it to be all in one sort, and as we came backe againe, there came a great Beare towards vs, against whom we

began

began to make defence, but she perceauing that, made away from vs, and we went to the place from whence she came, to see her den, where we found a great hole made in ẏ Ice, about a mãs lenght in depth, the entry thereof being very narrow, and with in, wide, there we thrust in our pickes to seeke if there was any thing within it, but perceauing it was emptie, one of our men crept into it, but not too farre, for it was fearefull to behold, after that we went along by the Sea side, and there we saw, that in the end of March, and the begining of Aprill the Ice was in such wondefull maner risen and piled vp one vpon the other, that it was wonderfull in such manner as if there had bin whole townes made of Ice, with towres and bulwarkes round about them.

The 16. of Aprill it was foule weather, the wind north-west, whereby the Ice began some-what to breake.

The 17. of Aprill it was faire cleere weather, with a south-west wind, and then seauen of vs went to the ship, and there we saw open water in the Sea, and then we went ouer the Ice-hilles as well as we could to the water, for in sir or seauen monthes we had not gone so neare vnto it, and when we got to ẏ water, there we saw a litle bird swiming therein, but as sone as it espied vs, it dined vnder the water, which we toke for a signe that there was more open water in the Sea, then there had bene before, and that the time approached that the water would open.

The 18. of Aprill, it was faire weather, the wind south-west, then we toke the higth of the Sunne, and it was eleuated aboue the Horizon 25. degrees and 10. minutes, his declination 11. degrees and 12. minutes, which being taken from the higth aforesaid, there rested 13. degrees and 58. minutes, which substracted from 90. degrees, the higth of the Pole was found to be 75. degrees, 58. minutes; then eleuen of vs went with a stead to fetch more wood, and brought it to the house: in the night there came as other Beare vpon our house, which we hearing, went all out with our armes, but the Beare ranne away.

The 19. of Aprill it was faire weather with a North wind, that day fiue of vs went into the bath, to bathe our selues, which did vs much good, and was a great refreshing vnto vs.

The 20. of Aprill, it was faire weather with a West wind, the same day fiue of vs went to the place where we fetcht wood,

with

The Nauigation into the North-seas.

with a kettle & other furniture vpon a slead, to wash our shirts in that place, because the wood lay ready there, and for that we were to vse much wood to melt the Ice, to heate our water, and to drie our shirtes, esseeming it a lesse labour, then to bring the wood home to the house which was great trouble vnto vs.

The 21. of Aprill it was faire weather, with an East wind, and the next day the like weather, but in the euening the wind blewe northerly.

The 23. of Aprill, it was faire weather, and a north-east wind, and the next day the like, with an East wind.

The 25. of Aprill, it was faire weather, the wind easterly, the same day there came a Beare to our house, and we shot her into the skin, but she runne awaie, which another Beare that was not farre from vs perceauing runne away also.

The 26. and 27. of Aprill it was faire weather, but an extreme great north-east wind.

The 28. of Aprill it was faire weather, with a North wind, then we toke the higth of the Sunne againe, and found it to be eleuated 28. degrees and 8. minutes, his declination 14. degrees and 8. minutes, which substracted from 90. degrees, there rested 76. degrees for the highth of the Pole.

The 29. of Aprill it was faire weather, with a south-west wind, then we plaid at colfe, both to the ship, and from thence againe homeward, to exercise our selues.

The 30. of Aprill it was faire weather, the wind south-west, then in the night we could see the Sunne in the North (when it was in the highest) iust about the Horizon, so that from that time we saw the Sunne both night and day.

The 1. of May, it was faire weather with a West wind, then we sod our last flesh, which for a long time we had spared, and it was still very good, and the last morsell tasted as well as the first, and we found no fault therein, but onely that it would last no longer.

The 2. of May, it was foule weather, with a storme out of the south-west, whereby the Sea was almost cleere of Ice, and then we began to speake about getting from thence, for we had kept house long enough there.

The 3. of May it was still foule weather, with a south-west wind

wind, whereby the Ice began wholy to driue away, but it lay fast about the ship, and when our best meate, as flesh, and other things began to faile vs, which was our greatest sustenance, and that it behooued vs to be somewhat strong, to sustaine the labour that we were to vndergoe, when we went from thence, the maister shared the rest of the Bacon amongst vs, which was a small barrell with salt Bacon in pickle, whereof euery one of vs had two ounces a day, which continued for the space of three weekes, and then it was eaten vp.

The 4 of May it was indifferent faire weather, ye wind southwest, that day fiue of vs went to the ship, and found it lying still as fast in the Ice as it did before, for about the midle of March it was but 75. paces from the open water, and then it was 500. paces from the water, and inclosed round about with high hilles of Ice, which put vs in no small feare, how we should bring our Scute and our boate through or ouer that way into the water: when we went to leaue that place, that night there came a Beare to our house, but as soone as she heard vs make a noise, she ranne away againe, one of our men that climbed vp in the chimney saw when she ranne away, so that it seemed that as then they were afraid of vs, and durst not be so bold to set vpon vs, as they were at the first.

The 5. of May, it was faire weather, with some snow, the wind East, that euening, and at night we saw the Sunne when it was at the lowest, a good way aboue the Earth.

The 6. of May, it was faire cleere weather, with a great south-west wind, whereby we saw the Sea open both in the East and in the West, which made our men exceeding glad, longing for to be gone from thence.

The 7. of May, it was foule weather, and snew hard, with a North wind, whereby we were closed vp againe in our house, whereupon our men were somewhat disquieted, saying that they thought they should neuer goe from thence, and therefore said they, it is best for vs as soone as it is open water to be gone from hence.

The 8. of May, it was foule weather, with great store of snow, the wind West, then some of our men agreed amongst themselues to speake vnto the master, and to tell him that it was more
then

The Nauigation into the North-seas.

then time for vs to be gone from thence, but they could not agrée vpon it, who should moue the same vnto him, because he had said that he would staie vntill the end of Iune, which was the best of the sommer, to sée if the ship would then be loose.

The 9. of May it was faire cléere weather, w̄ an indifferent wind out of the north-east, at which time the desire that our men had to be gone from thence, still more and more encreased, and then they agréed to speake to Willam Barents, to moue the maister to goe from thence, but he held them of with faire words, and yet it was not done to delay them, but to take the best counsell, with reason and good aduise, for he heard all what they could saie.

The 10. of May, it was faire weather with a North-west wind, y night the Sun by our cōmon compas being North, North-east, and at the lowest, we tooke the higth thereof, and it was eleuated 3 degrées and 45 minutes, his declination was 17 degrées and 45 minuts, from whence taking the higth aforesaid, there rested 14. degrées, which substracted from 90 degrées, there rested 7 6 degrées for the higth of the Pole.

The 11. of May, it was faire weather, the wind South-west, and then it was open water, in the sea, then our men prayed William Barents once againe to moue the Maister to make preparation to goe from thence, which he promised to do as soone as conuenient time serued him.

The 12. of May, it was foule weather, the wind North-west & then the water became still opener then it was, which put vs in good comfort.

The 13. of May, it was still weather, but it snowed hard with a North wind.

The 14. of May, we fetcht our last slead with fire wood, and stil ware our showes made of rugde on our féete, wherewith we did our selues much pleasure, and they furthered vs much: at the same time we spake to Willam Barents againe, to moue the maister about going from thence, which he promised he would doe.

The 15. of May, it was faire weather, with a west wind and it was agréed that all our men should goe out, to exercise their bodies with running, goeing, playing at colfe and other exercises, thereby to stirre their ioynts and make them nymble, meane time Barents spake vnto the maister, and showed him what the com-

pany

pany had said, who made him answeare that they should stay no longer then to the end of that Mounth, & that if then the ship could not be loosed, that preparation should be made to goe away with the Scute and the boate.

The 16 of May, it was faire weather, with a West-wind at which time, the company were glad of the answere that the Maister had giuen, but they thought the time too long, because they were to haue much time to make the boate and the Scute ready to put to Sea with them, and therefore some of them were of opinion that it would be best for them to sawe the boate in the middle, and to make it longer, which opinion thought it was not amisse, neuerthelesse it would be y worse for vs, for that although it should be so much the better for the sailing, it would be so much the vnfitter to be drawne ouer the Ice, which we were forced to doe.

The 17. and 18. of May, it was faire cléere weather, with a West wind, and then we began to reconne the daies that were set downe and appointed for vs to make preparation to be gone.

The 19. of May it was faire weather with an East wind, then foure of our men went to the ship, or to the sea side, to sée what way we should draue the Scute into the water.

The 20. of May, it was foule weather with a North-east wind, whereby the Ice began to come in againe, and at noone we spake vnto the Maister, & told him that it was time to make preparation to be gon, if we would euer get away from thence, whereunto he made answeare, that his owne life was as déere vnto him, as any of ours vnto vs, neuerthelesse he willed vs to make haste to prepare our clothes, and other things ready and fit for our boiage, and that in the meane time we should patch and amend them, that after it might be no hinderance vnto vs, and that we should stay till the Mounth of May was past, and then make ready the Scute and the boate, and al other things fit and conuenient for our Journey.

The 21. of May, it was faire weather, with a North-east wind, so that the Ice came driuing in againe, yet we made preparation, touching our things that we should weare, that we might not be hindred thereby.

The 22. of May, it was faire weather, with a North-west wind,
and

The Nauigation into the North-seas.

and for that we had almost spent all our wood, we brake the portall of our doore downe and burnt it.

The 23. of May, it was faire weather with an East wind, then some of vs went againe to the place where the wood lay to wash our shats.

The 24. of May, it was faire weather, with a South-east wind, whereby there was but a little open water.

The 25. of May, it was faire weather, with an East wind, then at noone time we toke the higth of the Sunne, that was eleuated aboue the Horizon 34 degrees and 46 minutes, his declination 20 degrees and 46 minutes, which taken from the higth aforesaid, there rested 14 degrees, which taken from 90 degrees, rested 76 degrees, for the higth of the pole.

The 26. of May, it was faire weather, with a great North-east wind, whereby the Ice came in againe.

The 27. of May, it was foule weather, with a great North-east wind, which draue the Ice mightely in againe, whereupon the Maister at the motion of the company willed vs to make preparation to be gon.

The 28. of May, it was foule weather, with a North-west wind, after noone it began to be somewhat better, then seuen of vs went vnto the ship, and fetcht such things from thence, as should serue vs for the furnishing of our Scute, and our boate, as the old fock sayle, to make a sayle for our boate, and our Scute, and some tackles, and other things necessarie for vs.

The 29. of May, in the morning, it was reasonable faire weather with a West wind, then ten of vs went vnto the Scute to bring it to the house to dresse it, and make it ready to sayle, but we found it deepe hidden vnder y̓ snow, & were faine with great paine and labour to dig it out, but when we had gotten it out of the snow, and thought to draw it to the house, we could not doe it, because we were too weake, wherewith we became wholely out of heart, doubting that we should not be able to goe forwarde with our labour, but the Maister encouraging vs, bad vs striue to doe more then we were able, saying that both our liues and our welfare consisted therein: and that if we could not get the Scute from thence, and make it ready, then he said we must dwell there as Burgers of Noua Zembla, and make our graues in that place, but

The Nauigation into the North-seas.

there wanted no good will in vs but onely strength, which made vs for that time to leaue of worke and let the Scute lye stil, which was no small greefe vnto vs, and trouble to thinke what were best for vs to doe, but after noone being thus comfortlesse come home, we toke hearts againe and determined, to tourne the boate that lay by the house with her keale vpwards, & to amend it that it might be ye fitter to carry vs ouer the sea, for we made full account yt we had a long troublesom voiage in hãd, wherin we might haue many crosses, and wherein we should not be sufficiently prouided, for all things necessarie, although we toke neuer so much care, and while we were busy about our worke, there came a great Beare vnto vs, wherewith we went into our house, and stood to watch her in our thrée dores, with harquebushes, and one stood in the chimney with a Musket, this Beare came boldlyer vnto vs then euer any had done before, for she came to the neather step yt went to one of our dores, and the man that stood in the dore saw her not, because he lookt towards the other dore, but they that stood within saw her, and in great feare called to him, wherewith he turned about, and although he was in a maze, he shot at her, and the bullet past cleane through her body, whereupon she ran away, yet it was a fearfull thing to sée, for the Beare was almost vpon him before he saw her, so that if the péece had failed to giue fir, (as often times they doe) it had cost him his life, and it may be yt the Beare would haue gottẽ into ye house: the Beare being gone somewhat from the house lay downe, wherewith we went all armed and killed her out right, and when we had ript open her belly: we found a péece of a Bucke therein with haire skin and all, which not long before, she had towrne and deuoured.

The 30. of May, it was indifferent faire weather, but very cold and close aire, the wind West, then we began to set our selues to worke about the boate to amend it, the rest staying in the house to make the sailes and all other things ready, that were necessarie for vs, but while we were busie working at our boate, there came a Beare vnto vs, wherewith we were forced to leaue worke,, but she was shot by our men, then we brake downe the plankes of the roffe of our house, to amend our boate withall, and so procéeded in our worke as well as we could, for euery man was willing to labour, (for we had sore longed for it) and did

more

The Nauigation into the North-seas.

more then we were able to doe.

The 31. of May, it was faire weather, but somewhat colder then before, the wind being south-west, whereby the Ice draue away, and we wrought hard about our boate, but when we were in the chiefest part of worke, there came an other Beare, as if they had smelt that we would be gone, and that therefore they desired to tast a peece of some of vs, for that was the third day, one after the other, that they set so fiercely vpon vs, so that we were forced to leaue our worke and goe into the house, and she followed vs, but we stood with our peeces to watch her, and shot three peeces at her, two from our dores, & one out of the chimney, which all three hit her, whereby she fared as the Dogge did with the pudding, but her death did vs more hurt then her life, for after we ript her belly, we drest her liuer and eate it, which in the taste liked vs well, but it made vs all sicke, specially three that were exceding sicke, and we verily thought that we should haue lost them, for all their skins came of, from the foote to the head, but yet they recouered againe, for the which we gaue God heartie thankes, for if as then we had lost these three men, it was a hundred to one, that we should neuer haue gotten from thence, because we should haue had too few men to draw and lift at our neede.

The 1. of June, it was faire weather, and then our men were for the most part sicke with eating the liuer of a Beare, as it is said before, whereby that day there was nothing done about the boate, and then there hung a pot still ouer the fire with some of the liuer in it, but the master tooke it, and cast it out of the dore, for we had enough of the sawce thereof: that day foure of our men, that were the best in health went to the ship, to see if there was any thing in it, that would serue vs in our voiage, and there found a barrell with gere, which we shared amongst our men, whereof euery one had two, and it did vs great pleasure.

The 2. of June, in the morning it was faire weather, with a south-west wind, and then fiue of vs went to see and finde out the best way, for vs to bring our boate and our Scute to the water side, for as then the Ice laie so high and so thicke one vpon the other, that it seemed vnpossible to draw, or get our boate and the Scute ouer the Ice, and the shortest and best way that we could

could find was straight from the ship to the water side, although it was full of hilles and altogether vneuen, and would be great labour and trouble vnto vs, but because of the shortnesse, we esteemed it to be the best way for vs.

The 3. of Iune, in the morning it was faire cleare weather the wind West, and the ice were somewhat better, and tooke great paines with the boate, that at last we got it ready, after we had wrought sixe daies vpon it: about euening it began to blow hard, and therewith the water was very open, which put vs in god comfort that our deliuerance would soone follow, & that we should once get out of that desolate, and fearefull place.

The 4. of Iune, it was faire cleere weather, and indifferent warme, & about ye South-east Sun, eleuen of vs went to our Scute where it then lay, and drew it to the ship, at which time the labour seemed lighter vnto vs then it did before whē we tooke it in hand, & were forced to leaue it off againe. The reason thereof was the opinion, that we had that the snow as then lay harder vpon the groūd and so was become stronger, and it may be that our courages were better, to see that the time gaue vs open water, and that our hope was that we should get from thence, and so three of our men stayd by the Scute to build her to our mindes, and for that it was a herring Scute, which are made narrow behind, therefore they sawed it of behinde, and made it abroad stearne, and better to broke the seas: they built it also somewhat higher, and drest it vp as well they could, the rest of our men were busy in the house to make all other things ready for our voiage, and that day drew two sleads with victuals, and other goods vnto the ship, that lay about halfe way betweene the house and the open water, that after they might haue so much ye shorter way, to carry the goods vnto ye water side, when we should goe away: at which time al the labour and paines that we tooke seemed light and easie vnto vs, because of the hope that we had to get out of that wild desart, irkesome fearefull, and cold country.

The 5. of Iune it was foule weather, with great store of haile and snow, the wind West, which made an open water, but as then we could doe nothing without the house, but within we made all things ready, as sailes, oares, mastes, sprit, rother, sword, and all other necessarie things.

The

The Nauigation into the North-seas.

The 6. of Iune, in the morning it was faire weather, the wind north-east, then we went with our Carpenters to the ship, to build vp our Scute, and carried two Sleades-full of goods into the ship, both victualles and marchandise, with other things, which we ment to take with vs; after that there rose very foule weather in the south-west, with snow, haile, and raine, which we in long time had not had, whereby the Carpenters were forced to leaue their worke, and goe home to the house with vs, where also we could not be drie, because we had taken of the deales, therewith to amend our boate & our Scute, there laie but a saile ouer it, which would not hold out the water, and the way that laie full of snow began to be soft, so that we left of our shoes made of rugge & silt, and put on our leather shoes.

The 7. of Iune, there blew a great north-east wind, whereby we saw the Ice come driuing in againe, but the Sunne being south-east it was faire weather againe, and then the Carpenters went to the Scute againe to make an end of their worke, and we picked the march'nts goods that we ment to take with vs, and made defences for our selues of the said packes to saue vs from the Sea in the open Scute.

The 8. of Iune, it was faire weather, and we drew the wares to the ship, which we had packed and made ready, and the Carpenters made ready the Scute, so that the same euening it was almost done, the same day all our men went to draw our boate to the ship, and made ropes to draw withall, such as we vse to draw with in Scutes, which we cast ouer our shoulders, and held fast with all our hands, and so drew both with our hands and our shoulders, which gaue vs more force, and specially the desire and great pleasure we toke to worke at that time, made vs stronger, so that we did more then, then at other times we should haue done, for that good will on the one side, and hope on the other side, increased our strenght.

The 9. of Iune, it was faire weather, with variable windes, then we washt our shirts, and all our linnen, against we should be ready to saile away, and the Carpenters were still busie to make an end of the boate and the Scute.

The 10. of Iune, we caried foure sleades of goods into the ship, the wind then being variable, and at euening it was northerly,

M and

and we were busie in the house to make all things ready, the wine that was left we put into litle vessels, that so we might deuide it into both our vessels, and that as we were inclosed by the Ice, (which we well knew would happen vnto vs) we might the easelier cast the goods vpon the Ice, both out and into the Scutes, as time and place serued vs.

The 11. of June, it was foule weather, and it blew hard north north-west, so that all that day we could doe nothing, and we were in great feare least the storme would carry the Ice and the ship both away together, (which might well haue come to passe:) then we should haue bæne in greater miserie then euer we were, for that our goods both victualles and others were then all in the ship, but God prouided so well for vs, that it fell not out so vnfortunatly.

The 12. of June, it was indifferent faire weather, then we went with hatchets, halberds, shouels and others instruments, to make the way plaine, where we should draw the Scute and the boate to the water side, along the way that lay full of knobbes and hilles of Ice, where we wrought sore, with our hatchets & other instruments, and while we were in the chiefest of our worke there came a great leane Beare out of the Sea, vpon the Ice towards vs, which we iudged to come out of Tartaria: for we had sæne of them twenty or thirty miles within the sea, & for that we had no muskets, but only one, which our Surgian carried. I ran in great haste towards the ship to fetch one or two, which the Beare perceiuing ran after me, and was very likely to haue ouer taken me, but our company sæing that, left their worke and ran after her which made the Beare turne towards them and left me, but when she ran towards them, she was shot into the body by the Surgian, and ran away, but because the Ice was so vneuen and hilly she could not go farre, but being by vs ouer taken we killed her out right, and smot her tæth out of her head, while she was yet liuing.

The 13. of June, it was faire weather, then the Maister and the Carpenters went to the ship, & there made the Scute & the boate ready, so that there rested nothing as then, but onely to bring it downe to the water side, the Maister and those that were with him, sæing that it was open water, and a good West wind, came

backe

The Nauigation into the North-seas.

backe to the house againe, and there he spake vnto William Barents (that had bin long sicke) and shewed him, that he thought it good, (seeing it was a fit time) to goe from thence, and so willed the company to driue the boate and the Scute downe to the water side, and in the name of God to begin our voiage, to saile from Noua Zembla, then William Barents wrote a letter, which he put into a Muskets charge, and hanged it vp in the chimney, shewing how he came out of Holland, to saile to the kingdome of China, and what had happened vnto vs, being there on land, with all our crosses, that if any man chanced to come thither, they might know what had happened vnto vs, and how we had bin forced in our extremity to make that house, & had dwelt 10 mounthes therein, and for that we were to put to sea in two small opē boates, & to vndertake a dangerous, & aduenterous voiage in hand, the maister wrote two letters, which most of vs subscribed vnto, signifing, how we had stayed there vpon the land in great trouble & miserie, in hope that our ship would be freed from the Ice, and that we should saile away with it againe, and how it fell out to the contrary, and that the ship lay fast in the Ice so that in the end the time passing away, and our victuals beginning to faile vs, we were forced for the sauing of our owne liues, to leaue the ship, and to saile away in our open boates, and so to commit our selues into the hands of God. Which done he put into each of our Scutes a letter, ȳ if we chanced to loose one another, or ȳ by stormes or any other misaduenture we hapened to be cast away, that then by the scute that escaped, men might know, how we left each other, and so hauing finished all things as we determined, we drew the boate to the water side, and left a man in it, and went and fetcht the Scute, and after that eleuen sleads with goods, as victuals and some wine that yet remained, and the Marchants goods which we preserued as wel as we cou'd. viz. 6. packs with fine wollen cloth, a chest with linnen, two packets of Veluet, two smal chests with mony, two drifats with the mens clothes, and other things, 12 barrels of bread, a barrell of cheese, a fletch of Bacon, two runlets of oyle, 6. small runlets of wine two runlets of vineger, with other packs belonging to ȳ sailers so that when they lay altogether vpon a heape, a man wou'd haue iudged that they would not haue gone into the Scutes which being all put into them, we went to the house, and first drew William Barents vpon a slead, to the place where our

M 2   hauing

The Nauigation into the North-seas.

Scutes lay, & after that we fetcht Claes Adrianson, both of them hauing bin long sicke, & so we entred into the Scutes, and deuided our selues, into each of them alike, and put into either of them a sicke man, then the Maister caused both the Scutes to ly close one by the other, and there we subcribed to the letters which he had written, the coppie whereof hereafter ensueth, and so committing our selues to the will and mercie of God, with a West North-west wind & an endifferent open water, we set saile and put to sea.

The coppie of their letter.

Hauing till this day stayd for the time and opportunity, in hope to get our ship loose, and now are cleane out of hope thereof, for that it lyeth fast shut vp and inclosed in the Ice, and in the last of March, and the first of Aprill, the Ice did so mightily gather together in great hils, that we could not deuise how to get our Scute and boate into the water, or where to find a conuenient place for it, and for that it seemed almost impossible to get the ship out of the Ice, therefore I and *William Barents* our pilot, and other the officers, & company of Sailors therunto belonging, considering with our selues which would be the best course for vs, to saue our owne liues, and some wares belonging to the Marchants, we could find no better meanes, thē to mend our boate and Scute, and to prouide our selues as well as we could of all things necessarie, that being ready, we might not loose or ouerslip any fit time and opportunity, that God should send vs, for that it stood vs vpon to take the fittest time, otherwise we should surely haue perished with hunger and cold, which as yet is to be feared will goe hard inough with vs, for that there are three or foure of vs that are not able to stirre to doe any thinge, and the best and strongest of vs are so weake, with the great cold and disseases that we haue so long time endured, that we haue but halfe a mans strength, and it is to be feared, that it will rather be worse then better, in regrad of the long voiage that we haue in hand, and our bread, wil not last vs longer then to the end of the Mounth of August, and it may easily fal out, that the voiage being contrary and crosse vnto vs, that before that time we shall not be able to get to any land, where we may procure any victuals or other prouisions for our selues as we haue hitherto done our best, therefore we thougth it our best course not to stay any longer here, for

that

The Nauigation into the North-seas.

by nature we are bound to seeke our owne good and securites, and so we determined hereupon, and haue vnder written this present letter with our owne hands, vpon the first of Iune 1597. and while vpon the same day we were ready and had a West wind and an indifferent open sea, we did in Gods name prepare our selues, and entred into our voiage, the ship lying as fast as euer it did inclosed in the Ice, notwithstanding that while we were making ready to be gon, we had great wind out of the West, North, and North-west, & yet find no alteration, nor bettering in the weather, & therefore in the last extremity, we left it. vpon the 13 of Iune.

Iacob hemskerke, Peter Peterson vos, Mr. Hans vos, Laurence Willmso, Pete Cr ornelison, Iohn Remarson, William Barets, Gerrat de Veer, Leonard Hendrickson, Iacob Ionson Scheadam, Iacob Ionso Sterrenburg.

The 14. of Iune in the morning, the Sunne easterly, we put ● from the land of Noua Zembla, and the fast Ice therunto adioyning, with our boate and our Scute, hauing a West wind, and ●●●●● east-north-east, all that day to the Ilands point, which ● ●s fiue miles. but our first beginning was not very good, for we entred fast into the Ice againe, which there laie very hard and ●●t, which put vs into no smal feare and trouble, and being there, ●●●e of vs wet on land, to know the scituation thereof, and there ●● toke many birds which we kild with stones vpon the cliftes.

The 15. of Iune, the Ice began to goe away, then we put to ●aile againe with a south wind, and past along by the head point, ●●d the flushingers point, streaching most north-east, and after ●●at North, to the point of desire, which is about 13. miles, and ●●●e we laie till the 16. of Iune.

The 16. of Iune, we set saile againe, and got to the Island of Orange, with a South wind, which is 8. miles distant from the ●●●nt of desire, there we went one land with two small barrels, ● kettle, to melt snow, & to put ỹ water into ỹ barrels, as also to ●●●e for birds & egges to make meate for our sicke men, and being ●●●re, we made fire with such wood as wée found there, and mel●● the snowe, but found no birds, but thrée of our men went ouer ●●e Ice to the other Island, and got thrée birds, and as we came ●●●●e againe, our Maister (which was one of the thrée) fell into

the

The Nauigation into the North-seas.

the Ice, where he was in great danger of his life, for in that place there ran a great streame, but by Gods helpe he got out againe and came to vs, and there dryed himselfe by the fire that we had made, at which fire we drest the birds, and carried them to the Scute, to our sicke men, and filled our two runlets with water that held about eight gallons a péece, which done, we put to the sea againe, with a South-east wind, and drowsie miseling weather, whereby we were al danki(?) & wet, for we had no shelter in our opē Scutes, and sailed West, and West and by South, to the Ice point, and being there, both our Scutes lying hard by each other, the maister called to William Barents, to know how he did, and William Barents made answeare and said, well God be thanked, and I hope before we get to Warehouse, to be able to goe, then he spake to me and said, Gerrit are we about the Ice point? if we be then I pray you lift me vp, for I must veiw it once againe, at which time we had sailed from the Island of Orange to the Ice point, about fiue miles, and then the wind was Westerly, and we made our Scuts fast to a great péece of Ice, and there eate somewhat, but the weather was still fouler and fouler, so that we were once againe inclosed with Ice, and forced to stay there.

The 17. of June in the morning, when we had broken our fastes, the Ice came so fast vpon vs, that it made our haires stare vpright vpon our heades, it was so fearefull to behold, by which meanes we could not make fast our Scutes, so that we thought verily, that it was a foreshewing of our last end, for we draue alway so hard with the Ice, and were so sore prest betwéen a flake of Ice, that we thought verily the Scutes would burst in a hundreth péeces, which made vs looke pittifully one vpon theother, for no counsell nor aduise was to be found, but euery minute of an houre, we saw death before our eies, at last being in this discomfort, & extréeme necessity, ỹ master said if we could take hold with a rope vpon the fast Ice, we might therewith, drawe ỹ Scute vp, and so get it out of the great drift of Ice, but as this counsell was good, yet it was so full of daunger that it was the hazard of his life that should take vpon him to doe it, & without doing it, was it most certaine, ỹ it would cost vs all our liues: this counsell as I said was good, but no man (like to the tale of ỹ mise) durst hang the bell about ỹ cats necke, fearing to be drowned, yet neces-

The Nauigation into the North-seas.

necessity required to haue it done, and the most danger made vs chuse the least, so that being in that perplexity, I being the lightest of all our company, tooke on me to fasten a rope vpon the fast Ice, and so creeping from one péece of driuing Ice to another, by Gods help got to the fast Ice, where I made a rope fast to a high hdwell, and they that were in the Scute, drew it thereby vnto the said fast Ice, and then one man alone could drawe more then all of them could haue done before, and when we had gotten thither, in all haste we tooke our sicke men out and layd them vpon the Ice, laying clothes and other things vnder them, and then tooke all our goods out of the Scutes, and so drew them vpon the Ice, whereby for that time we were deliuered from that great danger, making account that we had escaped out of deaths clawes, as it was most true.

The 18. of June, we repaired and amended our Scutes againe, being much brused and crushed with the racking of the Ice, and were forced to driue all the nailes fast againe, and to péece many things about them, God sending vs wood, wherewith we moult our pitch, and did all other things that belonged thereunto, that done, some of vs went vpon the land, to séeke for egges, which the sicke men longed for, but we could finde none, but we found some birds, not without great danger of our liues, betwéene the Ice and the firme land, wherein we often fell, and were in no small danger.

The 19. of June, it was indifferent weather, the wind northwest, and west south-west, but we were still shut vp in the Ice, and saw no opening, which made vs thinke that there would be our last aboade, and that we should neuer get from thence, but on the other side we comforted our selues againe, that séeing God had helped vs often times vnexpectedly, in many perils, and that his arme, as yet was not shortened, but that he could helpe vp, at his good will and pleasure, it made vs somewhat comfortable, and caused vs to speake chéerfully one vnto the other.

The 20. of June, it was indifferent weather, the wind West, and when the Sunne was south-east, Claes Adrianson, began to be extreme sicke, whereby we perceiued that he would not liue long, and the Boateson came into our Scute, and told vs in what case he was, and that he could not long continue aliue,
whereupon

The Nauigation into the North-seas.

whereupon William Barents spake & said I thinke I shal not liue long after him, & yet we did not iudge William Barents to be so sicke, for we sat talking one with the other, and spake of many things, and William Barents read in my Card, which I had made touching our voiage, at last he laid away the Card, and spake vnto me saying Gerrit giue me some drinke, & he had no sooner drunke, but he was taken with so sodain a qualme, that he turned his eies in his head, and died presently, and we had no time to call the maister, out of the Scute, to speake vnto him, and so he died before Claes Adrianson: the death of William Barents put vs in no small discomfort, as being the chiefe guide, and onely Pilot on whom we reposed our selues, next vnder God, but we could not striue against God, and therefore we must of force be content.

The 21. of June, the Ice began to driue away againe, and God made vs some opening with a south-south-west wind, and when the Sunne was north west, the wind began to blow south-east, with a good gale, and we began to make preparation, to goe from thence.

The 22. of June, in the morning, it blew a good gale out of the south east, and then the Sea was reasonable open, but we were forced to draw our Scutes ouer the Ice, to get vnto it, which was great paine and labour vnto vs; for first we were forced to draw our Scutes ouer a peece of Ice, of 50. paces long, and there put them into the water, and then againe to draw them vp vpon other Ice, and after drew them at the least 100. paces more ouer the Ice, before we could bring them to a good place, where we might easily get out, and being gotten vnto the open water, we committed our selues to God, and set saile, the Sunne being about east-north-east, with an indifferent gale of wind, out of the south, and south-south-east, and sailed west, and west and by south, till the Sunne was south, and then we were round about enclosed with Ice againe, and could not get out, but were forced to lie still, but not long after, the Ice opened againe, like to a sluce, and we past through it and set saile againe, and so sailed along by the land, but were presently enclosed with Ice, but being in hope of opening againe, meane time we eate some what, for the Ice went not away as it did before: after that we vsed all the meanes we could to breake it, but all in vaine,

and

The Nauigation into the North-feas.

and yet a good while after, the Ice opened againe, and we got out, and sailed along by the land, west and by south, with a south wind.

The 23. of Iune, we sailed still foreward west and by south, till the Sunne was south-east, and got to the Trust point, which is distant from the Ice point 25. miles, and then could goe no further, because the Ice laie so hard, and so close together, and yet it was faire weather: the same day we tooke the higth of the Sunne with the Astrolabium, and also with our Astronomicall ring, and found his higth to be 37. degrees, and his declination 23. degrees, and 30. minutes, which taken from the higth aforesaid, there rested 13. degrees and 30. minutes, which substracted out of 90. degrees, the higth of the Pole was 76. degrees and 30. minutes, and it was faire Sunne-shine weather, and yet it was not so strong as to melt the snow, that we might haue water to drinke, so that we set all our tin platers and other things ful of snow to melt, and so molt it, and put snow in our mouthes, to melt it downe into our throates, but all was not enough, so that we were compelled to endure great thirst.

The stretching of the land from the house where we wintered, along by the north side of *Noua Zembla*, to the straights of *VVeigats*, where we past ouer to the coast of *Russia*, and ouer the entrie of the white Sea to *Cola*, according to the Card here ensueing.

From the low land, to the Streame Baie, the course east and west: 4. miles.

From the Streame Baie, to the Ice hauen point, the course east and by north 3. miles.

From the Ice hauen point, to the Ilands point, the course east north-east 5. miles.

From the Ilands point, to the Flushingers point, the course north-east and by east 3. miles.

From the Flushingers point, to ye head point, the course north-east 4. miles.

From the head point, to the point of desire, the course south and north 6. miles.

From the point of Desire, to the Iland of Orange, north-west 8. miles.

K From

The Nauigation into the North-seas.

From the Islands of Orange, to the Ice point, the course west, and west and by south 5. miles.

From the Ice point, to the point of Thrust, the course west, and by south 25. miles.

From the point of Trust, to Passawes point, the course west, and west and by north 10. miles.

From the Passawe point, to the east end of the crosse Island, the course west and by north 8. miles.

From the east end of the crosse Island, to Williams Island, the course west and by south 3. miles.

From Williams Island, to the black point, the course West South-west, 6. miles.

From the black point, to the east end of the admirable Island, the course West South-west 7. miles.

From the east to the west point of the admirable Island, the course west southwest 5 miles.

From the West point of the admirable Island, to Cape Planto, the course South-west and by west, 10 miles.

From Cape de Planto, to Lombsbay, the course west South-west, 8. miles.

From Lombsbay to the staues point, the course west South-west 10. miles.

From the staues point to Langenesse, the course South-west & by South, 14. miles.

From Langenes to Cape de Cant, the course South-west and by South 6. miles.

From Cape de Cant, to the point with the black clifts, the course South and by west, 4. miles.

From the point with the black cliftes, to the black Island, the course South south east 3. miles.

From the black Island, to Constint-sarke, the course east and west 2 miles.

From constint sarke, to the Crosse point the course South south east 5 miles.

From crosse point, to S. Laurence bay, the course South south east 6 miles.

From S. Laurence bay, to Pel-hauen, the course South east 6. miles.

From

The Nauigation into the North-seas.

From Wel-hauen to the two Islands, the course South South-east 16. miles.

From the 2. Islands, where we crost ouer to the Russia coast, to the Islands of Matflo and Delgoye, the course South-west 30. myles.

From Matflo & Delgoye, to the cræke where we sailed the compasse round about, and came to the same place againe. 22. miles.

From that cræke to Colgoy, the course West North-west, 18. miles.

From Colgoy to the east point of Candenas, the course West North-west, 20. miles.

From the East point of Candenas, to the West side of the White sea, the course West North-west, 40 miles.

From the West point of the White sea, to the 7. Islands, the course North-west, 14. miles.

From the 7. Islands, to the West end of Kilduin, the course North-west, 20. miles.

From the west end of Kelduin, to the place where Iohn Cornelis came vnto vs, the course North-west and by West, 7. miles.

From thence to Cola, the course West Southerly 18. miles.

So that we sailed in the two open Scutes, some times in the Ice, then ouer the Ice, and through the sea, 381 miles flemish, which is 1143 miles Inglish.

The 24. of Iune the Sunne being Easterly, we rowed here and there in the Ice, to se where we might best goe out, but we saw no opening, but when the Sunne was South, we got into the sea, for the which we thanked God most heartilie, that he had sent vs an vnexpected opening, and then we sailed with an East wind, and went lustily forward, so that we made our account to get aboue the point of Nassawes close by the land, & we could easily see the point of Nassawes, and made our account to be about 3 miles from it, the wind being South and South South-west, then fire of our men went on land, and there found some wood, whereof they brought as much as they could into the Scutes, but found neither birds nor egges, with the which wood they sod a pot of water pap, (which we called Matsammorc) that we might eate some warme thing the wind blowing stil Southerly.

The 25. of Iune, it blew a great South-wind, and the Ice whereunto

The Nauigation into the North-seas.

whereunto we made our selues fast, was not very strong, whereby we were in great feare, that we should breake off from it, and driue into the sea, for when the Sun was in the West, a péece of that Ice brake of, whereby we were forced to dislodge, and make our selues fast to another péece of Ice.

The 26. of June, it still blew hard out of the South, and broke the Ice whereunto we were fast, in péeces, and we thereby draue into the sea, and could get no more to the fast Ice, whereby we were in a thousand dangers to be all cast away, and driuing in ye sort in the sea, we rowed as much as we could, but we could not get néere vnto the land, therefore we hoysed vp our sock, and so made vp with our saile, but our sock-mast brake, twice in péeces, and then it was worse for vs then before, and notwithstanding that there blew a great gale of wind, yet we were forced to hoyse vp our great saile, but the wind blew so hard into it, that if we had not presently taken it in againe we had sunke in the sea, or else our boate would haue bin filled with water, for the water began, to leap ouer borde, and we were a good way in the sea, at which time the waues went so hollow, that it was most fearful, and we therby saw nothing, but death before our eyes, and euery twinckling of an eye lookt when we should sincke. But God that had deliuered vs out of so many dangers of death, holpe vs once againe, & contrary to our expectations sent vs a North-west wind, and so with great danger we get to ye fast Ice againe, when we were deliuered out of that danger, and knew not where our other Scute was, we sailed one mile along by the fast Ice, but found it not, whereby we were wholy out of heart, & in great feare yt they were drowned, at which time it was mistie weather, and so sailing along, & hearing no newes of our other Scute, we shot of a Musket, wh they hearing shot of another but yet we could not sée each other, meane time approching néerer to each other, & the weather waxing somwhat clearer, as we & they shot once againe, we saw the smoake of their péece, & at last we met together againe, & saw the ly fast betwéen driuing & fast Ice, & when we got néere vnto thē, we went ouer the Ice, & holp them to vnlade the goods out of their Scute, and drew it ouer the Ice, and with much paine and trouble brought it into the open water againe, and while they were fast in the Ice, we found some wood vpon the land, by the sea side, and when we lay by each other we sod some bread and water together, and eate it vp warme,

which

The Nauigation into the North-seas.

which did vs much good.

The 17. of June, we set saile with an indifferent gale out of the east, & got a mile aboue the Cape de Nassaw, one the west side thereof, and then we had the wind against vs, and we were forced to take in our sailes, and began to rowe and as we went along close by the land, we saw so many Sea-horses lying vpon the Ice, that it was admirable, and a great number of birds, at the which we discharged muskets and killed twelue of the, which we fetcht into our Scutes, and rowing in that sort, we had a great mist, and then we entred into driuing Ice, so that we were compelled to make our Scutes fast vnto the fast Ice, and to stay there till the weather brake vp, the wind being west north-west, and right against vs.

The 28. of June, when the Sunne was in the east, we laid all our goods vpon the Ice, and then drew the Scutes vpon the Ice also, because we were so hardly prest on all sides, with the Ice, and the wind came out of the Sea vpon the land, and therefore we were in feare to be wholely inclosed with the Ice, and should not be able to get out thereof againe, and being vpon the Ice, we laid sailes ouer our Scutes, and laid downe to rest, appointing one of our men to keepe watch, and when the Sunne was north there came three Beares towards our Scutes, wherewith he that kept the watch cried, three Beares three Beares, at which noise we leapt out of our boates, with our muskets, that were laden with haile-shot, to shoote at birds, and had no time to discharge them, and therefore shot at them therewith, and although that kinde of shot could not hurt them much, yet they ranne away, and in the meane time they gaue vs leisure to lade our muskets with bullets, and by that meanes we shot one of the three, dead, which the other two perceauing ranne away, but within two houres after they came againe, but when they were almost at vs, and heard vs make a noise, they ranne away, at which time the wind was west and west and by north, which made the Ice driue with great force into the east.

The 29. of June, the Sunne being south-south-west, the two Beares came againe to the place where the dead Beare laie, where one of them tooke the dead Beare in his mouth, and went a great way with it ouer the rugged Ice, & then began to eate it,

R 3 which

which we perceauing shot a musket at her, but she hearing the noise thereof, ran away, and let the dead Beare lie, then foure of vs went thither, and saw that in so short a time she had eaten almost the halfe of her, we tooke the dead Beare and laid it vpon a high heape of Ice, that we might sée it out of our Scute, that if the Beare came againe we might shot at her, at which time we tried the great strenght of the Beare, that carried the dead Beare as lightely in her mouth, as if it had béene nothing, where as we foure had enough to doe to cary away the halfe dead Beare betwéene vs, then the wind still held west, which draue the Ice into the east.

The 30. of Iune, in the morning, when the Sunne was east and by north, the Ice draue hard east-ward, by meanes of the west wind, and then there came two Beares vpon a péece of Ice that draue in the Sea, and thought to set vpon vs, and made show as if they would leape into the water, and come to vs, but did nothing, whereby we were of opinion, that they were the same Beares, that had béene there before, and about the south-south-east Sunne, there came another Beare vpon the fast Ice, and made towards vs, but being neare vs, and hearing vs make a noise, she went away againe, then the wind was west-southwest, and the Ice began somewhat to falle from the land, but because it was mistie weather, and a hard wind, we durst not put to Sea, but staied for a better opportunitie.

The 1. of Iulie, it was indifferent faire weather, with a west-north-west wind, and in the morning the sunne béeing east, there came a beare from the driuing yce towards vs, and swam ouer the water to the fast yce whereon we lay, but when she heard vs, she came no nearer, but ran away, and when the sunne was southeast, the Ice came so fast in towards vs, that all the Ice whereon we lay with our Scutes and our goods, brake and ran one péece vpon another, whereby we were in no small feare, for at that time most of our goods fell into the water, but we with great diligence drew our Scutes further vpon the Ice towards the land, where we though to be better defended from the driuing of the Ice, and as we went to fetch our goods, we fell into the greatest trouble that euer we had before, for y we endured so great danger in the sauing thereof, that as we laid hold vpon on péece thereof, the rest sunke
downe

The Nauigation into the North-seas.

returne with the Ice, and many times the Ice brake vnder our owne feat, whereby we were wholy discomforted, and in a maner cleane out of all hope, expecting no issue thereof, in such sort that our trouble at that time surmounted all our former cares and impeachments, and when we thought to draw vp our boates vpon the Ice, the Ice brake vnder vs, and we were caried away with the Scute, and al by the driuing Ice, and when we thought to saue the goods, the Ice brake vnder our feet, and with that the Scute brak in many places, especially y which we had mēded, as y mast, y mast planke, and almost al the Scute, wherein one of our men that was sicke, and a chest of mony lay, which we with great danger of our liues got out from it, for as we were doing it, the Ice that was vnder our feet draue from vs, and slid vpon other Ice, whereby we were in danger to burst both our armes & our legs, at which time thinking, y we had bin cleane quit of our Scute, we beheld each other in pittiful maner, knowing not what we should doe, our liues depending thereon, but God made so god prouision for vs, y y peeces of Ice draue from each other, wherewith we ran in great haste into the Scute, and drew it to vs again in such case as it was, and layd it vpon the fast Ice by the boate, where it was in more securitie, which put vs vnto an exceeding and great and dangerous labor, from the time that the Sunne was south east, vntill it was west South west, and in al that time we rested not, which made vs extreame weary, and wholy out of comfort, for that it troubled vs sore, and it was much more fearfull vnto vs, then at that time when William Barents dyed, for there we were almost drowned, & that day we lost (which was sounke in the sea) two barrels of bread, a fat with linne cloth, a driefat with the Sailors clothes, our Astronomicall ring, a pack of Scarlet-cloth, a runlet of oyle, & some cheeses and a runlet of wine, which bongd with the Ice, so that there was not any thing thereof saued.

The 2. of Iulie, the sunne East, there came another beare vnto vs, but we making a noyse she ran away, and when the Sun was West South-west, it began to be faire weather. then we began to mend our Scute, with the planks wherewith we had made the turckmish, and while 6. of vs were busied about mending of our scute the other sixe went further into the land, to seeke for some wood, and to fetch some stones, to lay vpon the Ice, that we might

make

The Nauigation into the North-seas.

make a fire thereon, therewith to melt our pitch, which we should need about the Scute, as also to see if they could fetch any wood for a mast, which they found with certaine staues, and brought them where the Scutes lay, and when they came to vs againe, they shewed vs that they had found certaine wood that had bin clouen, & brought some wedges with them, wherwith the said wood had bin clouē, whereby it appeared that men had bin there, then we made al the haste we could to make a fire and to melt our pitch, and to do al other things that were necessary to be done for the repairing of our Scute, so that we got it ready againe, by that the Sunne was North-east, at which time also we rosted our birds, & made a god meale with them.

The 3. of July, in the morning the Sunne being East, two of our men went to the water, and there they found two of our oares our helme sticke, the pack of Scarlet cloth, the chest with linnen cloth, and a hat that fell out of the driefat, whereby we gest, that it was broken in peeces, which they perceiuing, toke as much with them as they could carry, and came vnto vs, shewing vs that they had left more goods behind them, whereupon the Maister with 5. mere of vs went thither, & drew al the goods vpon the firme Ice, y when we went away, we might take it with vs, but they could not carry the chest nor the pack of cloth (that were ful of water) because of their waight, but were forced to let them stand, till we went away, that the water might drop out of them, and so they did, the Sunne being South west: there came another great beare vnto vs, which the man that kept watch saw not, and had beene deuoured by her, if one of our other men that lay downe in the ship, had not espied her, and called to him that kept watch, to loke to himselfe, who therewith ran away, meane time the beare was shot into the body, but she escaped, and that time the wind was east, north-east.

The 4. of July it was so faire cleare weather, that from the time we were first in Noua Zembla, we had not the like, then we wa∫t the veluets that had beene wet with the salt water, in fresh water, drawne out of snow and then dryed them, and packt them vp againe, at which time the wind was west, & west southwest.

The 5. of July it was faire weather, the wind west, southwest,

the

The Nauigation into the North-Seas.

the same day dyed Iohn Franson of Harlem (Claes Adrians nephew, that dyed the same day when William Barents dyed) the sunne being then about North, north-west, at which time the Ice came mightily driuing in vpon vs, and then sixe of our men went into the land, and there fetcht some fire-wood to dresse our meate.

The 6. of Iuly it was misty weather, but about euening it began to cleere vp, and the wind was south-east, which put vs in some comfort, and yet we lay fast vpon the Ice.

The 7. of Iuly it was faire weather with some raine, the wind west, South-west, and at euening west, and by north, then wee went to the open water, and there killed thirtéene birts, which we toke vppon a péece of driuing Ice, and layd them vpon the fast Ice.

The 8. of Iuly it was close misty weather, then we drest the birds which we had killed, which gaue vs a princely mealetide, in the euening there blew a fresh gale of wind, out of the North east, which put vs in great comfort to get from thence.

The 9. of Iuly in the morning, the Ice began to driue, whereby we got open water on the land side, and then also the fast Ice thereon we lay, began to driue, whereupon the master and the men went to fetch the packe and the chest, that stood vpon the Ice, to put them into the Scute, and then drew the Scutes to the water, at least 340. paces, which was hard for vs to do, in regard that the labour was great, and we very weake, & when the Sun was south south east we set saile, with an east wind, but when the sunne was west, we were forced to make towards the fast Ice againe, because thereabouts it was not yet gon, y wind being south, and came right from the land, whereby we were in good hope that it would driue away, and that we should procéede in our voyage.

The 10. of Iuly, from the time that the sunne was east, north-east, till it was east, we toke great paines & labour to get through the Ice, and at last we got through, and rowed forth, vntill wée happened to fall betwéene two great flakes of Ice, that closed one with the other, so that we could not get through, but were forced to draw the Scutes vpon them, and to vnlade the goods, and then to draw them ouer to the open water on the other side, and then we must go fetch the goods also to the same place, being at

least

The Nauigation into the North-leas.

least 110. paces long, which was very hard for vs, but there was no remedy, for it was but a folly for vs to thinke of any wearines, and when we were in the open water againe, we rowed forward as well as we could, but we had not rowed long, before we fell betwéene two great flakes of Ice, that came driuing one against the other, but by Gods help, and our spédy rowing, we got from betwéene them, before they closed vp, and being through we had a hard west wind, right in our téeth so y of force we were constrained to make towards the fast Ice that lay by the shore, and at last with much trouble, we got vnto it, and being there, we thought to row along by the fast Ice, vnto an Island that we saw before vs, but by reason of the hard contrary wind, we could not goe farre, so that we were compelled to draw the Scutes and the goods vpon the Ice, to sée what weather God would send vs, but our courages were cooled, to sée our selues so often inclosed in y Ice being in great feare y by meanes of the long and continuall paines (which we were forced to take) we should lose all our strength, & by that meanes should not long be able to continue or hold out.

The 11. of July in the morning as we sate fast vpon the Ice, the sunne being North east, there came a great beare out of the water, running towards vs, but we watcht for her with thrée muskets, and when she came within 30. paces of vs, we shot all the thrée muskets at her, and killed her outright, so that she stirred not a foote, and we might sée the fat run out at the holes of her skinne, that was shot in with the muskets, swimme vpon the water like oyle, and so driuing dead vpon the water, we went vpon a flake of Ice to her, and putting a rope about her neck, drew her vp vpon the Ice, and smit out her téeth, at which time we measured her body, & found it to be eight foote thick, then we had a west winde with close weather, but when the sunne was South it began to cléere vp, then thrée of our men went to the Island that lay before vs, and being there, they saw the Crosse Island, lying westward from them, and went thither to sée if that sommer there had béene any Russian there, and went thither vpon the fast Ice, that lay betwéene the two Islands, and being in the Island, they could not perceiue that any man had béene in it since we were there, there they got 70. egges, but when they had them, they knew not wherein to carry them, at last one of them
put

The Nauigation into the North-seas.

put off his bréeches, and tying them fast below, they carried them betwéene two of them, and the third bare the musket: and so came to vs againe, after they had béene twelue houres out, which put vs no small feare to thinke what was become of them, they told vs that they had many times gone vp to the knées in water, vpon the Ice betwéene both the Islands: and it was at least 6. miles to and fro, that they had gone, which made vs wonder how they could indure it, séeing we were all so weake. With the egges that they had brought, we were al wel comforted, and fared like Lords, so that we fcond some reliefe in our great misery, and then we shared our last wine amongst vs, whereof euery one had thrée glasses.

The 12. of July in the morning, when the sunne was East, the wind began to blow east, and east north east, with misty weather, and at euening sir of our men went into the land, to séeke certaine stones, and found some, but none of the best sort, and comimng backe againe, either of them brought some wood.

The 13. of July it was a faire day, then seuen of our men went to the firme land, to séeke for more stones, & found some, at which time the wind was South-east.

The 14. of July it was faire weather, with a good south wind, and then the Ice began to driue from the land, whereby we were in good hope to haue an open water, but the wind turning westerly againe, it lay still. When the sunne was south-west, thrée of our men went to the next Island, that lay before vs, and there shot a Bercheynet, which they brought to the Scute, and gaue it amongst vs, for all our goods were common.

The 15. of July, it was misty weather, that morning the wind was south-east, but the sunne being west, it began to raine, and the wind turned west and west south-west.

The 16. of July there came a beare from the firme land, that came very néere vnto vs, by reason that it was as white as snow, whereby at first we could not discerne it to be a beare, because it shewed so like the snow, but by her stirring at last wee perceiued her, and as she came néere vnto vs, we shot at her, and hit her, but she ran away: that morning, the wind was west, and a ter that againe, east north-east with close weather.

The 17. July, about the south south east sunne, 5. of our men went

went againe to the neerest Island, to see if there appeared any open water, for our long staying there was no small griefe vnto vs, perceiuing not how we should get from thence, who being halfe way thither, they found a beare lying behind a peece of Ice, which the day before had beene shot by vs, but she hearing vs went away, but one of our men following her with a boate-hooke, thrust her into the skinne, wherewith the beare rose vp vpon her hinder feet, and as the man thrust at her againe, she stroke the Iron of the boat-hooke in peeces, wherewith the man fell downe vpon his buttocks, which our other two men seeing, two of them shot the beare into the body, and with that she ran away, but the other man went after her with his broken staffe, and stroke the beare vpon the backe, wherewith the beare turnd about against the man three times one after the other, and then the other two came to her, and shot her into the body againe, wherewith she sat downe vpon her buttocks, and could scant runne any further, ant then they shot once againe, wherewith she fell downe, and they shot her teeth out of her head: all that day the wind was north-east, & east north-east.

The 18. of July, about the east sunne, three of our men went vp vpon the highest part of the land, to see if there was any open water in the sea, at which time they saw much open water, but it was so farre from the land, that they were almost out of comfort, because it lay so farre from the land and the fast Ice, being of opinion that we should not be able to drawe the Scutes and the gœds so farre thither, because our strengthes stil began to decrease: and the sore labour and paine that we were forced to indure more and more increased, and comming to our Scutes, they brought vs that newes, but we being compelled thereunto by necessity abandoned all wearines and faint heartednes, & determined with our selues to bring the boates and the gœds to the water side, and to row vnto that Ice, where we must passe ouer to get to the open water, and when we got to it, we vnladed our scutes, and drewe them first ouer the Ice to the open water, and after that the gœds; it being at the least 1000. paces, which was so sore a labour for vs, that as we were in hand therewith we were in a manner ready to leaue off in the middle thereof, and feared that we should not goe through withall, but for that we had gone through so many dangers,

The Nauigation into the North-seas.

gers we hoped that we should not be faint therin, wishing it might be last trouble we should as then indure, & so w great difficulty got into the open water, about the south-west sunne, then we set saile, till the sunne was west and by south; & presently fell amongst the Ice againe, where we were forced to drawe vp the Scutes againe vpon the Ice, and being vpon it, we could see the crosse Island, which we gest to be about a mile from vs the wind then being east, and east north-east.

The 19. of July lying in that manner vpon the Ice, about the East Sunne, seuen of our men went to the Crosse Island, and being there they saw great store of ope water in West, wherewith they much reioyced, and made as great haste as they could to get to the Scutes againe, but before they came away they got a hundred egges, and brought them away with them, and comming to the Scutes, they shewed vs that they had seen, as much open water in the sea, as they could decerne, being in good hope, that that would be the last time that they should draw the Scutes ouer the Ice, and that it should be no more measured by vs and in that sort put vs in good comfort, whereupon we made speede to dresse our egges & ate them amongst vs, and presently the Sun being South south-west we fell to worke, to make all things ready, to bring the Scutes to the water, which were to be drawen at least 200. paces ouer the Ice, which we did with a good courage, because we were in good hope that it would be the last time, and getting to the water, we put to sea with Gods helpe, with an East, and East north east wind, & a good gale, so that with the west Sun, we past by the Crosse Island, which is distant from Cape de Nassawes 10. miles, and presently after that the Ice left vs, & we got cleere out of it, yet we saw some in the sea, but it troubled vs not and so we held our course West and by South, with a good gale of wind out of the East, and East North-east, so that we gest that betweene euery meale-tide we sailed eightene miles, wherewith we were exceedingly comforted, giuing God thanks, that he had deliuered vs out of so great and many difficulties, (wherein it seemed that we should haue bin ouerwhelmed,) hoping in his mercie, that from thence forth he would ayde vs to bring our voyage to an end.

The 20. of July, hauing still a good gale about the South-east Sunne, we past a long by the black point, which is twelue miles distant from the crosse Iland, and sailed West South west, and about the euening with the West Sunne, we saw the Admirable Iland, and about the North Sun past along by it, which is distant from the black point eight miles, and passing along by it, we saw about two hundred sea horses, lying vpon a flake of Ice, and we sayled close by them, and draue them from thence, which had almost cost vs deere, for they being mighty strong fishes, and of great force, swam towards vs, (as if they would be reuenged on vs for the dispight that we had don them (round about our Scuts with a great noyse, as if they would haue deuoured vs, but we escaped from them by reason, that we had a good gale of wind, yet it was not wisely done of vs, to wake sleeping wolues.

The 21. of July, we past by Cape Pluncio, about the East North-east Sune, w lyeth West South-west ight miles from ye Admirable Iland, & w the good gales we had about ye South-west Snu, we sailed by Langenes, 9 miles frō Cape Pluncio, there ye lād reacheth most South-west and we had a good North-east winde.

The 22. of July, we hauing so good a gale of wind, when we came to Cape de Cant, there we went on land to seeke for some birds egs, but we found none, so we sayled forwards, but after ye about ye South Sun we saw a clift, ye was ful of birds, thither we sailed & casting stones at them, we killed 22. birds, and got fifteene egges, which one of our men fetcht from the clift, and if we would haue stayed there any longer, we might haue taken a hundred or two hundred birds at least, but because the maister was somewhat further into sea-ward then we, and stayed for vs, and for that we would not loose that faire fore-wind, we sailed forwards a long by the land, and about the South-west Sunne, we came to another point, where we got a hundred twenty fiue birds, which we toke with our hands out of their neasts, and some we killed with stones and made them fal downe into the water, for it is a thing certaine ye those birds neuer vsed to see men, & that no man had euer sought or vsed to take them, for else they would haue flowne away, and that they feared no body. but the Foxes and other wilde beastes, that could not clime vp the high clifts, and that therefore they had made their nests the con, where they were out of feare of any beastes comming vnto them, for we were in no small daunger of breaking of our legges and armes, especially as we came downe

againe

The Nauigation into the North-seas.

againe, because the clift was so high and so steepe, those birds had euery one but one egge in their neasts, and that lay vpon the bare clift without any straw or other thing vnder them, which is to be wondred at, to thinke how they could breed thir young ones in so great cold, but it is to be thought and beleeued, that they therfore sit but vpon on egge, that so the heat which they giue in breeding so many, may be wholy giuen vnto one egge, and by that meanes it hath all the heat of the birde vnto it selfe, and there also we found many egges, but most of them were foule and bad, and when we left them, the wind fell flat against vs, and blew North-west, and there also we had much Ice, and we tooke great paines to get from the Ice, but we could not get aboue it, and at last by lauering we fell into the Ice, and being there we saw much open water towards the land, whereunto we made as well as we could, but our Maister (that was more to sea ward) perceiuing vs to be in the Ice thought we had gotten some hurt, and lauered to and againe along by the Ice, but at last seeing that we sailed therein, he was of opinion that we saw some open water, and that we made towards it (as it was true) and therefore he wound also towards vs, and came toland by vs where we found a good hauen, and lay safe almost from all winds, and he came thither about two houres after vs, there we went on land, and got some eggs and some wood to make a fire, wherewith we made ready the birds that we had taken, at which time we had a North west wind with close weather.

The 23. of July, it was darke and mistie weather, with a North wind, whereby we were forced to lye still in that creeke or hauen: meane time some of our men went on land, to seeke for some egges and stones, but found not many, but a reasonable number of good stones.

The 24. of July, it was faire weather, but the wind still Northerly, whereby we were forced to lye still, and about noone we tooke the higth of y Sun, with our astrolabium, and found it to be eluated aboue the Horizon 37. degrees & 20. min. his declination 20. degrees & 10. min. which substracted frō y higth aforesaid rested 17. degrees & 10 minutes, which taken from 90 degrees, the higth of the Pole was 73. degrees and 10. minutes, and for y we lay stil there, some of our men went often times on land, to seeke stones, and found some that were as good as euer any that we found. The

The Nauigation into the North-seas.

The 25. of July it was darke misty weather, the wind north, but we were forced to ly still, because it blew so hard.

The 26. of July it began to be faire weather, which we had not had for certaine daies together, the wind still north; and about the south sunne, we put to sea, but it was so great a crèeke that we were forced to put foure miles into the sea, before wèe could get about the point thereof: and it was most in the wind, so that it was midnight before wee got aboue it, sometimes sayling, and sometimes rowing : and hauing past it, we stroke our sailes, and rowed along by the land.

The 27. of July it was faire calme weather, so that we rowed all that day, through the broken Ice, along by the land, the wind being northwest, and at euening about the west sunne, we came to a place where there ran a great streame, whereby we thought that we were about Constinsarke, for we saw a great crèeke, and we werée of opinion ÿ it went through to the Tartarian sea, our course was most south-west: about the north sunne we past along by the crosse point, and sailed betwèen the firme land and an Island. & then went South south-east, with a Northwest wind and made good spéed, the maister with ÿ Scute being a good way before vs, but whē he had gotten about ÿ point of the Island, he staied for vs, & there we lay by ÿ clifts, hoping to take some birds, but got none, at which time we had sailed from Cape de Cant along by Constinsarke, to the crosse point 20. miles, our course South south-east, the wind North-west.

The 28. of July it was faire weather, with a North-east wind, then we sailed along by the land, and with the South-west sunne, got before S. Laurence Bay, or Sconce point, and sayled South south-east, 6. miles, and being there, we found two Russians Lodgies, or ships, beyond the point, wherewith we were not a little comforted, to thinke that we were come to the place where we found men, but were in some doubt of them, because they were so many, for at that time, wee sawe at least 30. men, and knew not what they were, there with much paine and labour, we got to the land, which they perceiuing, left off their worke, and came towards vs, but without any armes. and wèe also went on shore, as many as were well, for diuers of vs were very ill at ease, and weake by reason of a great scouring in their

bodyes,

The Nauigation into the North-seas.

bodies, and when wee met together, wee saluted each other in friendly wise, they after theirs, and we after our manner, and when we were met, both they and we lookt each other stedfastly in the face, for that some of them knew vs, and we them, to bee the same men which the yeare before, when we past through the Weigats, had béen in our ship: at which time we perceiued y they were abasht, and wondred at vs, to remember that at that time we were so well furnished with a great ship, that was excéedingly prouided of all things necessary, and then to sée vs so leane & bare, & with so small Scutes into that country: & amongst them there were two, that in friendly manner clapt y master & me vpon the shoulder, as knowing vs since y voyage: for there was none of all our men that was as then in that voiage, but we two onely, and asked vs for our Crable, meaning our ship, and we shewed them by signes as well as we could (for we had no interpreter) that we had lost our ship in the Ice, wherewith they sayd, Crable pro pal, (which we vnderstood to be, haue you lost your ship) and we made answere, Crable pro pal, which was as much as to say, that we had lost our ship, and many more words we could not vse, because we vnderstood not each other, then they made shew to be sorry for our losse, and to be grieued that we the yeare before had béene there with so many ships, and then to sée vs in so simple manner, & made vs signes that then they had drunke wine in our ship, and asked vs what drinke we had now, wherewith one of our men went into the scute and drew some water, and let them taste thereof, but they shakt their heads, and said No dobbre (that is, it is not good) then our master went néerer vnto them, and shewed them his mouth, to giue them to vnderstand that we were troubled with a loosnesse in our bellies, and to know if they could giue vs any councel to help it, but they thought we made shew that we had great hunger, wherewith one of them went vnto their lodging, and fetcht a round Rie loafe, weighing about 8. pounds, with some smored foules, which we accepted thankfully, and gaue them in exchange halfe a dozen of Muschuyt, then our master led two of the chiefe of them, with him into his Scute, & gaue them some of the wine that we had, being almost a gallon, for it was so néere out: and while we staied there, we were very familiar with them, and went to the place where they lay, & sod some of our mischuyt with

with water by their fire, that we might eate some warme thing downe into our bodies, and we were much comforted to see the Russians for that in thirteene moneths time, that wee departed from Iohn Cornelison, we had not seene any man, but onely monsterous and cruell wild beares: for that as then we were in some comfort, to see that we had lived so long, to come in company of men againe, and therewith we said vnto each other, now we hope it will fall out better with vs, seeing we haue found men againe, thanking God with all our hearts, that he had beene so gracious and mercifull vnto vs, to giue vs life vntill that time.

The 29. of July it was reasonable faire weather, & that morning the Russians began to make preparatiō to be gone, & to set saile: at which time they digd certaine barrels with traine oile out of the sieges, which they had buried there, and put it into their ships, and we not knowing whither they would go, saw them saile towards y̌ VVeigats: at which time also we set saile, & followed after them, but they sayling before vs, and we following them, along by the land, the weather being close and misty, we lost the sight of them, and knew not whether they put into any creeke or sayled forward, but we held on our course, South-south east with a North-west wind, and then South-east, betweene two Islands, vntill we were inclosed with Ice againe, and saw no open water, whereby we supposed that they were about the VVeigats, and that the North-west wind had driuen the Ice into that creeke, and being so inclosed with Ice, & saw no open water before vs, but with great labour and paines, we went back againe to the two Islands aforesaid, and there about the North-east sunne, we made our Scutes fast at one of the Islands, for as then it began to blowe hard.

The 30. of July lying at anchor, the wind still blew Northwest, with great store of raine, and a sore storme, so that although we had couered our Scutes with our sailes, yet we could not lye dry, which was an vnaccustomed thing vnto vs: for we had had no raine in long time before, and yet we were forced to stay there all that day.

The 31. of July, in the morning, about the North-east sunne, we rowed frō that Island to another Island, whereon there stood two crosses, whereby we thought that some men had laine there

about

The Nauigation into the North-seas.

about trade of merchandise, as the other Russians that we saw before had done, but we found no man there, the wind as then béeing North-west, whereby the Ice draue still towards the Weigats: there, to our great good, we went on land, for in that Island, we found great store of Leple leaues, which serued vs excéeding well, and it séemed that God had purposely sent vs thither: for as then we had many sicke men, and most of vs were so troubled with a scouring in our bodies, and were thereby become so weake, that we could hardly row, but by meanes of those leaues, we were healed thereof: for that as soone as we had eaten them, we were presently eased and healed, whereat we could not chose but wonder, & therefore we gaue God great thanks, for that, and for many other his mercies shewed vnto vs, by his great and vnexpected ayd lent vs, in that our dangerous voyage: and so as I sayd before, we eate them by whole handfuls together, because in Holland wée had heard much spoken of their great force, and as then found it to be much more then we expected.

The 1. of August the wind blew hard North-west and the Ice that for a while had driuen towards the entry of the Weigats, stayed and draue no more, but the sea went very hollow, whereby we were forced to remoue our Scutes on the other side of the Island, to defend them from the waues of the sea, and lying there we went on land againe to fetch more Leple leaues, whereby wée had bin so wel holpen, & stil more and more recouered our healths, and in so short time, that we could not chose but wonder thereat, so that as then some of vs could eate bisket againe, which not long before they could not do.

The 2. of August it was dark misty weather, the wind stil blowing stiffe northwest, at which time our victuals began to decrease, for as then we had nothing but a little bread and water, and some of vs a little chéese, which made vs long sore to be gone frō thence, specially in regard of our hunger, whereby our weake members began to be much weaker, and yet we were forced to labour sore, which were two great contraries: for it behoued vs rather to haue our bellies full, that so we might be the stronger, to indure our labour, but patience was our point of trust.

The 3. of August about the North sun, the weather being somwhat better, we agréed amongst our selues to leaue Noua Zembla and

The Nauigation into the North-seas.

and to crosse ouer to Russia, and so committing our selues to God, we set saile with a North-west wind, & sailed South South-west till the Sun was east, and then we entred into Ice againe, which put vs in great feare, for we had crost ouer and left the Ice vpon Noua Zembla, & were in good hope y we should not meet with any Ice againe, in so short space, at which time being in the Ice, with calme weather, whereby our Sailes could doe vs no great good, we stroke our sailes and began to row againe, and at last we rowed cleane through the Ice, not without great & sore labour, and about the South-west Sunne got cleere thereof, and entred into the large sea, where we saw no Ice, and then what with sailing and rowing we had made 20. miles, & so sailing forwards we thought to aproch neere vnto the Russian coast; but about the North-west Sunne, we entred into Ice againe, and then it was very cold, wherewith our hearts became very heauy, fearing that it would alwaies continew in that sort, and that we should neuer be freed thereof, and for that our boate could not make so good way, nor was not able to saile aboue the point of Ice, we were compelled to enter into the Ice, for that being in it, we perceiued open sea beyond it, but the hardest matter was to get into it, for it was very close, but at last we found a meanes to enter, and got in, and being entred it was somewhat better, and in the end with great paine and labour we got into the open water: our Maister that was in the scute, which sailed better then our boate got aboue the point of the Ice, and was in some feare that we were inclosed with y Ice, but God sent vs the meanes to get out from it, as soone as he could saile about the point thereof, and so we met together againe.

The 4 of August, about the South-east Sunne, being gotten out of the Ice, we sailed forward with a North-west wind, and held our course Southerly, and when the Sunne was South, at none time we saw the coast of Russia, lying before vs, whereat we were exceeding glad, and going neerer vnto it, we stroke our sailes and rowed on land, and found it to be very low land, like a bare strand that might be flowed ouer with the water; there we lay till the Sun was South-west, but perceiuing that there we could not much further our selues, hauing as the sailed from the point of Noua Zembla, (from whence we put off) thither, ful 30 miles, we sailed forward along by the coast of Russia, with an indifferet gale of wind

The Nauigation into the North-seas.

wind, and when the Sunne was North, we saw another Russien Iolle or ship, which we sailed vnto to speake with them, and being hard by them, they came al about hatches, and we cried vnto them Candinaes Candinaes (whereby we asked them if we were about Candinaes) but they cryed againe and sayd Pitzora Pitzora (to shew vs that we were there abouts) & for y we sailed along by the coast, where it was very drie, supposing that we held our course, west and by North, that so we might get beyond the point of Candinaes; we were wholy deceiued by our copas, that stood vpon a chest boud with yron bands, which made vs vary at least 2. points, whereby we were much more southerly then we thought our course had bin, & also farre more easterly, for we thought verily that we had not bin farre from Candinaes, and we were three daies sailing from it, as afer we perceiued, & for that we found our selues to be so much out of our way, we stayed there all night til day appeared.

The 5. of August, lying there, one of our men went on shore, and found the land further in, to be greene, and ful of trees, & from thence called to vs, to bid vs bring our peeces on shore, saying that there was wild deere to be killed, which made vs excæding glad, for then our victuales were almost spent, and we had nothing but some broken bread, whereby we were wholy out of comfort, and some of vs were of opinion that we should leaue the Scutes, and goe further into the land, or else they said, we should all die with hunger, for that many daies before we were forced to fast, and hunger was a sharpe sword, which we could hardly endure any longer.

The 6. of August, the weather began to be somewhat better, at which time we determined to row forward because the wind was against vs, that we might get out of the creeke, the wind being East South-east which was our course as then, and so hauing rowed about three miles we could get no further, because it was so full in the wind, and we al together heartlesse and faint; the land streatching further North-east then we made account it had done, whereupon we beheld each other in pittifull manner, for we had great want of victuals, and knew not how farre we had to saile before we should get any releese, for al our victuals was almost consumed.

The 7. of August, the wind being west North west, it serued vs vs well to get out of that créeke, and so we sailed forward East, and by North, till we got out of the créeke, to the place, and the point of land, where we first had bin, and there we made our Scutes fast againe: for the North-west wind was right against vs, whereby our mens hearts and courages were wholy abated, to sée no issue, how we should get from thence: for as then sicknesses, hunger, and no means to be found how to get from thence, consumed both our flesh and our bloud, but if we had found any reléefe, it would haue bin better with vs.

The 8. of August, there was no better weather, but still the wind was against vs, and we lay a good way one from the other, as we found best place for vs, at which time there was most dislike in our boate, in regard that some of vs were excéeding hungrie, and could not endure it any longer, but were wholy out of heart still wishing to die.

The 9. of August, it was all one weather, so that the wind blowing contrary, we were forced to lye still, and could goe no further, our gréefe still increasing more & more, at last two of our men went out of the Scute, wherein the Maister was, which we perceiuing, two of our men also landed, and went altogether about a mile into the countrie, and at last saw a banke, by the which there issued a great streame of water, which we thought to be the way from whence the Russians came, betwéene Candinaes & the firme land of Russia, and as our men came backe againe, in the way as they went along, they found a dead sea-horse, that stanke excéedingly, which they drew with thé to our Scute, thinking that they should haue a dainty morsell out of it, because they endured so great hunger, but we told thé that without doubt it would kil vs, & that it were better for vs, to endure pouerty and hunger for a time, then to venture vpon it, saying, that seeing God who in so many great extremitys had sent vs a happie issue, still liued, and was excéeding powerfull, we hoped and nothing doubting, that he would not altogether forsake vs, but rather helpe vs, when we were most in dispaire.

The 10. of August, it was stil a North-west wind with mistie & darke weather, so that we were driuen to lie still, at which time it was no néed for vs to aske one another how we fared, for we could well gesse it by our countenances.

The

The Nauigation into the North-seas.

The 11. of August, in the morning, it was faire calme weather, so that the Sunne being about north-east, the master sent one of his men to vs, to bid vs prepare our selues to set saile, but we had made our selues ready thereunto before he came, and began to rowe towards him, at which time for that I was very weake and no longer able to rowe, as also for that our boate was harder to rowe then the Scute, I was set in the Scute, to guide the helme, and one that was stronger, was sent out of the Scute into the boate to rowe in my place, that we might kéepe company together, and so we rowed till ye Sunne was south, and then we had a good gale of wind out of the south, which made vs take in our oares, and then we hoised vp our sailes, wherewith we made good way, but in the euening the wind began to blowe hard, where by we were forced to take in our sailes and to rowe towards the land, where we laid our Scutes vpon the Strand, and went on land to séeke for fresh water, but found none, and because we could goe no further, we laid our sailes ouer the boates to couer vs from the weather, at which time it began to raine very hard, and at midnight it thundred, and lightned, with more store of raine, wherewith our company were much disquieted, to sée that they found no meanes of reléese, but still entred into further trouble and danger.

The 12. of August, it was faire weather, at which time the Sunne being east, we saw a Russia Lodgie come towards vs, with al his sailes vp, wherewith we were not a little comforted, which we perceauing from the strand, where we laie with our Scutes, we desired the master that we might goe vnto him, to speake with him, and to get some victuales of them, and to that end we made as much haste as we could, to launche out our Scutes and sailed toward them, and when we got to them, the master went into the Lodgie, to aske them how farre we had to Cardinaes, which we could not well learne of them, because we vnderstood them not, they held vp their fiue fingers vnto vs, but we knew not what they ment thereby, but after we perceaued, that thereby they would shew vs, that there stood fiue Crosses vpon it, and they brought their compas out and shewed vs that it lay North west frō vs, which our compas also shewed vs, which reckning also we had made: but when we saw we could haue no

better

The Nauigation into the North-seas.

better intelligence from them, the master went further into their ship, & pointed to a barrell of fish ỹ he saw therein, making signes to know, whether they would sel it vnto vs, showing them a péece of 8. royles, which they vnderstanding, gaue vs 102. fishes, with some cakes, which they had made of meale, when they sod their fishe, and about the south Sunne we left them, being glad that we had gotten some victuales, for long before we had had but two ounces of bread a day, with a little water and nothing else, and with that we were forced to comfort our selues as well as we could: the fishes we shared amongst vs equally, to one as much as another, without any difference, & when we had left thẽ, we held our course west and by north, with a south, and a south and by east wind, and when the Sunne was west-south-west it began to thunder and raine, but it continued not long, for shortly after the weather began to cleare vp againe, and passing forward in that sort, we saw the Sunne in our common Compas, go downe north and by west.

The 13. of August, we had the wind against vs, being west-south-west, and our course was west and by north, whereby we were forced to put to the shore againe, where two of our men went on the land, to sée how it laie, and whether the point of Candinaes reacht not out from thence into the sea, for we gess that we were not farre from it, our men comming againe, showed vs that they had séene a house vpon the land, but no man in it, and said further that they could not perceaue, but that it was the point of Candinaes that we had séene, wherewith we were somewhat comforted, and went into our Scutes againe, and rowed along by the land, at which time hope made vs to be of good cōfort, & procured vs to doe more then we could well haue done, for our liues and maintenance consisted therein, and in that sort rowing along by the land: we saw an other Russian Iollie lying vpon the shore, which was broken in péeces, but we past by it, and a little after that, we saw a house at the water-side, wherevnto some of our men went, wherein also they found no man, but onely an ouen, and when they came againe to the Scute, they brought some leple leaues with them which they had found as they went, and as we rowed along by the point, we had a good gale of winde out of the east, at which time we hoised vp our sailes

The Nauigation into the North-seas.

sailes, & sailed foreward, and after none, about the south-west Sunne, we perceaued that the point, which we had séene, laie south-ward, whereby we were fully perswaded that it was the point of Candinaes, frō whence we went to saile ouer the mouth of the white sea, and to that end we boūded each other and deuided our candles, and all other things that we should néed amongst vs. to helpe our selues therewith, and so put of from the land, thinking to passe ouer the white sea, to the coast of Russia, and sailing in that sort, with a good winde, about midnight there rose a great storme out of the north, wherewith we stroke saile, and made it shorter, but our other boate that was harder vnder saile, (knowing not that we had lessened our sailes,) sailed foreward, whereby we straied one from the other, for then it was very darke.

The 14. of August, in the morning, it being indifferent good weather with a south-west wind, we sailed west north-west, and then it began to cleare vp, so that we saw our boate, and did what we could to get vnto her, but we could not, because it began to be mistie weather againe, and therefore we said vnto each other, let vs hold on our course, we shal finde them well enough, on the north coast, when we are past the white sea, our course was west-north-west, the wind being south-west and by west, and about the south-west Sunne, we could get no further, because the wind fel contrary, whereby we were forced to strike our sailes, and to row foreward, and in that sort rowing till the Sunne was west, there blew an indifferent gale of wind out of the east and therewith we set saile, and yet we rowed with two oares, till the Sunne was north-north-west, and then the wind began to blow somewhat stronger east, and east-south-east, at which time we tooke in our oares, and sailed forward west-north-west.

The 15. of August, wée saw the sunne rise east north-east, wherevpon we thought that our compasse varied somewhat, and when the sunne was east, it was calme weather againe, wherewith we were forced to take in our sailes, and to row againe, but it was not long before wee had a gale of winde out of the south-east, and then we hoysed vp our sailes againe, and went forward west and by south, and sayling in that manner, with a good fore-

A   winde

The Nauigation into the North-seas.

wind, when the sunne was South, we saw land, thinking that as then we had béene on the west side of the white sea, beyond Candinaes, and being close vnder the land, we saw fire Russian Lodgies, lying there, to whom we sailed, and spake with them, asking them how farre wée were from Kilduin, but although they vnderstood vs not well, yet they made vs such signes that we vnderstood by them that we were still farre from thence, and that we were yet on the East side of Candinaes: with that they stroke their hands together, thereby signifying y we must first passe ouer the white sea, and that our Scutes were to little to doe it, and that it would be ouer great daunger for vs to passe ouer it, with so small Scutes, and that Candinaes was still North-west from vs, then wee asked them for some bread, and they gaue vs a loafe, which wée eate hungerly vp as wée were rowing, but wée would not beléeue them, that we were still on the east side of Cardinaes, for we thought verily that wee had past ouer the white sea, and when we left them, we rowed along by the land, the wind béeing North, and about the North-west sunne, we had a good wind againe from the South-east, and therewith we sayled along by the shore, and saw a great Russian Lodgie, lying on the Starre-boord from vs, which we thought came out of the white sea.

The 16. of August in the morning, sayling forward North-west, wée perceiued that we were in a Créeke, & so made towards y Russian Lodgie, which we had séene on our starresboord, which at last with great labour and much paine, we got vnto, and comming to them about the South east sunne, with a hard wind, we asked them how farre we were from Sembla de Cool or Kilduin, but they shooke their heads, and shewed vs that we were on the east side of Zembla de Candinaes, but we would not beléeue them, and then we asked them some victuals, wherewith they gaue vs certaine plaice, for the which the maister gaue them a péece of money, and sailed from them againe, to get out of that hole, where wée were, as it reacht into the sea; but they perceiuing that we toke a wrong course, and that the flud was almost past, sent two men vnto vs, in a small boate, with a great loafe of bread which they gaue vs, and made signes vnto vs to come aboord of their ship againe, for that they intended to haue further spéech with vs, and to help vs, which we séeming not to refuse, and desiring not to be

vn-

The Nauigation into the North-seas.

vnthankfull, gaue them a péece of money, and a péece of linnen cloth, but they stayed still by vs, and they that were in the great Lodgie, held vp bacon and butter vnto vs, to moue vs to come a bord of them againe, and so we did: and being with them, they shewed vs that we were stil on the east side of the point of Candinaes, then we fetcht our card and let them sée it, by the which they shewed vs, that we were still on the east side of the white sea, and of Cardinaes, which we vnderstanding, were in some doubt with our selues, because we had so great a boiage to make ouer the white sea, and were in more feare for our companions that were in the boate, as also ý hauing sailed 22. miles along by the Russian coast, we had gotten no further, but were then to saile ouer the mouth of the white sea, with so small prouision, for which cause the master bought of ý Russians thrée sacks vv meale, two flitches and a halfe of bacon, a pot of Russia butter, and a runlet of honny for prouision for vs and our boate, when we should méet with it againe, & for ý in the meane time, the flod was past we sailed with the ebbe, out of the aforesaid Créeke, where the Russians boate came to vs, and entred into the sea with a god South-east wind, holding our course North, north-west, and there we saw a point that reacht out into the sea, which we thought to be Candinaes, but we sailed still forward, and the land reached North-west: in the euening the sunne being North-west: when we saw that we did not much god with rowing, and that the streame was almost past, we lay still, and sod a pot full of water and meale, which tasted excéeding well, because we had put some bacon fat and honny into it, so that we thought it to be a feastiuall day with vs, but still our minds ran vpon our boate, because we knew not where it was.

The 17. of August lying at anchor, in the morning at breake of day, we saw a Russian Lodgie that came sayling out of the white sea, to whom we rowed, that we might haue some instruction fro him, and when wée borded him, without asking or speaking vnto him, he gaue vs a loafe of bread, and by signes shewed vs as well as he could, that he had séene our companions, and that there was seuen men in the boate, but we not knowing well what they sayd, neither yet beléeuing them, they made other signes vnto vs, and held vp their seuen fingers, and pointed to our Scute, there

A 2   by

The Nauigation into the North-seas.

by shewing that there was so many men in the boate, and that they had sold them bread flesh, fish, and other victualls: and while we staid in their Lodgie, we saw a small compasse therein, which we knew that they had bought of our chiefe Boatson, which they likewise acknowledged, then we vnderstanding them well, askt them how long it was since they saw our boate, and whereabouts it was, they made signes vnto vs, that it was the day before: and to conclude, they shewed vs great friendship, for the which we thanked them, and so being glad of the good newes we had heard, we tooke our leaues of them, much reioycing that we heard of our companions welfare, and specially because they had gotten victuals from the Russians, which was the thing that we most doubted of, in regard that we knew what small prouision they had with them, which done, we rowed as hard as we could, to try if we might ouertake them, as being still in doubt, that they had not prouision inough, wishing that they had had part of ours: and hauing rowed al that day with great labour along by the land, about midnight we found a fall of fresh water, and then we went on land to fetch some, and there also we got some Leple leaues; and as we thought to row forward, we were forced to saile, because the flood was past, and still wee lookt earnestly out for the point of Cardinaes, and the fiue Crosses, whereof we had béene instructed by the Russians, but we could not sée it.

The 18. of August in the morning, the sunne being East, we puld vp our stone, (which we vsed in stéed of an anchor) and rowed along by the land, till the sunne was south, and then we saw a point of land, reaching into the sea, and on it certaine signes of crosses, which as we went néerer vnto, wee saw perfectly, and when the sunne was west, wee perceiued that the land reached West and South-west, so that thereby we knew it certainly to be the point of Candinaes, lying at the mouth of the white sea, which we were to crosse, and had long desired to sée it. This point is easily to be knowne, hauing fiue crosses standing vpon it, which are perfectly to be deerned, one the East side, in the South-east, and one the other side in the South-west, and when we thought to saile from thence, to the West side of the white sea towards the coast of Norway, we found that one of our runlets of fresh water was almost leakt out, and for that we had about 40. Duch miles

to

The Nauigation into the North-seas.

to saile ouer the sea, before we should get any fresh water, we sought meanes first to row on land, to get some, but because the waues went so high we durst not do it, & so hauing a good north-east wind, (which was not for vs to slack) we set forward in the name of GOD, and when the Sunne was North-west, we past the point, and all that night and the next day sailed with a good wind, and all that time rowed but while three glasses were run out, and the next night after ensuing, hauing still a good wind, in the morning about the East North-east Sunne, we saw land, on the West side of the white sea, which we found by the rushing of the sea vpon the land, before we saw it, and perceiuing it to be ful of clifts, and not low sandy ground with same hils, as it is on the east side of the white sea, we assured our selues that we were on ye west side of the white sea, vpon the coast of Lapeland, for the which we thanked GOD, that he had helped vs to saile ouer the white sea in thirty houres, it being forty Dutch miles at the least, our course being West with a North-east wind.

The 20. of August, being not farre from the land, the Northeast wind left vs, and then it began to blow stiffe North-west, at which time seeing we could not make much way by sailing forward, we determined to put in betweene certaine clifts, and when we got close to the land, we espied certaine crosses, with warders vpon them, whereby we vnderstood, that it was a good way, and so put into it, and being entred a litle way within it, we saw a great Russian lodgie lying at an anchor, whereunto we rowed as fast as we could, and there also we saw certaine houses wherein men dwelt, and when we got to the Lodgie, we made our selues fast vnto it, and cast our tent ouer the Scute, for as then it began to raine, then we went on land into the houses that stood vpon the shore, where they shewed vs great friendship, leading vs into their stoaues, and there dried our wet clothes, and then seething some fish, bade vs sit downe and eate somwhat with them. In those litle houses we found thirteene Russians who euery morning went out to fish in the sea, whereof two of them had charge ouer the rest, they liued very poorly, and ordinarily eate nothing but fish & bread: at euening when we prepared our selues to go to our scute againe, they prayed the maister and me to stay with them in their houses, which the maister thanked them for, would not do, but I staied stayed with them al that night: besides those thirtéene men, there was two Laplanders more, and thrée women with a child, that liued very poorely of the ouerplus which the Russians gaue them, as a péece of fish, and some fishes heades, which the Russians threw away, and they with great thankfulnesse tooke them vp, so that in respect of their pouertie, we thought our selues to bee well furnished: & yet we had litttle inough, but as it séemed, their ordinary liuing was in that manner, and we were forced to stay there, for that the wind being Northwest, it was against vs.

The 21. of August it rained most part of the day, but not so much after dinner as before, then our master brought good store of fresh fish, which we sod, and eate our bellies full, which in long time we had not done, and therewith sod some meale and water, in stéed of bread, whereby we were well comforted. Afternoone, when the raine began to lessen, we went further into the land, and sought for some Leple leaues, and then we saw two men vpon y hilles, whereupon we said one to the other, hereabouts there must more people dwel, for there came two men towards vs, but we regarding them not, went backe againe to our Scute, and towards the houses: the two men that were vpon the hilles (being some of our men that were in the boate) perceauing the Russian lodgie, came downe the hill towards her, to buy some victuales of them, who being come thither vnawares, and hauing no mony about them, they agréed betwéene them to put off one of their paire of breches, (for that as then we ware two or thrée paire, one ouer the other) to sel them for some victuales, but when they came downe the hill, and were somewhat néerer vnto vs, they espied our Scute lying by the lodgie, and we as then beheld them better, and knew them, wherewith we reioyced, and shewed each other of our procéedings, and how we had sailed to and fro in great necessitie and hunger, and yet they had béene in greater necessitie and danger then we and gaue God thankes, that he had preserued vs aliue, and brought vs together againe, and then we eate some thing together, and dranke of the cleare water, such as runneth along by Collen through the Rem, and then we agréed that they should come vnto vs, that we might saile together.

The 22. of August, the rest of our men with the boate came vnto vs, about the East South east Sunne, whereat we much reioyced

The Nauigation into the North-seas.

red, and then we prayed the Russians coke, to bake a sacke of meale for vs, and to make it bread, paying him for it, which he did, and in the meane time, when the fishermen came with their fishe out of the sea, our maister bought foure Cods of them, which we sod and eate, and while we were at meat, the chiefe of the Russians came vnto vs, and perceiuing that we had not much bread, he fetcht a loafe and gaue it vs, and although we desired them to sit downe and eate some meat with vs, yet we could by no means get them to graunt thereunto, because it was their fasting day, & for y̌ we had poured butter and fat into our fish: nor we could not get them once to drinke with vs, because our cup was somewhat greasie, they were so superstitious touching their fasting, and religion, neither would they lend vs any of their cups to drinke in, least they should likewise be greased at that time the wind was North-west.

The 23. of August, the Coke began to knead our meale, and made vs bread thereof, which being don, and the wind and weather beginning to be somewhat better, we made our selues ready to depart from thence, at which time, when the Russians came from fishing, our maister gaue their chiefe commander a good péece of mony, in regard of the frendship that he had shewed vs, and gaue some what also to the coke, for the which they yéelded vs great thankes, at which time the chiefe of the Russians, desired our maister to giue him some gunpowder which he did, and when we were ready to saile from thence, we put a sacke of meale into the boate, least we should chance to stray one from the other againe, that they might help them selues therewith, and so about euening when the Sunne was West, we set saile and departed from thence, when it began to be high water, & with a North-east wind, held our course North-west along by the land.

The 24. of August, the wind blew East, and then the Sunne being East, we got to the seuen Islands, where we found many fishermen, of whom we enquired after Cool and Kilduin, and they made signes that they lay West from vs, (which we likewise gest to be so, (and withall they shewed vs great frendship, and cast a Cod into our Scute, but for that we had a good gale of wind, we could not stay to pay them for it, but gaue them great thanks, much wondering at there great courtesy, and so with a good gale of

wind

The Nauigation into the North-seas.

wind, we arriued before the seuen Islands, when the Sun was South-west, and past betwen them and the land, and there found certaine fishermen, that rowed to vs, & asked vs where our Crable (meaning our ship) was, whereunto wee made answere with as much Russian Language as we had learned, & said, Crable pro Pal (ẏ is our ship is lost) which they vnderstanding said vnto vs, Cool Brabouse Crable whereby we vnderstood that at Cool there was certaine Neatherland ships, but we made no great account therof because our intent was to saile to VVare-house, fearing least the Russians or great Prince of the country, would stay vs there.

The 25. of August, sailing along by the land with a South-east wind, about the South Sun, we had a sight of Kilduin at whi' time we held our course West North-west, and sailing in t' manner betwene Kilduin and the firme land, about the South South-west Sunne, we got to the West end of Kilduin, and being there lookt if we could see any houses, or people therein, and at last we saw certaine Russian lodgies that lay vpon the strand, and there finding a conuenient place for vs to Anchor with our Scutes, while we went to know if any people were to be found, our maister put in with the land, and there found fiue or sir small houses, wherein the Laplanders dwelt, of whom we asked if that were Kilduin, whereunto they made answere, & shewed vs that it was Kilduin, & said ẏ at Coola there lay thre Brabants Crables or ships, whereof two were that day to set saile, which we hearing determined to saile to Ware-house, and about the West, South-west sunne, put off from thence with a South-east wind : but as we were vnder saile, the wind blew so stiffe, that wee durst not kepe the sea in the night time, for that the waues of the sea went so hollow, that we were still in doubt that they would smite the Scutes to the ground, and so toke our course behind two clifts, towards the land, and when we came there, wee found a small house vpon the shore, wherein there was thre men and a great dogge, which receiued vs very friendly, asking vs of our affaires, and how we got thither, whereunto we made answere, and shewed them that we had lost our ship, and that we were come thither to see if we could get a ship that would bring vs into Holland: whereunto they made vs answere as the other Russians had done,

that

The Nauigation into the North-seas.

that there was thrée ships at Coola, whereof two were to set saile from thence that day, then we asked them if they would goe with one of our men by land to Coola, to looke for a ship, wherewith we might get into Holland, and said we would reward them well for their paines, but they excused themselues and said, that they could not go from thence, but they sayd that they would bring vs ouer the hill, where we should finde certaine Laplanders whom they thought would go with vs, as they did: for the maister and one of our men, going with them ouer the hill, found certaine Laplanders there, whereof they got one to go, with our man, promising him two royals of eight for his pains, and so the Laplander going with him, tooke a péece on his necke, and our man a boatehooke, and about euening they set forward, the windas then being East, and East North-east.

The 26. of August it was faire weather the wind South east, at which time we drew vp both our Scutes vpon the land, and tooke all the goods out of them, to make them the lighter, which done, we went to the Russians and warmed vs, and there dressed such meates as we had, and then againe wée began to make two meales a day, when we perceiued that we should euery day find more people, and we dranke of their drinke which they call Quas, which was made of broken péeces of bread, and it tasted well: for in long time we had drunke nothing else but water: some of our men went further into the land & there found blew berries, and bramble berries, which they plucked and eate, and they did vs much good, for we found that they healed vs of our loosenesse, the wind still blew South-east.

The 27. of August, it was foule weather with a great storm, North, and North North-west, so that in regard that the Strand was low, and as also for that the spring tide was ready to come on, we drew our Scutes a great way vp vpon the land, which hauing done, wee went to the Russians to warme vs by their fire and to dresse our meate: meane time the maister sent one of our men to the sea side to our Scutes, to make a fire for vs vpon the Strand, that when we came we might finde it ready, and that in the meane time the smoake might be gone, and while one of our men was there, and the other was going thither, the water draue so high, that both our Scutes were smitten into the water, and in

great

The Nauigaion into the North-seas.

great danger to be cast away, for in the Scute there was but two men, and three in the boate, who with much labour and paine, could hardly keep the Scutes from being broken vpon the strand, which we seeing, were in great doubt, and yet could not help them, yet God be thanked, he had then brought vs so farre, that neuerthelesse we could haue gotten home, although wee should haue lost our Scutes, as after it was seene. That day, and all night it rained sore, whereby we indured great trouble and miserie, being throughly wet, and could neither couer nor defend our selues frō it, and yet they in the Scutes indured much more, being forced to bee in that weather, and still in daunger to bee cast vpon the shore.

The 28. of August it was indifferent good weather, and then we drew the Scutes vpon the land againe, that we might take the rest of the goods out of them, because the wind still blew hard north, and north-north-west, and hauing drawne the Scutes vp, we spread our sailes vpon them, to shelter vs vnder them, for it was still mistie, and rainie weather, much desiring to heare some newes of our man, that was gone to Cola with the Lapelander, to know if there were any shipping at Coola to bring vs into Holland, and while we laie there we went into the land and fetcht some blew berries and bramble berries to eate, which did vs much good.

The 29. of August it was indifferent faire weather, and we were still in good hope to heare some good newes from Cola, and alwaies looked vp towards the hill to see if our man and the Lapelander came, but seeing they came not, we went to the Russians againe, and there drest our meate, and then ment to goe to our Scutes to lodge in them all night, in the meane time we spied the Laplander cōming alone without our man whereat we wondred, and were somewhat in doubt, but when he came vnto vs, he shewed vs a letter that was writtten vnto our maister, which he opened before vs, the contents thereof being, that he that had written the letter wondred much at our arriuall in that place, and that long since he verily thought that we had beene all cast away, being exceeding glad of our happy fortune, and how that he would presently come vnto vs, with victuales and all other necessaries to succour vs withall, we being in no small admiration

who

The Nauigation into the North-seas.

who it might be, that shewed vs so great fauour and friendship, could not imagine what he was, for it appeared by the letter, that he knew vs well: and although the letter was subscribed, by me Iohn Cornelison Rip, yet we could not be perswaded, that it was the same Iohn Cornelison, who the yeere before had beene set out in the other ship with vs, and left vs about the Beare Iland: for those good newes we paid the Lapelander his hier, and beside that gaue him hoase, breeches and other furniture, so that he was apparelled like a Hollander: for as then we thought our selues to be wholy out of danger, and so being of good comfort, we laid vs downe to rest: Here I cannot chuse but shew you how fast the Lapelander went: for when hee went to Cola, as our companion told vs, they were two dayes and two nights on the way, and yet went apace, and when he came backe againe, he was but a day & a night cōming to vs which was wonderful, it being but halfe ye time, so that we said, & verily thought, that he was halfe a coniurer and he brought vs a partridge which he had killed by the way as he went.

The 30. of August it was indifferent faire weather, we still wondering who that Iohn Cornelison might be that had written vnto vs, and while we sate musing thereon, some of vs were of opinion that it might be the same Iohn Cornelison that had sayled out of Hollād in company with vs, which we could not be perswaded to beleeue, because we were in as little hope of his life as hee of ours, supposing that he had sped worse then we, and long before that had beene cast away, at last the master said, I will looke amongst my letters, for there I haue his name written, and that will put vs out of doubt, & so looking amongst them, we found that it was the same Iohn Cornelison, wherewith we were as glad of his safety & welfare, as he was of ours, and while we were speaking thereof, and that some of vs would not beleeue that it was the same Iohn Cornelison, we saw a Russian Ioll come rowing, with Iohn Cornelison and our companion, that wee had sent to Cola, who being landed, we receiued & welcomed each other, w great ioy & exceeding gladnesse, as if either of vs on both sides had seene each other rise from death to life again: for we esteemed him, & he vs to be dead long since: he brought vs a barrell of Roswicke beere, wine, aqua uite, bread, flesh, bacon, Salmon, suger, and other things

The Nauigation into the North-seas.

things which comforted and releeued vs much, and wee reioyced together for our so vnexpected meeting: at that time giuing God great thankes for his mercy shewed vnto vs.

The 31. of August it was indifferent faire weather, the wind Easterly, but in the euening it began to blow hard from the land, and then we made preparation to saile from thence to Cola, first taking our leaues of the Russians, and heartily thanking them for their curtesie shewed vnto vs, and gaue them a peece of money for their good wils, and at night about the North-sunne we sailed from thence with a high water.

The 1. of September in the morning, with the East sunne, we got to ye west side of the riuer of Cola & entered into it, where we rowed till the flood was past, and then we cast the stones that serued vs for anchors, vpon the ground, at a point of land till the flood came in againe: and when the sunne was south, wee set saile againe with the flood, & so sailed and rowed till midnight, and then we cast anchor againe till morning.

The 2. of September in the morning, we rowed vp the riuer, and as we past along we saw some trees on the riuer side, w comforted vs, and made vs as glad as if we had then come into a new world, for in all the time ye we had béene out, we had not séene any trées, & when we were by the the salt kettles, which is about thrée miles from Cola, we stayed there a while, & made merry, & then went forward againe, and with the West, North-west sun got to Iohn Cornelisons ship, wherein we entred and drunke: there wee began to make merry againe, with the sailers that were therein, and that had béene in the voiage with Iohn Cornelison the yeare before, and bad each other welcome: then we rowed forward, & late in the euening got to Cola, where some of vs went on land, and some stayed in the Scutes to loke to the goods: to whom we sent milke and other things to comfort & refresh them, and we were all excéeding glad that God of his mercy had deliuered vs out of so many dangers and troubles, and had brought vs thither in safety: for as then wee estéemed our selues to be safe: although ye place in times past, lying so far from vs was as much vnknowne vnto vs as if it had béene out of the world, & at that time being there, we thought ye we were almost at home.

The 3. of September we vnladed all our goods & there refreshed

our

The Nauigation into the North-seas.

our selues, after our toylesome and weary iourney, and the great hunger that we had indured, thereby to recouer our healthes and strengthes againe.

The 11. of September, by leaue and consent of the Wayart, gouernour for the great prince of Muscouia, we brought our Scute and our boate into the merchants house, and there let them stand for a remembrance of our long farre (& neuer before sailed way and that we had sailed in those open Scutes, almost 400. Dutch miles, through and along by the sea coasts to the towne of Coola, whereat the inhabitants thereof could not sufficiently wonder.

The 15. of Sep. we went in a Lodgie, wall our goods & our men to Iohn Cornelisons ship, which lay about halfe a mile from the towne, and that day sailed in the ship downe the riuer til we were beyond the narrowest part thereof which was about half the riuer, and there staied for Iohn Cornelison, and our Maister, that said they would come to vs the next day

The 17. of September Iohn Cornelison, and our Maister be being come abord, the next day about the East Sunne, we set saile out of the riuer Coola, & with GODS grace put to sea, to saile hom-wards, and being out of the riuer we sailed along by the land North-west, and by North, the wind being South.

The 19. of September, about the South Sunne, we got to Ware-house, and there ankored, and went on land, because Iohn Cornelison, was there to take in more goods, and staid there til the first of October, in the which time we had a hard wind out of the North and North west, & while we stayed there, we refreshed our selues somewhat better, to recouer our sicknesse and weaknesse againe, that we might grow stronger, which asked sometime, for we were much spent and exceeding weake.

The 6. of October, about euening, the Sunne being South-west, we set saile, and with GODS grace from VVare-house, for Holland, but for that it is a common and well knowne way, I will speake nothing thereof, only that vpon the 29. October, we ariued in the Mase, with an East north-east wind, & the next morning got to Masclandsluce, and there going on land, from thence rowed to Delfe, and then to the Hage, and from thence to Harlem, & vpon the first of Nouember about noone, got to Amsterdam, in the same clothes that we ware in Noua Zembla, with our caps

furd

The Nauigation into the North-seas.

furd with white Foxes skins, and went to the house of Peter Hasselaer, that was one of the marchants, that set out the two ships, which were conducted by Iohn Cornelison, and our Maister, and being there, where many men wondered to see vs, as hauing esteemed vs long before that to haue bin dead and rotten, the newes thereof being spread abroad in the towne, it was also caried to the Princes courte in the Hage, at which time the Lord Chancelor of Denmark, Ambassador for the said King, was then at dinner with Prince Maurice: for the which cause we were presently fetcht thither by the Scout, and two of the Burgers of the towne and there in the presence of those Ambassadors, and the Burger masters, we made rehearsall of our Journey both forwards and backewards, and after that euery man that dwelt thereabouts went home but such as dwelt not neere to that place, were placed in good lodgings for certaine daies, vntill we had receiued our pay, and then euery one of vs departed, and went to the place of his aboad.

The names of those that came home againe from this dangerous voiage, were.

Iacob Hemstreck Maister and Factor.
Peter Peterson Vos.
Geret de Veer.
Maister Hans Vos, Surgion.
Iacob Iohnson, Sterenburg.
Lenard Hendrickson.
Laurence VVilliamson.
Iohn Hilbrantson.
Iacob Iohnson hooghwont.
Peter Cornelison.
Iohn Vous Buysen.
and Iacob Euartsen.

FINIS.

The Hakluyt Society edition

London, 1876

THE
True and perfect De-
scription of three Voy-

ages, so strange and woonderfull,

that the like hath neuer been

heard of before:

Done and performed three yeares, one after the other, by the Ships
of *Holland* and *Zeland*, on the North sides of *Norway, Muscouia,* and
Tartaria, towards the Kingdomes of *Cathaia* & *China;* shewing
the discouerie of the Straights of *Weigates, Noua Zembla,*
and the Countrie lying vnder 80. degrees ; which is
thought to be *Greenland:* where neuer any man had
bin before : with the cruell Beares, and other
Monsters of the Sea, and the vnsupportable and extreame cold that is
found to be in those
places.

And how that in the last Voyage, the Shippe was so inclosed by
the Ice, that it was left there, whereby the men were forced to build a
house in the cold and desart Countrie of *Noua Zembla,* wherin
they continued 10. monthes togeather, and neuer saw nor
heard of any man, in most great cold and extreame
miserie ; and how after that, to saue their liues, they
were constrained to sayle aboue 350. Duch
miles, which is aboue 1000. miles English,
in litle open Boates, along and ouer the
maine Seas, in most great daunger,
and with extreame labour, vnspeakable troubles, and
great hunger.

Imprinted at London for *T. Pauier.*
1609.

TO THE RIGHT WOR-
shipfull, Sir *Thomas Smith* Knight, Gouer-
nour of the *Muscouy* Company, &c.

RIGHT WORSHIPFVLL: Being intreated by some of my Friends, and principally by M. Richard Hakluyt (a diligent obseruer of all Proceedings in this nature) to Translate and publish these three yeares Trauelles and Discoueries of the Hollanders to the North-east; I could not deuise how to consecrate my Labours so properly to any, as to your selfe, considering not onely the generall good affection the whole Kingdome takes notice, that you beare to all Honorable actions of this kinde, be they for Discouerie, Traffique, or Plantation; but also in respect of that particular charge, most worthily recommended to your care, ouer the Trade of the English in those Northeast Partes.

Many attempts and proffers (I confesse) there haue bin to find a passage by those poorest parts to the richest; by those barbarous, to the most ciuile; those vnpeopled, to the most popular; those Desarts, to the most fertile Countries of the World: and of them all, none (I dare say) vndertaken with greater iudgement, with more obdurate Patience, euen *aduersus Elementa, aduersus ipsam in illis locis rerum naturam*, then these three by the Hollanders.

If any of our Nation be employed that way in time to come, here they haue a great part of their Voiage layd open, and the example of that industrious people (first excited to this and other famous Voyages, by imitation of some of ours) for the conquering of all difficulties and dangers; those people (I say) that of all Christians, and for aught I know, of all Adams Posteritie, haue first nauigated to 81 Degrees of Northerly Latitude, and wintered in 76, where they had no Inhabitants, but Foxes, Beares, and Deare, to keepe them company.

And were it for nothing else, but to register the miraculous prouidence of the Creator, and his admirable and vnspeakable workes in these congealed Climats, vnknowen vtterly to the Ancients, and to demonstrate how much we are obliged to his omnipotent fauour, for planting vs in so temperate, so ciuill, and so Religious a part of the World, as this blessed Island; I thinke omission in this kinde were little lesse than Sacriledge.

As it is, I humbly desire you to vouch-safe it your protection, and to esteeme mee,

Alwayes deuoted to your seruice,

WILLIAM PHILLIP.

THE FYRST PART

OF THE

NAUIGATION INTO THE NORTH SEAS.

It is a most certaine and an assured assertion, that nothing doth more benefit and further the common-wealth (specially these countries[1]) then the art and knowledge of nauigation, in regard that such countries and nations as are strong and mightie at sea, haue the meanes and ready way to draw, fetch, and bring vnto them for their maintenaunce, all the principalest commodities and fruites of the earth, for that thereby they are inabled to bring all necessary things for the nourishment and sustentation of man from the vttermost partes of the world, and to carry and conuay such wares and marchendizes whereof they haue great store and aboundance vnto the same places, which by reason of the art of nauigation, and the commodities of the sea, is easily to be effected and brought to passe. Which nauigation as it dayly more and more increaseth (to the great woonder and admiration of those, that compare the sea-faring and nauigation vsed in our forefathers times, yea and that also that hath beene practised in our age, with that which now at this present is daily furthered and sought out), so there are continually new

As the art of nauigation more increaseth, so there are daily more new countries found out.

[1] Namely, the United Provinces of the Netherlands.

voiages made, and strange coasts discouered; the which although they be not done by the first, secōd, or third voiage, but after, by tract of time, first brought to their full effect, and desired commoditie, and the fruits thereof, by continuance of time reaped. Yet we must not be abasht, nor dismayed, at the labour, toile, trauaile, and dāgers sustayned in such uoiages, to that end made, although as I said before the benefit thereof be not had nor seene in the first, second, third, or more uoiages; for what labour is more profitable, and worthier praise and commendation, then that which tendeth vnto the common good and benefit of all men; Although such as are vnskilfull, contemners, and deriders of mens diligence and proceedings therein, at the first esteeme it an vnprofitable and needlesse thing, when as the end prooueth beneficiall and commodious. If the famous nauigators Cortesius, Nonius, and Megalanes,[1] and others, that in their times sought out and discovered the kingdomes, countries, and ilands farre distant from vs, in the extreamest parts of the world, for the first, second, or third voyage, that had succeeded vnfortunately with them, had left off and giuen ouer their nauigatiō, they had not afterward reaped nor enioyed the fruites, benefits, and commodities thereof. Alexander magnus (after he had woone all Grecia, and from thence entred into little and great Asia, and comming to the farthest parts of India, there found some difficultie to passe) sayd, If we had not gone forward, and persisted in our intent, which other men esteemed and held to be impossible, we had still remayned and stayed in the entry of Cilicia,[2] where as now we haue ouerrunne and past through all those large and spacious countries: for nothing is found and effected

Diligence and continuance effect that which is sought

We must not leaue of by some mens dislike or dispraise in our proceedings.

A thing not continued, can not be effected.

All things are effected in convenient time.

---

[1] The Amsterdam Latin version of 1598 has "*Columbus*, Cortesius, et Magellanus". But the emendation is unnecessary, since the author evidently intends Vasco Nuñez de Balboa, the discoverer of the Pacific.

[2] "Cicilia", in the English original, can only be an error of the press.

all at one time, neither is any thing that is put in practise, presently brought to an end. To the which end, Cicero wisely saith, God hath giuen vs some things, and not all things, that our successours also might have somewhat to doe. Therefore we must not leaue off, nor stay our pretence in the middle of our proceedings, as long as there is any commoditie to be hoped, and in time to be obtayned: for that the greatest and richest treasures are hardliest to be found. But to make no long digression from our matter, concerning the dayly furtheraunce of the most necessarie and profitable art of nauigation, that hath been brought to full effect, not without great charges, labour, and paines; ouerslipping and not shewing with how long and troublesome labour and toyle, continually had, the passages to the East and West Indies, America, Brasilia, and other places, through the straight of Magellanes, in the South Sea, twise or thrise passing vnder the Line,[1] and by those meanes other countries and ilands, were first found out and discouered.

Let vs looke into the White Seas,[2] that are now so commonly sayled (on the north side of Muscouia), with what cumbersome labour and toyle they were first discouered: What hath now made this voyage so common and easie? is it not the same, and as long a voyage as it was, before it was fully knowne and found out? I,[3] but the right courses, which at the first were to be sought, by crossing the seas from one land to another, and are now to be held aloofe

That which in the beginning is hard, by continuance of time is made easie and light.

---

[1] *Deur ende weer deur de Linie*—passing and repassing the Line.

[2] *De witte Zee*—the White Sea.

[3] The adverb of affirmation, now written *ay*. A striking instance of its use occurs in *Romeo and Juliet*:—

> "Hath Romeo slaine himself? say thou but I,
> And that bare vowell I shall poyson more
> Than the death-darting eye of Cockatrice;
> I am not I, if there be such an I."

into the seas and directly sayled, hath, of difficult and toylesome, made them easie and ready voyages.

This small discourse I thought good to set downe, for an introduction vnto the reader, in regard that I haue vndertaken to describe the three voyages made into the North Seas, in three yeares, one after the other, behind Norway, and along and about Muscouia, towardes the kingdome of Cathaia and China: whereof the two last I myself holpe to effect;[1] and yet brought them not to the desired end that we well hoped.

<small>The first finding is hard, but the second attempt is easier.</small>

First, to shew our diligent and most toylesome labour and paynes taken, to find out the right course; which we could not bring to passe, as we well hoped, wished, and desired, and possible might haue found it, by crossing the seas, if we had taken the right course; if the ice and the shortnesse of time, and bad crosses had not hindered vs: and also to stoppe their mouthes, that report and say, that our proceeding therein was wholly vnprofitable and fruitelesse; which peraduenture in time to come, may turne vnto our great profite and commoditie. For he which proceedeth and continueth in a thing that seemeth to be impossible, is not to be discommended: but hee, that in regarde that the thing seemeth to be impossible, doth not proceed therein, but by his faint heartedness and sloath, wholly leaueth it off.

<small>Not the nearness of the North Pole, but the Ice in the Tartarian sea, causeth the greatest cold.</small>

Wee haue assuredly found, that the onely and most hinderaunce to our voyage, was the ice, that we found about Noua Zembla,[2] vnder 73, 74, 75, and 76 degrees; and not so much vpon the sea betweene both the landes:[3] whereby

---

[1] Thus it appears that Gerrit de Veer was not on the *first* voyage, as has been supposed by some writers.

[2] By the Russians called *Nóvaya Zémlya*, i.e., "the New Land".

[3] Namely, between Nóvaya Zémlya and Spitzbergen, which latter was, by Barentsz and his companions, thought to be a part of Greenland.

it appeareth, that not the nearenesse of the North Pole, but the ice that commeth in and out from the Tartarian Sea,[1] about Noua Zembla, caused vs to feele the greatest cold. Therefore in regard that the nearenesse of the Pole was not the cause of the great cold that we felt, if we had had the meanes to haue held our appoynted and intended course into the north-east, we had peraduenture found some enteraunce: which course we could not hold from Noua Zembla, because that there we entred amongst great store of ice; and how it was about Noua Zembla, we could not tell, before we had sought it; and when we had sought it, we could not then alter our course, although also it is vncertaine, what we should have done, if we had continued in our north-east course, because it is not yet found out. But it is true, that in the countrie lying vnder 80 degrees,[2] (which we esteeme to be Greenland) there is both leaues and grasse to be seene; wherein, such beastes as feed of leaues and grasse, (as hartes, hindes, and such like beastes) liue: whereas to the contrary in Noua Zembla, there groweth nether leaues nor grasse, and there are no beastes therein but such as eate flesh,[3] as beares, and foxes, &c.; although Noua Zembla lyeth 4, 5, and 6 degrees more southerly from the Pole, then the other land aforesaid. It is also manifest, that vpon the south and north side of the line of the sunne on both sides, between both the tropicos, vnder 23 degrees and a halfe, it is as hot as it is right vnder the Line. What

Comparison of the heate under the line, with the cold under the North Pole.

---

[1] The Sea of Kara, east of Nóvaya Zémlya.

[2] This country, which was discovered by the Hollanders on their third voyage, has since proved to be Spitzbergen.

[3] The same is repeated by Sir John Barrow (*Chronological History of Voyages, etc.*, pp. 148, 185), who questions the fact asserted by Hudson, of his having seen reindeer in the island. But Lütke expressly declares (*Viermalige Reise, etc.*, Erman's *Translation*, pp. 43, 75, 314, 359), that these animals do exist in Nóvaya Zémlya, even beyond the 74th parallel of north latitude. See also Baer, in Berghaus's *Annalen*. vol. xvii, p. 300; vol. xviii, p. 25.

wonder then should it be, that about the North Pole also, and as many degrees on both sides, it should not bee colder then right vnder the Pole? I will not affirme this to bee true, because that the colde on both sides of the North Pole hath not as yet beene discouered and sought out, as the heat on the north and south side of the Line hath beene. Onely thus much I will say, that although we held not our direct pretended[1] course to the north-east, that therefore it is to be iudged, that the cold would haue let our passage through that way, for it was not the sea, nor the neerenesse vnto the Pole, but the ice about the land, that let and hindered vs (as I sayd before) for that as soon as we made from the land, and put more into the sea, although it was much *The resolute intent and opinions of William Barents.* further northward, presently we felt more warmth; and in yt opinion our pilote William Barents[2] dyed, who notwithstanding the fearful and intollerable cold that he endured, yet he was not discouraged, but offered to lay wagers with diuers of us, that by Gods helpe he would bring that pretended voiage to an end, if he held his course north-east from the North Cape. But I will leaue that, and shewe you of the three voyages aforesaid, begun and set forth by the permission and furtherance of the generall States of the vnited Prouinces, and of Prince Maurice, as admirall of the sea, and the rich towne of Amsterdam. Whereby the reader may iudge and conceaue what is to bee done, for the most profite and advantage, and what is to be left.

First you must understand, that in anno 1594 there was 4 ships set foorth out of the vnited Prouinces, whereof two were of Amsterdam, one of Zelandt, one of Enckhuysen, that were appointed to saile into the North Seas, to discouer the kingdomes of Cathaia, and China, north-ward from

[1] Intended.
[2] As is shown in the Introduction, the proper name of this able navigator is Willem Barentszoon, that is, William, the son of Barent or Bernard; which name, as usually contracted, was written Barentsz.

Norway, Muscouia, and about Tartaria; whereof William Barents, a notable skilfull and wise pilote, was commander ouer the ships of Amsterdam, and with them vpon Whit-sunday[1] departed from Amsterdam and went to the Texel.

Upon the fifth of June they sailed out of the Texel, and hauing a good wind and faire weather, vpon the 23 of June, they arrived at Kilduin in Muscouia,[2] which for that it is a place well knowen and a common voyage, I will make no further discription thereof.

The 29 of June, at foure of the clocke in the after noone, they set saile out of Kilduin, and so 13 [52] or 14 [56] miles[3] out-right sailed north-east, with a north north-west wind, and close weather.

The 30 of June they sayled east north-east 7 [28] miles, till the sunne was east south-east [about half-past six o'clock in the morning],[4] with a north wind, with 2 schower sailes,[5]

[1] May 29th, 1594.

[2] The island of Kildin, on the coast of Russian Lapland, in 69° 18' north latitude, and 34° 20' longitude east of Greenwich.

[3] Dutch or German miles of fifteen to the degree; so that one such mile is equal to four English sea miles, or geographical miles of sixty to the degree. To assist the reader, who might not always have this in mind, the English miles will throughout be inserted between brackets.

[4] A rude way of determining the time by the bearing of the sun, customary among seamen of all nations in those days, for want of portable time-pieces. Were the precise azimuth of the sun observed, no method could be more exact; but as no interval between the several points of the compass (which are 11° 15' apart) is taken into account, and as the sun's bearing is also subject to the variation of the compass, the result must be only approximative. From the compass-bearing alone, as recorded, it would be difficult for the reader to form anything like a correct idea of the actual time—for example, when, on the 30th of June, the sun was observed to be full south, it wanted more than an hour-and-a-quarter of mid-day. It is, therefore, deemed advisable to insert, after each observation of time by the sun, the time by the clock to the nearest quarter of an hour.

[5] *Schoverseylen*—the courses, or sails on the lower masts.

there they cast out their lead, at 100 fadome deepth, but found no ground.

From whence the same day they sailed east north-east[1] 5 [20] miles, till the sunne was full south [¾ past 10, A.M.], hauing the wind north, with 2 schower sailes, where once againe they cast out the lead 100 fadome deepe, but found no ground; and then from noone to night[2] the same day, they sailed east, and east and by north 13 [52] miles, till the sunne was north-west [¼ past 7, P.M.], and there casting out their lead, they had ground at 120 fadome, the ground being oasie,[3] and blacke durt.

The 1 of July, after they had sailed one quarter[4] 4 [16] miles east, and east and by north, early in the morning they cast out the lead, and found ground at 60 fadome, where they had an oasie small sandy ground; and within an houre after they cast out the lead againe, and had ground at 52 fadome, being white sande mixed with blacke, and some-what oasie: after that they had sailed 3 [12] miles east and by north, where they had ground at 40 fadome, being gray sand mixed with white. From thence they sailed 2 [8] miles east-ward, with a north north-east winde, there they had ground at 38 fadome, being red sand mixed with black, the sunne being south-east and by east [¼ past 7, A.M.]. From thence they sailed 3 [12] miles, east and by south, and east south-east til noone, where they had the sunne at 70 degrees and ¾,[5] there they cast out the lead againe, and had ground at 39 fadome, being small gray sand, mixed with blacke stippellen[6] and pieces of shels.

Then againe they sailed 2 [8] miles south-east, and then

[1] *O. ten n.*—east by north. [2] *Tots avonds*—till the evening.
[3] Oozy, muddy.
[4] *Een quartier*—one watch; the duration of which was, as usual, four hours.
[5] *I.e.*, they found themselves to be in 70° 45′ north latitude, by means of an observation of the sun.
[6] Small black specks.

woond[1] northward with an east north-east wind, and after sailed 6 [24] miles north-east all that day,[2] with a south-east wind, till the sunne was north north-west [¼ past 9 P.M.], the weather being cold; and the lead being cast foorth they found ground at 60 fadome, being small gray oasie sand, mixed with a little blacke, and great whole shels:[3] after that the same euening to the first quarter,[4] they sailed 5 [20] miles, east north-east, and north-east and by east, and after that east north-east, and north-east and by east 5 [20] miles, vntill the second of July in the morning, and there they had 65 fadome deepe, the ground oasie with black slime or durt.

The same day from morning till noone, they sailed 3 [12] or 4 [16] miles east north-east, the wind blowing stiffe south-east, whereby at noone they were forced to take[5] in the fore-saile, and driue with a schower saile,[6] in mistie weather, for the space of 3 [12] or 4 [16] miles, vntill euening, holding east, and east and by south: after that the winde blew south-west, and about 5 of the clocke in the after-noone, they cast out the lead, but had no ground at 120 fadome. That euening the weather cleared vp againe, and they sailed about 5 [20] miles before the wind, east north-east, for the space of 3 houres, and then againe it began to be mistie, so that they durst not saile forward, but lay hulling in the wind,[7] where vpon Sunday morning being the 3 of July, when the sunne was north-east [½ p. 1, A.M.], they cast out the lead and found ground at 125 fadome, being black durt or slime.

From thence they sailed 8 [32] miles east north-east, till

---

[1] *Wendense weder noordwaert over*—they again tacked to the north. Phillip uses throughout the expression "to wind" in the sense of "to tack".   [2] *Van deeldagh af*—from noon.
[3] *Groote holle schulpen*—large hollow shells.
[4] The first watch, beginning at 8 o'clock P.M.
[5] "Table."—*Ph.* Evidently a misprint.
[6] *Een schover zeyl*—one course, namely, the main-sail.
[7] *Wierpent aen de wint*—they hauled close to the wind.

the sunne was south-east [½ p. 7, A.M.], and casting out the lead, found ground at 140 fadom, being blacke slimie durt, at which time they tooke the high of the sun and found it to be 73 degrees and 6 minutes, and presently againe they cast out the lead, and had 130 fadome deepth, the ground being blacke slime. After that they sayled 6 [24] or 7 [28] miles further east north-east, till the sunne was north-west [½ p. 7, P.M.].

On Sunday in the morning, being the 3 of July, it was very faire and cleare weather, the wind blowing south-west, at which time William Barents found out the right meridien, taking the high of the sunne with his crosse-staffe,[1] when it was south-east, and found it to be eleuated in the south-east 28 degrees and a halfe, and when it had passed ouer west and by north, it was but[2] 28 degrees and a half aboue the horizon, so that it differed 5 points and a half, which being deuided there rested 2 points and ¾; so that their compasse was altered 2 points and ¾, as it appeared the same day, when the sunne was in her higth, betweene south south-west and south-west and by south, for the sun was south-west and by south, and yet was not declined, and they had 73 degrees and 6 minutes.

[1] *Graedt-boogh*—rendered *Radius astronomicus* in the Amsterdam Latin version of 1598, and *Ray nautique* in the French version of the same year and place—Cross-staff, Jacob's-staff, or fore-staff; a well known instrument, no longer in use among European navigators. But the Arab seamen on the east coast of Africa still employ a primitive instrument, which is essentially the same. It consists of a small quadrangular board, through which a string, knotted at various distances, is passed; each knot being at such a distance from the board, that when the latter is held by the observer before him, with the knot between his teeth and the string extended, the board (between its upper and lower edges) shall subtend the angle at which the pole-star is known to be elevated above the horizon at some one of the ports frequented by the observer. Inartificial as such an instrument may be, yet if, instead of a knotted string, a notched stick were used, on which the board might slide backwards and forwards, it would be the cross-staff of our early navigators.

[2] *Noch* (now spelt *nog*)—again.

The 4 of July in the morning, they sailed 4 [16] miles east and by north, and casting out the lead found ground at 125 fadome, being slimie. That night the weather was mistie againe, and in the morning the wind was east; then they sailed 4 [16] miles south-east and by south, till the sunne was east [½ p. 4, A.M.], and then againe they cast out the lead, and found ground at 108 fadome, black durt; then they wound north-ward, and sailed 6 [24] miles, north north-east, and north-east and by north, vntill the sunne was south south-west [¾ p. 11, A.M.], and then they saw the land of Noua Zembla, lying south-east and by east 6 [24] or 7 [28] miles from them, where they had black durty ground at 105 fadome. Then they woond southward againe, and sailed 6 [24] miles, south and by west, till the sunne was west north-west [5, P.M.], there they had 68 fadome deepe, with durtie ground as before, the wind being south-east.

Then they woond east-ward and sailed 6 [24] miles east and by south, at which time,[1] William Barents took the height of the sunne with his crosse-staffe,[2] when it was at the lowest, that is between north north-east and east and by north,[3] and found it to bee eleuated aboue the horizon 6 degrees and ⅓ part, his declination being 22 degrees and 55 minutes, from whence substracting the aforesaid heigth, there resteth 16 degrees and 35 minutes, which being substracted from 90 degrees, there resteth 73 degrees and 25 minutes; which was when they were about 5 [20] or 6 [24] miles from the land of Noua Zembla.

Then they woond east-ward and sailed 5 [20] miles, east and by south, and east south-east, and past by a long point of land that lay out into the sea,[4] which they named Langenes:

[1] *Den 4 Julij des nachts*—on the 4th of July, at night.

[2] *Graed-boogh.* See the preceding page, note 1.

[3] So in the original. But the sense requires "*north*-east and by north", that being the next point to N.N.E.

[4] *Een laghe uytstekenden hoeck*—a *low* projecting point. Through some misconception, Phillip repeatedly has "long" for "low".

and hard by that point east-ward there was a great bay, where they went a land with their boate, but found no people.

Three [12] or foure [16] miles from Langenes east north-east, there lay a long[1] point, and a mile [4 miles] east-ward from the said point there was a great bay, and upon the east side of the said bay, there lay a rock not very high aboue the water, and on the west side of the bay, there stood a sharpe little hill, easie to be knowne: before the bay it was 20 fadome deepth, the ground small blacke stones, like pease: from Langenes to Cape Bapo[2] east north-east it is 4 [16] miles.

From Cape Bapo to the west point of Lombsbay north-east and by north are 5 [20] miles, and betweene them both there are 2 creekes. Lombsbay is a great wide bay, on the west side thereof hauing a faire hauen 6, 7, or 8, fadome deepe, black sand: there they went on shore with their boate, and vpon the shore placed a beacon, made of an old mast which they found there; calling the bay Lombsbay, because of a certaine kind of beares[3] so called, which they found there in great aboundance.

The east point of Lombsbay is a long narrow point, and by it there lyeth an island, and from that long point to sea-

---

[1] *Laghe*—low.

[2] *Capo Baxo*—Low Point. From the long connection of the Netherlands with Spain, the Dutch navigators appear to have employed the Spanish language for trivial names like "Low Point", "Black Point", as being more distinctive than the vernacular.

[3] *Eenderley aert van voghelen*—a certain kind of *birds*. This strange mistake of the translator has given occasion to frequent comment. It is the more unaccountable, as the original work contains a pictorial representation of these birds,—*noordtsche papegagen*, or northern parrots, as they are there called,—in connection with the plan of Lomsbay; and it is also expressly stated, that the bay "has its name from the birds which dwell there in great numbers. They are large in the body and small in the wing, so that it is surprising how their little wings can carry their heavy bodies. They have their nests on steep rocks,

ward in, there is a great creeke.[1] This Lombsbay lyeth vnder 74 degrees and ⅓ part. From Lombsbay to the point of the Admirals Island,[2] they sailed 6 [24] or 7 [28] miles, north-east and by north. The Admirals Island is not very faire on[3] the east side, but a farre off very flat, so that you must shunne it long before you come at it; it is also very vneuen, for at one casting off the lead they had 10 fadome deepe, and presently at another casting of the lead they had but 6 fadome, and presently after that againe 10, 11, and 12 fadome, the streame running hard against the flats.

From the east end of the Admirals Island, to Cape Negro,[4] that is the Black Pointe, they sailed about 5 [20] or 6 [24] miles, east north-east; and a mile [4 miles] without the Black Point it is 70 fadome deepe, the ground slimie, as vpon Pamphius:[5] right eastward of the Blacke Point, there

in order to be secure from animals, and they sit on only one egg at a time. They were not afraid of us; and when we climbed up to any of their nests, the others round about did not fly away."

The bird in question is the Brunnich's Guillemot. *(Alca Arra.)* It is described and figured in the fifth volume of Gould's *Birds of Europe*, and in Yarrell's *British Birds*.

An assemblage of these birds, such as is here described by the author, "is called by the Russians a 'bazar'. Thus this Persian word has been carried by Russian walrus-hunters to the rocks of the icy sea, and there for want of human inhabitants applied to birds."—Baer, in Berghaus's *Annalen*, vol. xviii, p. 23.

[1] *Een laeghen slechten hoeck, ende daer leyt een cleijn Eylandeken by, van den hoeck af zeewaerts in, so was noch by oosten dien laeghen hoeck een groote wyde voert ofte inwijck*—A *low flat* point, and by it there lyeth a *small* island seawards from the point, and *also to the east of this low point* there is a great wide creek or inlet.

[2] *Het Admiraliteyts Eyland*—Admiralty Island.

[3] "One."—*Ph.*

[4] *Capo Negro.*

[5] Usually written *Pampus*. A bar of mud and sand near Amsterdam, at the junction of the Y with the Zuyder Zee. This simile calls to mind that of Mungo Park, who, on his discovery of the Niger, described it as being "as broad as the Thames at Westminster". Such homely comparisons, though by some they may be condemned as unscientific, often

are 2 sharpe pointed hills in the creeke, that are easie to be knowen.

The 6 of July, the sunne being north [½ p. 10, P.M.], they came right before the Blacke Point with faire weather: this Blacke Point lyeth vnder 75 degrees and 20 minutes. From the Placke Point to Williams Island,[1] they sailed 7 [28] or 8 [32] miles, east north-east, and between them both about halfe a mile, [2 miles] there lay a small island.

The 7 of July they sailed from Williams Island, and then William Barents tooke the height of the sunne with his crosse-staffe,[2] and found it to be eleuated aboue the horizon[3] in the south-west and by south 53 degrees and 6 minutes,[4] his declination being 22 degrees and 49 minutes, which being added to 53 degrees and 6 minutes, make 75 degrees and 55 minutes.[5] This is the right height of the pole of the said island. In this island they found great store of driff-wood, and many sea-horses, being a kinde of fish[6] that keepeth in the sea, having very great teeth, which at this day are vsed insteed of iuorie or elephants teeth: there also is a good road for ships, at 12 and 13 fadome deep, against all winds, except it be west south-west and west windes; and there they found a piece of a Russian ship,[7] and that day they had the wind east north-east, mistie weather.

---

speak more distinctly to the feelings of such as can appreciate them than the most elaborate descriptions.

[1] *Willems Eyland.*

[2] *Met zijn groote quadrant*—With his large quadrant.

[3] This is not correctly stated, since it is the sun's zenith distance, and not its elevation above the horizon, that was 53° 5'. The observation is, however, correctly worked out, subject only to the trifling error of 1'.

[4] The original has 53° 5' both here and two lines lower down. There is consequently an error of 1' in the calculation. The correction should be made on the result, instead of on the observation itself.

[5] So in the original; but it should be 75° 56'.

[6] *Een ghedierte*—an animal.

[7] A proof, among many others, that the west coast of Nóvaya Zémlya had previously been visited by the Russians.

The 9 of July they entered into Beeren-fort,[1] vpon the road vnder Williams Island, and there they found a white beare, which they perceiuing, presently entered into their boate, and shot her into the body with a musket; but the beare shewed most wonderfull strength, which almost is not to be found in any beast, for no man euer heard the like to be done by any lyon or cruel beast whatsoeuer: for notwithstanding that she was shot into the bodie, yet she leapt vp, and swame in the water, the men that were in the boate rowing after her, cast a rope about her necke, and by that meanes drew her at the sterne of the boat, for that not hauing seene the like beare before, they thought to haue carryed her aliue in the shippe, and to have shewed her for a strange wonder in Holland; but she vsed such force, that they were glad that they were rid of her, and contented themselves with her skin only, for she made such a noyse, and stroue in such sort, that it was admirable, wherewith they let her rest and gave her more scope with the rope that they held by her, and so drew her in that sort after them, by that meanes to wearie her: meane time, William Barents made neerer to her,[2] but the beare swome to the boate, and with her fore-feet got hold of the sterne thereof, which William Barents perceiuing, said, She will there rest her selfe; but she had another meaning, for she vsed such force, that at last she had gotten half her body into the boat, wherewith the men were so abashed, that they run into ye further end of the boate, and thought verily to have been spoiled by her, but by a strange means they were deliuered from her, for that the rope that was about her necke, caught hold vpon the hooke of the ruther, whereby the beare could get no further, but

[1] *Berenfort*—Bear Creek. It might be better written *Beren-voert;* as the word *voert*—which is apparently either the Danish *fiord*, or else the old form of the modern Dutch *vaart*—is used by the author (see page 13, note 1) as equivalent to *inwijck*, a creek or inlet.

[2] *Palde hem altemet wat aen*—poked him now and then (with the boat-hook).

so was held backe, and hanging in that manner, one of the men boldly stept foorth from the end of the scute,[1] and thrust her into the bodie with a halfe-pike; and therewith she fell downe into the water, and so they rowed forward with her to the ship, drawing her after them, till she was in a manner dead, wherewith they killed her out-right, and hauing fleaed her, brought the skinne to Amsterdam.

The 10 of July,[2] they sailed out of Beren-fort fro Williams Island, and the same day in the morning got to the Island of Crosses,[3] and there went on land with their pinnace, and found the island to bee barren, and full of cliffes and rocks, in it there was a small hauen, whereinto they rowed with their boat. This island is about halfe a mile [2 miles] long, and reacheth east and west; on the west end it hath a banke, about a third part of a mile [1⅓ mile] long, and at the east end also another banke: vpon this island there standeth 2 great crosses; the island lyeth about 2 [8] long miles from the firme land,[4] and vnder the east-end thereof there is good road at 26 fadome, soft ground;[5] and somewhat closer to the island on the strand, at 9 fadome, sandy ground.

From the Island of Crosses to the point of Cape Nassawe,[6] they sailed east, and east and by north, about 8 [32] miles: it is a long[7] flat point which you must be carefull to shunne, for thereabouts at 7 fadome there were flats or sholes, very farre from the land: it lyeth almost under 76 degrees and a halfe. From the west end of Williams Island to the Island with the Crosses is 3 [12] miles, the course north.[8]

From Nassaw Point they sailed east and by south, and

[1] *Van de voorschuyt*—from the fore-part of the boat.
[2] "20 of July."—*Ph.*
[3] *Het Eylandt mette Cruycen*—the Island with the Crosses.
[4] The mainland of Nóvaya Zémlya.
[5] *Steeck gront*—stiff ground.
[6] *Tot den Hoeck van Nassowen*—to Cape Nassau.
[7] *Laghe*—low. [8] *Noordt-oost*—north-east.

east south-east 5 [20] miles, and then they thought that they saw land in north-east and by east,[1] and sailed towards it 5 [20] miles north-east to discrie it, thinking it to be another land, that lay northward from Noua Zembla; but it began to blow so hard out of the west, that they were forced to take in their marsaile,[2] and yet the wind rose in such manner, that they were forced to take in all their sailes, and the sea went so hollow, that they were constrained to driue 16 houres together without saile, 8 [32] or 9 [36] miles east north-east.

The 11 of July their boat was by a great wave of the sea sunke to the ground, and by that meanes they lost it, and after that they drave without sailes 5 [20] miles, east and by south; at last, the sunne being almost south-east [½ p. 7, A.M.], the wind came about to the north-west, and then the weather began somewhat to clear up, but yet it was very mistie. Then they hoysed vp their sailes againe and sailed 4 [16] miles till night, that the sunne was north and by east [11, P.M.], and there they had 60 fadome deepth, muddie ground, and there they saw certaine flakes of ice,[3] at which time vpon the 12 of July they woond west, and held north-west, and sailed about a mile [4 miles] with mistie weather, and a north-west wind, and sailed up and downe west south-west 3 [12] or 4 [16] miles to see if they could find their boat againe: after that they wound againe with the wind,[4] and sayled 4 [16] miles south-east, till the sunne was south-

---

[1] "The existence of the land said to have been seen by the Hollanders to the eastward of Cape Nassau is exceedingly doubtful. They themselves make but slight mention of it, and not at all on the second (third) voyage. Perhaps they saw some projecting point of the land of Novaya Zemlya; or yet more probably they mistook a fog-bank for land."—Lütke, p. 21.

[2] *Marscylen*—topsails.

[3] *Eenighe ys schollen*—some pieces of drift ice.

[4] *Wenden zijt weder aen de wint*—they again hauled close to the wind.

west [1, P.M.], and then they were close by the land of Noua Zembla, that lay east and by north, and west and by south; from thence they wound ouer againe till noone, and sayled 3 [12] miles north and by west; and then, till the sunne was north-west [¾ p. 6, P.M.], they held north-west and by north 3 [12] miles; then they wound east-ward and sailed 4 [16] or 5 [20] miles north-east and by east.

The 13 of July at night, they found great store of ice, as much as they could descrie out of the top, that lay as if it had been a plaine field of ice;[1] then they wound west-ward ouer from the ice, and sailed about 4 [16] miles west south-west, till the sunne was east and by north [5 A.M.], and that they saw the land of Noua Zembla, lying south south-east from them.

Then they wound north-ward againe and sailed 2 [8] miles, till the sunne was east south-east [½ p. 6, A.M.], and then againe found great store of ice, and after that sailed south-west and by south 3 [12] miles.

The 14 of July they wound northward againe, and sayled with 2 schower sailes[2] north and by east, and north north-east 5 [20] or 6 [24] miles, to the height of 77 degrees

---

[1] *So veel als men uyten mars oversien mocht, altemael een effen velt ys.* This passage is deserving of special notice, on account of the following statement in Captain Scoresby's *Account of the Arctic Regions*:—"The term *field* was given to the largest sheets of ice by a Dutch whale fisher. It was not until a period of many years after the Spitzbergen fishery was established, that any navigator attempted to penetrate the ice, or that any of the most extensive sheets of ice were seen. One of the ships resorting to Smeerenberg for the fishery, put to sea on one occasion, when no whales were seen, persevered westward to a considerable length, and accidentally fell in with some immense flakes of ice, which, on his return to his companions, he described as truly wonderful, and as resembling fields in the extent of their surface. Hence the application of the term 'field' to this kind of ice. The discoverer of it was distinguished by the title of 'field finder'."—Vol. i, p. 243.

[2] See page 7, note 4.

and ⅓ part,[1] and entred againe amongst the ice, being so broad that they could not see ouer it, there they had no ground at 100 fadome, and then it blew hard west northwest.

From thence they wound south-ward, and sailed south south-west 7 [28] or 8 [32] miles, and came againe by the land, that shewed to be 4 or 5 high hilles. Then they wound northward, and till euening sayled north 6 [24] miles, but there againe they found ice.

From thence they wound south-ward, and sailed south and by west 6 [24] miles, and then againe entred into ice.

The 15 of July, they wound south-ward againe, sayling south and by west 6 [24] miles, and in the morning were by the land of Noua Zembla againe, the sunne being about north-east [¼ p. 1, A.M.].

From thence they wound north-ward againe, and sayled north and by east 7 [28] miles, and entred againe into the ice. Then they wound south-ward againe, the sunne being west [¾ p. 3, P.M.], and sailed south south-west, and south-west and by south 8 [32] or 9 [36] miles, vpon the 16 of July.

From thence they wound north-ward, and sailed north and by east 4 [16] miles; after that againe they wound west-ward, and sailed west and by south 4 [16] miles, and then they sailed north north-west 4 [16] miles, and then the wind blew north north-east, and it froze hard; this was upon the 17 of July.

Then they wound east-ward, and sailed east till noone, 3 [12] miles, and after that east and by south 3 [12] miles; from thence about euening they wound northward and sailed north and by east 5 [20] miles, till the 18 of July in the morning; then they sailed north and by west 4 [16] miles, and there entred againe amongst a great many flakes of

[1] 77° 20' N. lat.

ice,[1] from whence they wound southward, and close by the ice they had no groūd at 150 fadom.

Then they sayled about 2 houres south-east, and east south-east, with mystie weather, and came to a flake of ice,[2] which was so broad that they could not see ouer it, it being faire still weather, and yet it froze, and so sailed along by the ice 2 houres; after that it was so mistie, that they could see nothing round about them, and sailed south-west two [8] miles.

The same day William Barents tooke the height of the sun with his astrolabium, and then they were under 77 degrees and a ¼ of the Pole,[3] and sailed south-ward 6 [24] miles, and perceiued the firme land,[4] lying south from them.

Then they sailed till the 19 of July in the morning, west south-west, 6 [24] or 7 [28] miles, with a north-west wind and mistie weather; and after that south-west and south-west and by west 7 [28] miles, the sunne being 77 degrees 5 minutes lesse.[5] Then they sailed 2 [8] miles south-west, and were close by the land of Noua Zembla, about Cape Nassaue.[6]

From thence they wound north-ward and sailed north 8 [32] miles, with a west north-west wind and a mist, and till the 20 of July in the morning north-east and by north 3 [12] or 4 [16] miles; and when the sunne was east [½ p. 4, A.M.] they wound west, and till euening sailed south-west 5 [20] or 6 [24] miles, with mistie weather, and then south-west and by south 7 [28] miles, till the 21 of July in the morning.

Then they wound north-ward againe, and from morning

---

[1] *In groote menichte van ys schollen* —among a great quantity of drift ice.

[2] *Een velt ys*—a field of ice

[3] In 77° 15′ N. lat.

[4] The main land of Nóvaya Zémlya.

[5] 76° 55′ N. lat.

[6] *Capo de Nassauw*.

till euening sailed north-west and by west 9 [36] miles, with mistie weather, and againe north-west and by west[1] 3 [12] miles; and then wound south-ward, and till the 22 of July in the morning sailed south south-west 3 [12] miles, with mistie weather, and till euening south and by west, 9 [36] miles, all mistie weather.

After that they wound north-ward againe, and sailed north-west and by north 3 [12] miles, and then 2 [8] miles north-west;[2] and in the morning being the 23 of July the wind blew north-west, and then they cast out the lead, and had 48 fadome muddie ground.

Then they sailed 2 [8] miles north north-east and north and by east, and 2 [8] miles north-east, at 46 fadome deepe; after that they wound west-ward, and sailed west and by north 6 [24] miles; there it was 60 fadome deepe, muddy ground.

Then they wound eastward and sailed 3 [12] miles east and by north; then againe 9 [36] or 10 [40] miles east, and east and by south; and after that 5 [20] or 6 [24] miles east, and east and by south; and after that 5 [20] or 6 [24] miles more, east and by south, till euening, being the 24 of July; then againe 4 [16] miles south-east and by east, the wind being east north-east.

Then they woond north-ward, and till the 25 of July in the morning sailed north, and north and by west, 4 [16] miles; there they had 130 fadome deepe, muddie ground; then they sailed north-ward, where they had 100 fadome deepe, and there they saw the ice in the north-east; and then againe they sailed 2 [8] miles, north and by west.

Then they woond south-ward towards the ice, and sailed south-east one mile [4 miles]; after that they wound north-ward againe, and sailed north 6 [24] miles, and were so inclosed about with flakes of ice,[3] that out of the top they

---

[1] *N.W. ten N.*—N.W. by *north*.   [2] *N. ten W.*—N. *by* W.
[3] *Ys schollen*—drift ice

could not discerne any thing beyond it, and sought to get through the ice, but they could not passe beyond it, and therefore in the evening they wound south-ward againe, and sailed along by the ice, south and west by 5 [20] miles, and after that south south-east 3 [12] miles.

The 25 of July at night, they took the heigth of the sunne, when it was at the lowest between north and north-east,[1] and north-east and by north, it being eleuated aboue the horizon 6 degrees and $\frac{3}{4}$, his declinatiō being 19 degrees 50 minutes; now take 6 degrees $\frac{3}{4}$ from 19 degrees and 50 minutes, and there resteth 13 degrees 5 minutes, which substracted from 90 there resteth 77 degrees lesse 5 minutes.[2]

The 26 of July, in the morning, they sailed 6 [24] miles south south-east, till the sunne was south-west [1, P.M.], and then south-east 6 [24] miles, and were within a mile of the land of Noua Zembla, and then wound north-ward from the land, and sailed 5 [20] miles north-west[3] with an east wind; but in the euening they wound south-ward againe, and sailed south south-east 7 [28] miles, and were close by the land.

Then they wound north-ward againe, and sailed north north-east 2 [8] or 3 [12] miles; from thence they wound south-ward, and sailed south south-east 2 [8] or 3 [12] miles, and came againe to Cape Trust.[4]

Then they wounde againe from the land, north-east, about halfe a mile [2 miles], and were ouer against the sandes of 4 fadome deepe, betweene the rocke and the land, and there the sands were 10 fadome deepe, the ground being small black stones; then they sailed north-west a little while, till they had 43 fadome deepe, soft ground.

From thence they sailed north-east 4 [16] miles, upon the

---

[1] *N.N.O.—N.N.E.*   [2] 76° 55′ N. lat
[3] *N. ten W.—N. by W.*
[4] *Ende quamen weder by't landt aen de Cape des Troosts*—and came again close to the land at Cape *Comfort.*

27 of July, with an east south-east wind, and wound southward againe, where they found 70 fadome deepe, clay ground, and sayled south and south and by east 4 [16] miles, and came to a great creek; and a mile and a halfe [6 miles] from thence there lay a banke of sande of 18 fadome deepe, clay sandy ground, and betweene that sand or banke and the land it was 60 and 50 fadome deepe, the coast reaching east and west by the compasse.

In the euening they wound [stife[1]] north-ward, and sailed 3 [12] miles north north-east; that day it was mistie, and in the night cleare, and William Barents tooke the height of the sunne with his crosse-staffe,[2] and found it to be eleuated aboue the horizon 5 degrees 40 minutes, his declination being 19 degrees 25 minutes, from whence substracting 5 degrees 40 minutes, there resteth 13 degrees 45 minutes, which substracted from 90 rested 76 degrees 31 minutes[3] for the height of the Pole.

Upon the 28 of July, they sailed 3 [12] miles north north-east, and after that wound south-ward, and sailed 6 [24] miles south south-east, and yet were then 3 [12] or 4 [16] miles from the land.

The 28 of July, the height of the sun being taken at noone with the astrolobiū, it was found to be eleuated aboue the horizon 57 degrees and 6 minutes,[4] her declination being 19 degrees and 18 minutes, which in all is 76 degrees and 24 minutes, they being then about 4 [16] miles from the land of Noua Zembla, that lay all couered ouer with snow, the weather being cleare, and the wind east.

Then againe, the sunne being about south-west [1, P.M.],

---

[1] This word is not in the original; and it is inconsistent, as in the next line their course is stated to have been N.N.E.

[2] *Graedt-boogh.* See page 10, note 1.

[3] So in the original. It should be 76° 15'.

[4] In like manner as on the 7th July (see page 14), it is the sun's zenith distance that is here recorded instead of its altitude.

they wound north-ward, and sailed one mile [4 miles] north north-east, and then wound againe, and sailed another mile [4 miles] south-east, then they wound north-ward againe, and sailed 4 [16] miles north-east and north-east and by north.[1]

The same day[2] the height of the sunne being taken, it was found to be 76 degrees and 24 minutes, and then they sailed north-east 3 [12] miles, and after that north-east and by east 4 [16] miles, and vpon the 29 of July came into the ice againe.

The 29 of July the height of the sunne being taken with the crosse-staffe, astrolabium, and quadrant,[3] they found it to bee eleuated aboue the horizon 32 degrees, her declination being 19 degrees, which substracted from 32 there resteth 13 degrees of the equator, which being substracted from 90 there rested 77 degrees; and then the neerest north point of Noua Zembla, called the Ice Point,[4] lay right east from them.

There they found certaine stones that glistered like gold, which for that cause they named gold-stones,[5] and there also they had a faire bay with sandy ground.

Upon the same day they wound south-ward againe, and sailed south-east[6] 2 [8] miles betweene the land and the ice, and after that from the Ice Point east, and to the south-

[1] *Noordt oost ten oosten*—N.E. by east.

[2] *Des selfden nachts*—the same *night*. The sun was then constantly above the horizon.

[3] *Metten graedtboogh, astrolabium ende quadrant.*

[4] *De aldernoordelijckste hoeck van Nora Sembla genaemt Ys hoeck*—the *northernmost* point, etc.

[5] Most probably marcasite or iron pyrites. Frobisher's third voyage to "Meta Incognita", *with fifteen vessels*, was principally for the purpose of bringing home an immense quantity of this mineral, which he had discovered on his former voyages, and fancied to be rich in gold.—See Hakluyt's *Voyages*, vol. i, pp. 74, 91; and Admiral Sir Richard Collinson's edition of Sir Martin Frobisher's *Three Voyages*. (Hakluyt Society, 1867.)

[6] *Z. ten O.*—S. by E.

ward[1] 6 [24] miles to the Islands of Orange; and there they laboured forward[2] betweene the land and the ice, with faire still weather, and vpon the 31 of July got to the Islands of Orange. And there went to one of those islands, where they found about 200 walrushen or sea-horses, lying upon the shoare to baske[3] themselues in the sunne. This sea-horse is a wonderfull strong monster of the sea, much bigger then an oxe, which keepes continually in the seas, hauing a skinne like a sea-calfe or seale, with very short hair, mouthed like a lyon, and many times they lie vpon the ice; they are hardly killed vnlesse you strike them iust vpon the forehead; it hath foure feet, but no eares, and commonly it hath one or two young ones at a time. And when the fisher-men chance to find them vpon a flake of ice[4] with their yong ones, shee casteth her yong ones before her into the water, and then takes them in her armes, and so plungeth vp and downe with them, and when shee will reuenge herselfe vpon the boats, or make resistance against them, then she casts her yong ones from her againe, and with all her force goeth towards the boate; whereby our men were once in no small danger, for that the sea-horse had almost stricken her teeth into the sterne of their boate, thinking to ouerthrowe it; but by means of the great cry that the men made, shee was afraid, and swomme away againe, and tooke her yong ones againe in her armes. They haue two teeth sticking out of their mouthes, on each side one, each beeing about halfe an elle long, and are esteemed to bee as good as any iuorie or elophants teeth, specially in Muscouia, Tartaria, and there abouts where they are knowne, for they are as white, hard, and euen as iuory.[5]

[1] *Oost wel so zuydelijck*—east a little south.
[2] *Laveerden*—"laveered", i.e., advanced by repeated short tacks.
[3] "Baste"—*Ph*. A misprint.   [4] *Een schots ys*—a piece of drift ice.
[5] A critical history of this animal is given in "Anatomische und Zoologische Untersuchungen über das Wallross (*Trichechus Rosmarus*) &c. von Dr. K. E. v. Baer"—*Mémoires de l'Acad. Imp. des Sc. de St.*

Those sea-horses that lay basking[1] themselues vpon the land, our men, supposing that they could not defend themselues being out of the water, went on shore to assaile them, and fought with thē, to get their teeth that are so rich, but they brake all their hatchets, curtle-axes,[2] and pikes in pieces, and could not kill one of them, but strucke some of their teeth ont of their mouthes, which they tooke with them; and when they could get nothing against them by fighting, they agreed to goe aboard the ship, to fetch some of their great ordinance, to shoot at them therewith; but it began to blow so hard, that it rent the ice into great peices, so that they were forced not to do it; and therewith they found a great white beare that slept, which they shot into the body, but she ranne away, and entred into the water; the men following her with their boat, and kil'd her out-right, and then drew her vpon the ice, and so sticking a half pike vp-right, bound her fast vnto it, thinking to fetch her when they came backe againe, to shoot at the sea-horses with their ordinance;

Pétersb., 6me Sér., Sciences Math., Phys. et Nat., tom. iv, 2de part., Sc. Nat. (1838), pp. 97-235.

In Scoresby's *Account of the Arctic Regions*, vol. i, p. 504, it is said: "When seen at a distance, the front part of the head of the young walrus, without tusks, is not unlike the human face. As this animal is in the habit of rearing its head above water, to look at ships and other passing objects, it is not at all improbable that it may have afforded foundation for some of the stories of mermaids. I have myself seen a sea-horse in such a position, and under such circumstances, that it required little stretch of imagination to mistake it for a human being; so like indeed was it, that the surgeon of the ship actually reported to me his having seen a man with his head just appearing above the surface of the water."

[1] "Bathing"—*Ph.* A misprint.

[2] *Cortelassen*—cutlasses. Plate CIII, of Dr. Meyrick's *Ancient Arms and Armour* (vol. ii) contains a representation of an "Andrew Ferrara", which is described as "a coutel-hache, coutelaxe or coutelas". But the true original of the name is the Italian *cultellaccio* or *coltellaccio*, meaning literally a large (heavy) knife. *Cultellazius*, the Latinized form of this word, occurs in a list of forbidden weapons, in a statue of the city of Ferrara, A.D. 1268 See Muratori, *Antiq. Italic.*, vol. ii, col. 515.

but for that it began more and more to blow, and the ice therewith brake in peeces, they did nothing at all.

After that W. Barents had begun this uoyage vpon the fifth of June, 1594, and at that time (as I sayd before) set saile out of the Texell, the 23 of the same month arriving at Kilduin in Muscouia, and from thence tooke his course on the north side of Noua Zembla, wherein he continued till the first of August, with such aduentures as are before declared, till he came to the Island of Orange:[1] after he had taken all that paine, and finding that he could hardly get through, to accomplish and ende his pretended[2] voyage, his men also beginning to bee weary and would saile no further, they all together agreed to returne back againe, to meet with the other ships[3] that had taken their course to the Weygates, or the Straights of Nassawe,[4] to know what discoueries they had made there.

Theire returne backe againe.

[1] *Tottet Eylandt van Oraengien.* [2] Intended.
[3] Namely, those of Zeelandt and Enkhuysen, from which they had separated at Kildin on the 29th of June.
[4] *De Weygats ofte Strate de Nassou.* This name has given occasion to much curious criticism. The Dutch, not unnaturally, have sought its explanation in their own language, in which *waaien* means "to blow", "to be windy", and *gat* is "a strait" or "passage"; so that *waaigat* would be "a passage wherein the wind blows strongly". And it is indisputable that this name has, on various occasions, been so applied by the seamen of that nation. Thus, we find a *Waaigat* in Baffin's Bay, one in Spitzbergen, and another by the Straits of Magellan; and even the roads between the Helder and Texel have, from an early period, borne the same name. See "Prize Essay on the Netherlandish Discoveries," by R. G. Bennet and J. G. van Wijk, in *Nieuwe Verhandelingen von het Provincial Utrechtsche Genootschap, etc.*, vol. vi (1827), p. 41.

Others, instead of the Dutch *waaien*, have taken the German *weihen* as the root, and thus made *weihgat* to mean the "sacred straits".

J. R. Forster, in his *Voyages and Discoveries in the North* (Engl. edit.), p. 273, contends, however, that the name is of Russian origin, and explains it as follows:—"Barentz found afterwards in Nova Zembla some carved images on a head-land near the straits, in consequence of which he called it *Afgoeden-hoek*, the 'Cape of Idols'. Now, in the Sclavonian tongue, *wajat* means 'to carve', 'to make an image'. *Wajati-Noss* would, there-

The first of August they turned their course to saile backe againe from the Islands of Orange, and sailed west and west by south 6 [24] miles to the Ice Point.

From the Ice Point to the Cape of Comfort,[1] they sailed west and somewhat south 30 [120] miles: betweene them both there lyeth very high land, but the Cape of Comfort is very low flat land, and on the west end thereof there standeth foure or fiue blacke houels or little hilles like country houses.[2]

Upon the 3 of August, from the Cape of Comfort they

fore, be the 'Carved' or 'Image Cape'; and this seems to me to be the true origin of the word *Waigats*, which properly should be called *Waja-telstwoi Proliw*, 'the Image Straits'." So convinced was Forster of the correctness of his conjecture, that in another part of his work (p. 413) he did not hesitate to assert that the Russians themselves give to the Afgoeden-hoek the name of Waijati Nos; and this strange derivation of the word Waigats has found supporters not only among foreign, but even among Russian writers. See *Barrow*, p. 137; *Berch*, p. 30.

But Lütke, who has fully investigated the subject, adduces as proof against these fanciful etymologies, first (p. 30), that the name recorded by the Dutch themselves is Waigatz [Weygats], and not Waigat, the Russian termination *tsch* being changed by them into *tz*, in the same way as in Pitzora for Petschora, etc.; secondly, that the name Waigatsch properly belongs to the island alone, and not to the straits; thirdly, that this name was known to the Englishman Burrough in 1556, nearly forty years before the first voyage of the Hollanders; and lastly (p. 31), that the Russians have never called the Cape of Idols Waiyati Nos, but always Bolwánskyi Muis, from *bolwàn*, a rough image.

Lütke adds that the true derivation of the name in question is as difficult to be determined as that of Kolguew, Nokuew, Kildin, Warandei, etc., which are probably the remains of the languages of tribes now extinct. But, at the same time, he directs attention to Witsen's assertion (which appears to have been altogether overlooked by previous writers), that the island of Waigatsch received its name from one Iwan Waigatsch—"het Eiland Waigats, dat zijn naem heeft van Ivan, of Ian Waigats;"—a derivation which is very probable, and certainly far more reasonable than any of the etymologies above recited.

[1] *De Cape des Troosts*—Cape Comfort; the same which Phillip had previously translated "Cape Trust". See page 22, note 4.

[2] *Swarte heuvels ghelijck boeren huysen*—black hillocks, like peasants' huts.

wound north-ward, and sailed 8 [32] miles north-west and by north, and north north-west; and about noone they wound south-ward till euening, and sailed south and by west, and south-south-west 7 [28] miles, and then came to a long narrow point of land one Cape Nassaw.[1]

In the euening they wound north-ward againe, and sailed north and by east 2 [8] miles; then the winde came north, and therefore they wound west-ward againe, and sailed north north-west one mile [4 miles]; then the wind turned east, and with that they sailed from the 4 of August in the morning till noone west and by north 5 [20] or 6 [24] miles; after that they sailed till euening south-west 5 [20] miles and after that south-west 2 [8] miles more, and fell vpon a low flat land, which on the east-end had a white patche or peece of ground.

After that they sailed till morning, being the 5 of August, west south-west 12 [48] miles,[2] then south-west 14 [56] miles, and then west 3 [12] miles till the 6 of August.

The 6 of August they sailed west south-west 2 [8] or 3 [12] miles; then south-west, and south-west and by south, 4 [16] or 5 [20] miles; then south-west and by west 3 [12] miles, and then south-west and by west 3 [12] miles; and after that west south-west and south-west and by south 3 [12] miles, till the 7 of August.

The 7 of August till noone they sailed 3 [12] miles west south-west, then 3 [12] miles west, and then they wound south-ward till euening, and sailed 3 [12] miles south-east and south-east and by east, then againe west south-west 2 [8] miles, after that they sailed south 3 [12] miles, till the 8 of August in the morning, with a west south-west winde.

The 8 of August they sailed south-east and by south 10 [40] miles, and then south-east and by east vntil euening 5

---

[1] *Ende quamen by een laghen slechten hoeck te landt aen de Cape de Nassauwen*—and came to a low, flat point, at Cape Nassau.

[2] "5 miles"—*Ph.*

[20] miles, and then came to a low flat land, that lay south-west and by south, and north-east and by north, and so sailed 5 [20] miles more, and there they had 36 fadome deepe, 2 [8] miles from the land, the ground blacke sand; There they sailed towards the land, till they were at 12 fadome, and halfe a mile [2 miles] from the land it was stony ground.

From thence the land reacheth south-ward for 3 [12] miles, to the other low point that had a blacke rocke lying close by it; and from thence the land reacheth south south-east 3 [12] miles, to another point; and there lay a little low island from the point, and within halfe a mile [2 miles] of the land it was flat ground, at 8, 9, and 10 fadome deepe, which they called the Black Island,[1] because it showed blacke aboue; then it was very mistie, so that they lay in the wind[2] and sailed 3 [12] miles west north-west; but when it cleared vp, they wound towards the land againe, and the sunne being south [¼ to 11 A.M.], they came right against the Blacke Island, and had held their course east south-east.

There W. Barents tooke the height of the sunne, it being vnder 71 degrees and ⅓; and there they found a great creeke, which William Barents iudged to be the place where Oliuer Brunel[3] had been before, called Costincsarth.[4]

[1] *Het swarte Eylandt.*
[2] *Zijt aen de wint leyden*—they lay to the wind.
[3] *Oliphier Brunel.* A native of Brussels, properly named Oliver Bunel, who traded to the north coasts of Russia in a vessel from Enckhuysen, and was lost in the river Petchora. The process by which Bunel has been made to become an Englishman, under the name of "Bennel", "Brunell", or "Brownell", is explained in the Introduction.
[4] *Costincsarch*, in the original Dutch text; *Costinclarch*, in the Amsterdam French version of 1598; *Constint-sarch*, or *Constantin zaar*, as it is called by Witsen in his *Noord en Oost Tartarije*, p. 918; *Constant Search*, according to Forster's ingenious hypothesis, p. 415; *Coasting Search*, as suggested by Barrow, p. 159. This name, which has scarcely ever been written twice alike, and which has given occasion to so much speculation as to its origin, is properly *Kostin-schar*, i. e., "Kostin Straits, or Passage"; it being the channel by which the Meyduscharski Island (i.e., "the island lying between the straits"), is separated from

From the Blacke Island, they sailed south and south and by east to another small[1] point 3 [12] miles, on which point there stood a crosse, and therefore they called it the Crosse Point;[2] there also there was a flat bay, and low water,[3] 5, 6, or 7 fadome deep, soft ground.[4]

From Crosse Point they sailed along by the land south south-east 4 [16] miles, and then came to another small[5] point, which behinde it had a great creeke, that reached east-ward: this point they called the Fifth Point or S. Lau-

the main land of Novaya Zemlya. Lütke, from whom (p. 22) the above definition is taken, explains further (p. 245), that "among Novaya Zemlya navigators, *schar* is properly the name of a strait or passage, which goes directly through or across an island or country, forming a communication between two distinct seas. For one that merely separates an island from the mainland, or otherwise forms part of one sea alone, the appropriate designation is *salma*. Thus, Matotschkin Schar, Yugorskyi Schar, etc., are properly so called; but Kostin Schar, as a walrus hunter told me, 'is styled a *schar* only through stupidity, as its correct designation would be *Kostin Salma*'."

Nevertheless, in justice to those who first gave the name of Kostin *Schar* to this strait, it must be remarked, that it was regarded by them as actually passing through the mainland of Novaya Zemlya, and as forming a communication with the Kara Sea. It is thus shown in the early maps; and Witzen (p. 918) expressly states—"Het ys *dryft door Nova Zemla* heen, *en comt by Constint Sarch*, of Constantin Zaar, *uit*."

It is the passage to the south of the island which is more especially named Kostin Schar, or Kostin Salma. That to the north is the Podryésof Passage (Podrjesow Schar). See *Lütke*, p. 315.

As regards the etymology of the word *Schar*, Lütke says (p. 245) that he was unable to satisfy himself. "The Samoyedes themselves regard it as a foreign term; and by some it is thought to come from the Finnish word *Schar* or *Skar*." Can the *shard* of Spencer have any connection with it?

> "Upon that shore he spyéd Atin stand
> There by his maister left, when late he far'd
> In Phædria's flitt barck over that perlous shard."
> *Faerie Queene*, II, vi, 38.

[1] *Schlecten*—flat.
[2] *Cruijs-hoeck*.
[3] *Slecht water*—shallow water.
[4] *Steeck grondt*—stiff ground.
[5] *Sclechten*—flat.

rence Point.[1] From the Fifth Point they sailed to the Sconce Point[2] 3 [12] miles, south south-east, and there lay a long blacke rocke close by the land, whereon there stood a crosse; then they entered into the ice againe, and put inward to the sea[3] because of the ice. Their intent was to saile along the coast of Noua Zembla to the Wey-gates, but by reason that the ice met them they wound west-ward, and from the 9 of August in the euening, till the 10 of August in the morning, sayled west and by north 11 [44] miles, and after that 4 [16] miles west north-west, and north-west and by west, the winde being north; in the morning[4] they wound east-warde againe, and sailed vntill euening 10 [40] miles east and east and by south; after that east and east and by north 4 [16] miles, and there they saw land, and were right against a great creeke, where with their boat they went on land, and there found a faire hauen 5 fadome deepe, sandy ground. This creeke on the north side hath 3 blacke points, and about the 3 points[5] lyeth the road, but you must keepe somewhat from the 3 point, for it is stonie, and betweene the 2 and 3 point there is another faire bay, for north-west, north, and north-east winds, blacke sandy ground. This bay they called S. Laurence Bay, and there they tooke the height of the sunne, which was 70 degrees and ¾.

From S. Laurence Bay, south south-east 2 [8] miles to Sconce Point, there lay a long[6] blacke rocke, close by the land,[7] whereon there stood a crosse; there they went on land

[1] *Den vijfden hoeck ofte S. Laurens hoeck.*

[2] *Schans hoeck.* "Barrow (p. 141) calls this headland *Sion's* Point."— *Lütke*, p. 20. This is clearly a clerical or typographical error for "Sconce Point", of a character similar to that in the first (Paris) edition of the *Histoire Générale des Voyages*, cited by Barrow, p. 139, whereby "Baie de Loms"—Lomsbay—is converted into "Baie de St. Louis!"

[3] *Leydent zeewaerts in*—tacked to seaward.

[4] *Des middaeghs*—at noon.

[5] *Om den derden hoeck*—near the *third* point.   [6] *Laghe*—low.

[7] *Aent last rast:* a typographical error in the original Dutch. It should be *aent landt rast*.

with their boat, and perceiued that some men had bin there, and that they were fled to saue themselues;[1] for there they found 6 sacks with rie-meale buried in the ground, and a heap of stones by the crosse, and a bullet for a great piece, and there abouts also there stood another crosse,[2] with 3 houses made of wood, after the north-countrey manner: and in the houses they found many barrels of pike-staues,[3] whereby they coniectured that there they vsed to take salmons,[4] and by them stood 5 or 6 coffins, by graues,[5] with dead men's bones, the coffins standing vpon the ground all filled vp with stones; there also lay a broken Russia ship,[6] the keele thereof being 44 foot long, but they could see no man on the land: it is a faire hauen for all winds, which they called the Meale-hauen,[7] because of the meale that they found there.

From the black rocke or cliffe with the crosse, 2 [8] miles south south-east, there lay a low island a little into the sea, from whence they sailed 9 [36] or 10 [40] miles south south-

[1] *Om onsent wil gevlucht waren*—were fled on our account.

[2] *Ende een gotelincks schoot van daer stont noch een cruijs*—and a falconet-shot from thence stood another cross. Lütke (p. 20) criticises Barrow for saying (p. 141) that the Hollanders found here, among other things, "a large cannon shot"; but it is clear that the latter has merely modernized Phillip's words "a bullet for a great piece".

[3] *Veel tonnen duyghen*—a quantity of pipe-staves. Here is a curious double error. In the first place, as *duyghen* are "staves" (for casks), *tonnen-duyghen* are simply "cask-staves" or "pipe-staves", and not casks (barrels) of pipe-staves. And secondly, the word *pipe* has been misprinted *pike;* so that altogether, without referring to the original Dutch, it was quite impossible to imagine what was meant.

[4] *Daer deur wy vermoeden datter cenighen Salm-vang moeste zijn*—whence we conjectured that there must be some salmon fishery here.

[5] *By de graven*—by the graves.

[6] *Lodding* (intended for the Russian word *lodya*)—a boat.

[7] *Meel-haven*—apparently the Strogonov Bay of Lütke, who, in his account of his third voyage (p. 316), speaks of a tradition, according to which this was formerly the residence of some natives of Novogorod of that name. These settlers are not mentioned in the chronicles, nor is anything known respecting them, or the date or cause of their emi-

east; there the height of the sunne[1] was 70 degrees and 50 minutes, when it was south south-west.

From that island they sailed along by the land 4 [16] miles south-east and by south; there they came to 2 islands, whereof the uttermost lay a mile [4 miles] from the land; those islands they called S. Clara.

Then they entered into the ice again, and wound inward to sea, in the wind,[2] and sailed from the island[3] vntill evening, west south-west 4 [16] miles, the wind being north-west; that evening it was very mistie, and then they had 80 fadom deepe.

Then againe they sailed south-west and by west, and west south-west 3 [12] miles; there they had 70 fadome deepe, and so sayled till the thirteenth of August in the morning, south-west and by west foure [16] miles; two houres before they had ground at fiftie sixe fadome, and in the morning at fortie five fadome, soft muddy ground.

gration. But assuming the remains found by Barentsz and his companions to be those of the Strogonovs, he deems it not unreasonable to place their arrival some twenty or thirty years earlier than the visit of the Hollanders; which date would correspond with the reign of John the Terrible (Yoan Grosnui), a period when the Novogoroders had the greatest reason to emigrate into the regions far distant from their native country. Indeed, it is not improbable that some of them may, at that time, have been banished to Novaya Zemlya. Lütke adds: "It is worthy of remark that our walrus-hunters give the name of Meal Cape to the western headland of Strogonov Bay; which name would seem to have originated in the six sacks of rye-meal which Barentz saw there. The remains of the dwellings of the Strogonovs lie close to Meal Cape."—P. 317.

The same writer adverts also, but with disfavour, to the further tradition, that "the Strogonovs were visited by certain monsters with iron noses and teeth". But when it is considered that the walrus must have been previously unknown to these natives of Novogorod, it is not unreasonable to imagine that animal to have given rise to what might otherwise well be regarded as a fable.

[1] *Den 12 Aug.*—on the 12th of August (omitted).

[2] *Ende wendent tzeewaert in aen de wint*—and tacked to seaward, hugging the wind.

[3] *Van den eylanden*—from the islands.

Then they sayled till noone sixe [24] miles south-west, and had twentie foure fadome deepe, black sandie ground; and within one houre after they had two and twentie fadome deepe, browne reddish sand; then they sailed sixe [24] miles south-west, with fifteene fadome deepe, red sand; after that two [8] miles south-west, and there it was fifteene fadome deepe, red sand, and there they sawe land, and sayled forward south-west untill evening, till we were within halfe a mile [2 miles] of the land, and there it was seven fadome deepe, sandy ground, the land being low flat downes reaching east and west.

Then they wound from the land and sailed north, and north and by east 4 [16] miles; from thence they wound to land againe, and sayled til the 14 of August 5 [20] or 6 [24] miles south-west, sailing close by the land, which (as they gesse[1]) was the island of Colgoyen;[2] there they sailed by the lād east-ward 4 [16] miles; after that 3 [12] miles east, and east and by south; then the weather became mistie, whereby they could not see the land, and had shallow flat water[3] at 7 or 8 fadome; then they took in the marsaile[4] and lay in the wind[5] till it was cleare weather againe, and then the sunne was south south-west [¾ p. 11 a.m.], yet they could not see the land: there they had 100 fadome deepe, sandy ground; then they sailed east 7 [28] miles; after that againe 2 [8] miles east south-east, and south-east and by east; and againe till the 15 of August in the morning, 9 [36] miles east south-east; then from morning till noone they sailed 4 miles east south-east, and sailed over a flat or sand of 9 or 10 fadome deepe, sandy ground, but could see

[1] Guessed.
[2] The large island of Kólguev, situate between Kanin Nos (Cape Kanin) and the entrance of the River Petchora. Its north-western extremity, according to Lütke's observations (p. 324), is in 69° 29′ 30″ N. lat., and 48° 55′ E. long.
[3] *Vlack water*— shallow water.
[4] *Marseylen*—topsails.
[5] *Leyde aen de wind*—lay to the wind.

no land; and about an houre before noone it began to waxe deeper, for then wee had 12 and 13 fadome water, and then wee sayled east south-east 3 [12] miles, till the sunne was south-west [1 p.m.].

The same daye the sunne being south-west,[1] William Barents tooke the height thereof, and found it to be elevated above the horizon 35 degrees, his declination being 14 degrees and ¼, so y^t as there wanted 55 degrees of 90, which 55 and 14 degrees and ¼ being both added together, made 69 degrees 15 minutes, which was the height of the Pole in that place, the wind being north-west; then they sailed 2 [8] miles more east-ward, and came to the islands called Matfloe and Delgoy,[2] and there in the morning they meet with the other shippes of their company, being of Zelandt and Enck-huysen,[3] that came out of Wey-gates the same day; there they shewed each other where they had bin, and how farre each of them had sailed, and discouered.

The ship of Enck-huysen had past the straights of Wey-gates, and said, that at the end of Wey-gates he had found a large sea,[4] and that they had sailed 50 [200] or 60 [240] miles further east-ward, and were of opinion that they had been about the riuer of Obi,[5] that commeth out of Tartaria, and that the land of Tartaria reacheth north-east-ward againe from thence, whereby they thought that they were not far

[1] This note of the bearing of the sun is only approximative, since the observation of the variation of the needle made on July 3rd (p. 10), shows that the sun came to the meridian between S.S.W. and S.W. by S.

[2] Matvyéyeva Ostrov and Dolgoi Ostrov, that is, Matvyéyev's Island and Long Island.—*Lütke*, p. 20.

[3] These vessels were the Swan of Der Veere in Zeelandt, commanded by Cornelis Corneliszoon Nai, and the Mercury of Enckhuysen, commanded by Brandt Ysbrandtszoon, otherwise called Brandt Tetgales.

[4] *Een ruyme zee*—an open sea.

[5] *Ontrent de lenghte van de revier Obi*—about *the longitude of* the river Obi. In this, however, they were in error, as they were still only on the eastern side of the Kara Sea.—See *Lütke*, p. 32.

from Cape Tabin,[1] which is ye point[2] of Tartaria, that reacheth towards the kingdom of Chathai, north-east and then southward.[3] And so thinking that they had discouered inough for that time, and that it was too late in the yeare to saile any further, as also that their commission was to discouer the scituation, and to come home againe before winter, they turned againe towards the Wei-gates, and came to an island about 5 miles great, lying south-east from Wei-gates on the Tartarian side, and called it the States Island;[4] there they found many stones, that were of a cristale mountaine,[5] being a kind of diamont.

When they were met together (as I sayd before) they made signes of ioy, discharging some of their ordinance, and were merry, the other shippes thinking that William Barents had sailed round about Noua Zembla, and had come backe againe through the Wei-gates: and after they had shewed each other what they had done, and made signs of ioy for their meeting, they set their course to turne backe againe for Holland; and vpon the 16 of August they went vnder the islands of Matfloe and Delgoy, and put into the road, because the wind was north-west, and lay there till the 18 of August.

The 18 of August they set saile, and went forward west north-west, and almost west and by north, and so sailed 12 [48] miles; and then west and by south 6 [24] miles, and came to a sand of scarce 5 fadome deepe, with a north-west wind; and in the evening they wound northward, and sailed east north-east 7 [28] or 8 [32] miles, the wind being

[1] *De Caep Tabijn*—the northernmost extremity of Siberia, now known by the name of Cape Taimur or Taimyr. It is the *Tabis* of Pliny.

[2] *Uythoeck*—the furthest point.

[3] *Nae't z. o. en voort nae't zuyden*—towards south-east, and then southwards.

[4] *Staten Eylandt*—the Myasnoi Ostrov (Flesh Island) of the Russians.—*Lütke*, p. 31.

[5] *Van cristal montaigne*—of rock-crystal.

northerly; and then they wound westward, and sailed till the 19 of August in the morning, west 2 [8] miles; then 2 [8] miles south-west, and after that 2 [8] miles south-east; there they wound west-ward againe, and sailed till evening with a calme, and after that had an east winde, and at first sailed west north-west, and north-west and by west 6 [24] or 7 [28] miles, and had ground at 12 fadome: then till the 20 of August in the morning, they sayled west north-west, and north-west and by west, 7 [28] miles with an easterly wind; and then againe sailed west north-west, and north-west and by west 7 [28] miles; then west north-west 4 [16] miles, and draue[1] forward till euening with a calme: after that they sailed west north-west and north-west and by west 7 [28] miles, and in the night time came to a sand of 3 fadome deepe right against the land, and so sailed along by it, first one mile north, then 3 [12] miles north north-west, and it was sandy hilly land, and many points:[2] and then sailed on forward with 9 or 10 fadome deepe, along by the land till noone, being the 21 of August, north-west 5 [20] miles; and the west point of the land, called Candinaes,[3] lay north-west[4] from them 4 [16] miles.

From thence they sailed 4 [16] miles north north-west, and then north-west and by north 4 [16] miles, and 3 [12] miles more north-west, and north-west and by north, and then north-west 4 [16] miles, til the 22 of August in the morning: and that morning they sailed north-west 7 [28] miles, and so till euening west north-west and north-west and by west 15 [60] miles, the wind being north; after that 8 [32] miles more, west north-west; and then till the 23 of August at noone, west north-west 11 [44] miles, the same day at noone the sunne was eleuated aboue the horizon 31

---

[1] *Dreven*—drifted.   [2] *Steijlhoeckigh*—precipitous.
[3] Kanin Nos, or Cape Kanin, at the north-eastern extremity of the White Sea, in 68° 33' 18" N. lat., and 43° 16' 30" E. long.—*Lütke*, p. 341.
[4] *W.n.w.*—W.N.W.

degrees and ⅓ part, his declination was 11 degrees and ⅔ partes; so that it wanted 58 degrees and ⅔ of 90 degrees, and adding the declination being 11 degrees ⅔ to 58 degrees and ⅔ partes, then the height of the Pole was 70 degrees and ⅓ part: then they sailed north-west, and north-west and by west, till euening 8 [32] miles; and then north-west and by west, and west north-west 5 [20] miles; and then vntill the 24 of August in the morning, north-west and by west 6 [24] miles; after that west, and west south-west 3 [12] miles, and then passed close by the island of Ware-huysen[1] in the roade. From Ware-huysen hither-ward, because the way is well knowne, I neede not to write thereof, but that from thence they sailed altogether homeward, and kept company together till they came to the Texel, where the ship of Ze- *The end of this voyage* landt past by, and William Barents with his pinnace came vpon a faire day,[2] being the 16 of September, before Amsterdam, and the ship of Enck-huysen to Enck-huysen, from whence they were set foorth. William Barents' men brought a sea-horse to Amsterdam, being of a wonderfull greatnesse, which they tooke vpon a flake of ice, and killed it.

[1] *Waerhuysen*—Wardhous, at the north-eastern extremity of Finmark, is in 70° 22' N. lat., and 31° 5' 35" E. long.

[2] *Op kermis dagh*—on the day of the (Amsterdam) fair. During the time that Louis Bonaparte was King of Holland, the fair-day was changed from the 16th of September to the first Monday in the month, in honour of his birthday, which was the 2nd of September.

A BRIEFE DECLARATION OF
A SECOND NAUIGATION MADE IN ANNO 1595, Behinde Norway, Moscouia, and Tartaria, towards the kingdoms of Cathaia and China.

THE 4 ships aforesaid being returned home about harvest-time, in anno 1594, they were in good hope that the voiage aforesaid would be done, by passing along through the Straights of Weygates, and specially by the report made by the 2 ships of Zelandt and Enck-huysen, wherein John Huyghen of Linschoten was committed,[1] who declared the manner of their trauell in such sort,[2] that the Generall States and Prince Maurice resolued, in the beginning of the next yeare, to prepare certaine ships, not only (as they went before) to discouer the passage, but to send certaine wares and merchandises thither, wherein the marchants might lade what wares they would, with certaine factors to sell the saide wares, in such places as they should arriue, neither

---

[1] *Dae Jan Huyghen van Linschoten comis op was*—whereof John Hugh van Linschoten was commissary or supercargo. This well-known traveller was born at Haarlem in 1563, and went at an early age to Portugal, whence he embarked for India. There he remained several years. Shortly after his return to Holland, he was appointed to take part in the first expedition to the North Seas, and sailed on board the Mercury of Enckhuysen (see page 36, note 3). He likewise accompanied the second expedition, and wrote an account of both voyages, as is mentioned more at length in the Introduction. He also published an account of his voyage to the East Indies, etc. Linschoten was afterwards treasurer of the town of Enckhuysen, and died there in 1633.—*Biogr. Univ.*

[2] *Die de saeck vry wat breedt voort stelde*—who represented the matter very favourably.

paying fraight nor custome. Peter Plantins,[1] a learned cosmographer, being a great furtherer and setter forward of this uoiage, and was their chiefe instructer therein, setting downe the scituation of the coasts of Tartaria, Cathaia, and China; but how they lye it is not yet sufficiently discouered, for that the courses and rules by him set downe were not fully effected, by meanes of some inconueniencies that fell out, which, by reason of the shortnesse of time could not be holpen. The reasons that some men (not greatly affected to this uoyage) vse to propound, to affirme it not possible to be done, are taken (as they say) out of some old and aunceient writers: which is, y^t 350 miles[2] at the least of the North Pole on both sides are not to be sailed, which appeareth not to be true, for that the White Sea, and farther north-ward, is now sayled and daily fisht in, cleane contrary to the writings and opinions of auncient writers; yea, and how many places hath bin discouered that were not knowne in times past? It is also no marueile (as in the beginning of the first description of this uoyage I haue sayd),[3] that vnder the North Pole for 23 degrees, it is as cold on both sides, one as the other, although it hath not beene fully discouered. Who would beleeue that in the Periudan mountaines,[4] and the Alpes, that lye betweene Spaine, Italie, Germanie, and France, there is so great cold, that the snow thereon neuer melteth, and yet lye a great deale nearer the sunne, then the

---

[1] *Petrus Plancius*, a celebrated theologian and mathematician, born in 1552, at Drenoutre in Flanders. He was one of the principal promoters and advisers of the various expeditions fitted out by the Dutch in the first years of their independence, so much to the advancement of science and to their own honour and advantage. At the synod of Dort, in 1619, Plancius was commissioned to revise the Dutch translation of the Old Testament in the "States Bible". He died at Amsterdam on the 25th May, 1622.—*Biogr. Univ.*

[2] The original has 305 miles, which are equal to 1220 geographical miles. The distance meant is from the pole to the Arctic circle.

[3] Page 5.   [4] *Gheberchte van Pireneen*—the Pyrenees.

countries lying on the North Seas doe, being low countries.[1] By what meanes then is it so cold in those hilles? onely by meanes of the deepe uallies, wherein the snow lyes so deepe, that the sunne cannot shine vpon the ground, by reason that the high hilles keepe the sunne from shining on them. So it is (as I iudge) with the ice in the Tartarian Seas, which is also called the Ice Sea, about Noua Zembla, where the ice that commeth into those seas out of the riuers that are in Tartaria and Cathaia, can not melt, by reason of the great quantitie thereof, and for that the sun sheweth not high aboue those places, and therefore casteth not so great a heat, as it can easily melt: which is the cause that the ice lyeth there still, as the snowe doth in the hilles of Spaine aforesayd, and that the sayd ice maketh it farre colder there, then it is a greate deal neerer the Pole in the large seas;[2] and although those places that are not discouered, cannot bee so well described as if they were discouered, yet I thought good to say thus much for a memoriall; and now I will proceed to the declaration of the second uoyage made into the North Seas.[3]

In anno 1595, the generall States of the vnited prouinces, and Prince Maurice, caused seuen shippes to bee prepared to sayle through the Wey-gates, or the Straights of Nassaue,[4] to the kingdome of Cathaia and China: two out of Amsterdam, two out of Zelandt, two out of Enck-huysen, and one out of Roterdam: sixe of them laden with diuers kindes of wares, marchandizes, and with money, and factors to sell the said wares; the seuenth beeing a pinace, that had commission, when the other shippes were past about the Cape de Tabin[5] (which is the furthest point of Tartaria), or

[1] *Als dese aen de Noordt Zee ligghende Nederlanden*—than these (our) Netherlands, which lie on the North Sea.

[2] *In de ruyme Zee*—in the *open sea*.

[3] *By den Noorden om*—round by the north.

[4] *De Waygats oft Strate de Nassou.* See page 27, note 4. By the Russians these straits are called Yugórskyi Schar.—*Lütke*, p. 29.

[5] Cape Taimur. See page 37, note 1.

so farre that they might saile foorth southward without any let or hinderance of the ice, to turne backe againe, and to bring newes thereof. And I being in William Barents ship, that was our chiefe pilote,[1] and James Hems-kerke chiefe factor,[2] thought good to write downe the same in order as it is here after declared, as I did the first uoyage, according to the course and stretching of the land as it lyeth.

First, after we had been mustered at Amsterdam, and euery man taken an oath that was then purposely ministered vnto vs,[3] vpon the 18 of June wee sailed to the Texel, from thence to put to sea with other ships that were appointed to meet vs at a certaine day; and so to begin our uoiage in the name of God.

The 2 of July, wee set saile out of the Texel, in the morning at breake of day, holding our course north-west and by north, and sayled about sixe [24] miles.

After that wee sailed north north-west 18 [72] miles, till the 3 of July in the morning, being then as we esteemed

---

[1] *Die opperste Piloot was.*

[2] *Opper Comis*—chief commissary or supercargo. Jacob Heemskerck was a native of Amsterdam, of a family of distinction still resident there. He took part in both the second and third voyages. He was afterwards employed in the navy of Holland, and served his country with great honour. In 1607, having the rank of vice-admiral, he commanded a fleet of twenty-six vessels sent against the Spaniards, and on the 25th of April fell in with the Spanish fleet, consisting of twenty ships and ten galleons, commanded by Don Juan Alvarez Davila. The engagement took place before Gibraltar; and on the second broadside Heemskerck had a leg carried away by a cannon-shot. He, however, continued to encourage his men, and retained his sword till he died. The Dutch gained a complete victory; seven vessels of the Spaniards were burned, and most of the remainder sunk; their admiral being killed, and his son taken prisoner. A superb monument was erected to Heemskerck in the old church at Amsterdam.—*Moreri; Biogr. Univ.*

[3] *Ons den behoorlijcken eedt afghenomen is*—we had been *duly* sworn. There is no reason for supposing that any special oath was administered, but merely the usual oath of service.

vnder 55 degrees; then the wind being north-west, and north north-west, calme weather, we sailed west and west and by south 4 [16] miles, till the 4 of July in the morning: after that, the winde being north north-west and rather more northerly, wee sayled west and west and by north 15 [60] miles, till the 5 of July in the morning, and after that 8 [32] miles more, till the sunne was west [¼ to 4 P.M.]

Then we wound about and sailed 10 [40] miles north-east, till the 6 of July in the morning, and so held on our course for the space of 24 [96] miles till the 7 July, the sunne being south [¾ p. 10 A.M.], and held the same course for 8 [32] miles, till midnight.

Then wee wound about and sailed west south-west fourteene [56] miles, till the ninth of July in the morning; and then againe wee wound north-eastward till evening, and so sayled about tenne [40] miles.

And then eighteene [72] miles more, east-ward,[1] till the tenth of July in the euening; then we wound about againe and sailed south-west, eight [32] miles, till the 11 of July, the sunne then being south-east [½ p. 7 A.M.]

Then wee wound north and north and by east, about sixteene [64] miles, till the twelue of July,[2] and then north and by west tenne [40] miles.

The 13 of July wee wound about againe, and sailed south-west and west south-west 10 [40] miles, till about three houres before euening; then wee wound againe, and sailed north north-east 10 [40] miles, till the 14 of July, the sunne being south south-east [9 A.M.], and then north and by east and north north-east 18 [72] miles, till the 15 of July in the morning: after that north and by east 12 [48] miles vntill euening; then wee saw Norway, and then wee sayled north and by east 18 [72] miles, till the 16 of July in the euening; at that time the sunne being north-west [½ p. P.M.]; and

[1] *Noorden ten oosten*—N. by E.
[2] *Outrent zuyder son*—when the sun was about south. (Omitted.)

vpon the 17 of July, north-east and north-east and by north, 24 [96] miles, till the sunne was in the west [¾ p. 3 P.M.]

Then againe wee sayled north-east,[1] 20 [80] miles, till the 18 of July, the sunne being north-west; from thence wee sayled north-west and by north 18 [72] miles, till the 19 of July, when the sunne was west.

From thence againe we wound about, north-east and by north and north-east, till the 20 of July, while sixe glasses were run out, in the first quarter,[2] and then stayed for our pinnace, that could not follow vs because the wind blew so stiffe: that quarter[3] being out, we saw our company lying to lee-ward,[4] to stay for vs, and when wee were gotten to them, wee helde our course (as before) till euening and sailed about 30 [120] miles.

Then we sayled south-east and by east 26 [104] miles, till the 21 of July in the euening, when we set our watch, and held on the same course for 10 [40] miles till the 22 of July, the sun being south south-east [9 A.M.]: the same euening,[5] the sun being south south-west [¾ p. 11 A.M.], we saw a great whale right before our bough,[6] that lay and slept, which by the rushing of the ship that made towards it, and the noyse of our men, awaked and swamme away, or els wee must haue sailed full vpon her; and so wee sayled eight [32] miles, till the sunne was north north-west [¼ p. 9 P.M.].

The twenty-third[7] of July wee sayled south-east and by south fifteene [60] miles, till the sunne was south south-west

---

[1] *N. ten o.*—N. by E.

[2] *Tottet seste glas int eerste quartier.*—Six half-hour glasses of the first watch would make the reckoned time to be 11 P.M. But from the context it would rather seem that the *morning* watch is meant, so that the time would be 7 A.M.

[3] Watch.

[4] *Op de ly legghen*—lying to.

[5] *Des naenoens*—in the afternoon.

[6] The bow of the ship.

[7] "Thirteenth."—*Ph.*

and saw land about foure [16] miles from vs. Then wee wound of from the land, when the sunne was about south south-west, and sayled twentie-foure [96] miles till euening, that the sunne was north-west.[1]

After that we sayled north-ward tenne [40] miles, till the twenty-fifth[2] of July at noone, and then north north-west eight [32] miles, till mid-night; then wee wound about againe, and sayled east south-east and south-east and by south, till the twenty sixe of July, the sunne being south, and had the sunne at seauentie one degrees and ¼.[3]

The sunne being south south-west, wee wounde about againe and sayled north-east and by north, till the seauen and twentie of July, the sunne being south; being vnder 72 degrees and ⅓ partes.[4]

After that, wee sayled full north-east[5] 16 [64] myles, till the 28 of July, the sunne being east [½ p. 4 A.M.]. Then we wound about againe south and by east, till the sunne was north-west, and sayled 8 [32] miles. After that, south-east and by south 18 [72] miles, till the 29[6] of July at midnight.

After that, we wound about againe, east and by north, and sayled eight [32] miles, till the 30 of July, when the sunne was north [½ p. 10 P.M.]; then we wound south south-east, with[7] calme weather, till the 31 of July, that the sunne was west north-west[8] [5 P.M.], and sayled sixe [24] miles.

From thence wee sayled east-ward 8 [32] myles, till the first of August about midnight, in calme faire weather, and saw Trumpsand[9] south-east from vs, the sunne being north [¼ p. 10 P.M.], and wee being tenne [40] miles from the

[1] *Totten 24 n. w. son*—till N.W. sun [½ p. 7 P.M.] on the 24th.
[2] "Fifteenth."—*Ph.*
[3] 71° 15' N. lat.
[4] 72° 20' N. lat.
[5] *N. ten o.*—N. by E.
[6] "19."—*Ph.*
[7] *Meest*—mostly. (Omitted.)
[8] "North-west."—*Ph.*
[9] *Trompsont*—Troms-oe, a small island on the coast of Norway, in about 69° 40' N. lat.

land; and so sayled till the sunne was east [½ p. 7 P.M.], with a litle cold gale[1] out of the east north-east; and after that, south-east 9 miles and a halfe [38 miles], till the sunne was north-west.

Then we wound about againe, being halfe a mile [2 miles] from the land, and sayled east and by north three [12] miles, till the 3 of August, the sunne south-west [1 P.M.]; and then along by the land about 5 [20] miles.

Then we wound about again, because there lay a rocke or sand, that reached about a mile and a halfe [6 miles] out from the land into the sea, whereon Isbrant, the uize-admiral,[2] stroke with his shippe: but the weather being faire and good, he got off againe. When he stroke vpon it, he was a litle before vs: and when we heard him cry out, and saw his shippe in danger, wee in all haste wound about; and the wind being north-east and by east, and south-east, and south-east and by south,[3] wee sayled 5 [20] or 6 [24] myles along by the land, till the sunne was south, vpon the 4 of August.

Then we tooke the height of the sunne, and found it to be seauentie and one degrees and ¼. At which time till noone[4] wee had calme weather: and hauing the wind southerly wee sayled east and by north, till the fifth of August, the sunne being south-east [½ p. 7 A.M.], the North Cape[5] lying about two [8] miles east from vs; and when the sunne was north-

---

[1] *Met weynich coelts*—with little wind.

[2] *Ysbrandt de vice admirael.* The admiral was Cornelius Nai. They had both taken part in the former expedition. See page 36, note 3. The title of admiral did not denote any fixed rank, but was given to the commander of the principal ship, under whose orders the others were. We should now call him the commodore.

[3] *De windt was n. o. ten o. ende z. o. meest z. o. ende z.*—the wind was N.E. by E. and S.E., *but mostly S.E. and S.*

[4] *Middernacht*—midnight.

[5] *De Noordt-caep.* The northernmost point of Europe; unless, indeed, we regard Spitzbergen as forming a portion of this quarter of the globe. The North Cape is not a part of the continent, but it is the extremity of a small island named Mager-oe.

west [½ p. 7 P.M.], the Mother and her Daughters[1] lay southward from vs four [16] miles, and in that time we sailed about fourteene [56] miles.

Then we sailed east north-east till the 6 of August, when wee had the sunne west north-west [5 P.M.], and then Isbrandt, the uize-admiral, came to vs with his ship, and so bating some of our sayles,[2] wee sayled about 10 [40] miles.

Then wee hoysed vp our sayles againe,[3] till the sunne was north-west, and after that halde vp againe[4] with an east and east north-east wind, and sailed south and by west with a stiffe gale till the 7 of August, that the sunne was southeast; then there came a ship of Enckhuysen out of the White Sea, and then we esteemed that wee had sailed about 8 [32] miles.

The sunne being south [¾ p. 10 A.M.], the North Cape lay south-west and by south from vs about a mile and a halfe [6 miles], and the Mother and her Daughters south-west from vs about 3 [12] miles; then hauing an east and by north wind we wound about, and held our course north and by east, and sailed 14 [56] miles till the 8 of August, when the sunne was south-west [1 P.M.]; then we wound south and by east, and so held her course till the 9 of August, that the sunne was south; and then we saw a high point of land south-east from vs, and another high point of land south-ward,[5] about 4 [16] miles from vs, as we gest,[6] and so we sailed about 14 [56] miles: and then againe we

---

[1] *De Moer mette Dochters.* Three remarkable islands, so called, lying off the coast of Norway.

[2] *Doen quam tschip van Ysbrandt de vice admirael ende wy tsamen, ende maeckten malcanderen seer reddeloos*—then the ship of Ysbrand, the vice-admiral, and ours ran foul, and damaged each other very much.

[3] *Doen streecken wy de seylen*—then we *took in* our sails. The translator appears to have carried this expression into the preceding sentence, of which he evidently did not understand the meaning.

[4] Hauled them up again.

[5] *S. w.*—South-*west.*   [6] Guessed, *i.e.*, estimated.

wound north-east and by north, till the 10 of August, the sun being east [½ p. 4 A.M.], and sailed about 8 [32] miles; after that we wound south-ward againe, till the sunne was north-west [½ p. 7 P.M.], and sailed, as we gest, 10 [40] miles.

Then wee wound about againe, when the North Cape lay west and by south from vs about 9 [36] miles, the North-kyen[1] being south and by west from vs about 3 [12] miles, and sailed north north-east till the 11 of August, in very mistie weather 10 [40] miles, till the sunne was south [¾ p. 10 A.M.]

From thence wee wound about againe, with an east north-east wind, and sailed south-east and by south 8 [32] miles, till the sunne was south-west [1 P.M.] vpon the 12 of August; then the North-kyen lying south-west and by south from vs about 8 [32] miles, we lay and draue at sea, in calme weather,[2] till the 13 of August, when the sunne was south south-west [¾ p. 11 A.M.], and in that time sailed about 4 [32] miles.

Then we sailed south-east and by east about 4 glasses,[3] and the Iron-hogge with her companie (being marchants)[4] took their course south-ward, and wee sailed till the 14 of August (when the sunne was south) about 18 [72] miles, and from thence for the most part held one course till the 15 of August, the sunne being east, and there we cast out the lead and found 70 fadome deepe, and sailed 38 [152] miles till the sunne was south.

The sunne being south,[5] and the height thereof being

[1] *Noordtkien.* The extreme northern point of the main land of Norway, and consequently of the continent of Europe.
[2] *Soo dreven wy in stilte*—so we drifted in a calm.
[3] Two hours.
[4] These were some merchant vessels, bound for the White Sea, with which the expedition had fallen in, and which now parted from it.
[5] Here again, as on the 15th of August (see page 36, note 1), the note of the sun's bearing can only be regarded as approximative. It must, in fact, be understood to mean when the sun came to the meridian.

taken, it was found to be 70 degrees and 47 minutes; then in the night time wee cast out the lead, and found ground at 40 fadome, it being a bancke; the sunne being north-west [½ p. 7 P M], we cast out the lead againe and had ground at 64 fadome, and so wee went on east south-east till the 16 of August, the sunne being north-east [½ p. 1 A.M.], and there the line being out, we found no ground at 80 fadome; and after that we sailed east and east and by south, and in that time wee cast the lead often times out, and found ground at 60 and 70 fadome, either more or lesse, and so sailed 36 [144] miles, till the sunne was south.

Then we sailed east, and so continued till the 17 of August, the sunne being east [½ p. 4 A.M.] and cast out our lead, and found 60 fadome deepe, clay[1] ground; and then taking the height of the sunne, when it was south-west and by south, we found it to be 69 degrees and 54 minutes, and there we saw great store of ice all along the coast of Noua Zembla, and casting out the lead had 75 fadome soft[1] ground, and so sayled about 24 [96] miles.

After that we held diuers courses because of the ice, and sayled south-east and by east and south south-east for the space of 18 [72] miles, till the 18 of August, when the sunne was east, and then wee cast out the lead againe, and found 30 fadome soft[2] ground, and within two houres after that 25 fadome, red sand, with small shels;[3] three glasses[4] after that we had ground at 20 fadome, red sand with blacke shels,[5] as before; then we saw 2 islands, which they of Enckhuysen gaue the names of Prince Maurice and his brother,[6] which lay from us south-east 3 [12] miles,

---

[1] *Steeck*—stiff; that is, good for anchorage.   [2] *Steeck*—stiff.
[3] *Met veel cleyne stipkens*—with many small specks.
[4] An hour and a half.   [5] *Swarte stipkens*—black specks.
[6] *Zijn Excell. van Oraengien ende zijn broeder*—his Excellency of Orange and his brother. These islands were so named by Cornelius Nai on the first voyage. But, according to Linschoten, *Voyagie, ofte Schip-*

being low land, and then we sailed 8 [32] miles, till the sunne was south. [¾ p. 10 A.M.]

Then we sailed east, and oftentimes casting out the lead we found 20, 19, 18, and 17 fadome deepe, good grounde

---

vaert van by Noorden om, etc., fol. 19, retr, Orange Island was so called in honour of Prince Maurice's *father* and the Princess of Orange.

Lütke (p. 32) identifies Maurice Island with Ostrov Dolgoi or Long Island, and Orange Island with Bolschoi Selénets or Great Greenland; and he is of opinion that the Hollanders, or at all events Linschoten, had no knowledge of Matvyéyev Island. But this is hardly consistent with that able navigator's previous identification of the latter island with Matfloe, where (as is mentioned in page 36 of the present work) the vessels of Nai and Barentsz met on the first voyage. And, indeed, it may be demonstrated that Maurice Island is not Dolgoi, but Matfloe or Matvyéyev Island; that Orange Island is the small island, named Ostrov Golets, close to the northern extremity of Long Island or Dolgoi; and that Dolgoi itself is the Land of New Walcheren, which the Dutch hesitated to describe as an island or as a portion of the mainland, but which Lütke (p. 32) erroneously deems to be the latter.

Premising that Linschoten's vessel, like that of Barentsz, passed between Matfloe and Dolgoi, the following description of the *three* islands above mentioned, given by Linschoten, will be found to be as conclusive as it is clear and intelligible. In fol. 18, that writer says:—"The island that lay to the north of us appeared to be of a roundish form, and on the side past which we sailed it was to the sight a short mile [3 or 4 miles] in extent. To the south of this island, and about a long mile [4 or 5 miles] distant, lay another island, which was the smallest and likewise the middlemost of the three. And from this middlemost island, about a short mile [3 or 4 miles] distant to the S.E., lay the third or southernmost island, which in appearance was much the largest, and which, as we sailed past it, lay on our left hand, and seemed on that side to be about a long mile [4 or 5 miles] in extent; but when on the other side, as we looked southwards at it, its west coast extended as far as we could see from the topmast, so that we doubted whether it was part of the continent or an island." And in the chart which accompanies these remarks, Linschoten has the following note:—"Maurice Island lies with the Land of New Walcheren N.N.W. and S.S.E., about 2 [8] miles apart; and with the Island of Orange it lies N. and S., a long mile [4 or 5 miles] distant."

On referring to Lütke's chart, it will at once be manifest how closely Maurice Island, New Walcheren, and Orange Island, as thus described, correspond with Matvyéyev Island or Matfloe, Long Island or Dolgoi,

mixed with blacke shels,[1] and saw the Wey-gates (the sunne being west) [¾ p. 3 P.M.], which lay east north-east from vs about 5 [20] miles; and after that we sailed about 8 [32] miles.

Then we sailed vnder 70 degrees,[2] vntill we came to the Wey-gates, most part through broken ice; and when we got to Wey-gates, we cast out our lead, and for a long time found 13 and 14 fadome, soft[3] ground mixed with blacke shels;[4] not long after that wee cast out the lead and found 10 fadome deepe, the wind being north, and we forced to hold stifly aloofe,[5] in regard of the great quantity of ice, till about midnight; then we were forced to wind north-ward, because of certaine rocks that lay on the south side of Wey-gates, right before vs about a mile and a halfe [6 miles], hauing ten fadome deepe: then wee changed our course, and sailed west north-west for the space of 4 glasses,[6] after that we wound about againe east and east and by south, and so entred into Wey-gates, and as wee went in, we cast out the lead, and found 7 fadome deepe, little more or lesse, till the 19 of August; and then the sunne being south-east [½ p. 7 A.M.] we entered into the Wey-gates, in the road, the wind being north.

The right chanell betweene the Image Point[7] and the

---

and Golets Island, respectively; and if to this be added, that in that chart the passage between the islands is in about 69° 30′ N. lat., and that Linschoten, when distant from Maurice Island, by estimation, 10 [40] miles W. by N. or nearly W., found himself to be in 69° 34′ N. at., while William Barentsz, when 2 [8] miles W. from the islands, made his latitude to be 69° 15′ N., there will remain no room for doubt on the subject.

[1] *Meest steeck grondt met swarte stipkens ghemenght*—mostly stiff ground mixed with black specks.

[2] *Van de 70 graden*—from the 70th parallel of north latitude.

[3] *Steeck*—stiff.   [4] *Stipkens*—spots.

[5] *Ende was ghestadich hout loef ende draghende*—and we kept continually luffing and falling off before the wind.

[6] Two hours.

[7] *Beelthoeck*. See page 27, note 4.

Samuters land[1] was full of ice, so that it was not well[2] to be past through, and so we went into the road, which we called the Trayen Bay,[3] because we found store of trayen-oyle there: this is a good bay for the course of the ice,[4] and good almost for all windes, and we may saile so farre into it as we will at 4, 5, and 3 fadome, good anchor-ground: on the east side it is deepe[5] water.

The 20 of August, the height of the sunne being taken with the crosse-staffe,[6] wee found that it was eleuated aboue the horizon 69 degrees 21 minuts,[7] when it was south-west and by south, being at the highest, or before it began to descend.

The 21 of August we went on land within the Wey-gates[8] with foure and fiftie men, to see the scituation of the countrey, and being 2 [8] miles within the land, we found many vel-werck trayen, and such like wares,[9] and diuers footsteps of men and deere; whereby wee perceived that some men dwelt thereabouts, or else vsed to come thither.

And to assure vs the more thereof, wee might perceiue it by the great number of images, which we found there upon the Image or Beelthooke[10] (so called by us) in great aboun-

---

[1] *De Samiuten landt*—a part of the country of the Samoyedes, lying in the extreme north-east of the present government of Archangel.

[2] *Wel moghelijck*—well possible.

[3] *Traenbay*—Train-oil Bay.

[4] *Den ysganck*—the drifting of the ice.

[5] *Diepste*—the deepest.

[6] See page 10, note 2.

[7] A very unscientific, and indeed incorrect, mode of expressing the fact, that they were in 69° 21' N. lat., as resulting from an observation of the sun.

[8] *Opt lande van de Weygats*—on land from the Weygats. De Veer adopts the vulgar error adverted to in page 27 (note 4) of the present work, and calls the Straits of Nassau, instead of the island to the north of these straits, by the name of "Weygats".

[9] *Diversche sleden met velwerck, traen, ende dierghelijcke waer*—several sledyes with skins, train-oil, and such like wares.

[10] *Op den Beeldthoeck*—at Image Point.

dance, whereof ten dayes after we were better informed by the Samuters[1] and the Russians, when we spake with them.

And when wee entered further[2] into the land, wee vsed all the meanes we could, to see if we could find any houses, or men, by whom wee might bee informed of the scituation of the sea[3] there abouts; whereof afterwards wee had better intelligence by the Samuters, that tolde vs, that there are certaine men dwelling on the Wey-gates,[4] and vpon Noua Zembla; but wee could neither finde men, houses, nor any other things; so that to have better information, we went with some of our men further south-east into the land, towards the sea-side;[5] and as we went, we found a path-way made with mens feete in the mosse or marsh-ground, about halfe knee deepe, for that going so deepe wee felt hard ground vnder our feete, which at the deepest was no higher than our shoes; and as wee went forward to the sea coast, wee were exceeding glad, thinking that wee had seene a passage open, where wee might get through, because we saw so little ice there: and in the euening entering into our ship againe, wee shewed them that newes. Meanetime our maister[6] had sent out a boat to see if the Tartarian Sea[7] was open, but it could not get into the sea because of the ice, yet they rowed to the Crosse-point,[8] and there let the boate lye, and went ouer the land to the

[1] *Samiuten*—Samoyedes.
[2] *Van de Weygats*—from Weygats. (Omitted.)
[3] *De gheleghentheyt der zeevaert*—the particulars of the navigation.
[4] *Opt Waygats*. Here, however, De Veer speaks of the *Island* of Waigatsch.
[5] *Wy...verder z. o. aen trocken nae den oever van der zee*—we went further S.E. towards the sea-side. It is manifest, that while going towards the sea-side, they could not have gone further *into the land*.
[6] *Schipper*—captain or master of the vessel. Most probably William Barentsz is meant; though in page 63 Cornelis Jacobszoon is spoken of as the "schipper" of William Barentsz.
[7] The sea of Kara.
[8] *Cruijs-hoeck*; by the Russians called Sukhoi Nos.

INTO THE NORTH SEAS. 55

West Point,[1] and there perceiued that the ice in the Tartarian Sea lay full vpon the Russian coastes, and in the mouth of Wey-gates.

The twentie three of August wee found a lodgie[2] or boate of Pitzore,[3] which was sowed together with bast or ropes,[4] that had beene north-ward to seeke for some sea-horses teeth, trayen,[5] and geese, which they fetcht with their boat, to lade in certaine shippes that were to come out of Russia, through Wey-gates.

Which shippes they sayd (when they spake with vs), were to saile into the Tartarian Sea, by the riuer of Oby,[6] to a place called Vgolita[7] in Tartaria, there to stay all winter, as they vsed to doe euery yeere: and told vs that it would yet bee nine or tenne weekes ere it began to freeze in that place, and that when it once began to freeze, it would freeze so hard, that as then men might goe ouer the sea into Tartaria (along vpon the ice), which they called Mermare.[8]

[1] *De Twist hoeck*—Cape Dispute; so named, because, on the first voyage of Nai and Brandt Ysbrandtsz, a dispute arose between them as to whether or not the passage extended further eastward. Through a typographical error, the Dutch text has *de t Wist hoeck*, whence has arisen the *West* Point of the translator. This is the Kóninoi Nos of the Russians.

[2] See page 33, note 6.

[3] The Petchora, a considerable river, which rises in the Ural mountains, and flows into the Arctic Ocean to the S. of Novaya Zemlya.

[4] *Met bast tsamen ghenaeyet*—sewed together with bast:—the inner bark of the linden or lime-tree (*Tilia*), of which is formed the Russian matting, so well known in commerce. The word *bast*, which in German and Dutch means "bark", is in English frequently pronounced, and even written *bass*.

[5] *Trayn*—train-oil.

[6] *Voorby de reviere Oby*—beyond the river Oby.

[7] Linschoten has "to another *river*, which they said was called *Gillissy*", meaning the large river *Yenisei*, which carries a great portion of the waters of Siberia into the Arctic Ocean.

[8] *Dattet gat soude toe vriesen, ende alst begon te vriesen soudet dan stracks toe vriesen, ende datmen dan over ys mocht loopen tot in Tartarien over de zee, die zy noemden Mermare* — ere the passage would be

The 24 of August in the morning betimes, we went on board of the lodgie, to haue further information and instruction of the sea on the east side of Wey-gates, and they gaue vs good instruction such as you haue heard.

The 25 of August we went againe to the lodgie, and in friendly maner spake with them, we for our parts offering them friendship; and then they gaue vs 8 fat geese,[1] that lay in the bottome of their boat: we desired that one or two of them would goe with vs on board our ship, and they willingly went with vs to the number of seuen; and being in our ship they wondered much at the greatnesse and furniture of our ship: and after they had seene and looked into it in euery place,[2] we set fish,[3] butter, and cheese before them to eat, but they refused it, saying that that day was a fasting day with them; but at last when they saw some of our pickled-herrings, they eat them, both heads, tayles, skin, and guts;[4] and hauing eaten thereof, we gaue them a small ferkin of herrings, for the which they gaue vs great thankes, knowing not what friendship they should doe vs to requite our courtesie, and we brought them with our pinnace into the Traen-Bay.

About noone wee hoysed vp our anchors with a west north-west wind; the course or stretching of Wey-gates is east to the Cruis point,[5] and then north-east to the Twist point,[6] and somewhat more easterly: From thence the land of Wey-gates reacheth north north-east, and north and by

frozen over; and that when it once began to freeze, it would speedily be frozen over, so that they could walk over the ice to Tartary (Siberia) across the sea which they called Mermare.

[1] *Die zy seer veel...hadden*—whereof they had many. (Omitted.)
[2] *Van voren tot achteren*—from stem to stern.
[3] *Vleysch*—meat.
[4] *So hebbense daer alle t'samen van ghegheten, met hooft, met staert, met al, van boven afbytende*—they one and all partook of them; and, biting from the head downwards, ate head, tail, and everything.
[5] *Cruijs hoeck*—Cross Point. See page 54, note 8.
[6] *Twisthoeck*—Cape Dispute. See note 1 in the preceding page.

east, and then north, and somewhat westerly; we sayled north-east and east-ward[1] 2 [8] miles, by the Twist point, but then we were compelled to saile backe again, because of the great store of ice, and tooke our course to our road aforesaid; and sayling backe againe wee found a good place by the Crosse point to anchor in, that night.

The 26 of August in the morning we hoysed anchor, and put out our forke-saile,[2] and so sailed to our old road there to stay for a more conuenient time.

The 28, 29, and 30 of August till the 31, the winde for the most part was south-west, and William Barents our captaine sayled to the south side of Wey-gates, and there went on land,[3] where wee found certaine wilde men (called Samuters),[4] and yet not altogether wilde, for they being 20 in number staid and spake with our men, being but 9 together, about a mile [4 miles] within the land, our men not thinking to find any men there (for that we had at other times beene on land in the *Wey-gates, and saw none); at last, it being mistie weather, they perceiued men [5] fiue and fiue in a company, and we were hard by them before[6] we knew it. Then our interpreter went alone towards them to speake with them; which they perceiuing sent one towardes vs, who comming almost to our men, tooke an arrow out of his quiuer, offering to shoote at him; wherewith our interpretor, being without armes, was afraide, and cryed vnto him, saying (in Russian speach), shoote not, we are friends: which the other hearing, cast his bow and arrowes to the ground, therewith giuing him to vnderstand that he was well content to speake with our man: which done, our man

[1] *N. o. wel soo oostelijk*—north-east a little easterly.
[2] *De fock*—the foresail.
[3] *Aent vaste landt*—to the main land; namely, the coast of Russia.
[4] *Samiuten*—Samoyedes.
[5] *In twee hoopen*—in two bodies.
[6] Two lines of Phillip's translation, being from *, are printed twice by mistake.

called to him once againe, and sayd, we are friendes; whereunto he made answere and sayd, then you are welcome: and saluting one the other, bended both their heades downe towardes the ground, after the Russian manner. This done,[1] our interpreter questioned with him about the scituation and stretching of the sea east-ward through the straightes of Wey-gates; whereof he gaue vs good instruction, saying, that when they should haue past a poynt of land about 5 dayes sayling from thence (shewing[2] north-eastward), that after that, there is a great sea (shewing towardes the south-east vpward[3]); saying, that hee knew it very well, for that one had been there that was sent thither by their king with certaine souldiers,[4] whereof he had been captaine.

The maner of their apparell is like as we vse to paint wild men; but they are not[5] wilde, for they are of reasonable iudgement. They are apparelled in hartes[6] skins from the head to the feete, vnlesse it be the principallest of them, which are apparelled, whether they bee men or women, like vnto the rest, as aforesayd, vnlesse it bee on their heads, which they couer with certaine coloured cloth lyned with furre: the rest wear cappes of hartes or buckes skinnes, the rough side outwardes, which stand close to their heades, and are very fitte. They weare long hayre, which they plaite and fold and let it hang downe vpon their backes. They are (for the most part all) short and low of stature, with broad flat faces, small eyes, short legges, their knees standing outwards; and are very quicke to goe and leape. They trust not strangers: for although that wee shewed them all the

[1] *Dese gheleghentheyt ghevonden* — availing himself of this opportunity.
[2] *Wysende*—pointing.
[3] *Wysende nae't z. o. op*—pointing towards the south-east.
[4] *Met een partye volcks*—with a number of persons.
[5] *Effenwel niet*—not altogether.
[6] *Rheeden*—reindeer.

courtesie and friendship that wee could, yet they trusted vs not much: which wee perceiued hereby, that as vpon the first of September we went againe on land to them, and that one of our men desired to see one of their bowes, they refused it, making a signe that they would not doe it. Hee that they called their king, had centinels standing abroad, to see what was done in the countrie, and what was bought and sould. At last, one of our men went neerer to one of the centinels, to speake with him, and offered him great friendship, according to their accustomed manner; withall giuing him a bisket, which he with great thankes tooke, and presently eate it, and while he eate it, hee still lookt diligently about him on all sides what was done.

Their sleades[1] stood alwayes ready with one or two hartes in them, that runne so swiftly with one or two men in them, that our horses were not able to follow them. One of our men shot a musket towards the sea, wherewith they were in so great feare that they ranne and leapt like mad men; yet at last they satisfied themselues when they perceiued that it was not maliciously done to hurt them: and we told them by our interpretor, that we vsed our peeces in stead of bowes, whereat they wondered, because of the great blow and noyse that it gaue and made: and to shew them what we could doe therewith, one of our men tooke a flatte stone about halfe a handfull broad, and set it vpon a hill a good way off from him: which they perceiuing, and thinking that wee meant some-what thereby, 50 or 60 of them gathered round about vs, and yet some-what farre off; wherewith hee that had the peece, shotte it off, and with the bullet smote the stone in sunder, whereat they woondred much more then before.

After that we tooke our leaues one of the other, with great friendship on both sides; and when we were in our penace,[2] we al put off our hattes and bowed our heades vnto them,

[1] Sledges.   [2] Pinnace.

sounding our trumpet: they in their maner saluting vs also, and then went to their sleads againe.

And after they were gone from vs and were some-what within the land, one of them came ryding to the shore, to fetch a rough-heawed image, that our men had taken off the shore and carried into their boate: and when he was in our boate, and perceiued the image, hee made vs a signe that wee had not done well to take away that image; which wee beholding, gaue it to him again: which when he had receiued, he placed it vpon a hill right by the sea side, and tooke it not with him, but sent a slead to fetch it from thence. And as farre as wee could perceiue, they esteemed that image to be their god;[1] for that right ouer against that place in the Wey-gates, which we called Beelthooke,[2] we found certaine hundreds of such carued images, all rough, about the heads being somewhat round, and in the middle hauing a litle hill instead of a nose, and about the nose two cuttes in place of eyes, and vnder the nose a cutte in place of a mouth. Before the images, wee found great store of ashes, and bones of hartes; whereby it is to be supposed that there they offered vnto them.

Hauing left the Samuters, the sunne being south-ward,[3] William Barents, our captaine, spake to the admirall to will him to set sayle, that they might goe forward; but they had not so many wordes together, as was betweene them the day before;[4] for that when the admirall and vize-admirall had spoken with him,[5] the admirall seeming to be well contented therewith, said vnto him: Captaine,[6] what think you were best for vs to doe? he made answere, I thinke we

[1] *Sulcken beelden voor haer Goden*—such images for their gods.
[2] Image Point. See page 53.
[3] *Ontrent zuyder son*—the sun being about south.
[4] From this it is manifest that a previous dispute had taken place, which is not recorded.
[5] *Hem uyt ghehoort hadden*—had heard him out.
[6] *Willem Barentsz.* Nai did not call him captain, but addressed him by his name.

should doe well to set sayle, and goe forward on our uoyage, that wee may accomplish it. Whereunto the admirall answeared him, and sayd: Looke well what you doe, captaine:[1] at which time, the sunne was north-west [½ p. 7 P.M.].

The 2 of September, a litle before sunne rising, wee put foorth our anckor[2] to get out, for that the winde as then blew south south-west; it being good weather to get out, and ill weather to lie still: for we lay under a low bancke.[3] The admirall and vize-admirall seeing vs making out, began also to hoyse their anckors, and to set sayle.

When wee put out our focke-sayle,[4] the sunne was east and by south [¼ p. 5 A.M.]; and then we sayled to the Crosse-poynt, and there wee cast anckor to stay for the vize-admirals pinnace; which with much labour and paines in time got out of the ice, by often casting out of their anckor,[5] and in the euening shee got to vs. In the morning, about 2 houres before sunne rising, we set sayle, and by sunne rising we got within a mile [4 miles] east-ward of the Twist-poynt,[6] and sayled north-ward 6 miles, till the sunne was south [¾ p. 10 A.M.]. Then wee were forced to wind about, because of the great quantitie of ice, and the mist that then fell; at which time the winde blew so vncertaine that we could hold no course, but were forced continually to winde and turne about,[7] by reason of the ice and the vnconstantnesse of the wind, together with the mist, so that our course was vncertaine, and we supposed that we had sailed south-ward vp towardes the Samuters countrey, and then held our course south-west, till the watchers[8] were north-west from

[1] *Willem Barentsz, siet wat ghy seght*—mind what you say.
[2] *Ons werp ancker*—our kedge-anchor.
[3] *Op een laghen wal*—on a lee shore.   [4] Fore-sail.
[5] *Met diversche reyse zijn werp-ancker uyt te brenghen*—by repeatedly carrying out their kedger (and so warping out).
[6] Cape Dispute.
[7] *Mosten stedts wenden*—were forced continually to tack.
[8] *De Wachters*. The stars β and γ of the Little Bear were called by

vs; then we came to the point of the States Island,[1] lying east-ward about a musket shot from the land, having 13 fadome deepe.

The 4 of September, we hoysed anchor because of the ice, and sailed betwene the firme land and the States Island, where wee lay close by the States Island at 4 and 5 fadome deepe, and made our shippe fast with a cable cast on the shoare; and there we were safe from the course of the ice,[2] and diuers time went on land to get[3] hares, whereof there were many in that island.

The 6 of September, some of our men went on shore vpon the firme land to seeke for stones, which are a kinde of diamont,[4] whereof there are many also in the States Island: and while they were seeking ye stones, 2 of our mē lying together in one place, a great leane white beare came sodainly stealing out, and caught one of them fast by the necke, who not knowing what it was that tooke him by the necke, cried out and said, Who is that that pulles me so by the necke?

---

the earlier navigators of modern times le Guardie, les Gardes, the Guards, de Wachters, die Wächter, on account of their constantly going round the Pole, and, as it were, guarding it. See Ideler, *Untersuchungen über die Sternnamen*, p. 291. These names do not, however, appear to be used by seamen at the present day.

The Amsterdam Latin version of 1598 renders the expression of the Dutch text by "Ursa minor, quam nautæ *vigiles* vocant;" but, according to Ideler (loc. cit.), the corresponding term used by writers of the middle ages, is *Circitores*, signifying, according to Du Cange, "militares, qui castra circuibant, *qui faisoient la ronde, et la sentinelle avancée*, ut vulgo loquimur".

In Il Penseroso, Milton speaks of "outwatching the Bear", evidently alluding to the never-setting of the circumpolar stars:

"Arctos oceani metuentes æquore tingi."

The time on the 3rd of September, when "the watchers were north-west", was about ½ past 10 P.M.

[1] *Staten Eylandt.* See page 37, note 4.
[2] *Den ysgangk*—the drifting of the ice.
[3] *Schieten*—to shoot.
[4] Namely, pieces of rock-crystal. See page 37.

How a frightful, cruel, big bear tare to pieces two of our companions.

Wherewith the other, that lay not farre from him,[1] lifted vp his head to see who it was, and perceiuing it to be a monsterous beare, cryed and sayd, Oh mate, it is a beare! and therewith presently rose vp and ran away.

The beare at the first faling vpon the man, bit his head in sunder,[2] and suckt out his blood, wherewith the rest of the men that were on land, being about 20 in number, ran presently thither, either to saue the man, or else to driue the beare from the dead body; and hauing charged their peeces and bent their pikes,[3] set vpon her, that still was deuouring the man, but perceiuing them to come towards her, fiercely and cruelly ran at them, and gat another of them out from the companie, which she tare in peeces, wherewith all the rest ran away.

We perceiuing out of our ship and pinace that our men ran to the sea-side to save themselues, with all speed entered into our boates, and rowed as fast as we could to the shoare to relieue our men. Where being on land, we beheld the cruell spectacle of our two dead men, that had beene so cruelly killed and torne in pieces by the beare. Wee seeing that, incouraged our men to goe backe againe with vs, and with peeces, curtleaxes,[4] and halfe pikes, to set vpon the beare; but they would not all agree thereunto, some of them saying, Our men are already dead, and we shall get the beare well enough, though wee oppose not our selues into so open danger; if wee might saue our fellowes liues, then we would make haste; but now wee neede not make such speede, but take her at an aduantage, with most securitie for our selues, for we haue to doe with a cruell, fierce and rauenous beast. Whereupon three of our men went forward, the beare still

---

[1] *Die by hem in de cuijl lach*—that lay near him in the hollow.

[2] *De beyr beet den eenen terstond thooft in stucken*—the bear instantly bit the one man's head in pieces

[3] *Haer roers ende spietsen gevelt*—lowering their muskets and pikes.

[4] See page 26, note 2.

deuouring her prey, not once fearing the number of our men, and yet they were thirtie at the least: the three that went forward in that sort, were Cornelius Jacobson,[1] maister of William Barents shippe, William Gysen, pilote of the pinace, and Hans van Nufflen, William Barents purser:[2] and after that the sayd maister and pilote had shot three times and mist, the purser stepping somewhat further forward, and seeing the beare to be within the length of a shot, presently leauelled his peece, and discharging it at the beare, shot her into the head betweene both the eyes, and yet shee held the man still faste by the necke, and lifted vp her head, with the man in her mouth, but shee beganne somewhat to stagger; wherewith the purser and a Scotishman[3] drew out their courtlaxes, and stroke at her so hard that their courtlaxes burst,[4] and yet she would not leaue the man. At last William Geysen went to them, and with all his might stroke the beare vpon the snowt with his peece, at which time the beare fell to the ground, making a great noyse, and William Geyson leaping vpon her cut her throat. The seuenth of September wee buryed the dead bodyes of our men in the States Island, and hauing fleaed the beare, carryed her skinne to Amsterdam.

The ninth of September, wee set saile from the States Island,[5] but the ice came in so thicke and with such force, that wee could not get through; so that at euening wee came backe againe to the States Island, the winde being

[1] *Cornelis Jacobsz. de schipper van Willem Barentsz.* William Barentsz was not in the capacity merely of commander of his own vessel, but in that of pilot-major of the fleet.

[2] *Hans van Nuffelen, schryver van Willem Barentsz*—i.e., his clerk or writer.

[3] *Een Schotsman.* From the intercourse which then existed, as now, between the opposite coasts of the German Ocean, there is nothing surprising in the fact of their having had such a person with them. The name of this individual is not recorded.

[4] *In stucken spronghen*—shivered in pieces.

[5] *By de wal henen*—along the coast. (Omitted.)

westerly. There the admirale and the pinace of Roterdam fell on ground by certaine rockes, but gote off againe without any hurt.

The tenth of September wee sayled againe from the States Island towards the Wey-gates, and sent two boates into the sea to certifie vs what store of ice was abroad; and that euening we came all together into Wey-gates, and anckored by the Twist Point.[1]

The 11 of September in the morning, we sailed againe into the Tartarian Sea,[2] but we fell into great store of ice, so that wee sailed back againe to the Wey-gates, and anckored by the Crosse Point, and about mid-night we saw a Russian lodgie,[3] that sailed from the Beeltpoint[4] towardes the Samuters land. The 13 of September, the sunne being south [¾ p. 10 A.M.], there beganne a great storme to blow out of the south south-west,[5] the weather being mistie, melancholly,[6] and snowie,[7] and the storme increasing more and more, we draue through.[8]

The 14 of September the weather beganne to bee somewhat clearer, the winde being north-west, and the storme blowing stiffe[9] out of the Tartarian Sea; but at euening it was[10] faire weather, and then the wind blewe north-east. The same day our men went on the other side of Wey-gates on the firme land,[11] to take the depth of the channel, and entered into the bough behinde the islands,[12] where there stood a

[1] Cape Dispute. See page 55, note 1.
[2] The Sea of Kara. [3] Boat. [4] Image Point. See page 60.
[5] *W. z. w.*—W.S.W. [6] *Moddich*—dirty.
[7] *Met sneejacht*—with drifting snow.
[8] *Also dat wy deur dreven*—so that we drifted before it.
[9] *Die stroom quam stijf*—the *current* ran strong.
[10] *Ende was tot den avondt*—and till the evening it was.
[11] *Aent vaste landt*—to the main land.
[12] *Voeren heel in de bocht achter het eylandt mette steert*—went quite into the bay behind the island with the tail. This is a small island lying in the channel, with a long sand or shallow running out behind it like a tail. To the bay behind this island the Dutch gave the name of Brandts Bay.

little howse made of wood, and a great fall of water into the land.[1] The same morning we hoysed vp our anckor,[2] thinking once againe to try what we could doe to further our uoyage; but our admirall being of another minde, lay still till the fifteene of September.

The same day in the morning the winde draue in from the east end of the Wey-gates,[3] whereby wee were forced presently to hoyse anchors, and the same day sailed out from the west ende of the Wey-gates, with all our fleete, and made home-wardes againe, and that day past by the islands called Matfloe and Delgoy,[4] and that night wee sayled twelue [48] miles, north-west and by west, till Saterday in the morning, and then the winde fell north-east, and it began to snow.

The 16 of September, from morning to evening, wee sayled west north-west 18 [72] miles, at 42 fadome deepe; in the night it snowed, and there blew very much winde out of the north-east: the first quarter[5] wee had 40 fadome deepe, but in the morning we saw not any of our ships.

After that wee sailed all the night againe till the 17 of September in the morning, with two schower sailes,[6] north-west and by west and west north-west 10 [40] miles; the same day in the second quarter we had 50 fadome deepe, and in the morning 38 fadome deepe, sandy ground with blacke shels.[7]

Sunday in the morning wee had the winde north and north-west, with a great gale, and then the admirals pinnace kept vs company, and sailed by vs with one saile from morning to evening, south south-west and south-west and by south, for the space of 6 [24] miles.

[1] *Een groot afwater*—a great fall of water.
[2] *Ende de stengh om hoogh*—and set the top-mast. (Omitted.)
[3] *Quam het ys weder om het oosteijnt vande Weygats in dryven*—the ice came again drifting in round the east end of Weygats.
[4] See page 36, note 2. [5] Watch.
[6] Courses. [7] *Stippelen*—specks.

Then we saw the point of Candynaes[1] lying south-east from vs, and then wee had 27 fadome deepe, redde san' with blacke shels. Sunday at night wee put out our focke sayle,[2] and wound northward ouer, and sayled all that night till Munday in the morning, 7 [28] or 8 [32] miles north-east and north-east and by east.

The 18 of September in the morning, wee lost the sight of the pinnace that followed vs, and till noone sought after her, but wee could not finde her, and sailed[3] east-ward 3 [12] miles, and from noone till night wee sailed north and by east foure [16] miles. And from Munday at night till Tuesday in the morning, north-east and by north, seuen [28] miles; and from morning till noone, north-east and by north, 4 [16] miles; and from noone till night, north-east,[4] 5 [20] or 6 [24] miles, at 55 fadome deepe; the same euening wee woond south-ward, and sailed so till morning.

The 20 of September, wee sayled south and by west and south south-west, 7 [28] or 8 [32] miles, at 80 fadome deepe, black slimie ground; from morning till noone wee sailed with both our marsh sailes,[5] south-west and by west 5 [20] miles, and from noone to night west and by south 5 [20] miles.

The 21 of September from night[6] till Thurseday in the morning, wee sayled one quarter[7] west, and so till day, still west, 7 [28] miles, at 64 fadome deepe, oasie ground.

From morning till noone, south-west 5 [20] miles, at 65 fadome deepe, oasie ground: at noone wee wound north-ward againe, and for three houres sayled north-east two [8] myles: then we wound westward againe, and sayled till night, while halfe our second quarter was out,[8] with two schoure sayles,[9] south south-west and south-west and by south sixe [24]

---

[1] Kanin Nos. See page 38, note 3.
[2] De fock—the fore-sail.
[3] Dreven—drifted.
[4] N. ten o.—N. by E.
[5] Met beyde mars-seylen—with both top-sails.
[6] Van den avont—from evening.
[7] One watch or four hours.
[8] Till half our second watch was out; that is, till 2 A.M.
[9] Two courses. See page 7, note 4.

myles. After that, in the second quarter, wee wound northward, and sayled so till Fryday in the morning.

The 22 of September wee sayled north and by east and north north-east 4 [16] miles :[1] and from morning till noone, north-east, 4 [16] myles. Then wee wound west-ward againe, and sayled north-west and by west and north-west three [12] miles. After that, the first quarter,[2] north-west and by west, fiue [20] miles; the second quarter, west and by north, foure [16] miles; and till Saterday in the morning, being the 23 of September, west south-west and south-west and by west, foure [16] miles. From Saterday in the morning till euening wee sayled with two schoure sailes,[3] south-west and south-west and by west, 7 [28] or 8 [32] miles, the winde being north north-west. In the euening we wound northward, and sayled till Sunday in the morning, being the 24 of September, with two schoure sayles, very neare east, with a stiffe north north-west wind, 8 [32] miles; and from morning till noone, east and by south, three [12] miles, with a north winde. Then we wound west-ward, and till euening sayled west south-west three [12] miles; and all that night till Monday in the morning, the 25 of September, west and by south, sixe [24] miles, the winde being north. In the morning the wind fell north-east, and we sailed from morning till euening west and west and by north, 10 [40] miles, hauing 63 fadome deepe, sandy ground.

From euening till Tuesday in the morning, being the 26 of September, we sailed west 10 [40] miles, and then in the morning wee were hard by the land, about 3 [12] miles east-ward from Kildwin;[4] and then we wound off from the land, and so held off for 3 houres together; after that we wound towards the land againe, and thought to goe into

---

[1] This and the preceding sentence should properly form but one, which should read thus:—After that, in the second watch, we tacked northward, and sailed till Friday morning, the 22nd Sept., N. by E., etc.
[2] Watch.   [3] Courses.   [4] Kilduin. See page 7, note 4.

Kilduin, but we were too low;[1] so that after-noone we wound off from the land againe, and till euening sailed east north-east 5 [20] miles; and from euening til two houres before Wednesday in the morning, being the 27 of September, we sailed east 6 [24] miles; then we wound west-ward, and till euening sailed west and by north 8 [32] miles, and in the euening came againe before Kilduin; then wee wound farre off from the land, and sailed 2 quarters[2] north-east and by east and east north-east 6 [24] miles; and about[3] Friday in the morning, being the 28 of September, wee wound about againe, and sayled with diuers variable windes, sometimes one way, then another way, till euening; then wee gest[4] that Kilduin lay west from vs foure [16] miles, and at that time wee had an east north-east winde, and sayled north north-west and north-west and by north, till Satterday in the morning 12 [48] or 13 [52] miles.

The nine and twentieth of September in the morning, wee sayled north-west and by west foure [16] miles; and all that day till euening it was faire, still, pleasant, and sunne-shine weather. In the euening wee went west south-west, and then wee were about sixe [24] miles from the land, and sayled till Sunday in the morning, beeing the 30 of September, north north-west eight [32] miles; then wee wound towardes the land, and the same day in the euening entered into Ward-house,[5] and there wee stayed till the tenth of October. And that day wee set sayle out of Ward-house, and vpon the eighteene of Nouember wee arriued in the Maes.

The course or miles from Ward-house into Holland I haue not here set downe, as being needlesse, because it is a continuall uoiage knowne to most men.

[1] *Maer quamen te laech*—but fell short of it.
[2] Two watches, or eight hours.
[3] *Teghen*—towards.
[4] Guessed.
[5] *Waerhuys.* See page 39, note 1.

THE END OF THE SECOND VOYAGE.

THE THIRD VOYAGE NORTH-
WARD TO THE KINGDOMES OF CATHAIA
and China, in Anno 1596.

AFTER that the seuen shippes (as I saide before) were returned backe againe from their north uoiage, with lesse benefit than was expected, the Generall States of the United Prouinces consulted together to send certaine ships thither againe a third time,[1] to see if they might bring the sayd uoyage to a good end, if it were possible to be done: but after much consultation had, they could not agree thereon; yet they were content to cause a proclamation to be made,[2] that if any, either townes or marchants, were disposed to venture to make further search that way at their owne charges, if the uoyage were accomplished, and that thereby it might bee made apparent that the sayd passage was to be sayled, they were content to giue them a good reward in the countryes behalfe, naming a certaine summe[3] of money. Whereupon in the beginning of this yeare, there was two shippes rigged and set foorth by the towne of Amsterdam, to sayle that uoyage, the men therein being taken vp vpon two conditions: viz., what they should have if the uoyage were not accomplished, and what they should have if they got through and brought the uoiage to an end, promising them a good reward if they could effect it, thereby to incourage the men, taking vp as many vnmarryed men as they could, that they might not bee disswaded by means of their wiues and children, to leaue off the uoyage. Upon these

---

[1] *Of men noch ten derdemael van slandts wegen wederom eenige toerustinge soude doen*—whether any expedition should again for the third time be fitted out at the expense of the country.

[2] In the original no mention is made of any proclamation.

[3] *Een mercklijcke somme*—a considerable sum.

conditions, those two shippes were ready to set saile in the beginning of May. In the one, Jacob Heemskerke Hendrickson was master and factor for the wares and marchandise,[1] and William Barents chiefe pilote. In the other, John Cornelison Rijp[2] was both master and factor for the goods that the marchants had laden in her.

The 5 of May all the men in both the shippes were mustered, and vpon the tenth of May they sayled from Amsterdam, and the 13 of May got to the Vlie.[3] The sixteenth wee set saile out of the Vlie, but the tyde being all most spent[4] and the winde north-east, we were compelled to put in againe; at which time John Cornelisons ship fell on ground,[5] but got off againe, and wee anchored at the east ende of the Vlie.[6] The 18 of May wee put out of the Vlie againe with a north-east winde, and sayled north north-west. The 22 of May wee saw the islands of Hitland[7] and Feyerilland, the winde beeing north-east. The 24 of May wee had a good winde, and sayled north-east till the 29th of May; then the winde was against vs, and blewe north-east in our top-sayle.[8] The 30 of May we had a good winde,[9] and sailed north-east, and we tooke the height of the sunne with our crosse-staffe, and found that it was eleuated aboue the horizon 47 degrees and 42 minutes,[10] his declination was

[1] *Als schipper ende comis van de comanschappe, Jacob Heemskerck Heijndricksz.*—as captain and supercargo of the merchandize.

[2] *Jan Cornelisz. Rijp.*

[3] The Vlie passage is frequented by ships bound northward which do not draw much water.

[4] *De stroom verliep*—the tide ran out.

[5] *Raeckte aen de grondt*—ran a-ground.

[6] *Aen de oost zyde vant Vlie-landt*—on the east side of Vlielandt: the island at the entrance of the Vlie, between it and Texel.

[7] *De eylanden van Hitlandt ende Feyeril.* Hitlandt is the Dutch name for the Islands of Shetland, anciently called Hialtland. Feyeril is Fair Isle, between Shetland and Orkney.

[8] *Waeyde een topseijl*—it blew a top-sail breeze.

[9] *Graedtboogh.* See page 10, note 2.

[10] This was the sun's zenith distance, and not its elevation.

21 degrees and 42 minutes, so that the height of the Pole was 69 degrees and twentie-foure minutes.

The first of June wee had no night, and the second of June wee had the winde contrary; but vpon the fourth of June wee had a good winde out of the west north-west, and sayled north-east.

And when the sunne was about south south-east [½ p. 9 A.M.], wee saw a strange sight in the element:[1] for on each side of the sunne there was another sunne, and two raine-bowes that past cleane through the three sunnes, and then two raine-bowes more, the one compassing round about the sunnes,[2] and the other crosse through the great rundle;[3] the great rundle standing with the vttermost point[4] eleuated aboue the horizon 28 degrees. At noone, the sunne being at the highest, the height thereof was measured, and wee found by the astrolabium that it was eleuated aboue the horizon 48 degrees and 43 minutes,[5] his declination was 22 degrees and 17 minutes, the which beeing added to 48 degrees 43 minutes, it was found that wee were vnder 71 degrees of the height of the Pole.

John Cornelis shippe held aloofe from vs and would not keepe with vs, but wee made towards him, and sayled north-east, bating a point of our compasse,[6] for wee thought that wee were too farre west-ward, as after it appeared, otherwise wee should haue held our course north-east. And in the euening when wee were together,[7] wee tolde him that wee

[1] *Een wonderlijck hemel-teijcken* — a wonderful phenomenon in the heavens.

[2] *Wijdt rondtomme de sonnen*—at a distance round about the suns.

[3] *Dweers deur de groote ronde*—right through the great circle (of the former rainbow).

[4] *De onderste cant*—its lower edge.

[5] The error noticed in the preceding page (note 10) is here repeated.

[6] *Hielt de loef van ons, ende quam niet af tot ons, maer wy ghinghen hem een streeck int ghemoet*—kept to windward of us, and would not fall off towards us; but we altered our course one point to go to him.

[7] *By malcanderen quamen*—approached each other.

were best to keepe more easterly, because we were too farre west-ward; but his pilote made answere that they desired not to goe into the Straights of Weygates. There course was north-east and by north, and wee were about 60 [240] miles to sea-warde in from the land,[1] and were to sayle north-east[2] when wee had the North Cape in sight, and therefore wee should rather haue sailed east north-east and not north north-east, because wee were so farre westward, to put our selues in our right course againe: and there wee tolde them that wee should rather haue sayled east-ward, at the least for certaine miles, vntill wee had gotten into our right course againe, which by meanes of the contrary winde wee had lost, as also because it was northeast; but whatsoeuer wee sayde and sought to councell them for the best, they would holde no course but north north-east, for they alleaged that if wee went any more easterly that then wee should enter into the Wey-gates; but wee being not able [with many hard words][3] to perswade them, altered our course one point of the compasse, to meete them, and sayled north-east and by north, and should otherwise haue sayled north-east and somewhat[4] more east.

The fifth of June wee sawe the first ice, which wee wondered at, at the first thinking that it had been white swannes, for one of our men walking in the fore-decke,[5] on a suddaine beganne to cry out with a loud voyce, and sayd that hee sawe white swans: which wee that were vnder hatches[6] hearing, presently came vp, and perceiued that it was ice that came driuing from the great heape,[7] showing like swannes,

[1] *Tzeewaert vant landt*—out at sea away from the land.

[2] *Ende behoorden n. o. aen te gaen*—and ought to have sailed N.E.

[3] As henceforward the omissions in the translation become more numerous, it is thought better to insert the omitted passage or words in the text between brackets [ ], instead of placing them in the foot-notes

[4] *Jae noch*—yea, even.   [5] *Opt verdeck*—on deck.

[6] *Die onder waren*—who were below.

[7] *Dat van den grooten hoop quam dryven*—which came drifting from the great mass.

it being then about euening: at mid-night wee sailed through it, and the sunne was about a degree eleuated aboue the horizon in the north.

The sixth of June, about foure of the clocke in the afternoone, wee entred againe into the ice, which was so strong that wee could not passe through it, and sayled south-west and by west, till eight glasses were runne out;[1] after that wee kept on our course north north-east, and sayled along by the ice.

The seuenth of June wee tooke the height of the sunne, and found that it was eleuated aboue the horizon thirtie eight degrees and thirtie eight minutes, his declination beeing twentie two degrees thirtie eight minutes; which beeing taken from thirtie eight degrees thirty eight minutes, wee found the Pole to bee seuentie foure degrees: there wee found so great a store of ice, that it was admirable: and wee sayled along through it, as if wee had past betweene two lands, the water being as greene as grasse; and wee supposed that we were not farre from Greene-land, and the longer wee sayled the more and thicker ice we found.

The eight of June wee came to so great a heape of ice, that wee could not saile through it, because it was so thicke, and therefore wee wound about south-west and by west till two glasses were runne out,[2] and after that three glasses[3] more south south-west, and then south three glasses, to sayle to the island that wee saw, as also to shunne the ice.

The ninth of June wee found the islande, that lay vnder 74 degrees and 30 minutes,[4] and (as wee gest) it was about fiue [20] miles long.[5]

[1] During four hours.
[2] One hour.
[3] One hour and a half.
[4] The accuracy of William Barentszoon's observations is worthy of remark. According to the observations of Fabure in the "Recherche", the west point of Bear Island is in 74° 30′ 52″ N. lat., being virtually the same as Barentsz., with his rude instruments, had made it two centuries and a half previously. The longitude of the same point is 16° 19′ 10″ east of Paris, or 18° 39′ 32″ E. of Greenwich.
[5] 5 *mylen groot*—twenty English miles in circvmference.

The tenth of June wee put out our boate, and therewith eight of our men went on land; and as wee past by John Cornelisons shippe, eight of his men also came into our boate, whereof one was the pilote. Then William Barents [our pilot] asked him whether wee were not too much west-ward, but hee would not acknowledge it: whereupon there passed many wordes betweene them, for William Barents sayde hee would prooue it to bee so, as in trueth it was.

The eleuenth of June, going on land, wee found great store of sea-mewes egges vpon the shoare, and in that island wee were in great danger of our liues: for that going vp a great hill of snowe,[1] when we should come down againe, wee thought wee should all haue broken our neckes, it was so slipperie[2] but we sate vpon the snowe[3] and slidde downe, which was very dangerous for vs to breake both our armes and legges, for that at the foote of the hill there was many rockes, which wee were likely to haue fallen vpon, yet by Gods help wee got safely downe againe.

Meane time William Barents sate in the boate, and sawe vs slide downe, and was in greater feare then wee to behold vs in that danger. In the sayd island we found the varying of our compasse, which was 13 degrees, so that it differed a whole point at the least; after that wee rowed aboard John Cornelisons shippe, and there wee eate our eggs.

The 12 of June in the morning, wee saw a white beare, which wee rowed after with our boate, thinking to cast a roape about her necke; but when we were neere her, shee

---

[1] *Een steylen sneebergh*—a steep mountain of snow. This was not a glacier, but merely an accumulation of snow. The land of Bear Island appears to be not sufficiently elevated for the formation of glaciers. See Von Buch's Memoir "über Spirifer Keilhavii", in *Abhandl. d. K. Acad. d. Wissensch. zu Berlin*, 1846, p. 69; and its transl., in *Journ. Geol. Soc. Lond.*, vol. iii, part ii, p. 51.

[2] *Steijl*—steep.

[3] *Wy ghinghen op ons naers sitten.*

was so great¹ that we durst not doe it, but rowed backe again to our shippe to fetch more men and our armes, and so made to her againe with muskets, hargubushes, halbertes, and hatchets, John Cornellysons men comming also with their boate² to helpe vs. And so beeing well furnished of men and weapons, wee rowed with both our boates vnto the beare, and fought with her while foure glasses were runne out,³ for our weapons could doe her litle hurt; and amongst the rest of the blowes that wee gaue her, one of our men stroke her into the backe with an axe, which stucke fast in her backe, and yet she swomme away with it; but wee rowed after her, and at last wee cut her head in sunder with an axe, wherewith she dyed; and then we brought her into John Cornelysons shippe, where wee fleaed her, and found her skinne to bee twelue foote long: which done, wee eate some of her flesh; but wee brookt it not well.⁴ This island wee called the Beare Island.⁵

The 13 of June we left the island, and sayled north and somewhat easterly, the winde being west and south-west, and made good way; so that when the sunne was north [¼ p. 11 P.M.], we gest that wee had sayled 16 [64] miles north-ward from that island.

The 14 of June, when the sunne was north, wee cast out our lead 113 fadome deepe, but found no ground, and so sayled forward till the 15 of June, when the sunne was south-east [½ p. 8 A.M.], with mistie and drisling⁶ weather, and sayled north and north and by east; about euening it

---

¹ *Geweldich*—powerful.　　　² *Bock*—yawl.　　　³ Two hours.
⁴ *Maer ten bequam ons niet wel*—but it did not agree with us.
⁵ *Het Beyren Eylandt*. The Russian walrus-hunters call this island simply *Medvyed*, "the Bear". By the English it has been usually called Cherry Island. This name was given to it in 1604 by Stephen Bennet, who went thither in a ship belonging to Sir Francis Cherry, a rich merchant of London, to kill walruses for their oil, and who named the island after his patron.
⁶ *Hyselachtich*—hazy.

A wonder in the heavens, and how we caught a bear.

cleared up, and then wee saw a great thing driuing[1] in the sea, which we thought had been a shippe, but passing along by it wee perceiued it to be a dead whale, that stouncke monsterously; and on it there sate a great number of sea meawes. At that time we had sayled 20 [80] miles.

The 16 of June, with the like speed wee sayled north and by east, with mistie weather; and as wee sayled, wee heard the ice before wee saw it; but after, when it cleared vp, wee saw it, and then wound off from it, when as wee guest wee had sayled 30 [120] miles.

The 17 and 18 of June, wee saw great store of ice, and sayled along by it vntill wee came to the poynt, which wee could not reach,[2] for that the winde was south-east, which was right against vs, and the point of ice lay south-ward from vs: yet we laueared[3] a great while to get beyond it, but we could not do it.

The 19 of June we saw land againe. Then wee tooke the height of the sunne, and found that it was eleuated aboue the horizon 33 degrees and 37 minutes, her declination being 23 degrees and 26 minutes; which taken from the sayd 33 degrees and 37 minutes, we found that we were vnder 80 degrees and 11 minutes, which was the height of the Pole there.[4]

[1] Floating.
[2] *Daer wy niet boven conden comen*—which we could not weather.
[3] See page 25, note 2.
[4] There is an error in the calculation here, which may be best explained by repeating the calculation itself, as it was doubtless made:—

33° 37'		Elevation of the sun.
23° 26'		Declination of the sun.
10° 11'	{	Elevation of the equator, which being the complement of the elevation of the Pole, had
90° 0'		to be deducted from 90°.
80° 11'		

But in making the deduction, the 11' were carried down instead of being subtracted from 60'; and then, of course, 90°—10°=80°. The true difference is 79° 49', which is, consequently, the latitude observed.

This land was very great,[1] and we sayled west-ward along by it till wee were vnder 79 degrees and a halfe, where we found a good road, and could not get neere to the land because the winde blew north-east, which was right off from the land: the bay reacht right north and south into the sea.

The 21 of June we cast out our anchor at 18 fadome before the land; and then wee and John Cornelysons men rode on the west side of the land, and there fetcht balast: and when wee got on board againe with our balast, wee saw a white beare that swamme towardes our shippe; wherevpon we left off our worke, and entering into the boate with John Cornelisons men, rowed after her, and crossing her in the way, droue her from the land; where-with shee swamme further into the sea, and wee followed her; and for that our boate[2] could not make way after her, we manned out our scute[3] also, the better to follow her: but she swamme a mile [4 miles] into the sea; yet wee followed her with the most part of all our men of both shippes in three boates, and stroke often times at her, cutting and heawing her, so that all our armes were most broken in peeces. During our fight with her, shee stroke her clowes[4] so hard in our boate, that the signes thereof were seene in it; but as hap was, it was in the forehead of our boate:[5] for if it had been in the middle thereof, she had (peraduenture) ouer-throwne it, they haue such force in their clawes. At last, after we had fought long with her, and made her wearie with our three boates that kept about her, we ouercame her and killed

[1] The country thus visited for the first time was supposed by its discoverers to be a part of Greenland; but it is now known to be Spitzbergen.

[2] *Bock*. It is impossible to say what is the correct English name for this smaller boat: probably "yawl". *Bock* (or *pont*) is properly a "punt", which is clearly not intended.

[3] *Schuijt*. This being the generic term for small craft, might well be translated "boat". [4] Clawa.

[5] *Voor aen den steven*—forward in the stem (of the boat).

How a bear came unto our boat, and what took place with him.

her: which done, we brought her into our shippe and fleaed her, her skinne being 13 foote long.

After that, we rowed with our scute about a mile [4 miles] inward to the land,[1] where there was a good hauen and good anchor ground, on the east-side being sandie: there wee cast out our leade, and found 16 fadome deepe, and after that 10 and 12 fadom; and rowing further, we found that on the east-side there was two islands that reached east-ward into the sea: on the west-side also there was a great creeke or riuer, which shewed also like an island. Then we rowed to the island that lay in the middle, and there we found many red geese-egges,[2] which we saw sitting vpon their nests, and draue them from them, and they flying away cryed red, red, red:[3] and as they sate we killed one goose dead with a stone, which we drest and eate, and at least 60 egges, that we tooke with vs aboard the shippe; and vpon the 22 of June wee went aboard our shippe againe.

Those geese were of a perfit red coulor,[4] such as come into Holland about Weiringen,[5] and euery yeere are there taken

[1] *Te landtwaert in*—towards the land.

[2] *Rotgansen*—brent geese or "barnacle" geese, as they were called, owing to the absurd idea which formerly prevailed as to their origin.

[3] *Rot, rot, rot.* It is certainly singular that the translator should have attempted to render into English what is intended to represent the natural cry of these birds. But even in this strange attempt he made a mistake; for "red" is in Dutch *rood*, while *rot* means a *rout*, crowd, flock, rabble; so that, in the opinion of some, these geese are called *rotgansen* in Dutch, on account of their flocking together.

[4] *Dit waren oprechte rotgansen*—these were true brent geese. Apart from Phillip's very curious "translation", it is difficult to imagine how he could have supposed these geese to be of "a perfit *red* coulor". And it is scarcely less incomprehensible how Barrow, in his *Chronological History, etc.*, p. 147, should have reproduced this and other errors of Phillip without the slightest comment. By a contemporary writer, in the passage cited in the next page, the brent goose is well described as " a fowle bigger than a mallard, and lesser than a goose, having blacke legs and bill or beake, and feathers blacke and white, spotted in such manner as is our mag-pie". It is figured and also described in the fifth volume of Gould's *Birds of Europe*.

[5] *Wieringen*, an island of North Holland, near the Texel.

Red geese breed their yong geese under 80 degrees in Green-land. in abundance, but till this time it was neuer knowne where they [laid and] hatcht their egges; so that some men haue taken vpon them to write that they sit vpon trees[1] in Scotland, that hang ouer the water, and such egges as fall from them downe into the water[2] become yong geese and swimme there out of the water;[3] but those that fall vpon the land burst in sunnder and are lost:[4] but this is now found to be

[1] *Aen boomen wassen*—grow upon trees.

[2] *Ende de tacken die overt water hangen ende haer vruchten int water vallen*—and those branches which hang over the water, and the fruit of which falls into the water.

[3] *Swemmen daer hennen*—swim away.

[4] *Comen te niet*—come to nothing. This extraordinary fable concerning the origin of these geese, which was prevalent in the sixteenth century, and was credited by the best informed naturalists and most learned scholars, is, at the present day, retained in our memory principally by Izaak Walton's quotation from *Divine Weekes and Workes* of Du Bartas:—

"So, slowe Boötes vnderneath him sees,
In th' ycy iles, those goslings hatcht of trees;
Whose fruitfull leaues, falling into the water,
Are turn'd (they say) to liuing fowls soon after.
So, rotten sides of broken ships do change
To barnacles; O transformation strange!
'Twas first a greene tree, then a gallant hull,
Lately a mushrom, now a flying gull."

For the reason which will appear in the sequel, it is deemed advisable to reproduce here the elaborate description of "the goose tree, barnacle tree, or the tree bearing geese", given by the learned John Gerard, in his *Herball or Generall Historie of Plantes*, of which the first edition was published in 1597:—

"There are found in the north parts of Scotland and the islands adiacent, called Orchades, certain trees, whereon do grow certaine shells of a white colour tending to russet, wherein are contained little liuing creatures: which shells in time of maturitie do open, and out of them grow those little liuing things, which falling into the water do become fowles, which we call barnakles; in the north of England, brant geese; and in Lancashire, tree geese: but the other that do fall vpon the land perish and come to nothing. Thus much by the writings of others, and also from the mouths of people of those parts, which may very well accord with truth.

"But what our eyes haue seene, and hands haue touched, we shall

contrary, and it is not to bee wondered at that no man could tell where they breed[1] their egges, for that no man that euer we knew had euer beene vnder 80 degrees, nor that land vnder 80 degrees was neuer set downe in any card,[2] much lesse the red geese that breed therein.

[1] *Liggen*—lay.

[2] Chart. The original has, however, nothing about any "card", but says *noch noyt dat land op die placts bekent is geweest*—nor was that land ever known on the spot (that is to say, from personal observation).

---

declare. There is a small island in Lancashire called the Pile of Foulders, wherein are found the broken pieces of old and bruised ships, some whereof haue been cast thither by shipwracke, and also the trunks and bodies with the branches of old and rotten trees, cast vp there likewise; whereon is found a certaine spume or froth that in time breedeth vnto certaine shels, in shape like those of the muskle, but sharper pointed, and of a whitish colour; wherein is contained a thing in forme like a lace of silke finely wouen as it were together, of a whitish colour, one end whereof is fastned vnto the inside of the shell, euen as the fish of oisters and muskles are; the other end is made fast vnto the belly of a rude masse or lumpe, which in time commeth to the shape and forme of a bird: when it is perfectly formed the shell gapeth open, and the first thing that appeareth is the foresaid lace or string; next come the legs of the bird hanging out, and as it groweth greater it openeth the shell by degrees, til at length it is all come forth, and hangeth onely by the bill; in short space after it commeth to full maturitie, and falleth into the sea, where it gathereth feathers, and groweth to a fowle bigger than a mallard, and lesser than a goose, hauing blacke legs and bill or beake, and feathers blacke and white, spotted in such manner as is our mag-pie, called in some places a pie-annet, which the people of Lancashire call by no other name than a tree-goose: which place aforesaid, and all those parts adioyning, do so much abound therewith, that one of the best is bought for three pence. For the truth hereof, if any doubt, may it please them to repaire vnto me, and I shall satisfie them by the testimonie of good witnesses.

"Moreouer, it should seeme that there is another sort hereof; the historie of which is true, and of mine owne knowledge: for trauelling vpon the shore of our English coast betweene Douer and Rumney, I found the trunke of an old rotten tree, which (with some helpe that I procured by fishermens wiues that were there attending their husbands returne from the sea) we drew out of the water vpon dry land: vpon this rotten tree I found growing many thousands of long crimson bladders, in shape like vnto puddings newly filled, before they be sodden, which were

82   THE NAVIGATION

Note.   It is here also to be noted, that although that in this land, which we esteeme to be Greene-land, lying vnder 80 de-

---

very cleere and shining; at the nether end whereof did grow a shell fish, fashioned somewhat like a small muskle, but much whiter, resembling a shell fish that groweth vpon the rocks about Garnsey and Garsey, called a lympit: many of these shells I brought with me to London, which after I had opened I found in them liuing things without forme or shape; in others which were neerer come to ripenes I found liuing things that were very naked, in shape like a bird: in others, the birds couered with soft downe, the shell halfe open, and the bird ready to fall out, which no doubt were the fowles called barnakles. I dare not absolutely auouch euery circumstance of the first part of this history, concerning the tree that beareth those buds aforesaid, but will leaue it to a further consideration; howbeit that which I haue seene with mine eyes, and handled with mine hands, I dare confidently auouch, and boldly put downe for veritie. Now if any will obiect, that this tree which I saw might be one of those before mentioned, which either by the waues of the sea or some violent wind had been ouerturned, as many other trees are; or that any trees falling into those seas about the Orchades, will of themselues beare the like fowles, by reason of those seas and waters, these being so probable coniectures, and likely to be true, I may not without preiudice gainesay, or indeauor to confute."—(2nd edit.) p. 1588.

Difficult as it is to understand how a man of Gerard's genius and information could have been thus deceived, the perfect sincerity of his belief is not to be doubted. Seeing, then, how deep rooted this popular error must have been, it was no small merit of William Barentz and his companions that they should have been mainly instrumental in disabusing the public mind on the subject. That they were so, and that at the time they enjoyed the credit of being so, is manifest from the following note on the foregoing passage, made by Thomas Johnson, the editor of the second edition of the *Herball*, published in 1633 :—

"The barnakles, whose fabulous breed my author here sets downe, and diuers others haue also deliuered, were found by some Hollanders to haue another originall, and that by egges, as other birds haue: for they in their third voyage to find out the north-east passage to China and the Molucco's, about the eightieth degree and eleuen minutes of northerly latitude, found two little islands, in the one of which they found aboundance of these geese sitting vpon their egges, of which they got one goose, and tooke away sixty egges, etc. *Vide Pontani, Rerum et vrb. Amstelodam. Hist., lib.* 2, *cap.* 22."

Parkinson, too, in his *Theatrum Botanicum*, published in 1640 (p. 1306), gives our Dutch navigators full credit for having confuted "this admirable tale of untruth".

grees and more, there groweth leaues and grasse, and that there are such beasts therein as eat grasse, as harts, buckes, and such like beastes as liue thereon; yet in Noua Zembla, under 76 degrees, there groweth neither leaues nor grasse, nor any beasts that eate grasse or leaues liue therein,[1] but such beastes as eate flesh, as beares and foxes: and yet this land lyeth full 4 degrees [further] from the North Pole as Greeneland aforesaid doth.

The 23 of June we hoysted anchor againe, and sayled north-west-ward into the sea, but could get no further by reason of the ice; and so wee came to the same place againe where wee had laine, and cast anchor at 18 fadome: and at euening[2] being at anchor, the sunne being north-east and somewhat more east-warde, wee tooke the height thereof, and found it to be eleuated above the horizon 13 degrees and 10 minutes, his declination being 23 degrees and 28 minutes; which substracted from the height aforesaid,[3] resteth 10 degrees and 18 minutes, which being substracted from 90 degrees, then the height of the Pole, there was 79 degrees and 42 minutes.

After that, we hoysted anchor againe, and sayled along by the west side of the land,[4] and then our men went on land, to see how much the needle of the compasse varyed. Mean time, there came a greate white beare swimming towardes the shippe, and would haue climbed up into it if we had not made a noyse, and with that we shot at her with

---

[1] This remark, which has previously been made by the author in page 5, is not founded on fact, inasmuch as reindeer do exist in Novaya Zemlya, as is there shown in note 2. In addition to the authorities cited in that place, may be given that of Rosmuislov, who passed the winter of 1768-9 to the northward of 73° N. lat., and saw there large herds of wild reindeer.—*Lütke*, p. 77.

[2] *Des nachts*—at night.

[3] *De selfde getogen van de genomen hooghde.* This is erroneous. It should be "*from which* subtracted the height aforesaid".

[4] *By de westwal heenen*—along the west wall, *i.e.*, the western shore.

a peece, but she left the shippe and swam to the land, where our men were: which wee perceiuing, sayled with our shippe towardes the land, and gaue a great shoute; wherewith our men thought that wee had fallen on a rocke with our shippe, which made them much abashed; and therewith the beare also being afraide, swam off againe from the land and left our men, which made vs gladde: for our men had no weapons about them.

Touching the varying of the compasse, for the which cause our men went on land to try the certaintie thereof, it was found to differ 16 degrees.

The 24 of June we had a south-west winde, and could not get aboue the island,[1] and therefore wee sayled backe againe, and found a hauen that lay foure [16] miles from the other hauen, on the west side of the great hauen, and there cast anchor at twelue fadome deepe. There wee rowed a great way in, and went on land; and there wee founde two seahorses teeth that waighed sixe pound: wee also found many small teeth, and so rowed on board againe.

The 25 of June we hoysted anchor againe, and sayled along by the land, and went south and south south-west, with a north north-east winde, vnder 79 degrees. There we found a great creeke or riuer,[2] whereinto we sailed ten [40] miles at the least, holding our course south-ward; but we perceiued that there wee could not get through: there wee cast out our leade, and for the most part found ten fadome deepe, but wee were constrained to lauere[3] out againe, for the winde was northerly, and almost full north;[4] and wee perceaued that it reached to the firm land, which we supposed to be low-land, for that wee could not see it any thing farre, and therefore wee sailed so neere vnto it till that wee might see

[1] *Boven dat eylandt niet comen*—could not weather that island.
[2] *Een gheweldigen inham*—an extremely large bay or inlet.
[3] *Laveren.* See page 25, note 2.
[4] *Ende moesten n. aen*—and *we had to go* north.

it, and then we were forced to lauere [back], and vpon the 27 of June we got out againe.

The twenty eight of June wee gate beyonde the point that lay on the west-side, where there was so great a number of birds that they flew against our sailes, and we sailed 10 [40] miles south-ward, and after that west, to shun the ice.

The twenty nine of June wee sayled south-east, and somewhat more easterly, along by the land, till wee were vnder 76 degrees and 50 minutes, for wee were forced to put off from the land, because of the ice.

The thirteeth of June we sayled south and somewhat east, and then we tooke the height of the sun, and found that it was eleuated aboue the horizon 38 degrees and 20 minutes, his declination was 23 degrees and 20 minutes, which being taken from the former height, it was found that wee were vnder 75 degrees.[1]

The first of July wee saw the Beare-Island[2] againe, and then John Cornelison and his officers came aboard of our ship, to speak with vs about altering of our course; but wee being of a contrary opinion, it was agreed that wee should follow on our course and hee his: which was, that hee (according to his desire) should saile vnto 80 degrees againe; for hee was of opinion that there hee should finde a passage through, on the east-side of the land that lay vnder 80 degrees.[3] And vpon that agreement wee left each other, they sayling north-ward, and wee south-ward because of the ice, the winde being east south-east.

The second of July wee sailed east-ward, and were vnder 74 degrees, hauing the wind north north-west, and then wee wound ouer another bough[4] with an east north-east winde, and

[1] That is to say, the sun's declination 23° 20′, being taken from his elevation 38° 20′, leaves 15°, the complement of the elevation of the Pole, which latter is consequently 75°.
[2] See page 76.
[3] Namely, Spitzbergen, which they had just left.
[4] *Wendent over den anderen boech*—went upon the other tack.

sayled north-ward. In the euening, the sunne beeing about north-west and by north [9 P.M.], wee wound about againe (because of the ice) with an east winde, and sailed south south-east; and about east south-east sun[1] [¼ p. 7 A.M.] we wound about againe (because of the ice), and the sunne being south south-west [½ p. 12 P.M.] we wound about againe, and sailed north-east.

The third of July wee were vnder 74 degrees, hauing a south-east and by east wind, and sailed north-east and by north: after that we wound about againe with a south wind and sayled east south-east till the sunne was north-west [¼ p. 8 P.M.], then the wind began to be somewhat larger.[2]

The fourth of July wee sailed east and by north, and found no ice, which wee wondered at, because wee sailed so high;[3] but when the sunne was almost south, we were forced to winde about againe by reason of the ice, and sailed westward with a north-wind; after that, the sunne being north [11 P.M.], wee sailed east south-east with a north-east wind.

The fifth of July wee sailed north north-east till the sunne was south [11 A.M.]: then wee wound about, and went east south-east with a north-east winde. Then wee tooke the height of the sunne, and found it to bee eleuated aboue the horizon 39 degrees and 27 minutes, his declination being 22 degrees and 53 minutes, which taken from the high aforesaid, we found that wee were under the height of the Poole seuentie three degrees and 20 minutes.[4]

The seuenth of July wee cast out our whole lead-lyne, but found no ground, and sailed east and by south, the wind being

---

[1] In Phillips' translation, "sun" is omitted, and the words "and then" substituted, whereby the sense is completely altered.

[2] *Wat te ruymen*—to be somewhat more favourable.

[3] That is, to so high a latitude.

[4] *73 graden ende 20 minuten.* This is an error of the press. It should be 73° 26'.

north-east and by east, and were vnder 72 degrees and 12 minutes.

The eight of July we had a good north [by] west wind, and sailed east and by north, with an indifferent cold gale of wind,[1] and got vnder 72 degrees and 15 minutes. The ninth of July we went east and by north, the wind being west. The tenth of July, the sunne being south south-west [9 A.M.], we cast out our lead and had ground at 160 fadome, the winde being north-east and by north, and we sailed east and by south vnder 72 degrees.

The 11 of July we found 70 fadome deepe, and saw no ice; then we gest that we were right south and north from Dandinaes,[2] that is the east point of the White-Sea, that lay southward from vs, and had sandy ground, and the bancke stretched north-ward into the sea, so that wee were out of doubt that we were vpon the bancke of the White Sea, for wee had found no sandy ground all the coast along, but onely that bancke. Then the winde being east and by south, we sayled south and south and by east, vnder 72 degrees, and after that we had a south south-east winde, and sayled north-east to get ouer the bancke.

In the morning wee draue forward with a calme,[3] and found that we were vnder 72 degrees, and then againe wee had an east south-east winde, the sunne being about south-west [2 P.M.], and sayled north-east; and casting out our lead found 150 fadome deepe, clay ground, and then we were ouer the bancke, which was very narrow, for wee sayled but 14 glasses,[4] and gate ouer it when the sunne was about north north-east [¼ p. 12 A.M.].

The twelfth of July wee sayled north and by east, the

[1] *Een tamelijcken coelte*—a tolerable breeze.
[2] *Dandinaes*: evidently a misprint for Candinaes, or Kaniu Nos; respecting which, see page 38, note 3.
[3] *Dreven wy in stilte*—we drifted in a calm.
[4] Seven hours.

winde being east; and at euening,[1] the sunne being north north-east, we wound about againe, hauing the winde north north-east, and sayled east and by south till our first quarter[2] was out.

The thirteenth of July wee sayled east, with a north north-east wind: then we tooke the height of the sunne and found it to bee eleuated aboue the horizon 54 degrees and 38 minutes,[3] his declination was 21 degrees and 54 minutes, which taken from the height aforesaid, the height of the Pole was found to be 73 degrees; and then againe wee found ice, but not very much, and wee were of opinion that wee were by Willoughbies-land.[4]

The fourteenth of July wee sailed north-east, the winde being north north-west, and in that sort sayled about a dinner time[5] along through the ice, and in the middle thereof wee cast out our leade, and had 90 fadome deepe; in the next quarter wee cast out the lead againe and had 100 fadome deepe, and we sayled so farre into the ice that wee could goe no further: for we could see no place where it

[1] *Des nachts*—at night.   [2] Watch.
[3] 54 *graden ende* 38 *minuten*. This is a misprint. It should be "38 degrees and 54 minutes", from which deducting 21° 54', the sun's declination, there remains 27°, the complement of the height of the Pole; so that the latitude is 73°.
[4] *Willebuijs landt*. On the 14th of August, 1553, the unfortunate Sir Hugh Willoughby discovered land in 72° N. lat., 160 leagues E. by N. from Seynam on the coast of Norway. In consequence of this discovery, some of the old charts showed in this direction a separate coast line, to which they gave the name of Willoughby's Land. It is to this that De Veer alludes. It is, however, now fully established that no such land exists; and there is every reason for the opinion that the coast seen by Willoughby was that of Novaya Zemlya itself. This opinion is entertained by Lütke, as well as by most geographers at the present day. See Mr. Rundall's *Narratives of Voyages towards the North-West*, Introd., p. v.
[5] *Een eetmael langh*—during four and twenty hours. The English translator must be excused for not understanding this expression, when even the Amsterdam Latin version of 1598 has *durante prandio*. Whatever may be the derivation of the expression, there can be no doubt as to its real meaning.

opened, but were forced (with great labour and paine) to lauere out of it againe, the winde blowing west, and wee were then vnder seuentie foure degrees and tenne minutes.

The fifteenth of July wee draue through the middle of the ice with a calme,[1] and casting out our leade had 100 fadome deepe, at which time the winde being east, wee sayled [south-] west.

The sixteenth of July wee got out of the ice, and sawe a great beare lying vpon it, that leaped into the water when shee saw vs. Wee made towards her with our shippe; which shee perceiuing, gotte vp vpon the ice againe, wherewith wee shot once at her.

Then we sailed east south-east and saw no ice, gessing that wee were not farre from Noua Zembla, because wee sawe the beare there vpon the ice, at which time we cast out the lead and found 100 fadome deepe.

The seuenteenth of July we tooke the height of the sunne, and it was eleuated aboue the horizon 37 degrees and 55 minutes; his declination was 21 degrees and 15 minutes, which taken from the height aforesaid, the height of the Pole was 74 degrees and 40 minutes:[2] and when the sunne was in the south [11 A.M.], wee saw the land of Noua Zembla, which was about Lomsbay.[3] I was the first that espied

[1] *Dreven wy in stilte midden int ys*—we drifted in a calm, surrounded by the ice.

[2] Here, again, the same error is committed as on the 19th of June (see page 77, note 4). The calculation is as follows:—

37° 55′	Elevation of the sun.
21° 15′	Declination of the sun.
16° 40′	Complem. of elev. of Pole.
90° 0′	
74° 40′	Elevation of the Pole.

But which should be 73° 20′

[3] In this they were mistaken, owing to their error in the calculation of their observed latitude, as is shown in the preceding note. On their

it. Then wee altered our course, and sayled north-east and by north, and hoysed vp all our sailes except the fore-saile and the lesien.[1]

The eighteenth of July wee saw the land againe, beeing vnder 75 degrees, and sayled north-east and by north with a north-west winde, and wee gate aboue the point of the Admirals Island,[2] and sayled east north-east with a west winde, the land reaching north-east and by north.

The nineteenth of July wee came to the Crosse-Island,[3] and could then get no further by reason of the ice, for there the ice lay still close vpon the land, at which time the winde was west and blewe right vpon the land, and it lay vnder 76 degrees and 20 minutes. There stood 2 crosses vpon the land, whereof it had the name.

The twentieth of July wee anchored vnder the island, for wee could get no further for the ice. There wee put out our boate, and with eight men rowed on land, and went to one of the crosses, where we rested vs awhile, to goe to the next crosse, but beeing in the way we saw two beares by the other crosse, at which time wee had no weapons at all about vs. The beares rose vp vpon their hinder feete to see vs (for they smell further than they see), and for that they smelt us, therefore they rose vpright and came towards vs, wherewith we were not a little abashed, in such sort that wee had littie lust[4] to laugh, and in all haste went to our boate againe, still looking behinde vs to see if they followed vs, thinking to get into the boate and so put off from the

---

former visit to Lomsbay (see page 13) they made its latitude to be 74° 20′; so that now, instead of being near that spot, they must have been about a degree to the south of it. This corresponds, too, better with their observation on the following day; for it is not to be imagined that they should have been 24 hours under full-sail, and yet have made only 20 miles of northing on a N.E. by N. course.

[1] *Het voormarsseijl ende besaen*—the fore-topsail and spanker.
[2] *Het Admiraliteijts Eylandt*—Admiralty Island. See page 13.
[3] The "Island with the Crosses" of page 16.
[4] Desire.

land: but the master[1] stayed us, saying, hee that first beginnes to runne away, I will thrust this hake-staffe[2] (which hee then held in his hand) into his ribs,[3] for it is better for vs (sayd hee) to stay altogether, and see if we can make them afraid with whooping and hallowing; and so we went softly towards the boate, and gote away glad that wee had escaped their clawes, and that wee had the leysure to tell our fellowes thereof.

The one and twenteeth of July wee tooke the height of the sunne, and found that it was eleuated aboue the horizon thirtie fiue degrees and fifteene minutes; his declination was one and twentie degrees, which being taken from the height aforesaide, there rested fourteene degrees, which substracted from ninetie degrees, then the height of the Pole was found to be seuentie sixe degrees and fifteene minutes:[4] then wee found the variation of the compasse to be iust twentie sixe degrees. The same daye two of our men went againe to the crosse, and found no beares to trouble vs, and wee followed them with our armes, fearing lest wee might meet any by chance; and when we came to the second crosse, wee found the foote-steps of 2 beares, and saw how long they had followed vs, which was an hundreth foote-steps at the least, that way that wee had beene the day before.

The two and twentie of July, being Monday, wee set vp another crosse and made our marke[s] thereon, and lay there before the Cross Island till the fourth of August; meane time we washt and whited[5] our linnen on the shoare.

The thirtie of July, the sunne being north [½ p. 10 P.M.],

---

[1] *De schipper.*   [2] *Bootshaeck*—boat-hook.
[3] *Huijt*—body (literally "hide").
[4] Here are *two* errors. In the first place, the difference between the sun's elevation and declination is not 14°, but 14° 15'. This is, manifestly, an error of the press. Then, in the same way as on the 19th of June and 17th of July (see pages 77 and 89), 90°—14° 15' is made to be 76° 15', whereas it should be 75° 45', which is the true latitude.
[5] *Bleeckten*—bleached.

there came a beare so neere to our shippe that wee might hit her with a stone, and wee shot her into the foote with a peece, wherewith shee ranne halting away.

The one and thirteeth of July, the sunne being east north-east [¾ p. 2 A.M.], seuen of our men killed a beare, and fleased her, and cast her body into the sea. The same day at noone (by our instrument) wee found the variation of the nedle of the compasse to be 17 degrees.[1]

The first of August wee saw a white beare, but shee ranne away from vs.

The fourth of August wee got out of the ice to the other side of the island, and anchored there: where, with great labour and much paine, wee fetched a boate full of stones from the land.

The fifth of August wee set saile againe towardes Ice-point[2] with an east wind, and sailed south south-east, and then north north-east, and saw no ice by the land, by the which wee lauered.[3]

The sixth of August we gate about the point of Nas-sawe,[4] and sayled forward east and east and by south, along by the land.

The seuenth of August wee had a west south-west wind, and sayled along by the land, south-east and south-east and by east, and saw but a little ice, and then past by the Trust-point,[5] which wee had much longed for. At euening we had an east wind, with mistie weather, so that wee were forced to make our ship fast to a peece of ice, that was at least 36 fadome deep vnder the water, and more than 16 fadome

---

[1] This would seem to be a misprint for 27°, as all the other observations made in Novaya Zemlya tend to show that at that time the variation was from 2 to 2½ points. The subject is discussed in the Introduction.

[2] The northernmost point of Novaya Zemlya. See page 24.

[3] *Daer we langhs heenen laveerden*—along which we tacked.

[4] *Quamen wy boven de hoeck van Nassouwen* — we weathered Cape Nassau. See page 16.

[5] *De hoeck van Troost*—Cape Comfort. See page 22, note 4.

aboue the water; which in all was 52 fadome thick, for it lay fast vpon ground the which was 36 fadome deepe. The eight of August in the morning wee had an east wind with mistie weather.

The 9 of August, lying still fast to the great peece of ice, it snowed hard, and it was misty weather, and when the sunne was south [¾ p. 10 A.M.] we went vpon the hatches[1] (for we alwayes held watch): where, as the master walked along the ship, he heard a beast snuffe with his nose, and looking ouer-bord he saw a great beare hard by the ship, wherewith he cryed out, a beare, a beare; and with that all our men came vp from vnder hatches,[2] and saw a great beare hard by our boat, seeking to get into it, but wee giuing a great shoute, shee was afrayd and swamme away, but presently came backe againe, and went behinde a great peece of ice, whereunto wee had made our shippe fast, and climbed vpon it, and boldly came towardes our shippe to enter into it:[3] but wee had torne our scute sayle in the shippe,[4] and lay with foure peeces before at the bootesprit,[5] and shotte her into the body, and with that, shee ranne away; but it snowed so fast that wee could not see whither shee went, but wee guest that she lay behinde a high hoouell,[6] whereof there was many vpon the peece of ice.

The tenth of August, being Saterday, the ice began mightily to breake,[7] and then wee first perceiued that the great peece of ice wherevnto wee had made our shippe fast, lay on the ground; for the rest of the ice draue along by it,

---

[1] *Boven opt verdeck*—above on deck.

[2] *Quamen wy alle boven*—we all came on deck.

[3] *Nae ons toe, om voor by 't schip op te climmen*—towards us, in order to climb up the bow of the ship.

[4] *Wy hadden boven opt schip ons schuyten seijl gheschoren*—we had placed the sail of our boat on deck as a screen.

[5] *Voor opt braedspit*—forward on the *capstan*.

[6] *Een hooghen heuvel*—a high hummock of ice.

[7] *Te dryven*—to drift, or move.

wherewith wee were in great feare that wee should be compassed about with the ice,[1] and therefore wee vsed all the diligence and meanes that wee could to get from thence, for wee were in great doubt:[2] and being vnder sayle, wee sayled vpon the ice, because it was all broken vnder us,[3] and got to another peece of ice, wherevnto wee made our shippe faste againe with our sheate anchor,[4] which wee made fast vpon it, and there wee lay till euening. And when wee had supped, in the first quarter[5] the sayd peece of ice began on a sodaine to burst and rende in peeces, so fearefully that it was admirable; for with one great cracke it burst into foure hundred peeces at the least: wee lying fast to it,[6] weied our cable and got off from it. Vnder the water it was ten fadome deepe and lay vpon the ground, and two fadome above the water: and it made a fearefull noyse both vnder and aboue the water when it burst, and spread it selfe abroad on all sides.

And being with great feare[7] gotten from that peece of ice, we came to an other peece, that was sixe fadome deepe vnder the water, to the which we made a rope fast on both sides.

Then wee saw an other great peece of ice not farre from vs, lying fast in the sea, that was as sharp aboue as it had been a tower; whereunto wee rowed, and casting out our lead, wee found that it lay 20 fadome deepe, fast on the ground vnder the water, and 12 fadome aboue the water.

The 11 of August, being Sunday, wee rowed to another peece of ice, and cast out our lead, and found that it lay 18 fadom deepe, fast to the ground vnder the water, and 10

---

[1] *Int ys beknelt soude werden*—we should be crushed by the ice.

[2] *Ghevaer*—danger.

[3] *Dattet al craeckte watter ontrent was*—so that all round about us cracked.

[4] *Werp ancker*—kedge.   [5] Watch.

[6] *Met de steven daer aen*—with our stem (bow) on it.

[7] *Ghevaer*—danger.

fadome aboue the water. The 12 of August we sailed neere[1] vnder the land, ye better to shun ye ice, for y^t the great flakes that draue in the sea[2] were many fadome deepe under the water, and we were better defended from them being at 4 and 5 fadome water; and there ran a great current of water from the hill [s]. There we made our ship fast againe to a peece of ice, and called that point the small Ice Point.[3]

The 13 of August in the morning, there came a beare from[4] the east point of the land, close to our ship, and one of our men with a peece shot at her and brake one of her legs, but she crept[5] vp the hill with her three feet, and wee following her killed her, and hauing fleaed her brought the skinne aboard the ship. From thence we set saile with a little gale of winde,[6] and were forced to lauere, but after that it began to blow more[7] out of the south and south southeast.

The 15 of August we came to the Island of Orange,[8] where we were inclosed with the ice hard by a great peece of ice where we were in great danger to loose our ship, but with great labour and much paine we got to the island, the winde being south-east, whereby we were constrained to turne our ship;[9] and while we were busied thereabouts and made much noise, a beare that lay there and slept, awaked and came towards vs to the ship, so that we were forced to leaue our worke about turning of the ship, and to defend our selues against the beare, and shot her into the body, wherewith she ran away to the other side of the island, and

[1] *Noch naerder*—still nearer.
[2] *De grootste schotsen dryvende ys*—the largest pieces of drift ice.
[3] *Den cleynen Ys-hoeck*   [4] *Om*—round.
[5] *Huppelde*—limped.
[6] *Met weynich coelte*—with little wind.
[7] *Began't beter te coelen*—the wind freshened.
[8] *De Eylandt van Oraengien.* On the first voyage the *Islands* of Orange are spoken of. See page 25.
[9] *Het schip verlegghen*—to change the position of the ship.

swam into the water, and got vp vpon a peece of ice, where shee lay still; but we comming after her to the peece of ice where shee lay, when she saw vs she leapt into the water and swam to the land, but we got betweene her and the land, and stroke her on the head with a hatchet, but as often as we stroke at her with the hatchet, she duckt vnder the water, whereby we had much to do before we could kill her: after she was dead we fleaed her on the land, and tooke the skin on board with vs, and after that turned[1] our ship to a great peece of ice, and made it fast thereunto.

The 16 of August ten of our men entring into one boat, rowed to the firm land at Noua Zembla, and drew the boate vp vpon the ice; which done, we went vp a high hill to see the cituation of the land, and found that it reached south-east and south south-east, and then againe south, which we disliked, for that it lay so much southward: but when we saw open water south-east and east south-east, we were much comforted againe, thinking y^t wee had woon our voyage,[2] and knew not how we should get soone inough on boord to certifie William Barents thereof.

The 18 of August we made preparation to set saile, but it was all in vaine; for we had almost lost our sheat anchor[3] and two new ropes, and with much lost labour got to the place againe from whence we came: for the streame ran with a mighty current, and the ice drave very strongly vpon the cables along by the shippe, so that we were in fear that we should loose all the cable that was without the ship, which was 200 fadome at the least; but God prouided well for vs, so that in the end wee got to the place againe from whence we put out.

The 19 of August it was indifferent good weather, the

[1] *Brachten*—brought.
[2] *De reijs ghewonnen waer*—i.e., the object of the voyage was attained, and they had become entitled to the reward offered by the States General, as mentioned on page 70.
[3] *Werp-ancker*—kedge.

winde blowing south-west, the ice still driuing, and we set saile with an indifferent gale of wind,[1] and past by y ͤ Point of Desire,[2] whereby we were once againe in good hope. And when we had gotten aboue the point,[3] we sailed south-east into the sea-ward 4 [16] miles, but then againe we entred into more ice, whereby we were constrained to turn back againe, and sailed north-west vntil we came to y ͤ land againe, which reacheth frō the Point of Desire to the Head Point,[4] south and by west, 6 [24] miles: from the Head Point to Flushingers Head,[5] it reacheth south-west, which are 3 [12] miles one from the other; from the Flushingers Head, it reacheth into the sea east south-east, and from Flushingers Head to the Point of the Island[6] it reacheth south-west and by south and south-west 3 [12] miles; and from the Island Point to the Point of the Ice Hauen,[7] the land reacheth west south-west 4 [16] miles: from the Ice Hauens Point to the fall of water or the Streame Bay[8] and the low land, it reacheth west and by south and east and by north, 7 [28] miles: from thence the land reacheth east and west.

The 21 of August we sailed a great way into the Ice Hauen, and that night ankored therein: next day, the streame[9] going extreame hard eastward, we haled out againe from thence, and sailed againe to the Island Point; but for that it was misty weather, comming to a peece of ice, we made the ship fast thereunto, because the winde began to blow hard south-west and south south-west. There we

[1] *Een tamelijcke coelte*—an easy breeze.
[2] *De hoeck van Begheerte.* Cape Desire.
[3] *Boven den hoeck waren*—had weathered the Cape.
[4] *De Hooft-hoeck.*
[5] *Het Vlissingher hooft*—Flushing Head.
[6] *De hoeck vant Eylandt.* Subsequently called *Den Eylandts hoeck*, or Island Point.
[7] *De hoeck van den Yshaven*—Ice Haven Point.
[8] *Het afwater ofte Stroom Bay.*
[9] *Stroom*—current.

H

went[1] vp vpon the ice, and wondred much thereat, it was such manner of ice: for on the top it was ful of earth, and there we found aboue 40 egges, and it was not like other ice, for it was of a perfect azure coloure, like to the skies, whereby there grew great contentiō in words amongst our men, some saying that it was ice, others that it was frozen land; for it lay vnreasonable high aboue the water, it was at least 18 fadome vnder the water close to the ground, and 10 fadome aboue the water: there we stayed all that storme, the winde being south-west and by west.

The 23 of August we sailed againe from the ice south-eastward into the sea, but entred presently into it againe, and wound about[2] to the Ice Hauen. The next day it blew hard north north-west, and the ice came mightily driuing in, whereby we were in a manner compassed about therewith, and withall the winde began more and more to rise, and the ice still draue harder and harder, so that the pin of the rother[3] and the rother were shorne in peeces,[4] and our boate was shorne in peeces[5] betweene the ship and the ice, we expecting nothing else but that the ship also would be prest and crusht in peeces with the ice.

The 25 of August the weather began to be better, and we tooke great paines and bestowed much labour to get the ice, wherewith we were so inclosed, to go from vs, but what meanes soeuer we vsed it was all in vaine. But when the sun was south-west [½ p. 2 P.M.] the ice began to driue out againe with the streame,[6] and we thought to saile southward about Noua Zembla, [and so westwards] to the Straites of Mer-gates.[7] For that seeing we could there find no passage, we hauing past[8] Noua Zembla, [we] were of opinion that our

[1] *Clommen*—climbed. [2] *Keerden omme*—turned back.
[3] *De pen vant roer*—the tiller.
[4] *Stucken gheschoven werden*—were broken in pieces.
[5] *Gheschoven*—stove in. [6] *Stroom*—current.
[7] *Weygats*. [8] That is, now that we had passed.

How our ship stuck fast in the ice, whereby three of us were nearly lost.

labour was all in vaine and that we could not get through, and so agreed to go that way home againe; but comming to the Streame Bay, we were forced to go back againe, because of the ice which lay so fast thereabouts; and the same night also it froze, that we could hardly get through there with the little wind that we had, the winde then being north.

The 26 of August there blew a reasonable gale of winde, at which time we determined to saile back to the Point of Desire, and so home againe, seeing y$_t$ we could not get through [by the way towards] y^e Wergats,[1] although we vsed al the meanes and industry we could to get forward; but whē we had past by y^e Ice Hauen y^e ice began to driue w^t such force, y^t we were inclosed round about therewith, and yet we sought al the meanes we could to get out, but it was all in vaine. And at that time we had like to haue lost three men that were vpon the ice to make way for the ship, if the ice had held ye course it went; but as we draue back againe, and that the ice also whereon our men stood in like sort draue, they being nimble, as ye ship draue by thē, one of them caught hould of the beake head, another vpon the shroudes,[2] and the third vpon the great brase[3] that hung out behind, and so by great aduenture by the hold that they took they got safe into the shippe againe, for which they thanked God with all their hearts: for it was much liklier that they should rather haue beene carried away with the ice, but God, by the nimbleness of their hands, deliuered them out of that danger, which was a pittifull thing to behold, although it fell out for the best, for if they had not beene nimble they had surely dyed for it.

The same day in the euening we got to the west side of the Ice Hauen, where we were forced, in great cold, pouerty, misery, and griefe, to stay all that winter; the winde then being east north-east.

[1] *Weygats.*
[2] *De schoot*—the sheet.
[3] *De groote bras*—the main brace.

The 27 of August the ice draue round about the ship, and yet it was good wether; at which time we went on land, and being there it began to blow south-east with a reasonable gale, and then the ice came with great force before the bough,[1] and draue the ship vp foure foote high before, and behind it seemed as if the keele lay on the ground, so that it seemed that the ship would be ouerthrowne in the place; whereupon they that were in the ship put out the boate,[2] therewith to saue their liues, and withall put out a flagge to make a signe to vs to come on board: which we perceiuing, and beholding the ship to be lifted vp in that sort, made all the haste we could to get on board, thinking that the ship was burst in peeces, but comming vnto it we found it to be in better case than we thought it had beene.

The 28 of August wee gat some of the ice from it,[3] and the ship began to sit vpright againe; but before it was fully vpright, as William Barents and the other pilot went forward to the bough,[4] to see how the ship lay and how much it was risen, and while they were busie vpon their knees and elbowes to measure how much it was, the ship burst out of the ice with such a noyse and so great a crack, that they thought verily that they were all cast away, knowing not how to saue themselues.

The 29 of August, the ship lying vpright againe, we vsed all the meanes we could, with yron hookes[5] and other instru-

---

[1] The bow of the ship.   [2] *Bock*—yawl.
[3] *Weeck het ys wat wech*—the ice gave way a little.   [4] Bow.
[5] *Koe-voeten* — crow-bars: literally *cows'-feet*, from the resemblance which the bifurcated end bears to the cloven foot of that animal. In one of the printed accounts of the riots of 1780 (the reference to which cannot just now be found), it is mentioned that a *pig's-foot*—the "jemmy" little tool used by housebreakers—was employed in the destruction of Newgate, and surprise was expressed at the power of so small an instrument to move the large stones of which that building was constructed. The small iron hammer common in our printing-offices is likewise called a *sheep's-foot*; the reason for the name being in each case the same.

How the ice heaved up the fore part of our ship.

ments, to breake the flakes of ice that lay one heap'd vpō the other, but al in vaine; so that we determined to commit our selues to the mercie of God, and to attend ayde from him, for that the ice draue not away in any such sort that it could helpe vs.

The 30 of August the ice began to driue together one vpon the other with greater force than before, and bare against the ship w^h a boystrous south [by] west wind and a great snowe, so that all the whole ship was borne vp and inclosed,[1] whereby all that was both about and in it began to crack, so that it seemed to burst in a 100 peeces, which was most fearfull both to see and heare, and made all ye haire of our heads to rise vpright with feare; and after y^t, the ship (by the ice on both sides that joined and got vnder the same) was driued so vpright, in such sort as if it had bin lifted vp with a wrench or vice.[2]

The 31 of August, by the force of the ice, the ship was driuen vp 4 or 5 foote high at the beake head,[3] and the hinder part thereof lay in a clift[4] of ice, whereby we thought that the ruther would be freed from the force of the flakes of ice,[5] but, notwithstanding, it brake in peeces staffe[6] and all: and if that the hinder part of the ship had bin in the ice that draue as well as the fore part was, then all the ship[7] would haue bin driuen wholly vpon the ice, or possibly haue ran on groūd,[8] and for that cause wee were in great feare, and set our scutes and our boate[9] out vpon the ice, if neede were, to saue our selues. But within 4 houres after, the ice draue awaye of it selfe, wherewith we were exceeding glad, as if we had saued our liues, for that the ship was then on

[1] *Gheknelt*—squeezed.
[2] *Vysel*—a screw or jack.
[3] *Voorsteven*—stem.
[4] Crevice.
[5] *Het schuyven des ys*—from the action (pushing) of the ice.
[6] *Pen*—tiller.
[7] *Het gantsche voorschip*—the entire fore-part of the ship.
[8] *In den grondt ghecomen*—gone to the bottom.
[9] *Ons schuijt ende boot*—our boat and yawl.

float againe; and vpon that we made a new ruther and a staffe,¹ and hung the ruther out vpon the hooks, that if we chanced to be born² vpon the ice againe, as we had bin, it might so be freed from it.

The 1 of September, being Sunday, while we were at praier, the ice began to gather together againe, so that the ship was lifted vp [bodily] two foote at the least, but the ice brake not.³ The same euening⁴ the ice continued in yᵗ sort still driuing and gathering together, so that we made preparation to draw our scute and the boate ouer the ice vpon the land, the wind then blowing south-east.

The 2 of September it snowed hard with a north-east wind, and the ship began to rise vp higher vpō the ice,⁵ at which time the ice burst and crakt with great force, so that we were of opinion to carry our scute on land in that fowle weather, with 13 barrels of bread and two hogsheads⁶ of wine to sustaine our selues if need were.

The 3 of September it blew [just as] hard, but snowed not so much, yᵉ wind being north north-east; at which time we began to be loose from the ice whereunto we lay fast, so that the scheck brake from the steuen,⁷ but the planks wherewith the ship was lyned held the scheck fast and made it hang on;⁸ but the boutloofe and a new cable, if we had falled vpon the ice, brake by the forcible pressing of the ice,⁹ but held fast

---

¹ *Pen*—tiller.   ² *Borne*, carried.
³ *Het bleef noch al dicht*— it (*the ship*) remained quite tight.
⁴ *Naenoens*—afternoon.
⁵ *Te schuyren vant ys*—to be moved by the ice.
⁶ *Vaetkens*—small casks.
⁷ *Soo dat de scheck achter van den steren geschoven werde*—so that the ice-knees (chocks) started from the stern-post.
⁸ *Hielde de scheck noch dat zy daeraen bleef hangen*— kept the ice-knees still hanging on.
⁹ *Ende de bouteloef brack mede stucken met een nieu cabeltou dat wy op het ys hadden rast ghemaeckt*—and the bumpkin likewise broke away, with a new cable, which we had made fast to the ice. The *bouteloef* or *botteloef* (in English, *bumpkin*) is a piece of iron, projecting from the

againe in the ice; and yet the ship was staunch, which was wonder, in regard y^t ye ice draue so hard and in great heapes as big as the salt hills that are in Spaine,[1] and within a harquebus shot of the ship, betweene the which we lay in great feare and anguishe.

The 4 of September the weather began to cleare vp and we sawe the sunne, but it was very cold, the wind being north-east, we being forced to lye still.

The 5 of September it was faire sunshine weather and very calme; and at euening, when we had supt, the ice compassed about us aguine, and we were hard inclosed therewith, the ship beginning to lye upon the one side and leakt sore,[2] but by Gods grace it became staunch againe,[3] wherewith[4] we were wholly in feare to loose the ship, it was in so great danger. At which time we tooke counsell together and caried our old sock saile,[5] with pouder, lead, peeces, muskets, and other furniture on land, to make a tent [or hut] about our scute y^t we had drawē vpon the land; and at that time we carried some bread and wine on land also, with some timber,[6] therewith to mend our boate, that it might serve vs in time of neede.

stem of the ship, and used for the purpose of giving more breadth to the fore-sail. It is no longer met with in square-rigged vessels, but only in small craft. It would seem to be one of the last things to which a seaman would attach a cable; but it may have been merely temporarily, or for some reason that cannot now be discovered.

[1] *Jae, datter ys berghen dreven, soo groot als de soutberghen in Spaengien*—yea, there drifted icebergs by us, as big as the salt mountains in Spain. Allusion is evidently here made to the celebrated salt mines of Cardona, about sixteen leagues from Barcelona, where "the great body of the salt forms a rugged precipice, which is reckoned between 400 and 500 feet in height". See Dr. Traill's "Observations" on the subject, in *Trans. Geol. Soc.* (1st ser.), vol. iii, p. 404. Our author's familiar comparison of the icebergs to these salt rocks, may be taken as a proof that he had been in Spain, and was personally acquainted with the locality.

[2] *Ende leet veel*—and suffered much.
[3] *Bleeft noch dicht*—still remained tight. [4] *Dan*—for.
[5] *Fock*—foresail. [6] *Timmerghereetschap*—carpenter's tools.

The 6 of September it was indifferent faire sea-wether[1] and sun-shine, the wind being west, whereby we were somewhat comforted, hoping that the ice would driue away and that we might get from thence againe.

The 7 of September it was indifferent wether againe, but we perceiued no opening of the water, but to the contrary it[2] lay hard inclosed with ice, and no water at all about the ship, no not so much as a bucket full. The same day 5 of our men went on land, but 2 of them came back againe; the other three went forward about 2 [8] miles into the land, and there found a riuer of sweet water, where also they found great store of wood that had bin driuen thither, and there they foūd the foote-steps of harts and hinds,[3] as they thought, for they were clouen footed, some greater footed than others, which made them iudge them to be so.

The 8 of September it blew hard east north-east, which was a right contrary wind to doe vs any good touching the carrying away of the ice, so that we were stil faster in the ice, which put vs in no small discomfort.

The 9 of September it blew [strongly from the] northeast, with a little snowe, whereby our ship was wholly inclosed with ice, for yᵉ wind draue the ice hard against it, so that we lay 3 or 4 foote deepe in the ice, and our sheck in the after-steuer brake in peeces[4] and the ship began to be somewhat loose before, but yet it was not much hurt.

[1] *Oock tamelijck weder ende stilletgens*—also tolerable weather and calm.

[2] *Wy*—we.

[3] *Rheden ende Elanden*—deer and elks. It is unaccountable that, with this fact within his own personal knowledge, Gerrit de Veer should have expressly asserted, on two several occasions (pages 5 and 83), that there are no graminivorous animals in Novaya Zemlya, and pointedly distinguished between this country and Spitzbergen on that account. It is most probable that these animals had crossed over from Siberia on the ice.

[4] *Ons scheck aen de achter-steven brack altemet noch meer stucken*—and the ice-knees on the stern-post broke more and more in pieces.

In the night time two beares came close to our ship side, but we sounded our trumpet and shot at them, but hit them not because it was darke, and they ran away.

The 10 of September the wether was somewhat better, because the wind blew not so hard, and yet all one wind.

The 11 of September it was calme wether, and 8 of vs went on land, euery man armed, to see if that were true as our other three companions had said, that there lay wood about the riuer; for that seeing we had so long wound and turned about, sometime in the ice, and then againe got out, and thereby were compelled to alter our course, and at last sawe that we could not get out of the ice but rather became faster, and could not loose our ship as at other times we had done, as also that it began to be [near autumn and] winter, we tooke counsell together what we were best to doe according to the [circumstances of the] time, [in order] that we might winter there and attend such aduenture as God would send vs: and after we had debated vpon the matter, to keepe and defend ourselues both from the cold and the wild beastes, we determined to build a [shed or] house vpon the land, to keep vs therein as well as we could, and so to commit ourselves vnto the tuition of God. And to that end we went further into the land, to find out the conuenientest place in our opinions to raise our house vpon, and yet we had not much stuffe to make it withall, in regard that there grew no trees, nor any other thing in that country convenient to build it withall. But we leauing no occasion unsought, as our men went abroad to view the country, and to see what good fortune might happen unto vs, at last we found an unexpected comfort in our need, which was that we found certaine trees roots and all, (as our three companions had said before, which had been driuen vpon the shoare, either from Tartaria, Muscouia, or elsewhere, for there was none growing vpon that land; wherewith (as if God had purposely sent them vnto vs) we were

How God in our extremest need, when we were forced to live all the winter vpon the land, sent vs wood to make vs a house and to serue vs to burne in the cold winter.

much comforted, being in good hope that God would shew us some further fauour; for that wood served vs not onely to build our house, but also to burne and serve vs all the winter long; otherwise without all doubt we had died there miserably with extreme cold.

The 12 of September it was calme wether, and then our men went vnto the other side of the land, to see if they could finde any wood neerer vnto vs, but there was none.[1]

The 13 of September it was calme but very mistie wether, so that we could doe nothing, because it was dangerous for vs to go into the land, in regard that we could not see the wild beares; and yet they could smell vs, for they smell better than they see.

The 14 of September it was cleere sunshine wether, but very cold; and then we went into the land, and laid the wood in heapes one vpō the other, that it might not be couered over with yᵉ snow, and from thence ment[2] to carry it to the place where we intended to builde our house.

The 15 of September in the morning, as one of our men held watch, wee saw three beares, whereof the one lay still behind a piece of ice [and] the other two came close to the ship, which we perceiuing, made our peeces ready to shoote at them; at which time there stod a tob full of beefe[3] vpon the ice, which lay in the water to be seasoned,[4] for that close by the ship there was no water; one of the beares went vnto it, and put in his head [into the tub] to take out a peece of the beefe, but she fared therewith as the dog did with yᵉ pudding;[5] for as she was snatching at the beefe, she was shot into the head, wherewith she fell downe dead and neuer

---

[1] *Maer vonden daer gantsch weynich*—but found very little there.
[2] Meant, intended.   [3] *Vleysch*—meat.
[4] *Opt ys om te ververschen*—upon the ice, to freshen.
[5] *Maer het bequam hem als de houdt de worst*—but it agreed with her as the pudding (sausage) did with the dog. This is a Dutch proverb, made use of when any undertaking turns out badly; because the dog is said to have stolen a sausage, and to have been soundly beaten for his pains.

stir'd. [There we saw a curious sight]: the other beare stood still, and lokt vpon her fellow [as if wondering why she remained so motionless]; and when she had stood a good while she smelt her fellow, and perceiuing that she [lay still and] was dead, she ran away, but we tooke halberts and other armes with vs and followed her.[1] And at last she came againe towardes us, and we prepared our selues to withstand her, wherewith she rose vp vpon her hinder feet, thinking to rampe at vs; but while she reared herselfe vp, one of our men shot her into the belly, and with that she fell vpon her fore-feet again, and roaring as loud as she could, ran away. Then we tooke the dead beare, and ript her belly open; and taking out her guts we set her vpon her fore-feet, so that she might freeze as she stood, intending to carry her w^t vs into Holland if we might get our ship loose: and when we had set ye beare vpon her foure feet, we began to make a slead, thereon to drawe the wood to the place where we ment[2] to build our house. At that time it froze two fingers thicke in the salt water [of the sea], and it was exceeding cold, the wind blowing north-east.

The 16 of September the sunne shone, but towardes the euening it was misty, the wind being easterly; at which time we went [for the first time] to fetch wood with our sleads, and then we drew foure beames aboue[3] a mile [4 miles] vpon the ice and the snow. That night againe it frose aboue two fingers thicke.

The 17 of September thirteene of vs went where the wood lay with our sleads, and so drew fiue and fiue in a slead, and the other three helped to lift the wood behind, to make vs draw the better and with more ease;[4] and in that manner we

---

[1] *Loerden op hem of hy oock wederom comen soude*—and watched for her coming back.

[2] Meant. "Went."—*Ph.*   [3] *By nae*—nearly.

[4] *Ende drie bleven byt hout om dat te behouwen, soo werdet so veel te lichter int slepen*—and three remained behind with the wood, to hew it, so that it might be the lighter to draw.

drew wood twice a day, and laid it on a heape by the place where we ment to build our house.

The 18 of September the wind blew west, but it snowed hard, and we went on land againe to continue our labour to draw wood to our place appointed, and after dinner the sun shone and it was calme wether.

The 19 of September it was calme sunshine wether, and we drew two sleads full of wood sixe thousand paces long,[1] and that we did twice a day.

[The 20 of September we again made two journeys with the sledges, and it was misty and still weather.]

The 21 of September it was misty wether, but towards euening it cleared vp, and the ice still draue in the sea, but not so strongly as it did before, but yet it was very cold, [so that we were forced to bring our caboose[2] below, because everything froze above.]

The 22 of September it was faire still weather, but very cold, the wind being west.

The 23 of September we fetcht more wood to build our house, which we did twice a day, but it grew to be misty and still weather againe, the wind blowing east and east-north-east. That day our carpentur (being of Purmecaet[3]) dyed as we came aboord about euening.

The 24 of September we buryed him vnder the sieges[4] in the clift of a hill, hard by the water,[5] for we could not dig vp the earth by reason of the great frost and cold; and that day we went twice with our sleads to fetch wood.

The 25 of September it was darke weather, the wind blowing west and west south-west and south-west, and the

[1] *Verde—far.* The distance which, on the 16th September, they had estimated at nearly one Dutch mile.

[2] *Conbuys.* The cooking-place on board ship.

[3] *Purmerend.* A town in North Holland, about eight miles north of Amsterdam.

[4] *Cinghel*—shingle.

[5] *Een afwateringhe*—a fall or current of water.

How we built a house of wood, wherein to keep ourselves through the winter.

ice begā somewhat to open and driue away; but it continued not long, for that hauing driuen about the length of the shott of a great peece,¹ it lay three fadomes deepe vpon the ground: and where we lay the ice draue not, for we lay in the middle of the ice; but if we had layne in the [open or] maine sea, we would haue hoysed sayle, although it was thē late in the yeare. The same day we raised up the principles² of our house, and began to worke hard thereon; but if the ship had bin loose we would haue left our building and haue made our after steuen of our ship,³ that we might haue bin ready to saile away if it had bin possible; for that it grieued vs much to lye there all that cold winter, which we knew would fall out to be extreame bitter; but being bereaued of all hope, we were compelled to make necessity a vertue, and with patience to attend what issue God would send vs.

The 26 of September we had a west wind and an open sea, but our ship lay fast, wherewith we were not a little greeued; but it was God's will, which we most⁴ patiently bare,⁵ and we began to make up our house:⁶ part of our men fetch'd wood to burne, the rest played the carpenters and were busie aboute the house. As then we were sixteene men in all, for our carpenter was dead, and of our sixteene men there was still one or other sicke.

The 27th of September it blew hard north-east, and it frose so hard that as we put a nayle into our mouths (as when men worke carpenters worke they vse to doe), there would ice hang thereon when we tooke it out againe, and made the blood follow. The same day there came an old

---

¹ *Een gotelinghs schoot*—a falconet shot. See page 33, note 2.
² *Balcken*—the beams or principal timbers.
³ *Ons scheck ofte achtersteven vant schip wederom ghemaeckt*—repaired the ice-knees or stern-post of the ship.
⁴ Must.   ⁵ Bear.
⁶ *Thuys altemet dicht te maecken*—by degrees to close up (the sides of) the house.

beare and a yong one towards vs as we were going to our house, beeing altogether (for we durst not go alone), which we thought to shoot at, but she ran away. At which time the ice came forcibly driuing in, and it was faire sunshine weather, but so extreame cold that we could hardly worke, but extremity forced vs thereunto.

The 28 of September it was faire weather and the sun shon, the wind being west and very calme, the sea as then being open, but our ship lay fast in the ice and stirred not. The same day there came a beare to the ship, but when she espied vs she ran away, and we made as much hast as we could[1] to build our house.

The 29 of September in the morning, the wind was west, and after-noone it [again] blew east,[2] and then we saw three beares betweene vs and the house, an old one and two yong; but we notwithstanding drew our goods from the ship to the house, and so got before yᵉ beares, and yet they followed vs: neuertheless we would not shun the way for them, but hollowed out as loud as we could, thinking that they would haue gone away; but they would not once go out of their foote-path, but got before vs, wherewith we and they that were at the house made a great noise, which made the beares runne away, and we were not a little glad thereof.

The 30 of September the wind was east and east southeast, and all that night and the next day it snowed so fast that our men could fetch no wood, it lay so close and high one vpon the other. Then we made a great fire without the house, therewith to thaw the ground, that so we might lay it about the house that it might be the closer; but it was all lost labour, for the earth was so hard and frozen so deep into the ground, that we could not thaw it, and it would haue cost vs too much wood, and therefore we were forced to leaue off that labour.

[1] *Wy ghinghen vast voort*—we kept on hard at work.
[2] "Northly."—*Ph*.

The first of October the winde blew stiffe north-east, and after noone it blew north with a great storme and drift of snow, whereby we could hardly go in[1] the winde, and a man could hardly draw his breath, the snowe draue so hard in our faces; at which time wee could not see two [or three] ships length from vs.

The 2 of October before noone the sun shone, and after noone it was cloudy againe and it snew, but the weather was still, the winde being north and then south, and we set vp our house[2] and vpon it we placed a may-pole[3] made of frozen snowe.

The 3 of October before noone it was a calme son-shine weather, but so cold that it was hard to be endured; and after noone it blew hard out of the west, with so great and extreame cold, that if it had continued we should haue beene forced to leaue our worke.

The fourth of October the winde was west, and after noone north with great store of snow, whereby we could not worke; at that time we brought our [bower] ankor vpon the ice to lye the faster, when we lay[4] but an arrow shot from the [open] water, the ice was so much driuen away.

The 5 of October it blew hard north-west, and the sea was

---

[1] *Teghens*—against.

[2] *We rechten het huys op*—we erected (*i.e.*, completed the erection of) our house.

[3] *Een Meyboom*—a May-*tree*. According to Adelung, in his *Hochdeutsches Wörterbuch*, "Maybaum" is in many parts of Germany the vernacular name of the birch-tree, especially the common species (*Betula alba*), also called the May-birch, or simply "May",—as the hawthorn is called in England,—branches of which are used for ornamenting the houses and churches in the month of May.

The same name is given to the green branch of a tree, or at times the whole tree itself—frequently the birch, but not exclusively so—which is set up on occasions of festivity. This is the *meyboom* of the Dutch; and it would seem on the one hand to be the original of our English May-*pole*, and on the other to have degenerated into the *flag* which our builders are in the habit of hoisting on the chimneys of houses, when raised.

[4] *Alsoo wy nu...laghen*—because we now lay.

very open[1] and without ice as farre as we could discerne; but we lay still frozen as we did before, and our ship lay two or three foote deepe in the ice, and we could not perceiue otherwise but that we lay fast vpon the ground,[2] and there[3] it was three fadome and a halfe deepe. The same day we brake vp the lower deck of the fore-part[4] of our ship, and with those deales[5] we couered our house, and made it slope ouer head[6] that the water might run off; at which time it was very cold.

The 6 of October it blew hard west [and] south-west, but towardes euening west north-west, with a great snow [so] that we could hardly thrust our heads out of the dore by reason of ye great cold.

The 7 of October it was indifferent good wether, but yet very cold, and we calk't our house, and brake the ground about it at the foote thereof:[7] that day the winde went round about the compasse.

The 8 of October, all the night before it blew so hard and the same day also, and snowed so fast that we should haue smothered if we had gone out into the aire; and to speake truth, it had not beene possible for any man to haue gone one ships length, though his life had laine thereon; for it was not possible for vs to goe out of the house or ship.

The 9 of October the winde still continued north, and blew and snowed hard all that day, the wind as then blowing from the land; so that all that day we were forced to stay in the ship, the wether was so foule.

---

[1] *Heel open*—quite open.
[2] *Wy laghen tot den grondt toe bevroren*—we lay frozen right down to the ground.
[3] "Then."—*Ph.*   [4] *Het vooronder*—the forecastle.
[5] *Deelen*—planks.
[6] *In den mitten wat hoogher*—somewhat higher in the middle.
[7] *Ende braken het achteronder mede uyt, omt huijs voort dicht te maeckten*—and pulled down likewise the poop, in order (therewith) to go on closing up the house.

The 10 of October the weather was somewhat fairer and the winde calmer, and [it] blew south-west and west south-west;[1] and that time the water flowed two foote higher then ordinary, which wee gest to proceede from the strong[2] north wind which as then had blowne. The same day the wether began to be somewhat better, so that we began to go out of our ship againe; and as one of our men went out, he chaunced to meete a beare, and was almost at him before he knew it, but presently he ranne backe againe towards the ship and the beare after him: but the beare comming to the place where before that we killed another beare and set her vpright and there let her freeze, which after was couered ouer with ice[3] and yet one of her pawes reached aboue it, shee stood still, whereby our man got before her and clome[4] vp into the ship in great feare, crying, a beare, a beare; which we hearing came aboue hatches[5] to looke on her and to shoote at her, but we could not see her by meanes of the exceeding great smoake that had so sore termented vs while we lay vnder hatches in the foule wether, which we would not haue indured for any money; but by reason of the cold and snowy wether we were constrained to do it if we would saue our liues, for aloft in the ship[6] we must vndoubtedly haue dyed. The beare staied not long there, but run away, the wind then being north-east.

The same day about euening it was faire wether, and we went out of our ship to the house, and carryed the greatest part of our bread thither.

The 11 of October it was calme wether, the wind being south and somewhat warme, and then we carryed our wine and other victuals on land; and as we were hoysing the wine ouer-boord, there came a beare towards our ship that had laine behinde a peece of ice, and it seemed that we had

---

[1] " W. and S.W."—Ph.
[2] " First."—Ph.
[3] Sneeu—snow.   [4] Climbed.   [5] Boven—on deck.
[6] Boven opt schip—on the deck of the ship.

waked her with the noise we made; for we had seene her lye there, but we thought her to be a peece of ice; but as she came neere vs we shot at her, and shee ran away, so we proceeded in our worke.

The 12 of October it blew north and [at times] somewhat westerly, and then halfe of our men [went and] slept[1] in the house, and that was the first time that we lay in it; but we indured great cold because our cabins were not made, and besides that we had not clothes inough, and we could keepe no fire because our chimney was not made, whereby it smoaked exceedingly.

The 13 of October the wind was north and north-west, and it began againe to blow hard, and then three of vs went a boord the ship and laded a slead with beere; but when we had laden it, thinking to go to our house with it, sodainly there rose such a wind and so great a storme and cold, that we were forced to go into the ship againe, because we were not able to stay without; and we could not get the beere into the ship againe, but were forced to let it stand without vpon the sleade. Being in the ship, we indured extreame cold because we had but a few clothes in it.

The 14 of October, as we came out of the ship, we found the barrell of beere standing [in the open air] vpon the sleade, but it was fast frozen at the heads,[2] yet by reason of

---

[1] "Kept."—*Ph.*

[2] *Zijnde een iopen vat, aen den bodem stucken ghevroren*—which, being a cask of spruce beer, had burst at the bottom through the frost.

From a very early period a decoction, in beer or water, of the leaf-buds (*gemmæ seu turiones*) of the Norway spruce fir (*Abies excelsa*), as well as of the silver fir (*Abies picea*), has been used, formerly more than at present, in the countries bordering on the Baltic Sea, in scorbutic, rheumatic, and gouty complaints. See *Magneti Bibliotheca Pharmaceutico-Medica*, vol. i, p. 2; *Pharmacopœia Borussica* (German translation by Dulk), 3rd edit., vol. i, p. 796; Pereira, *Elements of Materia Medica*, 3rd edit., vol. ii, p. 1182.

These leaf-buds are commonly called in German, *sprossen*, and in Dutch, *jopen*; whence the beer brewed therefrom at Dantzig—*cerevisia*

the great cold the beere that purged out[1] frose as hard vpon the side[2] of the barrel as if it had bin glewed thereon, and in that sort we drew it to our house and set the barrel an end, and dranke it first vp; but we were forced to melt the beere, for there was scant[3] any vnfrozen beere in the barrell, but in that thicke yeast that was vnfrozen lay the strength of the beere,[4] so that it was too strong to drinke alone, and that which was frozen tasted like water; and being melted we mixt one with the other, and so dranke it, but it had neither strength nor tast.

The 15 of October the wind blew north and [also] east and east south-east [and it was still weather]. That day we made place to set vp our dore, and shouled[5] the snowe away.

The 16 of October the wind blew south-east and south,[6] with faire calme weather. The same night there had bin a beare in our ship, but in the morning she went out againe when she saw our men. At the same time we brake vp another peece of our ship,[7] to vse the deales about the protall,[8] which as then we began to make.

The 17 of October the wind was south and south-east, calme weather, but very cold; and that day we were busied about our portaile.

---

dantiscana, as it is styled in the Amsterdam Latin version of 1598— acquired the appellations of *sprossenbier* and *jopenbier*, of the former of which the English name, *spruce*-beer, is merely a corruption.

The "Dantzig spruce" of commerce, which is known at the place of its manufacture by the names of *doppelbier, jopenbier*, and even "sprucebier", is the representative at the present day of the medicated *sprossenbier* of former times; though, curiously enough, the ingredient from which it derived its distinctive appellation (*i.e.*, the *sprossen* or *jopen*) appears to be now left out in its preparation.

[1] *Uyt liep*—ran out.   [2] *Den bodem*—the bottom.
[3] Scarcely.
[4] *In de selvighe vochticheyt was de cracht vant gantsche bier*—in that liquid part lay the whole strength of the beer.
[5] Shovelled.   [6] "S.E. and by S.E."—*Ph.*
[7] *Braecken wy de kuiuyt wech*—we pulled down the cabin.
[8] *Het portael*—the entrance hall, or porch.

The 18 of October the wind blew hard east [and] south-east, and then we fetched our bread out of the scute which we had drawne vp vpon the land, and the wine also, which as then was not much frozen, and yet it had layne sixe weeks therein, and notwithstanding that it had often times frozen very hard. The same day we saw an other beare, and then the sea was so couered ouer with ice that we could see no open water.

The 19 of October ye wind blew north-east, and then there was but two men and a boy in the ship, at which time there came a beare that sought forcibly to get into the ship, although the two men shot at her with peeces of wood,[1] and yet she ventured vpon them,[2] whereby they were in an extreame feare; [and] each of them seeking to saue them selues, the two men leapt into the balust,[3] and the boy clomed into the foot mast top[4] to saue their liues; meane time some of our men shot at her with a musket, and then shee ran away.

The 20 of October it was calme sunshine weather, and then againe we saw the sea open,[5] at which time we went on bord to fetch the rest of our beere out of the ship, where we found some of the barrels frozen in peeces, and the iron heapes[6] that were vpon the josam barrels[7] were also frozen in peeces.

The 21 of October it was calme sunshine wether, and then we had almost fetched all our victuals out of the ship [to the house].

[1] *Met brandthouten smeten*—threw billets of firewood at her.

[2] *Quam hy effenwel seer vreeselijck tot haer aen*—came towards them in a most terrific manner.

[3] *Int ruijm*—in the hold.

[4] *Clam int fockewant*—climbed up the fore-rigging.

[5] *Eenige openinghe van water in de zee*—some open places of water in the sea.

[6] *Banden*—hoops.

[7] *De joopen vaten*—the spruce-beer casks. See page 114, note 2.

The 22 of October the wind blew coldly and very stiff north-east, with so great a snow that we could not get out of our dores.

The 23 of October it was calme weather, and the wind blew north-east. Then we went aboord our ship to see if the rest of our men would come home to the house; but wee feared y^t it would blow hard againe, and therefore durst not stirre with the sicke man, but let him ly still that day, for he was very weake.

The 24 of October the rest of our men, being 8 persons, came to the house, and drew the sicke man vpon a slead, and then with great labour and paine vve drew our boate[1] home to our house, and turned the bottome thereof vpwards, that when time serued vs (if God saued our liues in the winter time) wee might vse it. And after that perceiuing that the ship lay fast and that there was nothing lesse to be expected then the opening of the water, we put our [kedge-] anchor into the ship againe, because it should not be couered ouer and lost in the snow, that in the spring time[2] we might vse it: for we alwaies trusted in God that hee would deliuer vs from thence towards sommer time either one way or other.

Things standing at this point with vs, as the sunne (when wee might see it best and highest) began to be very low,[3] we vsed all the speede we could to fetch all things with sleades out of our ship into our house, not onely meate and drinke but all other necessaries; at which time the winde was north.

The 26 of October we fetcht all things that were necessary for the furnishing of our scute and our boate:[4] and when we had laden the last slead, and stood [in the track-ropes] ready to draw it to the house, our maister looked about him and

---

[1] *Bock*—yawl.
[2] *Teghens den somer*—towards the summer.
[3] *Te begheren*—to leave us.   [4] See page 78, notes 2 and 3.

saw three beares behind the ship that were comming towards vs, whereupon he cryed out aloud to feare[1] them away, and we presently leaped forth [from the track-ropes] to defend our selues as well as we could. And as good fortune was, there lay two halberds vpon the slead, whereof the master tooke one and I the other, and made resistance against them as well as we could; but the rest of our men ran to saue themselues in the ship, and as they ran one of them fell into a clift of ice,[2] which greeued vs much, for we thought verily that the beares would haue ran vnto him to deuoure him; but God defended him, for the beares still made towards the ship after the men y^t ran thither to saue themselues. Meane time we and the man that fel into the clift of ice tooke our aduantage, and got into the ship on the other side; which the beares perceiuing, they came fiercely towards vs, that had no other armes to defend vs withall but onely the two halberds, which wee doubting would not be sufficient, wee still gaue them worke to do by throwing billets [of fire-wood] and other things at them, and euery time we threw they ran after them, as a dogge vseth to doe at a stone that is cast at him. Meane time we sent a man down vnder hatches[3][into the caboose] to strike fire, and another to fetch pikes; but wee could get no fire, and so we had no meanes to shoote.[4] At the last, as the beares came fiercely vpon vs, we stroke one of them with a halberd vpon the snoute, wherewith she gaue back when shee felt her selfe hurt, and went away, which the other two y^t were not so great as she perceiuing, ran away; and we thanked God that wee were so well deliuered from them, and so drew our slead quietly to our house, and there shewed our men what had happened vnto vs.

[1] Frighten.
[2] *In een scheur tusschent ys in*—into a crevice in the ice.
[3] *Onder*—below. The caboose had been removed below on account of the extreme cold on deck, as is mentioned in page 108.
[4] Their firearms had matchlocks.

The 26 of October the wind was north and north northwest, with indifferent faire wether. Then we saw [much] open water hard by the land, but we perceiued the ice to driue in the sea still towards the ship.[1]

The 27 of October the wind blew north-east, and it snowed so fast that we could not worke without the doore. That day our men kil'd a white fox, which they flead, and after they had rosted it ate thereof, which tasted like connies[2] flesh. The same day we set vp our diall and made the clock strike,[3] and we hung vp a lamp to burne in the night time, wherein we vsed the fat of the beare, which we molt[4] and burnt in the lampe.

The 28 of October wee had the wind north-east, and then our men went out to fetch wood; but there fell so stormy wether and so great a snow, that they were forced to come home againe. About euening the wether began to breake vp,[5] at which time three of our men went to the place where we had set the beare vpright and there stood frozen, thinking to pull out her teeth, but it was cleane couered ouer with snow. And while they were there it began to snow so fast againe [with rough weather], that they were glad to come home as fast as they could; but the snow beat so sore vpon them that they could hardly see their way[6] and had almost lost their right way, whereby they had like to haue laine all that night out of the house [in the cold].

The 29 of October the wind still blew north-east, and then we fetch'd segges[7] from the sea side and laid them vpon the saile that was spread vpon our house, that it might be so

---

[1] *Overt schip heenen*—out beyond the ship.   [2] Rabbits.
[3] *Stelden wy onse orlogie wederom dat de clock sloech*—we set up our clock, so that it (went and) struck (the hour).
[4] Melted.
[5] *Tweer was ghebetert*—the weather improved.
[6] *Zy conden nyt haer ooghen niet sien*—they could not see out of their eyes.
[7] *Cinghel*—shingle.

much the closer and warmer: for the deales were not driuen close together, and the foule wether would not permit vs to do it.

The 30 of October the wind yet continued north-east, and the sunne was full aboue the earth a little aboue the horizon.[1]

The 31 of October the wind still blew north-east w^t great store of snow, whereby we durst not looke out of doores.[2]

The first of Nouember the wind still continued north-east, and then we saw the moone rise in the east when it began to be darke, and the sunne was no higher aboue the horizon than wee could well see it, and yet that day we saw it not, because of the close[3] wether and the great snow that fell; and it was extreame cold, so that we could not go out of the house.

The 2 of November[4] the wind blew west and somewhat south, but in the euening it blew north with calme wether; and that day we saw the sunne rise south south-east, and it went downe [about] south south-west, but it was not full aboue the earth,[5] but passed in the horizon along by the earth. And the same day one of our men killed a fox with a hatchet, which was flead, rosted, and eaten. Before the sunne began to decline wee saw no foxes, and then the beares vsed to go from vs.[6]

The 3 of Nouember the wind blew north-west w^t calme wether, and the sunne rose south and by east and somewhat more southerly, and went downe south and by west and

[1] *Doen ghingh de son heel dicht boven der aerden, weynich boven den horisont*—then the sun went quite close over the earth, but little above the horizon.

[2] *Niet een hooft dorsten uyt steecken*—not one of us durst put his head out of doors.

[3] *Doncker*—dark, overcast.

[4] "December."—*Ph.*

[5] *Hy quam met zijn volle rondicheyt niet boven*—it did not show (rise with) its whole disk.

[6] *Ende de beyren ghinghen doen mede wegh*—and then the bears also went away.

somewhat more southerly; and then we could see nothing but the upper part[1] of the sun above the horizon, and yet the land where we were was as high as the mast[2] of our ship.[3] Then we tooke the height of the sunne,[4] it being in the eleuenth degree and 41 minutes of[5] Scorpio,[6] his declination being 15 degrees and 24 minutes on the south side of the equinoctiall line.

The 4 of Nouember it was calme wether, but then we saw the sunne no more, for it was no longer aboue the horizon. Then our chirurgien[7] [prescribed and] made a bath, to bathe[8] vs in, of a wine pipe, wherein we entred one after the other, and it did vs much good and was a great meanes of our health. The same day we tooke a white fox, that often times came abroad, not as they vsed at other times; for that when the beares left vs at the setting of the sunne,[9] and came not againe before it rose,[10] the fox[es] to the contrary came abroad when they were gone.

The 5 of Nouember the wind was north and somewhat west, and then we saw [much] open water vpon the sea, but our ship lay still fast in the ice; and when the sunne had left vs we saw ye moone continually both day and night, and [it] neuer went downe when it was in the highest degree.[11]

The 6 of Nouember the wind was north-west, still wether,

---

[1] *Den boven cant*—the upper edge.

[2] *De mars*—the round top.

[3] The question of refraction, arising out of this and other observations, is discussed in the Introduction.

[4] *De son peijlden*—observed (*lit.* measured) the sun.

[5] "Off."—*Ph.*

[6] That is to say, the sun's longitude was 221° 48', or 41° 48' from the autumnal equinox.   [7] *Onse surgijn*—our surgeon.

[8] *Te stoven*—*lit.* to stew. This is the primary sense of the word *stew*, which afterwards, like its synonym *bagnio*, acquired a very different meaning. The bath used appears to have been a vapour bath.

[9] *Mette son*—with the sun.   [10] *Weder quam*—it returned.

[11] Under the parallel of 76°, the moon continues incessantly above the horizon about seven or eight days in each month.

and then our men fetcht a slead full of fire-wood, but by reason that the son was not seene it was very dark wether.

The 7 of Nouember it was darke wether and very still, the wind west; at which time we could hardly discerne the day from the night, specially because at that time our clock stood still, and by that meanes we knew not when it was day although it was day:[1] and our men rose not out of their cabens all that day[2] but onely to make water, and therefore they knew not [very well] whether the light they saw was the light of the day or of the moone, wherevpon they were of seueral opinions, some saying it was the light of the day, the others of the night; but as we tooke good regard therevnto, we found it to be the light of the day, about twelue of the clock at noone.[3]

The 8 of Nouember it was still wether, the wind blowing south and south-west. The same day our men fetcht another slead of firewood, and then also we tooke a white fox, and saw [much] open water in the sea. The same day we shared our bread amongst vs, each man hauing foure pound and ten ounces[4] for his allowance in eight daies; so that then we were eight daies eating a barrell of bread, whereas before we ate it vp in fiue or sixe daies. [As yet] we had no need to share our flesh and fish, for we had more store thereof; but our drinke failed vs, and therefore we were forced to share that also: but our best beere was for the most part wholly without any strength,[5] so that it had no sauour at all, and besides all this there was a great deale of it spilt.

[1] *Vermoeden wy geen dagh, doent al dagh was*—we thought that it was not day, when it already was day.

[2] *Hadde op dien dagh niet vyt de koy gheweest*—had not that day been out of bed.

[3] *So wast wel opt hooghste van den dagh*—it was truly the *height* of day.

[4] *Loot*—a loot or half-ounce; of which 32 go to the pound. The quantity mentioned above is equal to 4 pounds 11 ounces avoirdupois.

[5] *Was meest al de cracht uytgevroren*—had almost all its strength frozen out of it.

The 9 of Nouember the wind blew north-east and somewhat more northerly, and then we had not much day-light, but it was altogether darke.

The 10 of Nouember it was calme wether, the wind north-west; and then our men went into the ship to see how it lay, and wee saw that there was a great deale of water in it, so that the balast was couered ouer with water, but it was frozen, and so might not be pump't out.

The 11 of Nouember it was indifferent wether, the wind north-west. The same day we made a round thing[1] of cable yearn and [knitted] like to a net, [and set it] to catch foxes withall, that we might get them into the house, and it was made like a trap, which fell vpon the foxes as they came vnder it;[2] and that day we caught one.

The 12 of Nouember the wind blew east, with a little[3] light. That day we began to share our wine, euery man had two glasses[4] a day, but commonly our drink was water which we molt[5] out of snow which we gathered without the house.

The 13 of Nouember it was foule wether, with great snow, the wind east.

The 14 of Nouember it was faire cleare wether, with a cleare sky full of starres and an east-wind.

The 15 of November it was darke wether, the wind north-east, with a vading light.[6]

The 16 of Nouember it was [still] wether, with a temperate aire[7] and an east-wind.

---

[1] *Een ronden hoep*—a round hoop.

[2] *Dat men se in huys mochten toe halen ghelijck een val, als de vossen daer onder quamen*—so that when the foxes came under it, as in a trap, we might drag them into the house.

[3] *Met een betoghen lucht*—with a cloudy sky.

[4] *Locxkens*. In Sewel's *Dutch and Eng. Dict.* by Buys, *Lokje*, the modern form of this word, is thus defined:—"*a little hollow log*, such as seamen sometimes use to put sauce in, for want of another dish: hence it is that some will call any *saucer* with that name."

[5] Melted.   [6] *Een betoghen lucht*—a cloudy sky.

[7] *Een ghetemperden lucht*—a moderate sky.

The 17 of Nouember it was darke wether and a close aire,¹ the wind east.

The 18 of Nouember it was foule wether, the wind south-east. Then the maister cut vp a packe of course [woollen] clothes,² and divided it amongst the men that needed it, therewith to defend vs better from the cold.

The 19 of Nouember it was foule wether, with an east wind; and then the chest with linnin was opened and deuided amongst the men for shift,³ for they had need of them, for then our onely care was to find all the means we could to defend our body from the cold.

The 20 of Nouember it was faire stil weather, the wind easterly. Then we washt our sheets,⁴ but it was so cold that when we had washt and wroong⁵ them, they presently froze so stiffe [out of the warm water], that, although we lay'd them by a great fire, the side that lay next the fire thawed, but the other side was hard frozen; so that we should sooner haue torne them in sunder⁶ than haue opened them, whereby we were forced to put them into the seething⁷ water again to thaw them, it was so exceeding cold.

The 21 of Nouember it was indifferent⁸ wether with a north-east wind. Then wee agreed that euery man should take his turne to cleaue wood, thereby to ease our cooke, that had more than work inough to doe twice a day to dresse meat and to melt snowe for our drinke; but our master and the pilot⁹ were exempted from yᵗ work.

The 22 of Nouember the wind was south-est, [and] it was faire wether, then we had but¹⁰ seuenteene cheeses,¹¹ whereof

¹ *Een betoghen lucht*—a cloudy sky.
² A piece of coarse woollen cloth.
³ *Tot hemden*—for shirts.
⁴ *Hemden*—shirts.
⁵ Wrung.
⁶ *Se ghebroken*—broken them.
⁷ Boiling.
⁸ *Bequaem*—suitable, good.
⁹ *De schipper ende stuerman*; namely, Jacob Heemskerck and William Barentsz.
¹⁰ *Noch*—yet.
¹¹ *Koyen kasen* — lit. cow-cheeses, because they were made from the milk of cows, and not of sheep, as is not uncommon in the Netherlands.

one we ate amonst vs and the rest were deuided to euery man one for his portion, which they might eate when he list.

The 23 of Nouember it was indifferent good weather, the wind south-east, and as we perceiued that the fox[es] vsed to come oftener and more than they were woont, to take them the better we made certaine traps of thicke plancks, wheron we laid stones, and round about them placed peeces of shards[1] fast in the ground, that they might not dig vnder them; and so [we occasionally] got some of the foxes.

The 24 of Nouember it was foule wether, and the winde north-west,[2] and then we [again] prepared our selues to go into the bath, for some of vs were not very well at ease; and so foure of vs went into it, and when we came out our surgion[3] gave us a purgation, which did vs much good; and that day we took foure foxes.

[1] *Ejinde van sparren*—ends of spars.   [2] "North-east."—*Ph.*

[3] *De barbier*—the barber. This is the person who on a former occasion (page 121) was called *de surgijn*—the surgeon. In the general decline of science during the middle ages, surgery, as a branch of medicine, became neglected, and its practice, in the rudest form, fell into the hands of the barber; from whose ordinary avocations of cutting the hair, shaving the beard, paring the nails, etc., the step was not very great to the operations of tooth-drawing, bleeding, cupping, dressing wounds, setting broken limbs, etc. And, with these functions of the surgeon, the barber not unreasonably assumed his title also.

The rivalry between these barber-surgeons and the pure surgeons, who again sprang up on the revival of learning, is matter of history.

In England, a compromise between the two rival bodies was early effected by means of the union of the barber-surgeons and surgeons of London, by the statute of 32 Hen. VIII, c. 41 (A.D. 1540), which, while nominally amalgamating them, virtually effected the separation of the two professions; inasmuch as those members of the united corporation "using barbery"—as it was somewhat barbarously expressed—were prohibited from "occupying any surgery, letting of blood, or any other thing belonging to surgery, drawing of teeth only except"; while, on the other hand, surgeons were forbidden to "use barbery". And the natural consequence was their formal separation into two entirely distinct bodies by the Act of 18 Geo. II, c. 15 (A.D. 1745).

On the continent, the barber-surgeon retained his rank to a much later date; and in France, in particular, till the revolution of 1793.

The 25 of Nouember it was faire cleare wether, the winde west; and that day we tooke two foxes with a springe that we had purposely set vp.

The 26 of Nouember it was foule weather, and a great storme with a south-west wind and great store of snowe, whereby we were so closed vp in the house that we could not goe out, but were forced to ease ourselues within the house.

The 27 of Nouember it was faire cleare weather, the wind south-west; and then we made more springes to get foxs; for it stood vs vpon to doe it,[1] because they serued vs for meat, as if God had sent them purposely for vs, for wee had not much meate.

But, instead of abandoning the razor to the hair-dresser, he still claimed the right of wielding it, "as being a *surgical* instrument"; so that, in order to distinguish between the two, it was ordained by Louis XIV, that the barber-surgeon should have for his sign a brass basin, and should paint his shop-front red or black only, whereas the barber-hairdresser should display a pewter basin, and paint his shop-front in any other colour. Blue was the colour usually adopted by the barber-hairdressers, and to this colour their name has in consequence become attached. That the connexion between the two is still not lost sight of in France, is proved by the following extract from the *Comédies et Proverbes* of Alfred de Musset, p. 510:—

"*Madame de Léry.*—Autant j'adore le lilas, autant je déteste le bleu.
Mathilde.—C'est la couleur de la constance.
Madame de Léry.—Bah! c'est la couleur des perruquiers."

Un Caprice.

Those professors of shaving and hairdressing, whose *poles*, painted red or black alternating with white, still decorate our streets, commit therefore a great mistake in using either of these two colours. "True like the needle to the pole," as Lieutenant Taffril wrote to Jenny Caxon ("To cast up to her that her father's a barber and has a pole at his door, and that she's but a manty-maker hersel! Fy for shame!"), they should confine themselves to the colour of constancy—and of the hairdressers; unless, indeed, they should happen to unite tooth-drawing to their other avocations, in which case they might perhaps, in strict right, be entitled to set up the red or black stripe of the barber-surgeons.

[1] *Die gheleghentheyt diente van ons waer ghenomen te zijn*—it was important for us to avail ourselves of the opportunity.

The 28 of Nouember it was foule stormie weather, and the wind blew hard out of the north, and it snew hard, whereby we were shut vp againe in our house, the snow lay so closed before the doores.[1]

The 29 of Nouember it was faire cleare wether and a good aire,[2] ye wind northerly; and we found meanes to open our doore by shoueling away the snowe, whereby we got one of our dores open; and going out we found al our traps and springes cleane[3] couered ouer with snow, which we made cleane, and set them vp again to take foxes; and that day we tooke one, which as then serued vs not onely for meat, but of the skins we made caps to were[4] vpon our heads, therewith to keep them warm from the extreame cold.

The 30 of Nouember it was faire cleare weather, the wind west, and [when the watchers[5] were about south-west, which according to our calculation was about midday,] sixe of vs went to the ship, all wel prouided of arms, to see how it lay; and when we went vnder the fore decke,[6] we tooke a foxe aliue in the ship.

The 1 of December it was foule weather, with a south-west wind and great stoare of snow, whereby we were once againe stopt vp in the house, and by that meanes there was so great a smoke in the house that we could hardly make fire, and so were forced to lye all day in our cabens, but the cooke was forced to make fire to dresse our meat.

The 2 of December it was still foule weather, whereby we were forced to keep stil in the house, and yet we could hardly sit by the fire because of the smoake, and therefore stayed still [for the most part] in our cabens; and then we heated stones, which we put into our cabens to warm our feet, for that both the cold and the smoke were vnsupportable.

---

[1] *Alle de deuren waren toe ghewaeyt*—all the doors were blown to.
[2] *Een helderen lucht*—a clear sky.
[3] Quite.
[4] Wear.
[5] See page 61, note 8.
[6] *Ondert verdeck*—under the deck, *i.e.*, below.

The 3 of December we had the like weather, at which times as we lay in our cabans we might heare the ice crack in the sea, and yet it was at the least halfe a mile [two miles] from vs, which made a hugh noyse [of bursting and cracking], and we were of oppinion that as then the great hils of ice[1] which wee had seene in the sea in summer time [lying so many fathoms thick] brake one from the other.[2] And for that during those 2 or 3 days, because of the extream smoake, we made not so much fire as we commonly vsed to doe, it froze so sore within the house that the wals and the roofe thereof were frozen two fingers thicke with ice, and also in our cabans[3] where we lay. All those three daies, while we could not go out by reason of the foule weather, we set vp the [sand-]glas of 12 houres, and when it was run out we set it vp againe, stil watching it lest we should misse our time. For the cold was so great that our clock was frozen, and might[4] not goe although we hung more waight on it then before.

The 4 of December it was faire cleare weather, the wind north,[5] and then we began euery man by turne to dig open our dores that were closed vp with snow; for we saw that it would be often to doe, and therefore we agreed to work by turns, no man excepted but the maister and the pilot.

The 5 of December it was faire weather with an east wind, and then we made our springes[6] cleane againe to take foxes.

The 6 of December it was foule weather againe, with an easterly wind and extreame cold, almost not to be indured; whereupon wee lookt pittifully one vpon the other, being in great feare, that if the extremity of ye cold grew to be more and more we should all die there with cold, for that what

---

[1] Icebergs.

[2] *Op malcanderen stuwen ende gheschoven werden*—were drifting and heaping one upon the other.

[3] *Jae selfs in de koyen*—yea, even in the cots.

[4] *Mochte*—could.   [5] "North-east."—*Ph.*   [6] *Vallen*—traps.

The exact manner of the house wherein we wintered.

fire soeuer we made it would not warme vs: yea, and our sack,[1] which is so hotte,[2] was frozen very hard, so that when [at noon] we were euery man to haue his part, we were forced to melt it in[3] the fire, which we shared euery second day about halfe a pint for a man, wherewith we were forced to sustain onr selues, and at other times we drank water, which agreed not well with the cold, and we needed not to coole it with snowe or ice,[4] but we were forced to melt it out of the snow.

The 7 of December it was still foule weather, and we had a great storme with a north-east wind,[5] which brought an extreme cold with it; at which time we knew not what to do, and while we sate consulting together what were best for vs to do, one of our companions gaue vs counsell to burne some of the sea-coles[6] that we had brought out of the ship, which would cast a great heat and continue long; and so at euening we made a great fire thereof, which cast a great heat. At which time we were very careful to keepe it in,[7] for that the heat being so great a comfort vnto vs, we tooke care how to make it continue long; whereupon we agreed to stop vp all the doores and the chimney, thereby to keepe in the heate, and so went into our cabans[8] to sleepe, well comforted with the heat, and so lay a great while talking together; but at last we were taken with a great swounding and daseling in our heads,[9] yet some more then other some,

[1] *Sareetsche secke*—Xeres seco, or sherry-sack.
[2] *Heet*—hot, strong.   [3] *Over*—over.
[4] Independently of the quiet humour of this observation, it is worthy of remark, as showing that at that early period the cooling of wine by means of ice or snow was practised by the Dutch.
[5] *Een vlieghenden storm uyten n. o.*—a hurricane out of the N.E.
[6] *Steen-colen*—stone or mineral coal; so called to distinguish it from charcoal, the usual fuel on the continent.
[7] *Maer wy wachtede ons voor de weerstuijt niet*—but we did not guard ourselves against the consequences.
[8] Cots.
[9] *Een sodanighen duyselinghe*—a sudden dizziness.

which we first perceiued by a sick man and therefore the lesse able to beare it, and found our selues to be very ill at ease, so that some of vs that were strongest start[1] out of their cabans, and first opened the chimney and then the doores, but he that opened the doore fell downe in a swound[2] [with much groaning] vppon the snow; which I hearing, as lying in my caban[3] next to the doore, start vp[4] [and there saw him lying in a swoon], and casting vinegar in his face[5] recouered him againe, and so he rose vp. And when the doores were open, we all recouered our healthes againe by reason of the cold aire; and so the cold, which before had beene so great an enemy vnto vs, was then the onely reliefe that we had, otherwise without doubt we had [all] died in a sodaine swound.[6] After y^t, the master, when we were come to our selues againe, gaue euery one of vs a little wine to comfort our hearts.

The 8 of December it was foule weather, the wind northerly, very sharpe and cold, but we durst lay no more coles on as we did the day before, for that our misfortune had taught vs that to shun one danger we should not run into an other [still greater].

The 9 of December it was faire cleare weather, the skie full of starres; then we set our doore wide open, which before was fast closed vp with snowe, and made our springes ready to take foxes.

The 10 of December it was still faire star-light weather, the wind north-west.[7] Then we tooke two foxes, which were good meate for vs, for as then our victuals began to be scant and the cold still increased, whereunto their skins serued vs for a good defence.

---

[1] Started.   [2] Swoon.   [3] Cot.
[4] *Liep daer heenen*—ran thither.
[5] *Haelde flucks edick ende vreef hem dat in zijn aensicht*—quickly fetched some vinegar and rubbed his face with it.
[6] *In eenen swijm*—in a swoon.   [7] "North-east."—*Ph.*

The 11 of December it was faire weather and a clear aire,[1] but very cold, which he that felt not would not beleeue, for our shoos[2] froze as hard as hornes vpon our feet, and within they were white frozen, so that we could not weare our shooes, but were forced to make great pattens,[3] ye vpper part being ship[4] skins, which we put on ouer three or foure paire of socks, and so went in them to keepe our feet warme.

The 12 of December it was faire cleare weather, with [a bright sky and] a north-west wind, but extreame cold, so that our house walles and cabans where[5] frozen a finger thicke, yea and the clothes vpon our backs were white ouer with frost [and icicles]; and although some of vs were of opinion that we should lay more coles vpon the fire to warme vs, and that we should let the chimney stand open, yet we durst not do it, fearing the like danger we had escaped.

The 13 of December it was faire cleare wether, with an east wind. Then we tooke another foxe, and took great paines about preparing and dressing of our springes, with no small trouble, for that if we staied too long without the doores, there arose blisters[6] vpon our faces and our eares.

The 14 of December it was faire wether, the wind northeast and the sky full of starres. Then we tooke the height of ye right shoulder of the Rens,[7] when it was south southwest and somewhat more westerly (and then it was at the

---

[1] *Een helderen lucht*—a bright sky.
[2] Shoes.
[3] *Wyde clompen*—loose clogs or slippers.
[4] Sheep.
[5] Were.
[6] *Blaren ende buylen*—"blains and boils."
[7] *De Reus*—the Giant, as the constellation Orion is called, after the Arabic *El-djebbâr*. The star Bellatrix γ *Orionis*, which was here observed, is usually said to be in the *left* shoulder. It depends, however, upon which way "the Giant" is considered as looking. The exact declination of this star for the end of the year 1596 is $+ 5° 58',$[4] N.; so that, after allowing $2',_6$ for refraction, the complement of the height of the Pole is 14° 17', and the height of the Pole is 75° 43'.

It is not possible for Betelgueze, (a) in the *right* shoulder of Orion, to have been the star observed; for the latitude resulting from it would be upwards of 79°.

highest in our [common] compas), and it was eleuated aboue the horison twenty degrees and eighteen[1] minutes, his declination being six degrees and eighteene minuts on the north side of the lyne, which declination being taken out of the height aforesaid there rested fourteen degrees, which being taken out of 90 degrees, then the height of ye Pole was seuenty sixe degrees.

The 15 of December it was still faire [bright] weather, the wind east. That day we tooke two foxes, and saw the moone rise east south-east, when it was twenty-sixe daies old; [and it was] in the signe of Scorpio.

The 16 of December it was faire cleare weather, the wind [north] east. At that time we had no more wood in the house, but had burnt it all; but round about our house there lay some couered ouer with snow, which with great paine and labour we were forced to digge out and so shouell away the snow, and so brought it into the house, which we did by turns, two and two together, wherein we were forced to vse great speede, for we could not long endure without the house, because of the extreame cold,[2] although we ware[3] the foxes skinnes about our heads and double apparell vpon our backs.

The 17 of December the wind still held north-east, with faire weather, and so great frosts that we were of opinion that if there stood a barrel full of water[4] without the doore, it would in one night freeze from the top to the bottome.

The 18 of December the wind still held north-east, with faire wether. Then seuen of vs went out vnto the ship to see how it lay; and being vnder the decke, thinking to find a foxe there, we sought all the holes,[5] but we found none: but when we entered into the caben,[6] and had stricken fire to

[1] "Twenty-eight."—*Ph*.
[2] *De onuytspreklijcke ondraechelijcke coude*—the inexpressible, intolerable cold.   [3] Wore.
[4] *Een joopen vat met water*—a spruce-beer cask full of water.
[5] *Stopten eerst alle de gaten dicht toe*—first closely *stopped* all the holes.
[6] *Ruijm*—hold.

see in what case the ship was and whether the water rose higher in it, there wee found a fox, which we tooke and carried it home, and ate it, and then we found that in eighteene dayes absence (for it was so long since we had beene there) the water was risen about a finger high, but yet it was all ice, for it froze as fast as it came in, and the vessels which we had brought with vs full of fresh water out of Holland were frozen to the ground.[1]

The 19 of December it was faire wether, the wind being south. Then we put each other in good comfort that the sun was then almost half ouer and ready to come to vs againe, which we sore longed for, it being a weary time for vs to be without the sunne, and to want the greatest comfort that God sendeth vnto man here vpon the earth, and that which reioiceth euery liuing thing.

The 20 of Dece[mber] before noone it was faire cleare wether, and then we had taken a fox; but towards euening there rose such a [violent] storm [and tempest] in the south-west, with so great a snow, that all the house was inclosed therewith.

The 21 of December it was faire cleere wether, with a north-east wind. Then we made our doore cleane againe and made a way to go out, and clensed our traps for the foxes, which did vs great pleasure when we tooke them, for they seemed as dainty as uenison unto vs.

The 22 of December it was foule wether with great store of snow, the wind south-west, which stopt up our doore againe, and we were forced to dig it open againe, which was almost euery day to do.

The 23 of December it was foule wether, the wind south-west with great store of snow, but we were in good comfort that the sunne would come againe to vs, for (as we gest[2]) that day he was in Tropicus Capricorni, which is the furthest

---

[1] *Grondt*—bottom. [2] Calculated.

signe[1] that the sunne passeth on the south side of the line, and from thence it turneth north-ward againe. This Tropicus Capricorni lyeth on the south side of the equinoctial line, in twenty-three degrees and twenty-eight[2] minutes.

The 24 of December, being Christmas-euen, it was faire wether. Then we opened our doore againe and saw much open water in the sea: for we had heard the ice crack and driue, [and] although it was not day,[3] yet we could see so farre. Towards euening it blew hard out of the north-east, with great store of snow, so that all the passage that wee had made open before was [immediately] stopt vp againe.

The 25 of December, being Christmas day, it was foule wether with a north-west wind; and yet, though it was [very] foule wether, we hard[4] the foxes run ouer our house, wherewith some of our men said it was an ill signe; and while we sate disputing why it should be an ill signe, some of our men made answere that it was an ill signe because we could not take them, to put them into the pot to rost them,[5] for that had been a very good signe for vs.

The 26 of December it was foule wether, the wind northwest, and it was so [extraordinarily] cold that we could not warme vs, although we vsed all the meanes we could, with greate fires, good store of clothes, and with hot stones and billets[6] laid vpon our feete and vpon our bodies as we lay in our cabens;[7] but notwithstanding all this, in the morning our cabens were frozen [white], which made vs behold one the other with sad countenance. But yet we comforted our selues againe as well as we could, that the sunne was then as low as it could goe, and that it now began to come to vs againe,[8]

[1] *T'uyterste perck*—the utmost limit.   [2] "Eighteen."—*Ph.*
[3] *Hoe well datter gheen dagh was*—though there was no daylight.
[4] Heard.   [5] *In de pot ofte aent spit*—in the pot or on the spit.
[6] *Kenghels*—balls.   [7] Cots.
[8] *Dattet int afgaen vanden bergh was: te weten, dat de son zijn wegh wederom nae ons toe nam*—that we were now going down hill; that is to say, the sun was now on his way back to us.

and we found it to be true; for that the daies beginning to lengthen the cold began to strengthen, but hope put vs in good comfort and eased our paine.[1]

The 27 of December it was still foule wether with a north-west wind, so that as then we had not beene out in three daies together, nor durst not thrust our heads out of doores; and within the house it was so extreme cold, that as we sate [close] before a great fire, and seemed to burne[2] [our shins] on the fore side, we froze behinde at our backs, and were al white, as the country men[3] vse to be when they come in at the gates of the towne in Holland with their sleads,[4] and haue gone[5] all night.

The 28 of December it was still foule wether, with a west wind, but about euening it began to cleare vp. At which time one of our men made a hole open at one of our doores, and went[6] out to see what news abroad,[7] but found it so hard wether that he stayed not long, and told vs that it had snowed so much that the snow lay higher than our house, and that if he had stayed out longer his eares would un-doubtedly haue been frozen off.

[1] *De daghen die langhen zijn de daghen die stranghen, dan hoope dede pijn versoeten*—"the days that lengthen are the days that become more severe [?];" but "hope sweetened pain". These are two Dutch proverbs, strung together somewhat after the fashion of Sancho Panza. The former is equivalent to "as the day lengthens, so the cold strengthens", and "cresce 'l dì, cresce 'l freddo", cited in Ray's *English Proverbs*, p. 37.

[2] *Bynaest...verbranden*—almost burned.

[3] *Boers*—boors, peasants.

[4] *Ter poorten van de steden incomen*—come in *at the gates* of the towns. It would almost seem that in the text the word is *sleden* and not *steden*; so that the meaning would be, "come in at the gates *from their sledges*". But, as the fact is that the boors enter the gates in their carts, and that those who come in sledges must necessarily reach the town by the water side, where there are no gates, it can scarcely be doubted that the proper reading is *steden*. The translator appears to have wished to provide for both cases.

[5] *Onder weghen ghewcest zijn*—have been travelling.

[6] *Croop*—crept.

[7] *Hoet daer ghestelt was*—how matters stood there.

The 29 of December it was calme wether and a pleasant aire,[1] the wind being southward. That day he whose turne it was opened the doore and dig'd a hole through the snow, where wee went out of the house vpon steps as if it had bin out of a seller,[2] at least seuen or eight steps high, each step a foote from the other. And then we made cleane our springes [or traps] for the foxes, whereof for certain[3] daies we had not taken any; and as we made them cleane, one of our men found a dead fox in one of them that was frozen as hard as a stone, which he brought into the house and thawed it before the fire, and after fleaing it some of our men ate it.

The 30 of December it was foule wether againe, with a storme out of the west and great store of snow, so that all the labour and paine that we had taken the day before, to make steps to go out of our house and to clense our springes,[4] was al in vaine; for it was al couered over w^t snow againe higher then it was before.

The 31 of December it was still foule wether with a storme out of the north-west, whereby we were so fast shut vp into the house as if we had beene prisoners, and it was so extreame cold that the fire almost cast no heate; for as we put our feete to the fire, we burnt our hose[5] before we could feele the heate, so that we had [constantly] work inough to do to patch our hose. And, which is more, if we had not sooner smelt then felt them, we should haue burnt them [quite away] ere we had knowne it.

[Anno 1597]

After that, with great cold, danger, and disease,[6] we had brought the[7] yeare vnto an end, we entered into ye yeare of our Lord God 1597, ye beginning whereof was in ye same maner as ye end of anno 1596 had been; for the

---

[1] *Een betoghen lucht*—a cloudy sky.
[2] Cellar.
[3] Several.
[4] *De trappen te maecken*—to set the traps.
[5] Stockings.
[6] *Onghemack*—hardship.
[7] "This."—*Ph.*

wether continued as cold, foule, [boisterous], and snowy as it was before, so that vpon the first of January we were inclosed in the house, y⁶ wind then being west. At the same time we agreed¹ to share our wine euery man a small measure full, and that but once in two daies. And as we were in great care and feare that it would [still] be long before we should get out from thence, and we [sometimes] hauing but smal hope therein, some of vs spared to drink wine as long as wee could, that if we should stay long there we might drinke it at our neede.

The 2 of January it blew hard, with a west wind and a great storme, with both snow and frost, so that in four or five daies we durst not put our heads out of y⁶ doores; and as then by reason of the great cold we had almost burnt all our wood [that was in the house], notwithstanding we durst not goe out to fetch more wood, because it froze so hard and there was no being without the doore; but seeking about we found some [superfluous] pieces of wood that lay ouer the doore, which we [broke off and] cloue, and withall cloue the blocks² whereon we vsed to beate our stock-fish,³ and so holp our selues so well as we could.

The 3 of January it was all one weather [constantly boisterous, with snow and a north-west wind, and so exceedingly cold that we were forced to remain close shut up in the house], and we had little wood to burne.

The 4 of January it was still foule stormie weather, with much snow and great cold, the wind south-west, and we were forced to keepe [constantly shut up] in the house. And to know where the wind blew, we thrust a halfe pike out at y⁶ chimney wᵗ a little cloth or fether upon it; but [we had to look at it immediately the wind caught it, for] as soone as we thrust it out it was presently frozen as hard as a peece of

---

¹ *Begonnen*—began.   ² *Het block*—the block.
³ *Bergher visch:* so called because it comes principally from Bergen in Norway.

wood, and could not go about nor stirre with the wind [so that we said to one another how tremendously cold it must be out of doors].

The 5 of January it was somewhat still and calme weather.¹ Then we digd our doore open againe, that we might goe out and carry out all the filth that had bin made during the time of our being shut in the house, and made euery thing handsome, and fetched in wood, which we cleft; and it was all our dayes worke to further our selues as much as we could, fearing lest we should be shut up againe. And as there were three doores in our portall, and for y*t* our house lay couered ouer in snow, we took y*e* middle doore thereof away, and digged a great hole in the snow that laie without the house, like to a side of a vault,² wherein we might go to ease our selues and cast other filth into it. And when we had taken paines³ al day, we remembered our selues that it was Twelf Euen,⁴ and then we prayed our maister⁵ that [in the midst of all our troubles] we might be merry that night, and said that we were content to spend some of the wine that night which we had spared and which was our share euery second day, and whereof for certaine daies we had not drunke; and so that night we made merry and drunke to the three kings.⁶ And

---

¹ *Wasset weder wat besadicht*—the weather was somewhat milder.

² *Als een verwulfsel van een boogh ofte kelder*—like the arch of a vault or cellar.

³ *Gheslooft*—toiled.

⁴ *Drie Coninghen Avondt*—Three Kings' Even. The *fifth* of January, as being the *eve* of the Feast of the Epiphany, is properly "Twelfth Night". But, in England, the vigils or eves of all feast days between Christmas and the Purification having been abolished at the Reformation (see Wheatley, *Rational Illustration of the Book of Common Prayer*, Oxford, 1846, p. 165), this season of festivity, thus deprived of its religious character, was transferred to the evening *after* the feast; so that Twelfth Night was thenceforward kept on the evening of the 6th of January.

⁵ *Begheerden aen den schipper*—requested the skipper.

⁶ *Coninexken speelden*—drew for king (*lit.* played at kings).

therewith we had two pound of meale [which we had taken to make paste for the cartridges], whereof we [now] made pancakes with oyle, and [we laid to] euery man a white bisket[1] which we sopt in [the] wine. And so supposing that we were[2] in our owne country and amongst our frends, it comforted vs as well as if we had made a great banket[3] in our owne house. And we also made[4] tickets, and our gunner was king of Noua Zembla, which is at least two hundred [800] miles long[5] and lyeth betweene two seas.[6]

The 6 of January it was faire weather, the wind north-east. Then we went out and clensed our traps [and springes] to take foxes, which were our uenison; and we digd a great hole in the snow where our fire-wood lay, and left it close aboue like a vault [of a cellar], and from thence fetcht out our wood as we needed it.

The 7 of January it was foule weather againe, with a north-west wind and some snow, and very cold, which put vs in great feare to be shut up in the house againe.

The 8 of January it was faire weather againe, the wind north. Then we made our [traps and] springes ready to get more uenison, which we longed for. And then we might [sometimes begin to] see and marke day-light, which then began to increase, that the sunne as then began to come towards vs againe, which thought put vs in no litle comfort.

The 9 of January it was foule wether, with a north-west wind, but not so hard wether as it had bin before, so y[t] we might[7] go out of the doore to make cleane our springes; but it was no need to bid vs go home againe, for the cold taught

[1] *Een wittbroods beschuijt* — a (captain's) biscuit made of wheaten flour.
[2] Fancying ourselves to be.
[3] Banquet.
[4] *Uytgedeelt*—distributed.
[5] This estimated length includes the island of Waigatsch.
[6] Namely, the Northern Ocean and the Sea of Kara.
[7] Could.

vs by experience not to stay long out, for it was not so warm to get any good by staying in the aire.[1]

The 10 of January it was faire weather, with a north wind. Then seuen of vs went to our ship, well armed, which we found in the same state we left it in, and [in] it we saw many footsteps of beares, both great and small, whereby it seemed that there had bin more than one or two beares therein. And as we went under hatches, we strooke fire and lighted a candle, and found that the water was rysen a foote higher in the ship.

The 11 of January it was faire weather, the wind northwest[2] and the cold began to be somewhat lesse, so that as then we were bold to goe [now and then] out of the doores, and went about a quarter of a mile [one mile] to a hill, from whence we fetched certaine stones, which we layd in the fire, therewith to warme vs in our cabans.

The 12 of January it was faire cleare weather, the wind west.[3] That euening it was very cleare, and the skie full of stars. Then we tooke the height of Occulus Tauri,[4] which

---

[1] *Want de coude keerde ons noch wel niet langhe uyt blyven, om dattet buyten niet snick heet was*—for the cold itself was quite enough to teach us not to stay long out, inasmuch as out of doors it was not smoking hot.

[2] "N.E."—*Ph*. [3] "N.W."—*Ph*.

[4] *Oculus Tauri*. The exact declination for this year of *a Tauri* or Aldeberan is + 15° 40',$_2$: so that the complement of the height of the Pole, after allowing 1',$_7$ for refraction, is 14° 12',$_1$, and the height of the Pole is 75° 47',$_9$. The mean of this observation, and that of γ *Orionis*, on December 14th, 1596 (page 131), is 75° 45',$_5$, which may be regarded as being a very close approximation to the true latitude of the expedition's wintering-place. From the author's statement, it appears that William Barentsz was of opinion that they were to the north of the 76th parallel, instead of to the south, as this corrected calculation makes their position to be. This only shows the importance of recording and publishing all observations in their original form, regardless of their apparent results, however anomalous. When a traveller's observations are for years kept back, in order that they may be "revised", the world may not uncharitably surmise that eventually they will not be presented to it in their integrity.

is a bright and well knowne star, and we found it to be eleuated aboue yᵉ horison twenty nine degrees and fifty foure minutes, her declination being fifteene degrees fifty foure minutes on the north side of the lyne. This declination being substracted from the height aforesaid, then there rested fourteene degrees: which substracted from ninety degrees, then the height of the pole was seuenty sixe degrees. And so by measuring the height of that starre and some others, we gest that yᵉ sun was in the like height,[1] and that we were there vnder seuenty sixe degrees, and rather higher than lower.

The 13 of January it was faire still weather, the wind westerlie; and then we perceaued that daylight began more and more to increase, and wee went out and cast bullets at the bale of yᵉ flag staffe, which before we could not see when it turnd about.[2]

The 14 of January it was faire weather and a cleare light,[3] the wind westerlie; and that day we tooke a fox.[4]

The 15 of January it was faire cleare weather, with a west wind; and six of vs went aboord the ship, where we found the bolck-vanger,[5] which the last time that we were in the ship we stucke in a hole in the fore decke[6] to take foxes, puld out of the hole, and lay in the middle of the ship, and

---

[1] *Also dat dese metinghe vande voornoemde sterre ende eenighe andere sterren, soo mede de metinghe van de sonne, alle over een quamen dat wy—* so that the measurement of the above-named star and of some other stars, as well as the measurement of the sun, all agreed (in showing) that we......

It will be seen in the sequel that the observations of the sun agree rather in showing the contrary of what is above contended for.

[2] *Liepen uyt ende schoten de cloot met de cloot van de vlayh-spil, die wy voor heen niet conden sien loopen*—ran out and played at ball (*lit.* threw the ball) with the truck of the flag-staff, which before that time we had not been able to see run.

[3] *Stil weder met een betoghen lucht*—calm weather with a cloudy sky.

[4] *Twee vossen*—two foxes.

[5] *Bolckvanger*—a seaman's rough coat.   [6] *Verdeck*—deck.

al torne in peeces by the bears, as we perceiued by their foote-steps.

The 16 of January it was faire weather, the wind northerly; and then we went now and then out of the house to strech out our ioynts and our limbs with going and running,[1] that we might not become lame; and about noone time we saw a certaine rednes in the skie, as a shew or messenger of the sunne that began to come towards vs.

The 17 of January it was cleare weather, with a north wind, and then still more and more we perceiued that the sun began to come neerer vnto vs; for the day was somewhat warmer, so that when wee had a good fire there fell great peeces of ice downe from the walles [and roof] of our house, and the ice melted in our cabens and the water dropt downe, which was not so before how great soeuer our fire was; but that night it was colde againe.[2]

The 18 of January it was faire cleare weather with a southeast wind. Then our wood began to consume,[3] and so we agreed to burne some of our sea-coles, and not to stop up the chimney, and then wee should not neede to feare any hurt,[4] which wee did, and found no disease thereby; but we thought it better for vs to keepe the coles and to burne our wood more sparingly, for that the coles would serue vs better when we should saile home in our open scute.[5]

The 19 of January it was faire weather, with a north wind. And then our bread began to diminish, for that some of our barels were not full waight, and so the diuision was lesse, and we were forced to mak our allowance bigger with

[1] *Om ons leden wat te verstercken, met gaen, werpen ende loopen* — to strengthen our limbs a little with walking, throwing (the ball), and running.

[2] *Maer des nachts vroort wederom effen cout* — but at night it froze again just as cold (as before).

[3] *Begonde vast te minderen* — began to diminish fast.

[4] *Swymen* — swooning.

[5] *De open schuyten* — the open boats.

that which we had spared before. And then some of vs went abord the ship, wherein there was halfe a barrell of bread, which we thought to spare till the last, and there [quite] secretly each of them tooke a bisket or two out of it.

The 20 of January the ayre was cleare,[1] and the wind south-west. That day we staied in the house and cloue wood to burne, and brake some of our emptie barrels, and cast the iron hoopes vpon the top of the house.

The 21 of January it was faire [clear] weather, with a west wind. At that time taking of foxes began to faile vs, which was a signe that the beares would soone come againe, as not long after we found it to be true; for as long as the beares stay[ed] away the foxes came abroad, and not much before the beares came abroad the foxes were but little seene.

The 22 of January it was faire wether with a west wind. Then we went out againe to cast the bullet,[2] and perceiued that day light began to appeare, whereby some of vs said that the sun would soon appeare vnto vs, but William Barents to the contrary said that it was yet [more than] two weeks too soone.

The 23 of January it was faire calme weather, with a south-west wind. Then foure of vs went to the ship and comforted each other, giuing God thankes that the hardest time of the winter was past, being in good hope that we should liue to talke of those things at home in our owne country; and when we were in the ship we found that the water rose higher and higher in it, and so each of us taking a bisket or two with us, we went home againe.

The 24 of January it was faire cleare weather, with a west wind. Then I and Jacob Hermskercke, and another with vs, went to the sea-side on the south side of Noua Zembla, where, contrary to our expectation, I [the] first [of all][3] saw the

[1] *Wast een betoghen lucht ende stil*—the sky was cloudy and calm.
[2] *De cloot schieten*—to throw the ball.
[3] That is to say, they all three saw it, but Gerrit de Veer saw it first.

edge of the sun ;[1] wherewith we went speedily home againe, to tell William Barents and the rest of our companions that joyfull newes. But William Barents, being a wise and well experienced pilot, would not beleeue it, esteeming it to be about fourteene daies too soone for the sunne to shin in that part of the world;[2] but we earnestly affirmed the contrary and said we had seene the sunne [whereupon diuers wagers were laid].

The 20 and 26 of January it was misty and close[3] weather, so y^t we could not see anything. Then they that layd ye contrary wager w^t vs, thought that they had woon; but vpon the twenty seuen day it was cleare [and bright] weather, and then we [all] saw the sunne in his full roundnesse aboue the horison, whereby it manifestly appeared that we had seene it vpon the twenty foure day of January. And as we were of diuers opinions touching the same, and that we said it was cleane contrary to the opinions of all olde and newe writers, yea and contrary to the nature and roundnesse both of heauen and earth; some of vs said, that seeing in long time there had been no day, that it might be that we had ouerslept our selues, whereof we were better assured:[4] but concerning the thing in itselfe, seeing God is wonderfull in all his workes, we wille referre that to his almightie power, and leaue it vnto others to dispute of. But for that no man shall thinke vs to be in doubt thereof, if we should let this passe without discoursing vpon it, therefore we will make some declaration thereof, whereby we may assure our selues that we kept good reckening.

You must vnderstand, that when we first saw the sunne,

Marginal note: How the sun which they had lost the 4 of Nouember did appere to them againe vpon the 24 of January, which was very strange and contrary to al learned mens opinions.

---

[1] Which had not been visible since the 3rd of November, as is mentioned in page 121.

[2] *Dat de sonne aldaer ende op die hooghde openbaren souden*—that the sun should appear there and in that latitude.

[3] *Disich*—hazy.

[4] *Daer van wy wel anders versekert zijn*—with respect to which we well know the contrary.

it was in the fift degree and 25 minutes of Aquarius,[1] and it should haue staied, according to our first gessing,[2] till it had entred into the sixteenth degree and 27 minutes of Aquarius[3] before he should haue shewed[4] there vnto vs in the high of 76 degrees.

Which we striuing and contending about it amongst our selues, we could not be satisfied, but wondred thereat, and amongst vs were of oppinion that we had mistaken our selues, which neuerthelesse we could [not] be persuaded vnto, for that euery day without faile we noted what had past, and also had vsed our clocke continually, and when that was frosen we vsed our houre-glasse of 12 houres long. Whereupon we argued with our selues in diuers wise, to know how we should finde out that difference, and learne[5] the truth of the time; which to trie we agreed to looke into the Ephemerides made by Josephus Schala,[6] printed in Venice, for the

[1] This makes the date to have been the twenty-*fifth* of January. On the 24th, the sun was only in the fourth degree of Aquarius. And all the details furnished by the author concur in proving, that, in spite of his assertion of extreme precision as to the date, the conjunction of the moon and Jupiter,—and, inferentially, the first appearance of the sun also,—took place on the 25th of January, instead of the 24th, as stated.

On January 25th, at midday, when the sun's longitude was $305° 25',1$, or $5° 25',1$ of Aquarius, its declination was—$18° 57',4$: consequently, its centre was $4° 42',4$, and its upper edge $4° 26',4$, below the horizon. The mean refraction at the horizon cannot, however, be estimated at more than $34',9$, or, with an assumed temperature of—$8°$ Fahren., $39',3$; so that the extraordinary and anomalous refraction amounts to no less than $3° 49'$.

[2] *Ons eerste gissinghe*—our first calculation.

[3] That is to say, till February 6th. But on that day, the sun's declination being—$15° 56',4$, it was $1° 41'$ below the horizon in $75° 45'$ N. lat., and therefore still invisible there. In lat. $76°$ it would have been as much as $1° 56'$.

In $75° 45'$ N. lat. the sun's upper edge would have been properly first visible on February 9th, when the sun was in $10° 29',2$ of Aquarius, or longitude $319° 29',2$; its declination then being—$15° 0',5$, with an assumed refraction of half a degree.

[4] Appeared.   [5] "Leave."—*Ph.*

[6] *Josephus Schala.* The title of the work here referred to, as given in

yeeres of our Lord 1589 till A. 1600, and we found therein that vpon the 24 day of January, (when the sunne first appeared vnto vs) that at Venice, the clocke being one in the night time,[1] the moone and Jupiter were in coniunction.[2] Whereupon we sought to knowe when the same coniunction should be ouer or about the house where we then were; and at last we found, yt the 24 day of January was the same day whereon the coniunction aforesaid happened in Venice, at one of the clocke in the night, and with vs in the morning when ye sun was in the east:[3] for we saw manifestly that the two

---

De Lalande's *Bibliographie Astronomique*, p. 120, is "Josephi Scala, Siculi, Ephemerides ex Tabulis Magini, ab anno 1589 ad annum 1600 continuatæ, una cum introductionibus Ephemeridum Josephi Moletii. Venetiis, 1589, 4to." It is not in the library of the British Museum, nor in that of the Royal Astronomical Society. This is, however, of no moment; as Mr. Vogel, to whose kindness I am indebted for so much valuable assistance, has calculated the time of the conjunction at Venice, and makes it differ only 57 seconds from Scala's computed time.

[1] In the astronomical reckoning of time, the date was certainly January 24th; but, then, "one in the night time" of that day—which would correctly be called January 24 days 13 hours—corresponds with 1 o'clock in the morning of January 25th, in the civil reckoning of time.

[2] January 23^d 12^h, mean time, Paris, corresponding with midnight between January 23rd and 24th in the civil reckoning of time,—which at Venice would be 20 minutes to 1 o'clock in the morning of January 24th,—the moon's longitude was 19° 57',$_3$ and her latitude + 2° 0,$_7$, while Jupiter's longitude was 32° 12',$_0$ and his latitude —1° 4',$_6$; so that there was no conjunction on that day. On the other hand, January 24^d 12^h 59^m 3^s mean time, Venice, corresponding with 57 seconds to one o'clock in the morning of January 25th, the position of the two planets was as follows:—

    Moon. Longitude 32° 17',$_3$ Latitude + 2° 58',$_3$
    Jupiter   ,,   32° 17',$_3$,,   — 1° 4',$_3$

that is to say, they were then in conjunction; their position in the heavens being near the star *a* Arietis.

[3] This can only be understood in a general sense, as meaning that it was somewhere about six o'clock in the morning. For at the time of the conjunction, the sun was more than 20° below the horizon; and as the dawn is not perceptible till the sun is about 18° from the horizon, they could not have possessed even this imperfect means of observing its general bearing, without the aid of the anomalous refraction.

planets aforesaid aproached neere vnto each other,[1] vntill such time as the moone and Jupiter stood iust ouer the other,[2] both in the signe of Taurus,[3] and that was at six of the clocke in the morning;[4] at which time the moone and Jupiter were found by our compas to be in coniunction, ouer our house, in the north and by east point, and the south part of the compass was south-south-west, and there we had it right south,[5] the moone being eight daies old; whereby it ap-

[1] *Want wy sagen gestadich op de vorrnoemde twee planeten dat se altemet malcanderen naerderden*—for we looked constantly at the two planets aforesaid, (and saw) that, from time to time, they approached each other. This is very loosely expressed. The author meant to say that they looked from time to time, and saw the two planets constantly approach.

[2] The moon stood 3° 47′,7 above Jupiter. At the time of the conjunction, the declination of the latter planet was + 11° 17′,2; so that in 75° 45′ N. lat. it must have set 37° 20′ west of the northern meridian. And yet it was observed in 11° 15′ west, when in fact it was 2° 44′,1, *below the horizon!* This is very remarkable. For, as is well known, the setting of even the brightest stars is not perceptible. They always vanish before they reach the horizon. The peculiar state of the atmosphere, which at noon of the same day had raised the sun's disc nearly 4°, allowed a star to be observed which had set 1 hour and 48 minutes previously.

[3] The longitude of the conjunction was 32° 17′,3, or 2° 17′,3 of the sign of Taurus, with reference to the old division of the ecliptic; though, owing to the retrogression of the equinoctial points whereby Aries has taken the place of Taurus, the conjunction actually occurred in the former sign, as is stated in note 2 of the preceding page.

[4] Their clock having stopped, and a twelve-hours sand-glass being their only time-keeper, it would be too much to expect precision in their immediate determination of the time of observation. But, fortunately, by placing on record the moon's azimuth at the time of the conjunction, they furnished the means of calculating the true time within very reasonable limits. The result shows that they were rather more than an hour slow, as it wanted 1 minute and 48 seconds of five o'clock.

[5] The moon's bearing by compass being N. by E. (11° 15′ E.), and the variation of the compass 2 points (22° 30′) W., the moon's azimuthal distance from the northern meridian was 11° 15′ W. From this *datum* Mr. Vogel has calculated the time of the observation, and makes it to be January 24^d 16^h 58^m 12^s mean time, or 4^h 58^m 12^s after midnight on January 25th. The difference between this time and that of the conjunction at Venice (0^h 59^m 3^s after midnight) is, of course, the

148   THE NAVIGATION

peareth that the sunne and the moone were eight points different,[1] and this was about sixe of the clocke in the morning:[2] this place differeth from Venice fiue houres in longitude, whereby we maye gesse[3] how much we were nearer east[4] then the citie of Venice, which was fiue houres, each houre being 15 degrees, which is in all 75 degrees that we were more easterly then Venice. By all which it is manifestly to be seene that we had not failed in our account, and that also we had found our right longitude by the two planets aforesaid; for the towne of Venice lieth vnder 37 degrees and 25 minutes in longitude, and her declination[5] is 46 degrees and 5 minutes;[6] whereby it followeth that our place of Noua Zembla lieth vnder 112 degrees and 25 minutes in longitude, and the high of the Pole 76 degrees; and so you haue the right longitude and latitude. But from

difference of longitude between the two places; it being $3^h\ 59^m\ 9^s$, or 59° 47' E. And Venice being 12° 21' 21" E. from Greenwich, it results that "the house of safety", at the north-eastern extremity of Novaya Zemlya, is in 72° 8' long. E. of Greenwich, or 89° 48' E. of Ferro; its latitude being 75° 45' N.

As the moon's bearing and the variation of the compass are both given only to the nearest point, there is a *possibility* of error to the extent of half a point, whereby the longitude might vary as much as 5°, or 20 minutes in time. But there is every reason for believing the variation, as stated, to be very nearly correct; or, if in error, it is in defect, which would have the effect of decreasing the eastern longitude.

[1] Apart. Their actual distance from each other was only 87° in longitude.

[2] This is not correct. The moon passed the meridian at $5^h\ 38^m\ 54^s$ after midnight, and the conjunction was observed $40^m\ 42^s$ before that planet came to the meridian. It was, therefore, only $4^h\ 58^m\ 12^s$ A.M. of January 25th.

[3] *Reeckenen*—reckon or calculate. The word "guess" is still used in this sense by the Americans.

[4] *Oosterlijcker*—more easterly.   [5] Latitude.

[6] The correct position of Venice is 30° 0' 58" E. of Ferro, or 12° 21' 21" E. of Greenwich, and 45° 25' 49" N. lat. It is curious that the latitude of so well-known a place should have been stated as much as 40' in error.

the vttermost [east] point of Noua Zembla to yͤ point of Cape de Tabin,¹ the vttermost point of Tartaria, where it windeth southward, the longitude differeth 60 degrees.² But you must vnderstand that the degrees are not so great as they are vnder the equinoxial line; for right vnder the line a degree is fifteene [60] miles; but when you leaue the line, either northward or southward, then the degrees in longitude do lessen, so that the neerer that a man is to the north or south Pole, so much the degrees are lesse: so that vnder the 76 degrees northward, where wee wintered, the degrees are but 3 miles and ⅔ parts [14⅔ miles],³ whereby it is to be marked⁴ that we had but 60 degrees to saile to the said Cape de Tabin, which is 220 [880] miles, so⁵ the said cape lieth in 172 degrees in longitude as it is thought: and being aboue it,⁶ it seemeth that we should be in the straight of Anian,⁷ where we may saile bouldlie into the south, as the land

¹ *Tot de Cape de Tabijn*—to Cape Taimur. See page 37, note 1.

² Cape Taimur being in about 100° E. long., and the Hollanders' wintering quarters in 72° E. long., the difference of longitude is apparently less than 30 degrees. But this is of no importance, as their determination of the position of that cape was merely speculative, there being at that time no data whatever for fixing its correct position; nor is it indeed exactly known even at the present day.

³ This is substantially correct. The exact measurement is 3·64 [14·66] miles. Under the 76th parallel of latitude a degree contains 13,859·414 toises (du Peru), and at the equator, 57,108·519 toises.—Encke, "Ueber die Dimensionen des Erdkörpers," *Berliner Jahrbuch für* 1852, p. 369.

⁴ *Af te meten*—to be calculated.

⁵ *So verde*—in so far as; *i. e.*, assuming that.

⁶ *Daer boven zijnde*—having passed beyond it.

⁷ *De Strate Anian*. The passage between the continents of Asia and America, now known as Behring's Strait, was formerly so called. It was supposed to be in about 60° N. lat., and the northern coast of America was imagined to stretch from thence to Hudson's Strait in a direction nearly east and west. Maldonado is said to have visited the Strait of Anian in 1588. A translation of the narrative of this pretended discovery is given in Barrow's *Chronological History*, Appendix ii, p. 24 *et seq*. See also the *Quarterly Review*, vol. xvi, p. 144 *et seq*.

reacheth. Now what further instructions are to be had to know where we lost the sun[1] vnder ye said 76 degrees upon the fourth of Nouember, and saw it again vpon the 24 of January, I leaue that to be described[2] by such as make profession thereof: it suffiseth vs to haue shewed that it failed vs not to appeare at the ordinary time.[3]

The 25 of January it was darke clowdy weather, the wind westerlie, so that the seeing of the sunne the day before was againe doubted of; and then many wagers were laid, and we still lookt out to see if the sunne appeared. The same day we sawe a beare (which as long as the sunne appeared not vnto vs we sawe not) comming out of the southwest towards our house; but when we shouted at her she came no neerer, but went away againe.

The 26 of Janurie it was faire cleere weather, but in the horrison there hung a white or darke cloude,[4] whereby we could not see the sun; whereupon the rest of our companions thought that we had mistaken our selues upon the 24 day, and that the sunne appeared not vnto vs, and mocked vs; but we were resolute in our former affirmation that we had seene the sunne, but not in the full roundnesse. That euening the sicke man that was amongst vs was very weake, and felt himselfe to be extreame sick, for he had laine long time,[5] and we comforted him as well as we might, and gaue him the best admonition y^t we could,[6] but he died not long after midnight.

The 27 of Januarie it was faire cleere weather, with a

---

[1] *Wat nu dan belanght dat men verstaen sal van tghene verhaelt is, dat wy de sonne...verloren*—Now, as regards the understanding of what has been related as to our having lost the sun, etc.

[2] *Disputiren*—discussed.

[3] *Dattet ons in den tijdt niet ghemisten heeft*—that we were not mistaken with respect to the time.

[4] *Een banck oft donckeren wolck*—a fog-bank or a dark cloud.

[5] *Een langh suer leyher ghehabt*—long lain seriously ill.

[6] *Seyden hem wat goets voor*—spoke kindly to him.

south-west winde: then in the morning we digd a hole in the snowe, hard by the house, but it was still so extreame cold that we could not stay long at worke, and so we digd by turnes euery man a litle while, and then went to the fire, and an other went and supplyed his place, till at last we digd seauen foote depth, where we went to burie the dead man; after that, when we had read certaine chapters and sung some psalmes,[1] we all went out and buried the man; which done, we went in and brake our fasts.[2] And while we were at meate, and discoursed amongst our selues touching the great quantitie of snowe that continually fell in that place, wee said that if it fell out that our house should be closed vp againe with snowe, we would find the meanes to climbe out at the chimney; whereupon our master[3] went to trie if he could clime vp through the chimney and so get out, and while he was climbing one of our men went forth of the doore to see if the master were out or not, who, standing vpon the snowe, sawe the sunne, and called vs all out, wherewith we all went forth and saw the sunne in his full roundnesse a litle aboue the horrison,[4] and then it was without all doubt that we had seene the sunne vpon the 24 of Januarie, which made vs all glad, and we gaue God hearty thankes for his grace shewed vnto us, that that glorious light appeared vnto vs againe.

The 28 of January it was faire [clear] weather, with a west wind; then we went out many tymes to exercise our selues, by going, running, casting of the ball (for then we

[1] *Daer nae deden wy een maniere van een lijck-predikinghe met lesen ende psalmen te singhen*—after that, we made a sort of funeral discourse, read prayers and sang psalms.

[2] *Aten de vroo cost*—ate the funeral meal. [3] Skipper.

[4] The refraction must have continued to be about as great as it was on January 25th. For, though in the interval the sun's declination had increased 46',6, yet they now saw it in its "full roundness", which is equal to about 32', and also "a little above the horizon", for which the remaining 15' can hardly be too large an allowance.

might see a good way from vs), and to refresh our ioynts,[1] for we had long time sitten dull,[2] whereby many of vs were very loase.[3]

The 29 of January it was foule weather, with great store of snow, the wind north-west, whereby the house was closed vp againe with snow.

The 30 of January it was darke weather, with an east-wind, and we made a hole through the doore, but we shoueled not the snow very farre from the portaile,[4] for that as soone as we saw what weather it was, we had no desire to goe abroad.

The 31 of January it was faire calme weather, with an east-wind; then we made the doore cleane, and shoueled away the snow, and threw it vpon the house, and went out and saw[5] the sunne shine cleare, which comforted vs; meane time we saw a beare, that came towards our house, but we went softly in and watcht for her till she came neerer, and as soone she was hard by we shot at her, but she ran away againe.

[1] *Om ons leden wat radder te maecken*—to make our joints somewhat more supple.

[2] *Verkrenpelt geseten*—sitten without motion.

[3] *Daer deur datter veel gebreck van den scheurbuijck ghecreghen hadden*—whereby several had fallen sick of the scurvy.

The derivation of the term "scurvy"—*schärbuk*, Low German; *scharbock*, High German; *skörbjugg*, Swedish; *scorbutus*, modern Latin,—is variously attempted to be explained. See Adelung, *Hochdeutsches Wörterbuch*; Mason Good, *Study of Medicine*, vol. ii, p. 870; Lind, *Treatise on the Scurvy*, 3rd Edit., p. 283. The last-named writer says:—"Most authors have deduced the term from the Saxon word *schorbok*, a griping or tearing of the belly [properly *scheuren*, 'to scour', and *bauch*, 'belly']; which is by no means so usual a symptom of this disease; though, from a mistake in the etymology of the name, it has been accounted so by those authors." It is in this sense that the expression has been understood by the English translator.

[4] *Het portael*—the entrance porch.

[5] Phillip has here inserted the word "not", which is not in the original, and is besides inconsistent.

The 1 of February, being Candlemas eve, it was boisterous weather with a great storme and good store of snow, whereby the house was closed vp againe with snow, and we were constrained to stay within dores; the wind then being north-west.

The 2 of February it was [still the same] foule weather, and as then the sun had not rid vs of all the foule weather, whereby we were some what discomforted, for that being in good hope of better weather we had not made so great prouision of wood as wee did before.

The 3 of February it was faire weather with an east winde, but very misty, whereby we could not see the sun, which made vs somewhat melancholy to see so great a miste, and rather more then we had had in the winter time; and then we digd our doore open againe and fetcht the wood that lay without about the dore into the house, which we were forced with great paine and labour to dig out of the snow.

The 4 of February it was [again] foule weather with great store of snow, the wind being south-west, and then we were close up again with snow; but then we tooke not so much paines as we did before to dig open the doore, but when we had occasion to goe out we clome[1] out at the chimney and eased our selues, and went in againe the same way.

The 5 of February it was still foule weather, the wind being east with great store of snow, whereby we were shut vp againe into the house and had no other way to get out but by the chimney, and those that could not clime out were faine to helpe themselues within as well as they could.

The 6 of February it was still foule stormie weather with store of snow, and we still went out at the chimney, and troubled not ovr selues with the doore, for some of vs made it an easie matter to clime out at the chimney.

The 7 of February it was still foule weather with much snow and a south-west wind, and we thereby forced to

[1] Climbed.

keepe the house, which griued¹ vs more than when the sun shined not, for that hauing seen it and felt the heat thereof, yet we were forced not to inioy² it.

The 8 of February it began to be fairer weather, [the sky being bright and clear, and] the wind being south-west; then we saw the sun rise south south-east and went downe south south-west;³ [well understood] by yᵉ compas that we had made of lead and placed to the right meridian of that place, but by our common compas according⁴ it differed two points.

The 9 of February it was faire cleare weather, the wind south-west, but as then we could not see the sunne, because it was close weather in the south, where the sunne should goe downe.⁵

The 10 of February it was faire cleare weather [and calm], so that we could not tell where the wind blew, and then we began to feele some heat of the sunne; but in the euening it began to blow somewhat cold⁶ out of the west.

The 11 of February it was faire weather, the wind south; yᵗ day about noone there came a beare towards our house, and we watcht her with our muskets, but she came not so neere that wee could reach her. The same night we heard some foxes stirring, which since the beares began to come abroad againe we had [not] much seen.

The 12 of February it was cleare weather and very calme, the wind south-west. Then we made our traps [and springes] cleane againe; meane-time there came a great beare towards our house, which made vs all goe in, and we leauelled at her with our muskets, and as she came right before our dore we shot her into the breast clean through the heart, the bullet

---

¹ Grieved. ² Enjoy.
³ The sun ought properly not to have been visible till the following day. See page 145, note 3.
⁴ That is to say, according to our common compass.
⁵ *Opgaen moest*—should *rise* or appear.
⁶ *Begont een weynich te coelen*—a little breeze sprang up.

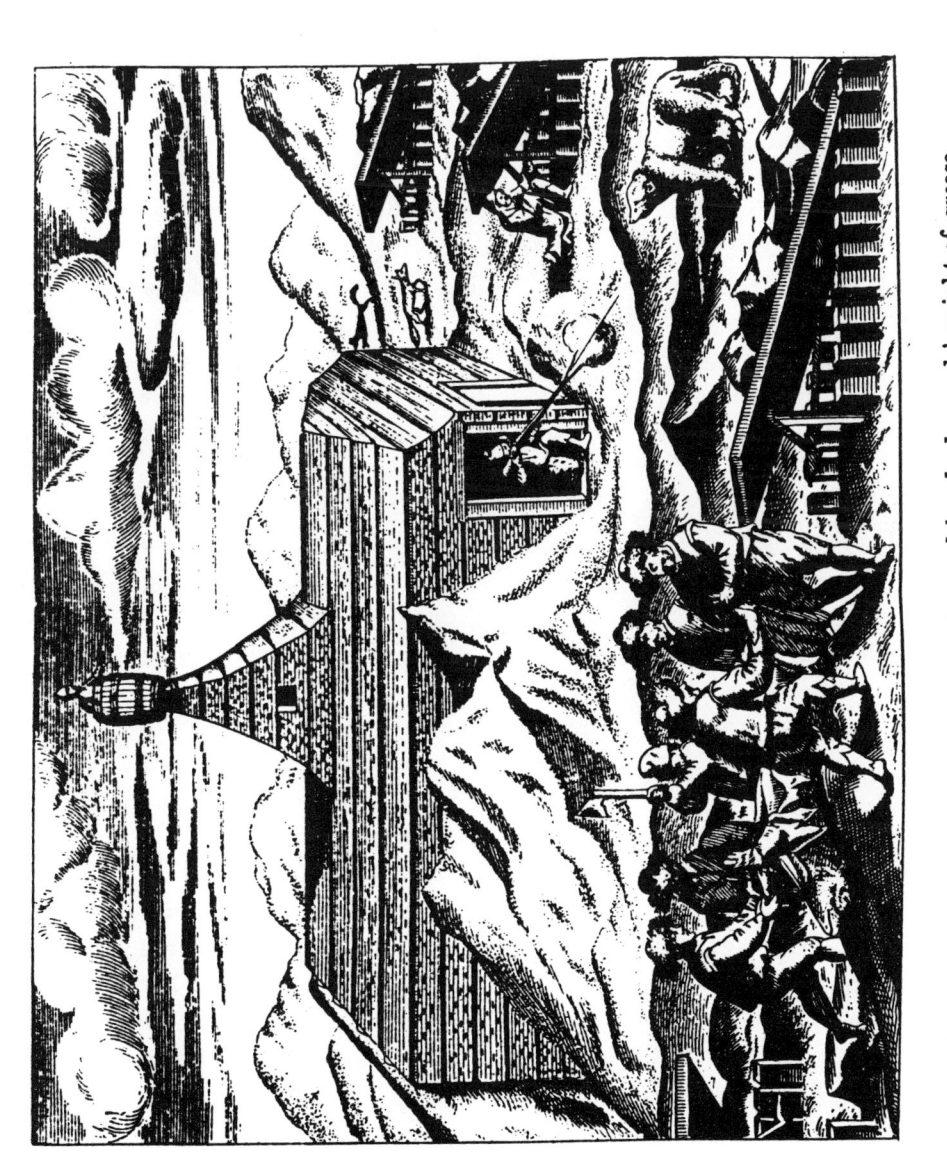

How we shot a bear, wherefrom we got a good hundred pounds' weight of grease.

passing through her body and went out againe at her tayle, and was as flat as a counter¹ [that has been beaten out with a hammer]. The beare feeling the blow, lept backwards, and ran twenty or thirty foote from the house, and there lay downe, wherewith we lept all out of the house and ran to her, and found her stil aliue; and when she saw vs she reard vp her head, as if she would gladly haue doone vs some mischefe;² but we trusted her not, for that we had tryed her strength sufficiently before, and therefore we shot her³ twice into the body againe, and therewith she dyed. Then we ript vp her belly, and taking out her guts, drew her home to the house, where we flead her and tooke at least one hundred pound of fat out of her belly, which we molt⁴ and burnt in our lampe. This grease did vs great good seruice, for by that meanes we still kept a lampe burning all night long, which before we could not doe for want of grease; and [further] euery man had meanes to burne a lamp in his caban for such necessaries as he had to doe. The beares skin was nine foote long and 7 foote broad.

The 13 of February it was faire cleare weather with a hard west wind, at which time we had more light in our house by burning of lamps, whereby we had meanes to passe the time away by reading and other exercises, which before (when we could not distinguish day from night by reason of the darknesse, and had not lamps continually burning) we could not doe.

The 14th of February it was faire cleere weather with a hard west wind before noone, but after noone it was still weather. Then fiue of vs went to the ship to see how it laie, and found the water to encrease in it, but not much.

¹ *Een copere duijt*—a copper doit. This was formerly the smallest Dutch coin, of the value of about half a farthing. It no longer exists under the present decimal system.

² *Al oft hy sien wilde wiet hem gedaen hadde*—as if she wished to see who had done it to her.

³ "Their."—*Ph.*   ⁴ Melted.

The 15 of February it was foule weather, with a great storme out of the south-west, with great store of snowe, whereby the house was closed vp againe. That night the foxes came to deuoure the dead body of the beare, whereby we were in great feare that all the beares thereabouts would come theather,[1] and therefore we agreed, as soone as we could, to get out of the house, to bury the dead beare deepe vnder the snowe.

The 16 of February it was still foule weather, with great store of snow and a south-west wind. That day was Shroue Twesday;[2] then wee made our selues some what merry in our great griefe and trouble, and euery one of vs dranke a draught of wine in remembrance that winter began to weare away, and faire weather[3] to aproache.

The 17 of February it was still foule weather and a darke sky, the wind south. Then we opened our dore againe and swept away the snow, and then we thrue[4] the dead beare into the hoale where we had digd out some wood, and stopt it vp, that the beares by smelling it should not come thither to trouble vs, and we set vp our springs[5] againe to take foxes; and the same day fiue of us went to the ship to see how it laie, which we found all after one sort;[6] there we found foote-steps of many beares, as though they had taken it vp for their lodging when we had forsaken it.

The 18 of February it was foule weather with much snow and very cold, the wind being south-west; and in the night

---

[1] Thither.

[2] *Vastelavont*, properly *Vastenavond*; formerly called in this country also, Fastern's or Fasten's Even. The "Fasting*ham* Tuiesday," and "Fastyng*onge* Tuesday," cited in Brand's *Observations on Popular Antiquities*, vol. i, p. 58, from Langley's *Polidore Vergile*, fol. 103, and Blomefield's *Norfolk*, vol. ii, p. 111, respectively, seem to be merely corruptions of this expression.

[3] *De vrolijcke tijt*—the *merry* time of year; the spring.

[4] Threw, cast.   [5] Springes or traps.

[6] In the same state as before.

time, as we burnt lampes and some of our men laie [late] awake, we heard beasts runne vpon the roofe of our house, which by reason of the snowe made the noise of their feete sound more than otherwise it would haue done, the snow was so hard [and cracked so much that it gave a great sound], whereby we thought they had beene beares; but when it was day we sawe no footing but of foxes, and we thought they had beene beares, for the night, which of it selfe is solitarie and fearefull, made that which was doubtfull to be more doubtfull and worse feared.[1]

The 19 of February it was faire cleere weather with a south-west wind. Then we tooke the hight of the sunne, which in long time before we could not doe because the horizon was not cleere, as also for that it mounted not so high nor gaue not so much shadowe as we were to haue[2] in our astrolabium, and therefore we made an instrument that was halfe round, at the one end[3] hauing 90 degrees marked thereon, whereon we hung a third[4] with a plumet of lead, as the water compasses[5] haue, and therewith we tooke the hight of the sunne when it was at the highest and found that it was three degrees eleuated aboue the horizon, his declination eleuenth degrees and sixteene minutes, which beeing added to the height aforesaid made 14 degrees and 16 minutes, which substracted from 90 degrees, there rested 75 degrees and 44 minutes for the higth of the Pole; but the aforesaid three degrees of higth being taken at the lowest side of the sunne, the 16 minutes might well be added to the higth of the Pole, and so it was just 76 degrees, as we had measured it before.[6]

[1] *Tghene dat eyselijck scheen noch eyselijcker*—that which was frightful appeared more frightful.
[2] *Behoefden*—required.
[3] *Op d'eene helft*—on the one half.   [4] Thread.
[5] *Waterpassen*—levels, such as are used by builders.
[6] We have here a remarkable instance of what might be called "cooking", were it not that everything is done in perfect good faith, and that

158   THE NAVIGATION

The 20 of February it was foule weather with great store of snow, the wind south-west; whereby we were shut vp againe in the house, as we had been often times before.

The 21 of February it was still foule weather, the wind north-west and great store of snow, which made vs greiue more then it did before, for we had no more wood, and so were forced to breake of[1] some peeces of wood in the house, and to gather vp some that lay troden vnder feet, which had not bin cast out of the way, whereby for that day and the next night we holp[2] our selues indifferent well.

The 22 of February it was clere faire weather with a

---

the means are afforded us of rectifying the error into which the observer fell through the desire to establish his preconceived idea, founded on the supposed results of his observations of December 14th and January 12th (See pages 131 and 140), that the latitude of the place of observation was to the north of 76°.

It is quite true that, as the sun's lower edge was observed, its semidiameter has to be added. But the effect of this is to increase, not the height of the Pole, but its complement; which, adopting the observer's own figures, would be 14° 16′ + 16′ = 14° 32′, so that the height of the Pole would be only 75° 28′. There is, however, another correction to be made, namely, for refraction, of which at that early period no account was taken; and this being as much as $15'._1$, the discrepancy is thereby so much reduced. The correct calculation of the observation will therefore be as follows:—

Sun's lower edge	3°	0′
,, semi-diameter		16
	3	16
Refraction		$15,_1$
True altitude of sun's centre	3	$0,_9$
Sun's declination	— 11	15
Complement of height of Pole	14	$15,_9$
Latitude	75°	$44,_1$

Which differs only $1'_5$ from the mean of the two observations of the 14th December and 12th January.

[1] Off.   [2] Helped.

south-west wind. Then we made ready a slead to fetch more wood, for need compelled vs thereunto; for, as they say, hunger driueth the wolfe out of his den.[1] And eleuen of vs went together, all well appointed with our armes; but coming to the place where wee should haue the wood, we could not come by it by reason it laie so deepe vnder the snow, whereby of necessitie we were compelled to goe further, where with great labour and trouble we got some; but as we returned backe againe therewith, it was so sore labour vnto vs that we were almost out of comfort, for that by reason of the long cold and trouble that we had indured, we were become so weake and feeble that we had little strength, and we began to be in doubt that we should not recover our strengths againe[3] and should not be able to fetch any more wood, and so we should haue died with cold; but the present necessitie and the hope we had of better weather increased our forces, and made vs doe more then our strengthes afforded. And when we came neere to our house, we saw much open water in the sea, which in long time we had not seene, which also put vs in good comfort that things would be better.

The 23 of February it was calme and faire weather, with a good aire,[4] the wind south-west, and then we tooke two foxes, that were as good to vs as venison.

The 24[5] of February it was still weather, and a close aire,[6] the wind south-west. Then we drest our springes [and traps] in good sort for the foxes, but tooke none.

---

[1] *Uytet wout*—out of *the wood*. The French say, "la faim chasse le loup hors du bois"; and in several other languages it is the same. In English the corresponding expression is, "hunger will break through stone walls." See *National Proverbs, etc.*, by Caroline Ward, p. 62.

[2] "Cod."—*Ph.*

[3] *Ons de cracht begheven soude*—we should *lose* our strength.

[4] *Met een betoghen lucht*—with a cloudy sky.

[5] "25."—*Ph.*

[6] *Donckere lucht*—a dark sky.

The 25 of February it was foule weather againe and much snow, with a north wind, whereby we were closed vp with snow againe, and could not get out of our house.

The 26 of February it was darke weather, with a south-west wind, but very calme: and then we opened our dore againe and exercised our selues with going and running and to make our ioints supple, which were almost clinged together.[1]

The 27 of February it was calme weather, with a south wind, but very cold. Then our wood began to lessen, which put vs in no small discomfort to remember what trouble we had to drawe the last slead-full home, and we must doe the like againe if we would not die with cold.

The 28 of February it was still weather with a south-west wind. Then ten of vs went and fetcht an other slead-full of wood, with no lesse paine and labor then we did before; for one of our companions could not helpe vs, because that the first ioint of one of his great toes was frozen of, and so he could doe nothing.

The first of March it was faire still weather, the wind west but very cold, and we were forced to spare our wood, because it was so great labor for vs to fetch it; so that when it was day we exercised our selues as much as we might, with running, going and leaping; and to them that laie in their cabins[2] we gaue hote[3] stones to warme them, and towards night we made a good fire, which we were forced to indure.[4]

The 2 of Marche it was cold cleere weather, with a west wind. The same day we tooke the higth of the sunne, and found that it was eleuated aboue the horizon sixe degrees and 48 minutes, and his declination was 7 degrees and 12

---

[1] *Vercleumt*—benumbed.
[2] *In de koy*—a-bed.   [3] Hot.
[4] *Daer my ons mede lyden moesten*—wherewith we were forced to be satisfied.

minutes, which[1] substracted from 90 degrees, resteth 76 degrees for the higth of the Pole.[2]

The 3 of March it was faire weather [and calm], with a [south-] west wind; at which time our sickemen were somewhat better and sat vpright in their cabins to doe some thing to passe the time awaie, but after they found[3] that they were too ready to stirre before their times.

The 4 of March it was faire weather with a west wind. The same day there came a beare to our house, whom we watcht with our peeces as we did before, and shot at her and hit her, but she run away. At that time fiue of us went to our ship, where we found that the beares had made worke, and had opened our cookes cubberd,[4] that was couered ouer with snow, thinking to find some thing in it, and had drawne it [a good way] out of the ship, where we found it.

The 5 of March it was foule weather againe, with a southwest wind: and as in the euening we had digd open our dore and went out, when the weather began to break vp,[5] we saw much open water in the sea, more then before which put vs in good comfort that in the end we should get away from thence.

The 6 of March it was foule weather, with a great storme out of the south-west and much snow. The same day some of vs climbed out of the chimney, and perceaued that in the sea and about the land there was much open water, but the ship lay fast still.

[1] Namely, the sum of the sun's elevation and southern declination, being fourteen degrees.

[2] With 7′,5 for refraction, and —7° 10′,8 for the sun's declination, the above observation gives 76° 8′,7 for the height of the Pole. If no allowance was made at the time for the sun's semi-diameter, 16′ will have to be deducted, which will make the true latitude to be 75° 52′,7.

[3] *Twelck haer naemaels niet ten besten verghingh*—which did them no good afterwards.

[4] *Het cocx luijck*—the cook's locker.

[5] *Wat ghebetert was*—was somewhat better.

The 7 of March it was still foule weather and as great a wind, so that we were shut vp in our house, and they that would goe out must clime vp through the chimney, which was a common thing with vs, and still we sawe more open water in the sea and about the land, whereby we were in doubt[1] that the ship, in that foule weather and driuing of the ice, would be loose[2] while we were shut vp in our house, and we should haue no meanes to helpe it.

The 8 of Marche it was still foule weather, with a southwest storme and great store of snow, whereby we could see no ice north-east nor round about in the sea, whereby we were of opinion that north-east from vs there was a great sea.[3]

The 9 of March it was foule weather, but not so foule as the [two] day[s] before, and lesse snow; and then we could see further from vs and perceiue that the water was open in the north-east, but not from vs towards Tartaria, for there we could still see ice in the Tartarian Sea, otherwise called the Ice Sea, so that we were of opinion that there it was not very wide; for, when it was cleere weather, we thought many times that we saw the land, and showed it vnto our companions, south and [south] south-east from our house, like a hilly land, as land commonly showeth it selfe when we see it [from afar off].[4]

[1] *Beducht*—afraid.

[2] The words "for as then the ice drave" are introduced here unnecessarily by Phillip.

[3] *Een ruyme zee moeste zijn*—there must be an *open* sea.

[4] There is little doubt of their having actually seen the country round the estuaries of the rivers Obi and Yenisei. Lütke says (p. 42) that "the distance of the two countries from one another is not known exactly, but there is reason for believing it to be less than 120 Italian miles. That the Hollanders really saw Siberia, and not (as some imagine) the Island of Maksimok, is corroborated by the tradition, which is mentioned even by Witsen (pp. 762, 897, 922), that at times Novaya Zemlya is, in like manner, seen from the Siberian coast.'

The 10 of March it was cleere weather, the wind north. Then we made our house cleane, and digd our selues out and came forth; at which time we saw [quite] an open sea, whereupon we said vnto each other that if the ship were loose we might venture to saile awaie, for we were not of opinion to doe it with our scutes,[1] considering the great cold that we found there. Towards euening, nine of vs went to the ship with a slead to fetch wood, when al our wood was burnt; and found the ship in the same order that it laie, and fast in the ice.

The 11 of March it was cold, but faire sunne-shine weather, the wind north-east; then we tooke the higth of the sunne with our astrolabium, and found it to be eleuated aboue the horizon ten degrees and 19 minutes, his declination was three degrees 41 minutes, which being added to the higth aforesaid, made 14 degrees, which substracted from 90 degrees, there resteth 76 degrees for the higth of the Pole.[2] Then twelue of vs went to the place where we vsed to goe, to fetch a slead of wood, but still we had more paine and labour therewith, because we were weaker; and when we came home with it and were very weary, we praid the master[3] to giue either of vs a draught of wine, which he did, wherewith we were somewhat releeued and comforted, and after that were the willinger[4] to labour, which was vnsupportable for vs if mere extremitie had not compelled vs thereunto, saying often times one vnto the other, that if the wood were to be bought for mony, we would giue all our earnings or wages for it.

The 12 of March it was foule weather, y^e wind north-east; then the ice came mightily driuing in, which [by] the south-

---

[1] Boats.
[2] Here, as before, the correct result will be (refraction $5'{,}1$; declination—$3°\ 41'{,}6$) $76°\ 4'{,}5$; or, deducting $16'$ for the sun's semi-diameter, $75°\ 48'{,}5$.
[3] Skipper.
[4] More willing.

west windo had bin driuen out, and it was then as could[1] as it had bin before in the coldest time of winter.

The 13 of March it was still foule weather, with a storme out of the north-east and great store of snow, and the ice mightely driuing in with a great noyse, the flakes rustling against each other fearfull to heare.

The 14 of March it was still foule weather with a great east north-east wind, whereby the sea was [again] as close[2] as it had bin before, and it was extreame cold, whereby our sicke men were very ill,[3] who when it was faire weather were stirring too soone.[4]

The 15 of March it was faire weather, the wind north. That day we opened our dore to goe out, but the cold rather increased then diminished, and was bitterer then before it had bin.

The 16 of March it was faire cleare weather, but extreame cold with a north wind, which put vs to great extremity, for that we had almost taken our leaues of the cold, and then it began to come againe.

The 17 of March it was faire cleare weather, with a north-wind, but stil very cold, wherby wee were wholy out of comfort to see and feele so great cold, and knew not what to thinke, for it was extreame cold.

The 18 of March it was foule cold weather with good store of snow, the wind north-east, which shut vs vp in our house so that we could not get out.

The 19 of March it was still foule and bitter cold weather, the wind north-east, the ice in the sea cleauing[5] faster and thicker together, with great cracking and a hugh[6] noyse, which we might easily heare in our house, but we delighted not much in hearing thereof.

[1] Cold.
[2] Closed up (with ice).
[3] *Wederom instorteden*—relapsed.
[4] Namely, on the 3rd of the month, as is mentioned in page 161.
[5] *Parste*—pressed.
[6] Huge, immense.

The 20 of March it was foule weather, bitter cold, and a north-east wind, then our wood began [by degrees] to consume,[1] so that we were forced to take counsell together;[2] for without wood we could not liue, and yet we began to be so weake that we could hardly endure the labour to fetch it.

The 21 of March it was faire weather, but still very cold, the wind north. The same day the sunne entred into Aries in the equinoxciall lyne, and at noone we tooke the hight of the sunne and found it to be eleuated 14 degrees aboue the horizon, but for that the sun was in the middle lyne and of the like distance from both the tropiks, there was no declination, neither on the south nor north side; and so the 14 degrees aforesaid being substracted from ninty degrees, there rested 76 degrees for the hight of the Pole.[3] The same

---

[1] *Op te gaen*—to be used up.

[2] *Also dat goet raedt doen duer was*—so that then good advice was dear. This is a proverbial saying; the meaning of which is, that, as they did not know what to do, good advice would have been very valuable.

[3] If we assume the smaller amount of error to be the more probable, we must regard this observation as having been made on the 20th of March, instead of the 21st. The observer found the sun's altitude to be 14°, believing it to be then on the equinoctial, and therefore without declination. But at mean noon in Novaya Zemlya, the sun's declination on March 20th was — 0° 8′,₅, and on March 21st + 0° 14′,₉, the sun having crossed the equinoctial between 10 and 11 o'clock of the intervening night. The corrected calculation for *both* days will therefore be as follows:—

	March 20th.	March 21st.
Altitude of the sun	14° 0′	14° 0′
Refraction	3,₈	3,₈
	13 56,₂	13 56,₂
Sun' declination	— 8,₈	+ 14,₉
Complement φ	14 5	13 41,₃
φ	75° 55′	76° 8′,₇
Or, deduct. the sun's semi-diam.	75° 36′	75° 52′,₇

day we made shooes of felt or rudg,[1] which we drew vpon our feet,[2] for we could not goe in our shooes by reason of the great cold, for the shooes on our feet were as hard as hornes; and then we fetcht a slead-ful of wood home to our house, with sore and extreame labour and with great extremity of cold, which we endured as if March[3] went to bid vs farewell. But[4] our hope and comfort was that the cold could not still continue in that force,[5] but that at length the strength thereof[6] would be broken.

The 22 of March it was cleere still weather, the wind north-east, but very cold; whereupon some of vs were of advice, seeing that the fetching of wood was so toylesome vnto vs, that euery day once we should make a fire of coales.

The 23 of March it was very foule weather, with infernall bitter cold,[7] the wind north-east, so that we were forced to make more fire as we had bin at other times, for then it was as cold as ever it had bin, and it froze very hard in the flore and vpon the wales of our house.[8]

The 24 of March it was a like cold, with great store of snow and a north wind, whereby we were once againe shut vp into the house, and then the coales serued vs well, which before by reason of our bad vsing of them we disliked of.

[1] *Van vilten ofte ruyghe hoeden*—of felt, or rough hats. It is probable that these were sheets of the rough material, which they had for use among the ship's stores.

[2] *Over de coussen aentrocken*—drew on over our stockings.

[3] *Als of de Maert haer foy hadde willen besetten*—as if March (before leaving them) had meant to pay them off—*lit.* to give them their fee.

[4] "For."—*Ph.*

[5] *Dat de coude so fel alse was, niet altijt dueren soude*—that the cold, severe as it was, would not last for ever.

[6] *Haer den neck*—its *neck*.

[7] *Met helle bittere koude*—with a *clear* sharp cold. The author is not open to the reproach of having, in the whole course of his narrative, made use of such an expression as that which the translator has here erroneously attributed to him.

[8] *Aen den solder ende wanden van binnen thuijs*—on the ceiling and walls inside the house.

The 25 of March it was still foule weather, the wind west, the cold still holding as strong as it was, which put vs in much discomfort.

The 26 of March it was faire cleere weather [with a west wind], and very calme; then we digd our selues out of the house againe and went out, and then we fetcht an other slead of wood, for the great cold had made vs burne vp all that we had.

The 27 of March it was faire weather, the wind west and very calme; then the ice began to driue away againe, but the ship lay fast and stird not.

The 28[1] of March it was faire weather, the wind southwest, whereby the ice draue away very fast [and we had much open water]. The same day sixe of vs went abord the ship to see how it lay, and found it still in one sort; but we perceiued that the beares had kept an euil fauoured house therein.[2]

The 29 of March it was faire cleere weather, with a northeast wind; then the ice came driuing in againe. The same day we fetcht another slead of wood, which we were euery day worse alike to doe[3] by reason of our weaknesse.

The 30 of March it was faire cleere weather, with an east wind, wherewith the ice came driving in againe. After noone there came two beares by our house, but they went along to the ship and let vs alone.

The 31 of March it was still faire weather, the wind northeast, wherewith the ice came still more and more driuing in, and made high[4] hilles by sliding one vpon the other.

The 1 of Aprill it blew stil[5] out of the east, with faire weather, but very cold; and then we burnt some of our

[1] "18."—*Ph.*
[2] *Daer in gheweldich huijs ghehouden hadden*—had made great havoc there.
[3] *Dat wy hoe langer hoe qualijcker doen conden*—which we were less and less able to do.
[4] *Gheweldighen*—huge, immense. [5] *Stijf*—strongly.

coales, for that our wood was too troublesome for vs to fetch.

The 2 of Aprill it was faire weather, the wind north-east and very calme. Then we tooke the higth of the sunne, and found it to eleuated aboue the horizon 18 degrees and 40 minutes, his declination being foure degrees and 40 minutes, which being substracted from the higth aforesaid, there rested 14 degrees, which taken from 90 degrees, the higth of the Pole was 76 degrees.[1]

The 3 of Aprill it was faire cleere weather, with a northeast wind and very calme; then we made a staffe to plaie at colfe,[2] thereby to stretch our jointes, which we sought by all the meanes we could to doe.

The 4 of Aprill it was faire weather, the wind variable. That daie we went all to the ship, and put out [through the hawse] the cable that was made fast to the [bower] anchor, to the end that if the ship chanced to be loose [or to drift] it might hold fast thereby.

The 5 of Aprill it was foule weather with a hard northeast wind, wherewith the ice came mightily in againe and slid in great peeces one vpon the other; and then the ship laie faster then it did before.

---

[1] On April 2nd at mean noon, Novaya Zemlya, the sun's declination was + 4° 56′,8, which, with the observed height (corrected for refraction = 18° 37′,2), would give 76° 19′,5 as the latitude; or, deducting 16′ for the sun's semi-diameter, 76° 3′,5. It is, however, not unlikely that the observation was made on April 1st, when indeed the sun's declination was + 4° 40′ at mean noon *at Venice*, though at mean noon at the place of observation (about four hours earlier) it was only 4° 33′,6. In this case, the latitude would be 75° 56′,4; or 75° 40′,4, if the sun's lower edge was observed.

[2] *Een colf om daer mede te colven*—literally, "a *colf* to *colve* with." The well-known game of colf or golf derives its name from the hooked stick or *club* (German, *kolbe*; Dutch, *colf* or *kolf*) with which it is played. A detailed description of the game, as played in Holland, is given in Sir John Sinclair's *Statistical Account of Scotland*, vol. xvi. p. 28, *note*. See also Jameson's *Scottish Dict.*, art. GOLF.

The 6 of Aprill it was still foule weather, with a stiffe north-west wind. That night there came a beare to our house, and we did the best we could to shoot at her, but because it was moist weather and the cocke foistie,[1] our peece would not giue fire, wherewith the beare came bouldly toward the house, and came downe the staires[2] close to the dore,[3] seeking to breake into the house; but our master held the dore fast to, and being in great haste and feare, could not barre it with the peece of wood that we vsed thereunto;[4] but the beare seeing that the dore was shut, she went backe againe, and within two houres after she came againe, and went round about and vpon the top of the house, and made such a roaring that it was fearefull to heare, and at last got to the chimney, and made such worke there that we thought she would haue broken it downe, and tore the saile[5] that was made fast about it in many peeces with a great and fearefull noise; but for that it was night we made no resistance against her, because we could not see her. At last she went awaie and left vs.

The 7 of Aprill it was foule weather, the wind south-west. Then we made our muskets ready, thinking the beare would haue come againe, but she came not. Then we went up vpon the house, where we saw what force the beare had vsed to teare away the saile, which was made so fast vnto the chimney.

The 8 of Aprill it was still foule weather, the wind south-west, whereby the ice draue away againe and the sea was open, which put vs in some comfort that we should once get away out of that fearefull place.

[1] *Deur dattet damper weer ende teruijt vochtich was*—because it was damp weather and the *powder* moist.
[2] The *steps* cut in the snow, as is mentioned in page 136.
[3] *Nae de deur vant huijs toe*—*towards* the door of the house.
[4] *Dat boven de deur was*—that was above the door.
[5] The house was covered with a sail, on which was placed shingle from the beach, to keep it weather tight, as is described in page 119.

The 9 of Aprill it was faire cleere weather, but towards euening it was foule weather, the wind south-west, so that stil ye water became opener, whereat we much reioysed, and gaue God thanks that he had saued vs from the aforesaid[1] cold, troublesome, hard, bitter, and vnsupportable winter, hoping that time would giue vs a happy issue.

The 10 of Aprill it was foule weather, with a storme out of the north-east, with great store of snowe; at which time the ice that draue away came in againe and couered all the sea ouer.[2]

The 11 of Aprill it was faire weather, with a great north-east wind, wherewith the ice still draue one peece vpon another and lay in high hilles.

The 12[3] of Aprill it was faire cleere weather, but still it blew hard north-east as it had done two dayes before, so that the ice lay like hilles one upon the other, and then was higher and harder then it had bin before.

The 13 of Aprill it was faire cleere weather with a north wind. The same day we fetcht a slead with wood, and euery man put on his shooes that he had made of felt or rudg,[4] which did vs great pleasure.

The 14 of Aprill it was faire cleare weather with a west wind; then we saw greater hilles of ice round about the ship then euer we had seene before, which was a fearefull thing to behold, and much to be wondred at that the ship was not smitten in pieces.

The 15 of Aprill it was faire calme weather with a north wind; then seauen of vs went aboard the ship, to see in what case it was, and found it to be all in one sort; and as we came backe againe there came a great beare towards vs,

---

[1] *Voorgaende*—late, previous.
[2] *Vervulde de gantsche zee*—filled the entire sea.
[3] "21st."—*Ph.*
[4] *Van den houden ghemaect hadden*—had made of the hats or felt. See page 166, note 1.

against whom we began to make defence, but she perceauing that, made away from us, and we went to the place from whence she came to see her den,[1] where we found a great hole made in ye ice, about a mans length in depth, the entry thereof being very narrow, and within wide; there we thrust in our pickes[2] to feele if there was any thing within it, but perceauing it was emptie, one of our men crept into it, but not too farre, for it was fearefull to behold. After that we went along by the sea side, and there we saw that in the end of March and the beginning of Aprill the ice was in such wonderfull maner risen and piled vp one vpon the other that it was wonderfull, in such manner as if there had bin whole townes made of ice, with towres and bulwarkes round about them.

The 16 of Aprill it was foule weather, the wind north-west, whereby the ice began some-what to breake.[3]

The 17 of Aprill it was faire cleere weather with a south-west wind; and then seauen of vs went to the ship, and there we saw open water in the sea, and then we went ouer the ice hilles as well as we could to the water, for in six or seauen monthes we had not gone so neare vnto it; and when we got to ye water, there we saw a litle bird swiming therein, but as soone as it espied vs it diued vnder the water, which we tooke for a signe that there was more open water in the sea then there had beene before, and that the time approached that the water would [be] open.

The 18 of Aprill it was faire weather, the wind south-west. Then we tooke the higth of the sunne, and it was eleuated aboue the horizon 25 degrees and 10 minutes, his declination 11 degrees and 12 minutes, which being taken from the higth aforesaid, there rested 13 degrees and 68 minutes, which substracted from 90 degrees, the higth of the Pole

---

[1] *Om te sien of hy daer eenighe holen hadde*—to see whether she had any holes there.

[2] *Spiesen*—pikes.   [3] *Af te setten*—to go away.

was found to be 75 degrees, 58 minutes.[1] Then eleuen of vs went with a slead to fetch more wood, and brought it to the house. In the night there came an other beare vpon our house, which we hearing, went all out with our armes, but [through the noise we made] the beare ranne away.

The 19 of Aprill it was faire weather with a north wind. That day fiue of vs went into the bath to bathe our selues,[2] which did vs much good and was a great refreshing vnto vs.

The 20 of Aprill it was faire weather with a west wind. The same day five of vs went to the place where we fetcht wood, with a kettle and other furniture[3] vpon a slead, to wash our shirts in that place, because the wood lay ready there, and for that we were to vse much wood to melt the ice, to heate our water and to drie our shirtes, esteming it a lesse labour then to bring the wood home to the house, which was great trouble vnto vs.

The 21 of Aprill it [still] was faire weather with an east wind; and the next day the like weather, but in the euening the wind blewe northerly.

The 23 of Aprill it was faire [clear] weather [with a bright sky] and a [strong] north-east wind; and the next day the like, with an east wind.

The 25 of Aprill it was faire [clear] weather, the wind easterly. The same day there came a beare to our house, and we shoot her into the skin,[4] but she runne awaie, which another beare that was not farre from vs perceauing [she came not nearer to us but] runne away also.

The 26 and 27 of Aprill it was faire weather, but an extreeme great north-east wind.

---

[1] The declination here given is that of April 19th. The corrected calculation for the 18th, with refraction $2'_{,0}$ and declination $+ 10°\ 50'_{,1}$, gives $75°\ 42'_{,1}$; or $75°\ 26'_{,1}$, if the sun's semi-diameter has to be deducted. On April 19th, the declination was $+ 11°\ 10'_{,1}$, whereby the height of the Pole would be $76°\ 2'_{,1}$; or, deducting the sun's semi-diameter, $75°\ 46'_{1}$.

[2] *Ende stoofden ons*—and stewed ourselves. See page 121, note 8.

[3] *Ghereetschap*—utensils.

[4] *Huijt*—literally "hide", but used in the sense of "body".

The 28 of Aprill it was faire weather with a north wind. Then we tooke the higth of the sunne againe, and found it to be eleuated 28 degrees and 8 minutes, his declination 14 degrees aud 8 minutes,[1] which substracted from 90 degrees, there rested 76 degrees for the higth of the Pole.[2]

The 29 of Aprill it was faire weather with a south-west wind. Then we plaid at colfe[3] [and at ball], both to the ship and from thence againe homeward, to exercise our selues.

The 30 of Aprill it was faire weather [with a bright sky], the wind south-west; then in the night wee could see the sunne in the north, when it was in the highest,[4] iust aboue the horizon, so that from that time we saw the sunne both night and day.[5]

The 1 of May it was faire weather with a west wind; then we sod our last flesh,[6] which for a long time we had spared, and it was still very good, and the last morsell tasted as well

---

[1] There is an omission here in the original. The following words require to be supplied:—"which substracted from the said elevation, there rested 14 degrees."

[2] With the sun's declination $+14°\ 8'.7$, ahd refraction $1'.8$, the corrected calculation will give $76°\ 2',5$; or, deducting $16'$ for the sun's semidiameter, $75°\ 46',5$.

[3] See page 168, note 2.

[4] *Opt hooghste was.* An oversight of the author. He meant to say that the sun was *on the meridian* in the north; where, of course, it must have been at the *lowest*, instead of the highest.

[5] Had the latitude of the place of observation been really more than $76°$ the sun ought to have been visible above the horizon at midnight on the 28th April, as its declination was then already more than $14°$; and as on the 30th April its declination was $14°\ 55'$, it ought to have had its *lower* edge full $39'$ above the horizon at the time when at the place of observation it is said to have been visible "just above the horizon". This is without taking into account the refraction, which under ordinary circumstances, would have made its visible altitude about $36'$ more. Hence it is quite clear that they were not so far north as $76°$.

[6] *Coockten wy onse laetste vleysch*—we cooked the last of our meat (beef).

as the first, and we found no fault therein but onely that it would last no longer.[1]

The 2 of May it was foule weather with a [seuere] storme out of the south-west, whereby the sea was almost cleere of ice, and then we began to speake about[2] getting from thence, for we had kept house long enough there.

The 3 of May it was still foule weather with a south-west wind, whereby the ice began wholy to driue away, but it lay fast about the ship. And when our best meate, as flesh and other things, began to faile vs,[3] which was our greatest sustenance, and that it behooued vs to be somewhat strong, to sustaine the labour that we were to vndergoe when we went from thence, the master shared the rest of the bacon[4] amongst vs, which was a small barrell with salt bacon in pickle,[5] whereof euery one of vs had two ounces a day, which continued for the space of three weekes, and then it was eaten up.[6]

The 4 of May it was indifferent faire weather, ye wind south-west. That day fiue of vs went to the ship, and found

---

[1] *Maer hadt maer een manghel, dattet niet langher deuren wilde*—only it had but one fault, which was, that it would not last any longer. Whenever a joke is intended by the author,—who, although a serious, matter-of-fact Dutchman, was evidently a bit of a wag,—it is, by some fatality, sure to be spoilt by the translator.

[2] *Te jancken*—to hanker after.

[3] *Ende also de beste spijs, als vleysch ende grutten ende anders, ons ontbrack*—and as our best food, such as beef, barley, and such like, failed us. *Gort* or *grutten*, for porridge, form an important item in the supplies of Dutch seamen. When the Dutch whale-fishery was in a more flourishing state, the sailors of the vessels employed in it used to be saluted by the boys in the streets of Amsterdam with the cry of—*Traan-bok! Stroop in je gort tot Pampus toe.*—"Train-oil Billy! Treacle in your porridge as far as Pampus;" meaning, that after they had passed Pampus (see page 13, note 5), which is only two hours from Amsterdam, they would, during the rest of the voyage, get their porridge without treacle.

[4] *Speck*—pork.

[5] *Een cleijn vactgien met peeckelspeck*—a small cask of salt pork.

[6] *Doen wast mede op*—then that also was gone.

it lying still as fast in the ice as it did before;[1] for about the midle of March it was but 75 paces from the open water, and then[2] it was 500 paces from the water and inclosed round about with high hilles of ice, which put vs in no small feare how we should bring our scute and our boate through or ouer that way into the water when we went to leaue that place. That night there came [again] a beare to our house, but as soone as she heard vs make a noise she ranne away againe; one of our men that climbed vp in the chimney saw when she ranne away, so that it seemed that as then they were afraid of vs, and durst not be so bold to set vpon vs as they were at the first.

The 5 of May it was faire weather with some snow, the wind east. That euening and at night we saw the sunne, when it was at the lowest, a good way aboue the earth.

The 6 of May it was faire cleere weather with a great south-west wind, whereby we saw the sea open both in the east and in the west, which made our men exceeding glad, longing sore to be gone from thence.

The 7 of May it was foule weather and snew hard, with a north wind, whereby we were closed vp againe in our house, whereupon our men were somewhat disquieted, saying that they thought they should neuer goe from thence,[3] and therefore, said they, it is best for vs as soone as it is open water to be gone from hence.

The 8 of May it was foule weather with great store of snow, the wind west; then some of our men agreed amongst themselues to speake vnto the master,[4] and to tell him that it was more then time for vs to be gone from thence;[5] but they could not agree vpon it who should moue the same vnto

---

[1] *Meer als te voren*—more than before. [2] *Nu*—now.
[3] *Segghende: dit weer sal hier nimmermeer vergaen*—saying, this weather will never more pass away here.
[4] The skipper, namely, Jacob Heemskerck.
[5] *Van daer te sien comen*—to see about getting from thence.

him,[1] because he had said that he would staie[2] vntill the end of June, which was the best of the sommer, to see if the ship would then be loose.

The 9 of May it was faire cleere weather with an indifferent wind out of the north-east; at which time the desire that our men had to be gone from thence still more and more encreased, and then they agreed to speake to William Barents to moue the master to goe from thence, but he held them of with faire words [and quieted them]; and yet it was not done to delay them,[3] but to take the best counsell with reason and good aduise, for he heard all what they could saie.[4]

The 10 of May it was faire weather with a north-west wind; y^t night, the sun by our common compas being north north-east and at the lowest, we tooke the higth thereof, and it was eleuated 3 degrees and 45 minutes, his declination was 17 degrees and 45 minuts, from whence taking the higth aforesaid, there rested 14 degrees, which substracted from 90 degrees, there rested 76 degrees for the higth of the Pole.[5]

The 11 of May it was faire weather, the wind south-west, and then[6] it was [quite] open water in the sea, when our men prayed William Barents once againe to moue the maister to make preparation to goe from thence, which he promised to do as soone as conuenient time serued him.

The 12 of May it was foule weather, the wind north-west;

---

[1] *Maer elck outsach sich den schipper dat te kennen te gheven* — but each was reluctant to make the skipper acquainted with it.

[2] *Vermidts dat hy hem hadde laten verluyden dat hy begeerde te wachten* — because he had given them to understand that he desired to wait.

[3] *Niet muytischer wyse* — not in a mutinous manner.

[4] *Want zy lieten haer gaerne ghesegghen* — for they let themselves easily be talked over.

[5] The corrected calculation, with declination + 17° 44′,9 and refraction 12′,2, will give 75° 47′,9. If the sun's lower edge was observed, 16′ will, in this instance, have to be *added* to the latitude, which thereby becomes 76° 3′,9.

[6] *Daer deur* — whereby.

and then the water became still opener then it was, which put vs in good comfort.

The 13 of May it was still weather, but it snowed hard with a north[-west] wind.

The 14 of May [it was fine clear weather with a north wind. Then] we fetcht our last slead with fire wood, and stil ware[1] our shooes made of rugde[2] on our feete, wherewith we did our selues much pleasure, and they furthered vs much. At the same time we spake to William Barents againe to mooue the maister about going from thence, which he promised he would doe [on the following day].

The 15 of May it was faire weather with a west wind, and it was agreed that all our men should go out to exercise their bodies with running, goeing,[3] playing at colfe[4] and other exercises, thereby to stirre their ioynts and make them nymble. Meane time [William] Barents spake vnto the maister and showed him what the company had said,[5] who made him answeare that they should stay no longer than to the end of that mounth, and that if then the ship could not be loosed, that preparation should be made to goe away with the scute and the boate.[6]

The 16 of May it was faire weather with a west-wind; at which time the company were glad of the answere that the maister had giuen, but they thought the time too long, because they were to haue much time[7] to make the boate and

[1] Wore.
[2] *Van de ruyghe hoetgens*—of the rough hats (felt). See page 166, note 1.
[3] *I.e.*, walking.   [4] *Colven.* See page 168, note 1.
[5] *Sprack Willem Barentzoon den schipper aen wat der ghesellen goeden raedt was*—William Barentsz told the skipper what the crew thought was best (to be done).
[6] *De schuijt ende bock*—the boat and yawl. Heemskerck's first thought, as supercargo, evidently was to save, if possible, the ship and property entrusted to him by the owner; and by waiting till the fine weather came and the sea was open, he hoped to be able to do this.
[7] *Dat men veel tijts behoeven soude*—because much time would be requisite.

the scute ready to put to sea with them, and therefore some of them were of opinion that it would be best for them to sawe the boate[1] in the middle and to make it longer; which opinion, though[2] it was not amisse, neuerthelesse it would be ye worse for vs, for that although it should be so much the better for the sailing, it would be so much the vnfitter to be drawne ouer the ice, which we were forced [afterwards] to doe.

The 17 and 18 of May it was faire cleere weather with a west wind, and then we [almost] began to reconne[3] the daies that were set downe and appointed[4] for vs to make preparation to be gone.

The 19 of May it was faire weather with an east wind; then foure of our men went to the ship or to the sea side, to see what way we should draue the scute into the water.[5]

The 20 of May it was foule weather with a north-east wind, whereby the ice began to come in [strongly] againe; and at noone we spake vnto the maister, and told him that it was time to make preparation to be gon, if he would euer get away from thence;[6] whereunto he made answeare that his owne life was as deere vnto him as any of ours vnto vs, neuerthelesse he willed vs to make haste to prepare our clothes and other things ready and fit for our voiage, and that in the meane time we should patch and amend them, that after it might be no hinderance vnto vs, and that we should stay till the mounth of May was past, and then make ready the scute and the boate and al other things fit and conuenient for our iourney.

[1] *Bock*—yawl; it being the smaller boat of the two.
[2] "Thought"—*Ph*.
[3] Reckon, count.
[4] *Dat den tijt aenquam*—till the time should arrive.
[5] *De schuyten te water soude moghen brenghen*—should be able to get the boats afloat.
[6] *Oft eens tijdt quam dat wy wech comen mochten*—if the time should ever come when we might get away.

The 21 of May it was faire weather with a north-east wind, so that the ice came driuing in againe, yet we made preparation touching our things that we should weare, that we might not be hindred thereby.

The 22 of May it was faire weather with a north-west wind; and for that we had almost spent all our wood, we brake the portall of our dore[1] downe and burnt it.

The 23 of May it was faire weather with an east wind; then some of [us] went againe to the place where the wood lay, to wash our sheets.[2]

The 24 of May it was faire weather with a south-east wind, whereby there was but little open water.

The 25 of May it was faire weather with an east wind. Then at noone time we tooke the higth of the sunne, that was eleuated aboue the horizon 34 degrees and 46 minutes, his declination 20 degrees and 46 minutes, which taken from the higth aforesaid, there rested 14 degrees, which taken from 90 degrees[3] resteth 76 degrees for the higth of the Pole.[4]

---

[1] *Den wandt rant portael*—the sides of the porch or entrance.

[2] *Hemden*—shirts.

[3] *Die dan wederom ghetoghen van de ghenomen hoochte*—which then being taken from the observed height. This error in the original text is corrected in the translation.

[4] The declination here given (correctly 20° 46',5) is that of the 24th May; that of the 25th being 20° 57',6. The amended calculation for both days will be as follows:—

	May 24th	May 25th.
Observed altitude of sun	34° 46',0	34° 46',0
Refraction	− 1',4	− 1',4
	34° 44',6	34° 44',6
Sun's declination	+ 20° 46',5	+ 20° 57',6
Complement φ	13° 58',1	13° 47',0
φ	76° 1',9	76° 13',0
Or, allowing for the sun's semi-diameter	75° 45',9	75° 57',0

Regarding the several observations of stars as well as of the sun (except

The 26 of May it was faire weather with a great northeast wind, whereby the ice came [drifting] in againe [with great force].

The 27 of May it was foule weather with a great northeast wind, which draue the ice mightely in againe, whereupon the maister, at the motion[1] of the company, willed vs [immediately to begin] to make preparation to be gon.

The 28 of May it was foule weather with a north-west wind; after noone it began to be somewhat better. Then seuen of vs went vnto the ship, and fetcht such things from thence as should serue vs for the furnishing of our scute and our boate, as the old fock sayle[2] to make a sayle[3] for our boate and our scute, and some tackles and other things necessarie for vs.[4]

The 29 of May in the morning it was reasonable fair

those of March 20th, April 2nd and 18th, and May 24th, which are uncertain), as being all equally good, subject only to correction for refraction and amended declination, the result will be 75° 57',5. Or, assuming that the sun's *lower* edge was observed in every case, but not allowed for (and the observations of the stars leave little room for doubting that such must have been the case), and taking the sun's semi-diameter at 16', and including also the observations of the two stars, we have 75° 49',5. In either case the latitude will be rather to the *south* than to the north of the 76th parallel. But, as all the latter observations of the sun were made under an erroneous impression, and evidently with a desire that they should correspond with what was believed to be the truth, the safest plan will be to content ourselves with the observations of the two stars and the *first* observation of the sun on February 19th, the result of which will be:—

γ	Orionis	75°	43',0
α	Tauri	75°	47',9
☉		75°	44',1
			135

Which gives exactly 75° 45' as the latitude of the spot.

[1] *Aenstaen*—urgent request.
[2] *Fock*—foresail.   [3] *De seylen*—the sails.
[4] *Eenigh loopende wandt ende trosgens ende anders meer*—some running rigging, ropes, and various other things.

How we made ready to sail back again to Holland.

weather with a west wind; then ten of vs went vnto the scute to bring it to the house to dresse it and make it ready to sayle,[1] but [on coming to it] we found it deepe hidden vnder ye snow, and were faine with great paine and labour to dig it out, but when we had gotten it out of the snow, and thought to draw it to the house, we could not doe it, because we were too weake, wherewith we became wholely out of heart, doubting that we should not be able to goe forwarde with our labour; but the maister encouraging vs bad vs striue to do more then we were able, saying that both our liues and our wellfare consisted therein, and that if we could not get the scute from thence and make it ready, then he said we must dwell there as burgers[2] of Noua Zembla, and make our graues in that place. But there wanted no good will in vs, but onely strength, which made vs for that time to leaue of worke and let the scute lye stil, which was no small greefe vnto vs and trouble to thinke what were best for vs to doe. But after noone, being thus comfortlesse come home, wee tooke hearts againe, and determined to tourne the boate[3] that lay by the house with her keale vpwards, and [we began] to amend it [and to heighten the gunwales, so] that it might be ye fitter to carry vs ouer the sea, for we made full account y^t we had a long troublesom voiage in hand, wherin we might haue many crosses, and wherin we should not be sufficiently prouided for all things necessarie, although we tooke neuer so much care; and while we were busy about our worke, there came a great[4] beare vnto vs, wherewith we went into our house and stood to watch her in our three dores with harquebushes, and one stood in the chimney with a musket. This beare came bold-

[1] *Nae de schuyt ghegaen om die ontrent het huijs te vertimmeren*—went to the boat, in order to repair it near the house.

[2] *Burghers*—burgesses, citizens; that is to say, they must consider Novaya Zemlya as their place of permanent residence.

[3] *De bock*—the yawl. [4] *Vreeselijcken*—frightful.

lyer¹ vnto vs than euer any had done before, for she came to the neather² step yᵗ went to one of our doores, and the man that stood in the doore saw her not because he lookt towards the other doore, but they that stood within saw her and in great feare called to him, wherewith he turned about, and although he was in a maze he shot at her, and the bullet past cleane through her body, whereupon she ran away. Yet it was a fearfull thing to see, for the beare was almost vpon him before he saw her, so that if the peece had failed to giue fire, (as often times they doe) it had cost him his life, and it may be yᵗ the beare would haue gotten into yᵉ house. The beare being gone somewhat from the house, lay downe, wherewith we went all armed [with guns, muskets, and half-pikes] and killed her outright, and when we had ript open her belly we found a peece of a bucke therein, with haire, skin and all,³ which not long before she had towrne⁴ and deuoured.

The 30 of May it was indifferent faire weather, but very cold and close aire,⁵ the wind west; then we began [again with all our men that were fit for it] to set our selues to worke about the boate⁶ to amend it, the rest staying in the house to make the sailes and all other things ready that were necessarie for vs. But while we were busie working at our boate, there came [again] a beare vnto vs, wherewith we were forced to leaue worke, but she was shot by our men. Then we brake downe the plankes of the rooffe of our house, to amend our boate withall,⁷ and so proceeded in our worke as well as we could; for every man was willing to labour, for we had sore longed for it, and did more then we were able to doe.

The 31 of May it was faire weather, but somewhat colder

---

¹ More boldly.   ² Nether, lower.
³ *Stucken van robben met huijt ende hayr*—pieces of seals, with the skin and hair.   ⁴ Torn.
⁵ *Niet seer kout maer doncker*—not very cold, but dark.
⁶ *Bock*—yawl.
⁷ *Om de bock daer mede op te boyen*—wherewith to raise the gunwale of our yawl.

then before, the wind being south-west, whereby the ice draue away, and we wrought hard about our boate; but when [we] were in the chiefest part of worke, there came an other beare, as if they had smelt that we would be gone, and that therefore they desired to tast a peece of some of vs,[1] for that was the third day, one after the other, that they set so fiercely vpon vs; so that we were forced to leaue our worke and goe into the house, and she followed vs, but we stood with our peeces to watch her, and shot three peeces at her, two from our dores and one out of the chimney, which all three hit her, whereby she fared as the dogge did with the pudding;[2] but her death did vs more hurt then her life, for after we ript her belly we drest her liuer and eate it, which in the taste liked vs well, but it made vs all sicke, specially three that were exceeding sicke, and we verily thought that we should haue lost them, for all their skins came of from the foote to the head, but yet they recouered againe, for the which we gave God heartie thankes, for if as then we had lost these three men, it was a hundred to one[3] that we should neuer haue gotten from thence, because we should haue had too few men to draw and lift at our neede.

[June, 1597.]

The 1 of June it was faire [beautiful] weather, and then our men were for the most part sicke with eating the liuer of a[4] beare, as it is said before, whereby that day there was nothing done about the boate; and then there hung a pot still ouer the fire with some of the liuer in it, but the master tooke it and cast it out of the dore, for we had enough of the sawce thereof.[5] That day foure of our men

[1] *Van ons eerst de smaeck begeerden te hebben*—they desired first to have a taste of us.

[2] *Also dat hem dit bequam als de hont de worst*—so that it agreed with her as the sausage did with the dog. This homely Dutch proverb has already been explained in page 106, note 5.

[3] *Mischien*—perhaps.

[4] *Den*—the.

[5] *Genoech van die sause*—enough of *that* sauce.

that were the best in health went to the ship, to see if there was any thing in it that would serue vs in our voiage, and there found a barrell with geep,[1] which we shared amongst our men, whereof every one had two, and it did vs great pleasure.

The 2 of June, in the morning, it was faire weather with a south-west wind; and then sixe of vs went to see and finde out the best way for vs to bring our boate and our scute to the water side, for as then the ice laie so high and so thicke one vpon the other, that it seemed [almost] unpossible to draw or get our boate and the scute ouer the ice, and the shortest and best way that we could find was straight from the ship to the water side,[2] although it was full of hilles and altogether vneuen and would be great labour and trouble vnto vs, but because of the shortnesse we esteemed it to be the best way for vs.

The 3 of June, in the morning, it was faire cleare [sunny] weather, the wind west; and then we were [again become] somewhat [stronger and] better [of our sickness], and tooke great paines with the boate,[3] that at last we got it ready after we had wrought sixe daies vpon it. About euening it began to blow hard, and therewith the water was very open, which put vs in good comfort that our deliuerance would soone follow, and that we should once get out of that desolate and fearefulle place.

The 4 of June it was faire cleere [sunny] weather and

---

[1] *Geep.* A well known fish (*Belone vulgaris*, Cuvier), which is called in English by a variety of trivial names:—gar-fish, gane-fish, sea-pike, mackerel-guide, mackerel-guard, green-bone, horn-fish, horn-back, horn-beak, horn-bill, gore-bill, long-nose, sea-needle. Considerable quantities are brought to the London markets in the spring from the Kent and Sussex coasts. In Holland they are now only used as bait for other fish. See Yarrell, *History of British Fishes*, vol. i, p. 393.

[2] *Nae't open water toe*—towards the open water.

[3] *Ende arbeyden met alle macht aen den boek*—and worked with all our might on the yawl.

indifferent warme;[1] and about y*e* south-east sun [½ p. 7 A.M.] eleuen of vs went to our scute [on the beach] where it then lay, and drew it to[wards] the ship, at which time the labour seemed lighter vnto vs then it did before when we tooke it in hand and were forced to leaue it off againe. The reason thereof was the opinion that we had that the snow as then lay harder vpon the ground and so was become stronger, and it may be that our courages were better to see that the time gaue vs open water, and that our hope was that we should get from thence; and so three of our men stayd by the scute to build her to our mindes, and for that it was a herring scute, which are made narrow behind, therefore they sawed it [a little] of behinde, and made it a broad stearne and better to broke the seas;[2] they built it also somewhat higher, and drest it vp as well they could.[3] The rest of our men were busy in the house to make all other things ready for our voiage, and that day drew two sleads with victuals and other goods [from the house] vnto the ship, that lay about halfe way betweene the house and the open water, [so] that after they might haue so much y*e* shorter way to carry the goods vnto y*e* water side, when we should goe away. At which time al the labour and paines that we tooke seemed light and easie vnto vs, because of the hope that we had to get out of that wild, desart, irkesome, fearefull, and cold country.

The 5 of June it was foule [uncomfortable] weather with great store of haile and snow, the wind west, which made an open water; but as then we could doe nothing without the house, but within we made all things ready, as sailes, oares,

[1] *Niet seer koud*—not very cold.

[2] *Maecktense met een spiegel, om also bequamer te zijn inde zee te ghebruijcken*—made it with a square stern, in order that it might be a better sea-boat.

[3] *Ende maecktense also vaerdich opt bequaemste dat men mocht*—and so got it ready in the fittest manner in their power.

mastes, sprit, rother, swerd,[1] and all other necessarie things.

The 6 of June in the morning it was faire weather, the wind north-east. Then we went with our carpenters to the ship to build vp our scute, and carried two sleades-full of goods into the ship, both victualles and marchandise, with other things, which we ment to take with vs. After that there rose very foul weather in the south-west, with snow, haile, and [also] raine, which we in long time had not had, whereby the carpenters were forced to leaue their worke and goe home to the house with vs, where also we could not be drie, [for] because we had taken of the deales [from the house], therewith to amend our boate and our scute; there laie but a saile ouer it, which would not hold out the water, and the way that laie full of snow began to be soft, so that we left of our shoes made of rugge and felt[2], and [again] put on our leather shoes.

The 7 of June there blew a great north-east wind, whereby we saw the ice come driuing in againe; but the sunne being south-east [½ p. 7 A.M.] it was faire weather againe, and then the carpenters went to the scute againe to make an end of their worke, and we packed the marchants goods that we ment to take with vs [the best and most valuable goods], and made defences for our selues of the said packes to saue vs from the sea[3] [as we had to carry them] in the open scute.

The 8 of June it was faire weather, and we drew the wares to the ship which we had packed and made ready; and the car-

---

[1] *Swaert* (now written *zwaarden*) lee-boards or whiskers. These are the boards still seen on the sides of Dutch flat-bottomed vessels, which serve to keep them steady, and to prevent them from drifting to leeward, when sailing with a side wind, or lying to.

[2] *Van hoeden.* See page 166, note 1.

[3] *Ende maeckten daer presentinghen over om van een zee waters beschermt te zijn*—and placed tarpaulings over them, to protect *them* (the goods) from the sea-water.

penters made ready the scute, so that the same euening it was almost done. The same day all our men went to draw our boate[1] to the ship, and made ropes to draw withall, such as we vse to draw with in scutes,[2] which we cast ouer our shoulders and held fast with all our hands,[3] and so drew both with our hands and our shoulders, which gaue vs more force, and specially the desire and great pleasure we tooke to worke at that time made vs stronger, so that we did more then then at other times we should haue done, for that good will on the one side and hope on the other side encreased our strenght.

The 9 of June it was faire weather with variable windes. Then we washt our shirts and all our linnen against we should be ready to saile away, and the carpenters were still busie to make an end of the boate and the scute.[4]

The 10 of June we carried foure sleades of goods into the ship, the wind then being variable; and at euening it was northerly, and we were busie in the house to make all things ready. The wine that was left we put into litle vessels,[5] that so we might deuide it into both our vessels,[6] and that as we were inclosed by the ice,[7] (which we well knew would happen vnto vs) we might the easelier cast the goods vpon the ice, both out and into the scutes, as time and place serued vs.

The 11 of June it was foule weather and it blew hard north north-west, so that all day we could doe nothing, and we were in great feare least the storme would carry the ice and the ship both away together (which might well haue come to passe); then we should haue beene in greater mise-

---

[1] *Bock*—yawl.   [2] *Sleden*—sledges.

[3] *Dat men noch effenwel onse handen daer aen mochten slaen*—so that we could likewise grasp them with our hands.

[4] *Om de buydenningen [buijkdenningen] in den bock ende schuyte te maecken*—to make the bottom-boards (ceiling) of the yawl and boat.

[5] *Cleyne raetgiens*—small casks.   [6] *Schuyten*—boats.

[7] *So mede als wy altemet int ys beset mochten werden*—in order that whenever we should be enclosed by the ice.

rie than euer we were, for that our goods, both victualles and others, were then all in the ship; but God prouided so well for vs that it fell not out so unfortunatly.

The 12 of June it was indifferent faire weather; then we went with hatchets, halberds,[1] shouels and others instruments, to make the way plaine where we should draw the scute and the boate to the water side, along the way that lay full of knobbes and hilles of ice,[2] where we wrought sore with our hatchets and other instruments.[3] And while we were in the chiefest of our worke, there came a great leane beare out of the sea vpon the ice towards vs, which we iudged to come out of Tartaria, for we had [before] seene of them twenty or thirty [80 or 120] miles within the sea; and for that we had no muskets but only one which our surgian[4] carried, I ran in great haste towards the ship to fetch one or two, which the beare perceiuing ran [quickly and boldly] after me, and was very likely to haue ouer taken me, but our company seeing that, left their worke and ran [quickly] after her, which made the beare turn towards them and left me; but when she ran towards them, she was shot into the body by the surgian, and ran away, but because the ice was so uneuen and hilly she could not go farre, but being by vs ouer taken we killed her out right, and smot[5] her teeth out of her head while she was yet liuing.

The 13 of June it was faire weather; then the maister and the carpenters went to the ship, and there made the scute and the boate ready, so that there rested nothing as then but onely to bring it downe to the water side. The maister and those that were with him, seeing that it was open water and a good west wind, came back to the house againe, and there

---

[1] *Met bylen, houweelen ende allerley ghereetschap*—with hatchets, pickaxes, and all sorts of implements.

[2] *Ys ende ysberghen*—ice and icebergs.

[3] *Met houwen, smyten, schoppen, graven ende wechwerpen*—with chopping, throwing, pushing, digging, and clearing away.

[4] *Barbier*. See page 125, note 3. [5] Smote, struck.

How we prepared a way whereby we brought our boats and goods to the sea.

he spake vnto William Barents (that had bin long sicke), and shewed him that he thought it good (seeing it was a fit time) to goe from thence, and so willed the company[1] to driue[2] the boate and the scute downe to the water side, and in the name God to begin our voiage to saile from Noua Zembla. Then William Barents wrote a letter, which he put into a muskets charge[3] and hanged it vp in the chimney, shewing how we[4] came out of Holland to saile to the kingdome of China, and what had happened vnto vs being there on land, with all our crosses, that if any man chanced to come thither, they might know what had happened vnto vs [how we had fared], and how we had bin forced in our extremity to make that house, and had dwelt 10 mounthes therein. And for that we were [now forced] to put to sea in two small open boates and to vndertake a dangerous and aduenterous voiage in hand, the maister [also] wrote two letters, which most of vs subscribed vnto, signifying how we had stayed there vpon the land in great trouble and miserie, in hope that our ship would be freed from the ice and that we should saile away with it againe, and how it fell out to the contrary, and that the ship lay fast in the ice; so that in the end, the time passing away and our victuals beginning to faile vs, we were forced, for the sauing of our owne liues, to leaue[5] the ship and to saile away in our open boates, and so to commit our selues into the hands of God. Which done, he put into each of our scutes a letter,[6] y*t* if we chanced to loose one another or y*t* by stormes or any other misaduenture we

---

[1] *Ende besloten doen onderlinghen metten gemeenen maets*—and they then resolved jointly with the ship's company.

[2] *Brengen*—to bring, to take.

[3] *Ende heeft Willem Barentsz. te voren een cleijn cedelken gheschreven, ende in een muskets mate ghedaen*—and William Barentsz had previously written a small scroll, and placed it in a *bandoleer*.

[4] "He".—*Ph.*   [5] Abandon.

[6] *Van welcke brief elcken schuyte een hadde*—of which letters each boat had one.

hapened to be cast away, that then by the scute that escaped
men might know how we left each other. And so, hauing
finished all things as we determined, we drew the boate¹ to
the water side and left a man in it, and went and fetcht the
scute,² and after that eleuen sleads with goods, as victuals
and some wine that yet remained, and the marchants goods
which we preserued as wel as we could,³ viz., 6 packs with
[the] fine[st] wollen cloth, a chest with linnen, two packets
wᵗ ueluet, two smal chests with mony, two drifats⁴ with the
mens clothes [such as shirts], and other things, 13 barrels of
bread, a barrell of cheese,⁵ a fletch of bacon, two runlets of
oyle, 6 small runlets of wine, two runlets of vinegar, with
other packs [and clothes] belonging to yᵉ sailers [and many
other things]; so that when they lay altogether upon a
heape, a man would haue iudged that they would not haue
gone into the scutes. Which being all put into them, we
went to the house, and first drew William Barents vpon a
slead to the place where our scutes lay, and after that we
fetcht Claes Adrianson,⁶ both of them hauing bin long sicke.
And so we [being] entred into the scutes and deuided our
selues into each of them alike, and put into either of them a
sicke man, then the maister caused both the scutes to ly close
one by the other, and there we subscribed to the letters
which he had written [as is above mentioned], the coppie
whereof hereafter ensueth. And so committing our selues to
the will and mercie of God, with a west north-west wind and
an endifferent open water, we set saile and put to sea.

¹ *Bock*—yawl.   ² Boat.
³ *Daer wy alle naersticheyt toe deden, om die so veel te berghen alst moghelijck was*—of which we took every care to preserve as much as was possible.
⁴ *Harnas tonnen*—coffers, trunks.
⁵ *Soetemelcx kaes*—in modern Dutch, *zoetemelksche kaas*—lit. sweet-milk cheese. This is the ordinary Dutch cheese, well known in England, and which on a former occasion (page 124, note 11) was described as *koyenkaas*. It is the produce principally of North Holland.
⁶ *Claes Andriesz.*—Nicholas, the son of *Andrew*, or Andrewson.

The Coppie of their Letter.

HAUING till this day stayd for the time and opportunity, in hope to get our ship loose, and now are cleane out of hope thereof,[1] for that it lyeth fast shut vp and inclosed in the ice, and in the last[2] of March and the first[3] of April the ice did so mightily gather together in great hils, that we could not deuise[4] how to get our scute and boate into the water and[5] where to find a conuenient place for it. And for that it seemed almost impossible to get the ship out of the ice, therefore I and William Barents our pilot,[6] and other the officers and company of sailors thereunto belonging, considering with our selues which would be the best course for vs to saue our owne liues and some wares belonging to the marchants, we could find no better meanes then to mend our boate and scute, and to prouide our selues as well as we could of all things necessarie, that being ready we might not loose or ouerslip any fit time and opportunity that God should

---

[1] *Daer als nu weynich oft geen hope toe en is*—whereof there is now little or no hope.

[2] End.   [3] Beginning.

[4] *Dat we vast overleggen*—that we considered well.

[5] "Or."—*Ph.*

[6] *Daerome hebbe ic met Willem Barentsz. de hoogh-bootsman ende ander officie luyden met alle ander gasten*—therefore I, with William Barentsz. (and), the chief-boatswain and other officers, with the rest of the crew. At first sight it might appear that William Barentsz. is described as "hoogh-bootsman". This is evidently the idea of the translator, though he takes on himself to paraphrase the term by "our pilot". But the statement on the 20th June (page 198), that the chief-boatswain came on board the boat in which William Barentsz. was, just before the latter's death, clearly proves that two different persons are here intended: so that, in order to avoid ambiguity, a conjunction, or at least a comma, should be inserted between the two. From the list of the ship's company given in page 193, it may be safely inferred that the "chief-boatswain", or first mate, as we should now call him, was Pieter Pieterszoon Vos. It is he, most probably, who on the 28th August, 1596 (page 100) is called "the other pilot".

send vs; for that it stood us vpon[1] to take the fittest time, otherwise we should surely haue perished with hunger and cold, which as yet is to be feared will goe hard inough with vs, for that there are three or foure of vs that are not able to stirre to doe any thinge,[2] and the best and strongest of us are so weake with the great cold and diseases that we haue so long time endured, that we haue but halfe a mans strength; and it is to be feared that it will rather be worse then better, in regard of the long voiage that we haue in hand, and our bread wil not last vs longer then to the end of the mounth of August, and it may easily fal out, that the voiage being contrary and crosse vnto vs, that before that time we shall not be able to get to any land, where we may procure any victuals or other prouisions for our selues, as we haue hitherto done our best;[3] therefore we thought it our best course not to stay any longer here, for by nature we are bound to seeke our owne good and securities. And so we determined hereupon, and haue vnder written this present letter with our owne hands,[4] vpon the first of June 1597. And while vpon the same day we were ready and had a west wind [with an easy breeze] and an indifferent open sea, we did in Gods name prepare our selues and entred into our voiage, the ship lying as fast as euer it did inclosed in the ice, notwithstanding that while we were making ready to be gon, we had great wind out of the west, north, and north-west, and yet find no alteration nor bettering in the weather, and therefore in the last extremity we left it.[5] [Dated] vpon the 13 of June [and signed by] Jacob Hemskerke, Peter Peterson Vos,

[1] It was requisite for us.
[2] *Daer wy inden arbeyt geen hulpe af en hebben*—from whom in our work we have no help.
[3] *Als we al schoon van dees ur af ons best deden*—even if from this moment we did our best.
[4] *Ende int generael van ons allen onderteijcknet, gedaen ende besloten*—and in general by us all subscribed, done, and concluded.
[5] *Hebben wijt cyndelijck verlaten*—we have at length abandoned it.

Mr. Hans Vos,[1] Laurence Willinsō, Peter Cornelison, Iohn Remarson, William Barēts, Gerrat de Veer, Leonard Hendrickson, Iacob Ionson Scheadam, Iacob Ionsō Sterrenburg.[2]

[1] *Meester Hans Vos.* This is the barber-surgeon, of whom mention has been made in page 125, note 3. The title of "meester", representing the Latin *magister*, shows that he was a member of a learned profession, who had not improbably taken his degree of "Magister Artium Liberalium", at an university. In Hungary, at the present day,—as we learn from the evidence of C. A. Noedl, on the recent trial of C. Derra de Meroda against Dawson and others, in the notorious affair of the Baroness von Beck,—"if a man wishes to become *a surgeon*, he must attend six Latin schools [meaning, apparently, that he must keep six terms at the High School or University], *and learn to cut hair*".—*Morning Post,* July 29th, 1852.

In the journal of Captain James, printed in Mr. Rundall's *Narrative of Voyages towards the North-West* (page 199), is the following entry, under the date of November 30th, 1631:—" Betimes, in the morning, I caused the chirurgion to cut off my hair short, and to shave away all the hair of my face... The like did all the rest." This was at a period when, as appears from the muster-roll of Captain Waymouth's expedition, given in page 238 of the same volume, the rating of the surgeon, who thus acted as barber to the ship's company, was next after "the preacher", and before the master and the purser.

[2] The names, as here given, are neither correctly written nor placed in the order in which they stand in the original text. They are there ranged in six short columns of two names each, except the last, which has only one name; but the translator has read them as if written in two lines across the page. Correctly placed and written, the names are as follows:—

Iacob Heemskerck.
WILLEM BARENTZ.
Pieter Pietersz. Vos.
Gerrit de Veer.
Meester Hans Vos.
Lenaert Hendricksz.
Laurens Willemsz.
Iacob Iansz. Schiedam.
Pieter Cornelisz.
Iacob Iansz. Sterrenburch.
Ian Reyniersz.

There were four others, who did not sign, most likely from their inability to write, or from ill-health.

The 14 of June in the morning, the sunne easterly [½ p. 4 A.M.], we [by God's mercy] put of from the land of Noua Zembla and the fast ice therevnto adioyning, with our boate and our scute,[1] hauing a west wind, and sailed east northeast all that day to the Ilands Point,[2] which was fiue [20] miles; but our first beginning was not very good, for we entered fast into the ice againe, which there laie very hard and fast, which put vs into no smal feare and trouble; and being there, foure of us went on land, to know the scituation thereof, and there we tooke many[3] birds, which we kild with stones vpon the cliftes.[4]

The 15 of June the ice began to goe away; then we put to saile againe with a south wind, and past along by the Head Point[5] and the Flushingers Point,[6] streaching most northeast, and after that north, to the Point of Desire,[7] which is about 13 [52] miles, and there we laie till the 16 of June.

The 16 of June we set saile againe, and got to the Island[s] of Orange[8] with a south wind, which is 8 [32] miles distant from the Point of Desire; there we went one land with two small barrels and a kettle, to melt snow and to put ye water into ye barrels, as also to seeke for birds and egges to make meate for our sicke men; and being there we made fire with such wood as wee found there, and melted the snowe, but found no birds; but three of our men went ouer the ice to the other island, and got three birds, and as we came backe againe, our maister (which was one of the three) fell into the ice, where he was in great danger of his life, for in that place there ran a great streame;[9] but by Gods helpe he got out againe and came to vs, and there dryed himselfe by the fire that we had made, at which fire we drest the

---

[1] *Met ons bock ende schuijt.* [2] *De Eylandts hoeck.*
[3] *Vier*—four. The translator evidently red *reel*. [4] Cliffs.
[5] *Hooft-hoeck.* [6] *Vlissingher hooft*—Flushing Head.
[7] *De Capo van Begeerte*—Cape Desire.
[8] *De Eylanden van Oraengien.*
[9] *Een geweldighen stroom*—a strong current.

birds, and carried them to the scute to our sicke men, and filled our two runlets with water that held about eight gallons[1] a peece; which done, we put to the sea againe with a south-east wind and drowsie miseling weather,[2] whereby we were al dankish[3] and wet, for we had no shelter in our open scutes, and sailed west and west and by south to [opposite] the Ice Point.[4] And being there, both our scutes lying hard by each other, the maister[5] called to William Barents to know how he did, and William Barents made answeare and said, Well, God be thanked, and I hope before we get to Warehouse to be able to goe.[6] Then he spake to me and said, Gerrit, are we about the Ice Point? If we be, then I pray you lift me vp, for I must veiw it once againe;[7] at which time we had sailed from the Island[s] of Orange to the Ice Points about fiue [20] miles; and then the wind was[8] westerly, and we made our scuts fast to a great peece of ice[9] and there eate somewhat; but the weather was still fouler and fouler, so that we were once againe inclosed with ice and forced to stay there.

The 17 of June in the morning, when we had broken our fastes, the ice came so fast[10] vpon vs that it made our haires stare[11] vpright vpon our heades, it was so fearefull to behold;

[1] *Minghelen.* A measure of rather more than an English *quart.*
[2] *Mottich, leelich weder*—nasty drizzly weather.
[3] *Wasich*—damp.
[4] *Ys-hoeck.*
[5] *De schipper*; namely, Jacob Heemskerck.
[6] *Al wel, maet, ick hope noch te loopen eer wy te Waerhuys comen*—quite well, mate. I still hope to be able to run before we get to Wardhuus. It is a matter of interest that the last words of such a man as William Barentsz. should be correctly given.
[7] *Gerrit, zijn wy ontrent den Yshoeck, soo beurt my noch eens op; ic moet dien hoeck noch eens sien*—Gerrit, if we are near the Ice Point, just lift me up again. I must see that Point once more. The Ice Point is the northernmost point of Novaya Zemlya (see page 24, note 4): hence the interest felt in it by the sick man, who, in spite of his courageous talk, was doubtless aware that he should never see it again.
[8] *Liep ten westen*—went round to the west.
[9] *An de schotsen*—to the drift ice.
[10] *Soo vreeselijck*—so frightfully.
[11] Stand.

by which meanes we could not make fast[1] our scutes, so that we thought verily that it was a foreshewing of our last end; for we draue away so hard with the ice, and were so sore prest betweene a flake of ice, that we thought verily the scutes would burst in a hundredth peeces, which made vs looke pittifully one upon the other, for no counsell nor aduise was to be found,[2] but euery minute of an houre[3] we saw death before our eies. At last, being in this discomfort and extreeme necessity, ye master said[4] if we could take hold with a rope vpon the fast ice,[5] we might therewith drawe ye scute vp, and so get it out of the great drift of ice. But as this counsell was good, yet it was so full of daunger, that it was the hazard of his life that should take vpon him to doe it; and without doing it, was it most certaine y^t it would cost us all our liues. This counsell (as I said) was good, but no man (like to the tale of ye mise) durst hang the bell about ye cats necke, fearing to be drowned; yet necessity required to haue it done, and the most danger made vs chuse the least. So that being in that perplexity [and as a drowned calf may safely be risked],[6] I being the lightest of all our company tooke on me to fasten[7] a rope vpon the fast ice; and so creeping from one peece of driuing ice to another, by Gods help got to the fast ice, where I made a rope fast to a high howell,[8] and they that were in the scute drew it thereby vnto

---

[1] *Redden*—save.

[2] *Goet raet was duer* — good counsel was dear. A proverbial expression, explained in page 165, note 2.

[3] *Ooghenblick*—instant.   [4] *Werter geseyt*—it was said (by some one).

[5] *Een trots ofte tou aent vaste ys conden vast cryghen*—could make fast a tackle or rope to the firm ice.

[6] *Een ghedrenckt calf goet te waghen is.* This is another Dutch proverb, which Gerrit de Veer modestly applies to himself, as signifying that his loss would not be much felt. The translator, not understanding the allusion or the force of the proverb, left it out; but on the other hand he, somewhat unnecessarily, introduced in the preceding passage the words "like to the tale of the mise", which are not in the original.

[7] *Te brenghen*—to carry.   [8] *Een hoogen heurel*—a high hummock.

How we were nearly wrecked, and with great danger had to betake ourselves to the ice.

the said fast ice, and then one man alone could drawe more than all of them could have done before. And when we had gotten thither, in all haste we tooke our sicke men out and layd them vpon the ice, laying clothes and other things vnder them [for them to rest on], and then tooke all our goods out of the scutes, and so drew them vpon the ice, whereby for that time we were deliuered from that great danger, making account that we had escaped out of death's clawes,[1] as it was most true.

The 18 of June we repaired and amended our scutes againe, being much bruised and crushed with the racking of the ice, and were forced to driue all the nailes fast againe, and to peece many things about them,[2] God sending vs wood wherewith we moult our pitch, and did all other things that belonged thereunto. That done, some of vs went vpon the land[3] to seeke for egges, which the sick men longed for, but we could find none, but we found foure birds, not without great danger of our liues betweene the ice and the firme land, wherein we often fell, and were in no small danger.

The 19 of June it was indifferent weather, the wind north-west, and [during the day west and] west south-west, but we were still shut vp in the ice and saw no opening, which made us thinke that there would be our last aboade, and that we should neuer get from thence; but on the other side we comforted our selues againe, that seeing God had helped vs oftentimes unexpectedly in many perils, and that his arme as yet was not shortened, but that he could [still] helpe vs[4] at his good will and pleasure, it made vs somewhat comfortable, and caused vs to speake cheerfully one unto the other.

The 20 of June it was indifferent weather, the wind west,

[1] *Des doots kaecken*—the jaws of death.
[2] *Allen de naeden hebben wy mede moeten versien ende dicht maecken, ende diversche presendinghe legghen*—we had likewise to examine and close all the *seams*, and to lay on pieces of tarpauling in various places.
[3] *Te landtwaert in*—towards the land.
[4] "Up".—*Ph.*

and when the sunne was south-east [½ p. 7 A.M.] Claes Adrianson[1] began to be extreme sicke, whereby we perceiued that he would not liue long, and the boateson[2] came into our scute[3] and told vs in what case he was, and that he could not long continue aliue; whereupon William Barents spake and said, I thinke I shal not liue long after him ;[4] and yet we did not ivdge William Barents to be so sicke, for we sat talking one with the other, and spake of many things, and William Barents read in my card which I had made touching our voiage,[5] [and we had some discussion about it]; at last he laid away the card and spake vnto me, saying, Gerrit, give me some drinke ;[6] and he had no sooner drunke but he was taken with so sodain a qualme, that he turned his eies in his head and died presently, and we had no time to call the maister out of the [other] scute to speake vnto him ; and so he died before Claes Adrianson [who died shortly after him]. The death of William Barents put vs in no small discomfort, as being the chiefe guide and onely pilot on whom we reposed our selues next vnder God ;[7] but we could not striue against God, and therefore we must of force be content.

The 21 of June the ice began to driue away againe, and God made vs some opening with [a] south south-west wind; and when the sunne was [about] north west the wind began to blow south-east with a good gale, and we began to make preparations to go from thence.

The 22 of June, in the morning, it blew a good gale out of the south-east, and then the sea was reasonable open, but we

---

[1] *Claes Andriesz.* See page 190, note 6.
[2] *De hoogh-bootsman*—the chief boatswain.   [3] *Bock*—yawl.
[4] *My dunckt tsal met my mede niet langhe dueren*—methinks with me too it will not last long.
[5] *Las in mijn caertgien dat ic van onse reyse gemaect hadde*—looked at my little chart, which I had made of our voyage.
[6] *Gerrit, geeft my eens te drincken*—Gerrit, give me something to drink.
[7] The words "next under God" are not in the text.

were forced to draw our scutes ouer the ice to get vnto it, which was great paine and labour vnto vs, for first we were forced to draw our scutes ouer a peece of ice of 50 paces long, and there put them into the water, and then againe to draw them vp vpon other ice, and after draw them at the least 300[1] paces more ouer the ice, before we could bring them to a good place, where we might easily get out. And being gotten vnto the open water, we committed our selues to God and set saile, the sunne being about east-north-east, with an indifferent gale of wind out of the south and south-south-east, and sailed west and west and by south, till the sunne was south, and than we were round about enclosed with ice againe, and could not get out, but were forced to lie still. But not long after the ice opened againe like to a sluce[2] and we passed through it and set saile againe, and so sailed along by the land, but were presently enclosed with ice; but, being in hope of opening againe, meane time we eate somewhat, for the ice went not away as it did before. After that we vsed all the meanes we could to breake it, but all in vaine; and yet a good while after the ice opened againe [of itself], and we got out and sailed along by the land, west and by south, with a south wind.

The 23 of June we sailed still forward west and by south till the sunne was south-east, and got to the Trust Point,[3] which is distant from the Ice Point 25 [100] miles, and then could go noe further because the ice laie so hard and so close together; and yet it was faire weather. The same day we tooke the hight of the sunne with the astralabium and also with our astronomicall ring, and found his hight to be 37 degrees, and his declination 23 degrees and 30 minutes, which taken from the hight aforesaid, there rested 13 degrees and 30 minutes, which substracted out of 90 degrees, the hight of the Pole was 76 degrees and 30

---

[1] "100."—*Ph.*   [2] *Sluijs*—lock, sluice.
[3] *Capo de Troosts*—Cape Comfort. See page 22, note 4.

minutes.[1] And it was faire sunne-shine weather, and yet it was not so strong as to melt the snow that we might haue water to drink; so that we set all our tin platers and other things[2] full of snow [in the sun] to melt, and so molt it [by the reflection of the sun, so that we had water to drink]; and [we also] put snow into our mouthes, to melt it downe into our throates;[3] but all was not enough, so that we were compelled to endure great thirst.

The stretching of the land from the house[4] where we wintered, along by the north side of Noua Zembla to the Straights of Waigats, where we passed ouer to the coast of Russia, and ouer the entry of the White Sea to Cola,[5] according to the card[6] here ensueing.

From the Low Land[7] to the Streame Baie,[8] the course east and west . . . 4 [16] miles.

From the Streame Baie to the Ice-hauen Point,[9] the course east and by north . 3 [12] miles.

From the Ice-hauen Point to the Islands Point,[10] the course east north-east . . 5 [20] miles.

From the Islands Point to the Flushingers Point,[11] the course north-east and by east . 3 [12] miles.

From the Flushingers Point to yᵉ Head Point,[12] the course north-east . . 4 [16] miles.

[1] The elevation of the sun, corrected for refraction, was 36° 58',7 and its declination + 23° 29',4; so that the elevation of the Pole was 76° 30',7.

[2] *De tinnen plateelen met alle het coperwerck*—the tin cans with all the copper vessels.

[3] *Voor ons drincken*—for our drink.

[4] *Streckinghe van't huijs af*—direction (of our course) from the house, etc.

[5] Cola. A small sea-port of Russian Lapland, in the government of Archangel, 540 miles N. of St. Petersburg. Population 1000.

[6] Chart.   [7] *Het layhe landt.*   [8] *Stroom-bay.*
[9] *Yshavens hoeck.*   [10] *Eylandts hoeck.*
[11] *Vlissenger hooft*—Flushing Head.   [12] *Hooft hoeck.*

From the Head Point to the Point of Desire,[1] the course south and north . . 6 [24] miles.

From the Point of Desire to the Island[s] of Orange,[2] north-west . . . 8 [32] miles.

From the Islands of Orange to the Ice Point,[3] the course west and west and by south 5 [20] miles.

From the Ice Point to the Point of Thrust[4] the course [west and] west and by south . 25 [100] miles.

From the Point of Trust to Nassawes Point,[5] the course[6] west and by north . 10 [40] miles.

From the Nassawe Point to the east end of the Crosse Island,[7] the course west and by north . . . . . 8 [32] miles.

From the east end of the Crosse Island to Williams Island,[8] the course west and by south 3 [12] miles.

From Williams Island to the Black Point,[9] the course west south-west . . . 6 [24] miles.

From the Black Point, to the east end of the Admirable Island,[10] the course west south-west . . . . . 7 [28] miles.

From the east to the west point of the Admirable Island, the course west south-west . 5 [20] miles.

From the west point of the Admirable Island to Cape Planto,[11] the course south-west and by west . . . . 10 [40] miles.

From Cape de Planto to Lombs-bay,[12] the course west south-west . . . 8 [32] miles.

---

[1] *De Hoeck van Begheerten*—Cape Desire.
[2] *De Eylanden van Oraengien.*
[3] *De Yshoeck.*   [4] *Capo de Troosts*—Cape Comfort.
[5] *Capo de Nassauwen*—Cape Nassau.   [6] "West and."—*Ph.*
[7] *Het Cruijs Eylandt.*   [8] *Willems Eylandt.*
[9] *De Swarten Hoeck*—Cape Negro. See page 13.
[10] *Het Admiraliteyts Eylandt*—Admiralty Island.
[11] *Capo Plancio*—Cape Plancius. See page 219, note 4.
[12] *Lomsbay.* See page 12.

From Lombs-bay to the Staues Point,[1] the course west south-west . . . 10 [40] miles.

From the Staues Point to [Cape de Prior or] Langenesse,[2] the course south-west and by south . . . . . 14 [56] miles.

From [Cape Prior or] Langenes to Cape de Cant,[3] the course south-west and by south 6 [24] miles.

From Cape de Cant to the Point with the black clifts,[4] the course south and by west . 4 [16] miles.

From the Point with the black cliftes to the Black Island,[5] the course south south-east 3 [12] miles.

From the Black Island to Constint-sarke,[6] the course east and west . . . 2 [8] miles.

From Constint-sarke,[7] to the Crosse Point,[8] the course south south-east . . . 5 [20] miles.

From Crosse Point to S. Laurence Bay,[9] the course south-east[10] . . . 6 [24] miles.

From S. Laurence Bay[11] to Mel-hauen,[12] the course [south] south-east . . 6 [24] miles.

From Mel-hauen to the Two Islands,[13] the course south south-east . . . 16 [64] miles.

From the 2 Islands, where we crost ouer to the Russia coast, to the Islands of Matfloo and Delgoye,[14] the course south-west[15] . 30 [120] myles.

---

[1] *De Staten Hoeck*—States Point.

[2] *Capo de Prior oft Langhenes.* See page 11.

[3] *Capo de Cant.* See page 219.

[4] *De Hoeck met de swarte clippen*—the Point with the black *cliffs*.

[5] *Het Swarte Eylandt*   [6] *Costintsarck.* See page 30, note 4.

[7] *Constinsarck.* A fatality seems to attend the spelling of this name.

[8] *Cruishoeck.* See page 31.   [9] *S. Laurens Bay.* See page 32.

[10] "S.S.E."—*Ph.*   [11] *S. Lauwersbay.*

[12] *Meelhaven.* See p. 33.

[13] *De twee Eylanden.* On the first voyage they were named St. Clara. See page 34.

[14] *Matfloo ende Delgoy.* See page 36, and also note 6 in page 50.

[15] The true course is almost south-*east*.

From Matfloo and Delgoye to the creeke[1] where we sailed the compasse [almost] round aboute, and came to the same place againe . 22 [88] miles.

From that creeke to Colgoy,[2] the course west north-west . . . . 18 [72] miles.

From Colgoy to the east point of Camdenas,[3] the course west north-west . 20 [80] miles.

From the east point of Camdenas to the west side of the White Sea, the course west north-west . . . . . 40 [160] miles.

From the west point of the White Sea to the 7 Islands,[4] the course north-west . 14 [56] miles.

From the 7 Islands, to the west end of Kilduin,[5] the course north-west . . 20 [80] miles.

From the west end of Kelduin to the place where John Cornelis came vnto vs,[6] the course north-west and by west . . . 7 [28] miles.

From thence to Cola,[7] the course most[8] southerly . . . . . 18 [72] miles.

So that we sailed in two open scutes, some times in the ice, then ouer the ice, and through the sea . . . 381 [1524] miles.[9]

The 24 of June, the sunne being easterly, we rowed here and there [round about] in the ice, to see where

[1] *Inham*—inlet.
[2] *Colgoy*—the Island of Kolguev. See page 35, note 2.
[3] *Candenas*—Kanin Nos. See page 38, note 3.
[4] *De 7 Eylanden.* "The Seven Islands (*Sem Ostrovi*) lie about 16 leagues S.E. by S., by compass, from Tieribieri Point, and by varying the appearance serve to distinguish this part of the coast."—Purdy, *Sailing Directions for the Northern Ocean*, p. 82.
[5] See page 7, note 4.   [6] Namely, on August 30th, 1598.
[7] *Coel.* See page 200, note 5.   [8] "West."—*Ph.*
[9] Phillip has inserted here "381 miles Flemish, which is 1143 miles Inglish". The miles of the text are German or Dutch miles of 15 to the degree, as is stated in page 7, note 1.

we might best goe out, but we saw no opening; but when the sunne was south we got through into the sea, for the which we thanked God most heartilie that he had sent vs an vnexpected opening; and then we sailed with an east wind and went lustily forward, so that we made our account to get aboue¹ the Point of Nassawes;² [but we were again prevented by the ice which beset us, so that we were obliged to stop on the east side of the Point of Nassau] close by the land, and we could easily see the Point of Nassawes, and made our account to be about 3 [12] miles from it, the wind being south and south south-west. Then sixe of our men went on land and there found some wood, whereof they brought as much as they could into the scutes, but found neither birds nor egges; with the which wood they sod³ a pot of water pap (which we called matsammore⁴), that we might eate some warme thing, the wind blowing stil southerly, [and the longer it blew the stronger it grew.]

The 25th of June it blew a great south wind, and the ice whereunto we made our selues fast was not very strong, whereby we were in greate feare that we should breake off from it and driue into the sea; for [in the evening], when the sun was in the west, a peece of that ice brake of, whereby we were forced to dislodge and make our selues fast to another peece of ice.

The 26 of June it still blew hard out of the south, and broke the ice whereunto we were fast in peeces, and we thereby draue into the sea, and could get no more to the fast ice, whereby we were in a thousand dangers to be all cast away; and driuing in yᵗ sort in the sea, we rowed as

---

¹ Beyond.   ² See page 92.   ³ Boiled.

⁴ *Matsammore.* Evidently a corruption of the Spannish *mazamorra*, which word, according to the *Diccionario* of the Royal Spanish Academy, means " biscuit powder, or biscuit broken and rendered unserviceable; also the pottage or food (made with bread or biscuit) which was given to the galley-slaves". The adoption of Spanish words by the Dutch is accounted for in page 12, note 1.

much as we could, but we could not get neere vnto the land, therefore we hoysed vp our fock;[1] and so made vp with our saile;[2] but our fock-mast[3] brake twice in peeces, and then it was worse for vs than before,[4] and notwithstanding that there blew a great gale of wind, yet we were forced to hoyse vp our great sayle,[5] but the wind blew so hard into it that if we had not presently taken it in againe we had sunke in the sea,[6] or else our boate would haue bin filled with water [so that we must have sunk]; for the water began to leap ouer borde,[7] and we were a good way in the sea, at which time the waues went so hollow [and so short] that it was most fearful, and we thereby saw nothing but death before our eyes, and euery twinckling of an eye lookt when we should sincke. But God, that had deliuered us out of so many dangers of death, holpe vs once againe, and contrary to our expectations sent vs a north-west wind, and so with great danger we got to ye fast ice againe. When we were deliuered out of that danger, and knew not where our other scute[8] was, we sailed one mile [4 miles] along by the fast ice, but found it not, whereby we were wholy out of heart and in great feare y^t they were drowned; at which time it was mistie weather. And so sailing along, and hearing no newes of our other scute,[9] we shot of a musket, w^h they hearing shot of another, but yet we could not see each other; meane time approaching nearer to each other, and the weather waxing somewhat cleerer, as we and they shot once againe, we saw the smoke of their peeces, and at last we met together againe, and saw them ly fast between driuing and

---

[1] Foresail.
[2] *Leyden op ons seylen toe*—tried to do it with our sailes.
[3] Foremast.   [4] *Arger als een gat*—worse than a leak.
[5] *Grootseyl*—main-sail.
[6] *In den grondt gheslaghen gheweest*—been capsized.
[7] *Al over boort in te loopen*—to run quite over the gunwale.
[8] *Ons ander macker*—our other companion.
[9] *Onser macker*—our companion.

fast ice. And when we got near vnto them, we went ouer the ice and holp them to vnlade the goods out of their scute, and drew it ouer the ice, and with much paine and trouble brought it into the open water againe; and while they were fast in the ice, we[1] found some wood vpon the land by the sea side, and when we lay by each other we sod[2] some bread and water together and eate it vp warme, which did vs much good.

The 27[3] of June we set saile with an indifferent gale out of the east, and got a mile [4 miles] aboue the Cape de Nassaw one the west side thereof, and then we had the wind against vs, and we were forced to take in our sailes and began to rowe. And as we went along [the firm ice] close by the land, we saw so many sea-horses lying vpon the ice [more than we had ever seen before] that it was admirable,[4] and a great number of birds, at the which we discharged 2 muskets and killed twelue of them, which we fetcht into our scutes. And rowing in that sort, we had a great mist, and then we entred into [the] driuing ice, so that we were compelled to make our scutes fast vnto the fast ice, and to stay there till the weather brake vp,[5] the wind being west northwest and right against vs.

The 28th of June, when the sunne was in the east, we laid all our goods vpon the ice, and then drew the scutes vpon the ice also, because we were so hardly prest on all sides with the ice, and the wind came out of the sea vpon the land, and therefore we were in feare to be wholly inclosed with the ice, and should not be able to get out thereof againe. And being vpon the ice, we laid sailes[6] ouer our scutes, and laie downe to rest, appointing one of our men to keepe watch; and when the sunne was north there

---

[1] *Hadden zy—they* had.   [2] Boiled.   [3] "17th."—*Ph.*
[4] *Jae zy waren ontelbaar*—nay, they were numberless.
[5] *Dattet op claerde*—till it cleared up.
[6] *Van de seylen een tente opgheslaghen*—made a tent of our sails.

came three beares towards our scutes, wherewith he that kept the watch cried [out lustily], three beares, three beares; at which noise we leapt out of our boates with our muskets, that were laden with haile-shot[1] to shoote at birds, and had no time to discharge[2] them, and therefore shot at them therewith; and although that kinde of shot could not hurt them much yet they ranne away, and in the meane time they gaue vs leisure to lade our muskets with bullets, and by that meanes we shot one of the three dead, which the other two perceauing ranne away, but within two houres after they came againe, but when they were almost at vs and heard us make a noise, they ranne away; at which time the wind was west and west and by north, which made the ice driue with great force into the east.

The 29th of June, the sunne being south south-west, the two beares came againe to the place where the dead beare laie, where one of them tooke the dead beare in his mouth, and went a great way with it ouer the rugged ice, and then began to eate it; which we perceauing, shot a musket at her, but she hearing the noise thereof, ran away, and let the dead beare lie. Then four of vs went thither, and saw that in so short a time she had eaten almost the halfe of her; [and] we tooke the dead beare and laid it vpon a high heap of ice, [so] that we might see it out of our scute, that if the beare came againe we might shoot at her. At which time we tried[3] the great strenght of the beare, that carried the dead bear as lightely in her mouth as if it had beene nothing, whereas we foure had enough to doe to cary away the halfe dead beare betweene vs. Then the wind still held west, which draue the ice into the east.

The 30 of June in the morning, when the sunne was east and by north, the ice draue hard eastward by meanes of the west wind, and then there came two beares vpon a

---

[1] *Haghel*—small shot.   [2] *Verladen*—re-load.
[3] *Berouden*—found out; experienced.

peece of ice that draue in the sea, and thought to set vpon
vs, and made show as if they would leape into the water and
come to vs, but did nothing, whereby we were of opinion
that they were the same beares that had beene there before; and about the south-south-east sunne there came an
other beare vpon the fast ice, and made [straight] towards
vs; but being neare vs, and hearing vs make a noise, she
went away againe. Then the wind was west-south-west,
and the ice began somewhat to falle from the land; but
because it was mistie weather and a hard wind, we durst not
put to sea, but staid for a better opportunitie.

The 1 of Julie it was indifferent faire weather, with a west-
north-west wind; and in the morning, the sunne being east,
there came a beare from the driuing yce and swam over the
water to the fast yce whereon we lay; but when she heard vs
she came no nearer, but ran away. And when the sunne was
south-east, the ice came so fast in towards vs, that all the ice
whereon we lay with our scutes and our goods brake and
ran one peece vpon another, whereby we were in no small
feare,[1] for at that time most of our goods fell into the water.
But we with great diligence drew our scutes[2] further vpon
the ice towards the land, where we thought to be better defended from the driuing of the ice, and as we went to fetch
our goods we fell into the greatest trouble that euer we had
before, for y^t we endured so great danger in the sauing
thereof, that as we laid hold vpon one peece thereof the rest
sunke downe with the ice, and many times the ice brake
vnder our owne feet; whereby we were wholy discomforted
and in a maner cleane out of all hope, expecting no issue
thereof, in such sort that our trouble at that time surmounted
all our former cares and impeachments. And when we
thought to draw vp our boates[3] vpon the ice, the ice brake
vnder vs, and we were caried away with the scute and al[4] by

---

[1] *Swaricheyt*—difficulty. [2] *Den bock*—the yawl. [3] *Ibid.*
[4] *Met schuijt ende al*—boat and all.

the driuing ice; and when we thought to saue the goods the ice brake vnder our feet, and with that the scute brak in many places, especially y^t which we had mended;[1] as ye mast, ye mast planke,[2] and almost all the scute,[3] wherein one of our men that was sick and a chest of mony lay, which we with great danger of our liues got out from it; for as we were doing it, the ice that was vnder our feet draue from vs and slid vpon other ice,[4] whereby we were in danger to burst both our armes and our legs. At which time, thinking y^t we had been cleane quit of our scute,[5] we beheld each other in pittiful maner, knowing not what we should doe, our liues depending thereon; but God made so good prouision for vs, y^t ye peeces of ice draue from each other, wherewith we ran in great haste vnto the scute[6] and drew it to vs again in such case as it was, and layd it vpon the fast ice by the boate,[7] where it was in more security, which put us unto an exceeding and great and dangerous labor from the time that the sunne was south-east vntill it was west southwest, and in al that time we rested not, which made vs extreame weary and wholy out of comfort, for that it troubled vs sore, and it was much more fearfull vnto vs then at that time when William Barents dyed; for there we were almost drowned, and that day we lost (which was sounke in the sea) two barrels of bread, a chest w^t linnen cloth, a driefat[8] with the sailors [best] clothes, our astron[omi]cale ring, a pack of scarlet cloth, a runlet of oyle, and some cheeses, and a runlet of wine, which bongd with the ice,[9] so that there was not anything thereof saued.

[1] *Dat wy daer aenghemaeckt hadden*—where we had added to it.
[2] *Mast-banck*—standing-thwart.
[3] *Al de schuijt*—the whole boat.
[4] *Ondert ander ys heen*—away under the other ice.
[5] We had entirely lost our boat.
[6] Boat. [7] Yawl. [8] *Harnas ton*—coffer; trunk.
[9] *Dat deurt ys den bodem ingheschoren werdt*—which was stove in by the ice.

The 2 of Julie, the sunne east, there came another beare vnto vs, but we making a noyse she ran away; and when the sun was west south-west it began to be faire weather. Then we began to mend our scute[1] with the planks wherewith we had made the buyckmish;[2] and while 6 of vs were busied about mending of our scute, the other sixe went further into the land, to seeke for some wood, and to fetch some stones to lay vpon the ice, that we might make a fire thereon, therewith to melt our pitch, which we should need about the scute, as also to see if they could fetch any wood for a mast [for the boat], which they found with certain stones,[3] and brought them where the scutes lay. And when they came to vs againe they shewed vs that they had found certain wood which had bin clouen,[4] and brought some wedges with them wherewith the said wood had been clouen, whereby it appeared that men had bin there. Then we made all the haste we could to make a fire, and to melt our pitch, and to do al other things that were necessary to be done for the repairing of our scute, so that we got it ready againe by that the sunne was north-east; at which time also we rosted[5] our birds [which we had shot], and made a good meale with them.

The 3 of July in the morning, the sunne being east, two of our men went to the water, and there they found two of our oares, our helme sticke,[6] the pack of scarlet cloth, the chest with linnen cloth, and a hat that fell out of the driefat,[7] whereby we gest[8] that it was broken in peeces; which they perceiuing, tooke as much with them as they could carry, and came vnto us, showing vs that they had left

---

[1] Boat. [2] *De buijckdenningh*—the bottom boards.
[3] "Staues."—*Ph.* A misprint.
[4] *Behouwen*—hewn; *i.e.*, laboured with an axe.
[5] *Coockten*—cooked; *lit.* boiled.
[6] *De helmstock*—the tiller of the rudder.
[7] *Harnas ton*—coffer; trunk.
[8] *Verstonden*—understood; became aware.

more goods behind them, whereupon the maister with 5 more of vs went thither, and drew al the goods vpon the firme ice, y^t when we went away we might take it with vs; but they could not carry the chest nor the pack of cloth (that were ful of water) because of their waight, but were forced to let them stand till we went away, that the water might drop out[1] of them [and we might afterwards fetch them], and so they did.[2] The sunne being south-west there came another great beare vnto vs, which the man that kept watch saw not, and had beene deuoured by her if one of our other men that lay downe in the ship[3] had not espied her, and called to him that kept watch to looke to himselfe, who therewith ran away. Meane time the beare was shot into the body, but she escaped; and that time the wind was east north-east.

The 4 of July it was so faire cleare weather, that from the time we were first in Noua Zembla we had not the like. Then wee washt the veluets, that had been wet with the salt water, in fresh water drawne out of snow, and then dryed them and packt them vp againe; at which time the wind was west and west south-west.

The 5 of July it was faire weather, the wind west south-west. The same day dyed John Franson[4] of Harlem (Claes Adrians[5] nephew, that dyed the same day when William Barents dyed[6]) the sunne being then about north north-west; at which time the ice came mightily driuing in vpon vs, and then sixe of our men went into the land, and there fetcht some fire-wood to dresse our meate.

The 6 of July it was misty weather, but about euening it began to cleere vp, and the wind was south-east, which put vs in some comfort, and yet we lay fast vpon the ice.

[1] *Afloopen*—run out; drain out.
[2] *Alst gheschiet is*—as it (afterwards) happened; as we afterwards did.
[3] *Van de schuijt af*—from out of the boat.
[4] *Jan Fransz.*—John, the son of Francis.
[5] *Claes Andriesz.* See page 190, note 6.
[6] See page 198.

The 7 of July it was faire weather with some raine, the wind west south-west, and at euening west and by north. Then wee went to the open water, and there killed[1] thirteene birds, which wee tooke vppon a peece of driuing ice,[2] and layd them vpon the fast ice.

The 8 of July it was close[3] misty weather; then we drest the foules[4] which we had killed, which gaue us a princely mealetide.[5] In the euening there blew a fresh gale of wind, out of the north-east, which put vs in great comfort to get from thence.

The 9 of July, in the morning, the ice began to driue, whereby we got open water on the land side, and then also the fast ice whereon we lay began to driue; whereupon the master and yᵉ men went to fetch the pack and the chest that stood vpon the ice, to put them into the scute, and then drew the scutes to the water at least 340 paces, which was hard for vs to do, in regard that the labour was great and we very weake. And when the sun was south south-east we set saile with an east wind; but when the sunne was west we were forced to make towards the fast ice againe, because thereabouts it was not yet gon;[6] yᵉ wind being south and came right from the land, whereby we were in good hope that it would driue awaye, and that we should proceede in our voyage.

The 10 of July, from the time that the sunne was east north-east till it was east, we tooke great paines and labour to get through the ice; and at last we got through, and rowed forth[7] vntill wee happened to fall betweene two great flakes[8] of ice, that closed one with the other,

---

[1] *Schoten*—shot.

[2] *Die wy op een schots ys nae dryrende, dan opraepten, ende op't vaste ys brachten*—which we then picked up by floating after them on a piece of drift ice, and brought upon the firm ice.

[3] *Mottich*—dirty.

[4] Fowls; birds.

[5] *Maeltijt*—meal; repast.

[6] *Afgheweecken*—given way.

[7] *Voort*—on; forward.

[8] *Velden*—fields.

so that we could not get through, but were forced to draw the scutes vpon them, and to vnlade the goods, and then to draw them ouer to the open water on the other side, and then we must go fetch the goods also to the same place, being at least 110 paces long, which was very hard for vs; but there was no remedy, for it was but a folly for vs to thinke of any werines. And when we were in the open water againe, we rowed forward as well as we could, but we had not rowed long before we fell betweene two great flakes of ice, that came driuing one against the other, but by Gods help and our speedy rowing we got from betweene them before they closed vp, and being through, we had a hard west wind right in our teeth, so that of force we were constrained to make towards the fast ice that lay by the shore, and at last with much trouble we got vnto it. And being there, we thought to row along by the fast ice vnto an island that we saw before vs; but by reason of the hard contrary wind we could not goe farre, so that we were compelled to draw the scutes and the goods vpon the ice, to see what weather[1] God would send vs; but our courages were cooled to see ourselues so often inclosed in ye ice, being in great feare y^t by meanes of the long and continuall paines (which we were forced to take) we should loose all our strength, and by that meanes should not long be able to continue or hold out.

The 11 of July in the morning as we sate fast vpon the ice, the sunne being north-east, there came a great beare out of the water running towards vs, but we watcht for her with three muskets, and when she came within 30 paces of vs we shot all the three muskets at her and killed her outright, so that she stirred not a foote, and we might see the fat run out at the holes of her skinne, that was shot in with the muskets, swimme vpon the water like oyle; and [she] so driving[2] dead upon the water, we went vpon a flake of ice to her, and putting a rope about her neck

[1] *Uytcomst*—issue.   [2] Floating.

drew her vp vpon the ice and smit out her teeth; at which time we measured her body, and found it to be eight foote thick.[1] Then we had a west wind with a close[2] weather; but when the sunne was south it began to cleere vp; then three of our men went to the island that lay before vs, and being there they saw the Crosse Island[3] lying westward from them, and went thither to see if that sommer there had been any Russian there, and went thither vpon the fast ice that lay betweene the two islands; and being in the island, they could not percieue that any man had beene in it since we were there. There they got 70 [burrow-ducks'[4]] egges, but when they had them they knew not wherein to carry them; at last one of them put off his breeches, and tying them fast below, they carried them betweene two of them, and the third bare the musket; and so [they] came to vs againe, after they had been twelue hours out, which put vs in no small feare to think what was become of them. They told vs that they had many times gone vp to the knees in water vpon the ice betweene both the islands, and it was at least 6 [24] miles to and fro that they had gone, which made vs wonder how they could indure it, seeing we were all so weake. With the egges that they had brought we were al wel comforted, and fared like lords, so that we found some reliefe in our great misery,[5] and then we shared our last wine amongst us, whereof euery one had three glasses.[6]

The 12 of July in the morning, when the sunne was east, the wind began to blow east and east north-

[1] That is, in girth.   [2] *Mottich*—dirty; drizzly.
[3] *Het Cruijs Eylandt*. See page 16.
[4] *Bergh-eenden*—lit. mountain-ducks. This is the common shieldrake or burrow-duck (*Tadorna vulpanser*): Gould, *Birds of Europe*, vol. v, pl. 357. The trivial name "Bar-gander" (bergander) is manifestly a corruption of the Dutch name, and not of "Burrow-gander", as has been supposed.
[5] *Also dattet altemet kermis was tusschen onsen smert*—so that there was sometimes a holiday in the midst of our sorrows.
[6] *Drie minghelen*—three minghelen, equal to nearly one gallon.

east, with misty weather; and at euening six of our men went into the land¹ to seeke certaine stones,² and found some, but none of the best sort; and comming backe againe, either of them brought some wood.

The 13 of July it was a faire day; then seuen of our men went to the firme land to seeke for more stones, and found some; at which time the wind was south-east.

The 14 of July it was faire weather with a good south wind, and then the ice began to driue from the land, whereby we were in good hope to haue an open water; but the wind turning westerly againe, it lay still [firm]. When the sunne was south-west, three of our men went to the next island that lay before vs, and there shot a bercheynet,³ which they brought to the scute and gaue it amongst vs, for all our goods were [in] common.

The 15 of July it was misty weather; that morning the wind was south-east, but the sunne being west it began to raine, and the wind turned west and west south-west.

The 16 of July there came a beare from the firme land that came very neere vnto vs, by reason that it was as white as snow, whereby at first we could not discerne it to be a beare, because it shewed so like the snow; but by her stirring at last wee perceiued her, and as she came neere vnto vs we shot at her and hit her, but she ran away. That morning the wind was west, and after that againe east north-east, with close⁴ weather.

The 17 of July, about the south south-east sunne, 5 of our men went againe to the nearest island to see if there appeared any open water, for our long staying there was no small griefe vnto vs, perceiuing not how we should get from thence; who being halfe way thither, they found a beare

---

¹ *Aent landt*—on shore.
² *Steentgiens*—pebbles, or probably pieces of rock-crystal. See page 37.
³ *Berch-eyndt*—burrow-duck. See note 4, in the preceding page.
⁴ *Mottich*—drizzly.

lying behind a peece of ice, which the day before had beene shot by vs, but she hearing vs went away; but one of our men following her with a boate-hooke, thrust her into the skinne,[1] wherewith the beare rose vp vpon her hinder feet, and as the man thrust at her againe, she stroke the iron of the boat-hooke in peeces, wherewith the man fell downe vpon his buttocks. Which our other two men seeing, two of them shot the beare into the body, and with that she ran away, but the other man went after her with his broken staffe, and stroke the beare vpon the backe, wherewith the beare turned about against the man three times one after the other; and then the other two came to her, and shot her into the body againe, wherewith she sat downe vpon her buttocks, and could scant[2] runne any further; and then they shot once againe, wherewith she fell downe, and they smot[3] her teeth out of her head. All that day the wind was north-east and east north-east.

The 18 of July, about the east sunne, three of our men went vp vpon the highest part of the land, to see if there was any open water in the sea; at which time they saw much open water, but it was so farre from the land that they were almost out of comfort, because it lay so farre from the land and the fast ice; being of opinion that we should not be able to drawe the scutes and the goods so farre thither, because our strengthes stil began to decrease,[4] and the sore labour and paine that we were forced to indure more and more increased. And comming to our scutes, they brought vs that newes; but we, being compelled thereunto by necessity, abandoned all wearines and faint heartednes, and determined with our selues to bring the boates and the goods to the water side, and to row vnto that ice where we must passe ouer to get to the open water. And when we got to

[1] *In zijn huijt*—in the body.
[2] Scarcely.
[3] Smote; struck.
[4] *Hoe langher hoe meer ons begaven*—failed us more and more.

it, we vnladed our scutes, and drewe them first [the one and then the other] ouer the ice to the open water, and after that the goods, it being at the least 1000 paces; which was so sore a labour for vs, that as we were in hand therewith we were in a manner ready to leaue off in the middle thereof, and feared that wee should not goe through withall; but for that we had gone through so many dangers, we hoped y* we should not be faint therin, wishing y* it might be y* last trouble y* we should as then indure, and so w* great difficulty got into the open water about the south-west sunne. Then we set saile till the sunne was west and by south, and presently fell amongst the ice againe, where we were forced to drawe vp the scutes againe vpon the ice; and being vpon it, we could see the Crosse Island, which we gest to be about a mile [4 miles] from vs, the wind then being east and east north-east.

The 19 of July, lying in that manner vpon the ice, about the east sunne seuen of our men went to the Crosse Island, and being there they saw great store of open water in y* west, wherewith they much reioyced, and made as great haste as they could to get to the scutes againe; but before they came away they got a hundred egges, and brought them away with them. And comming to the scutes, they shewed vs that they had seen as much open water in the sea as they could decerne; being in good hope that that would be the last time that they should draw the scutes ouer the ice, and that it should be no more measured by vs,[1] and in that sort put vs in good comfort. Whereupon we made speede to dresse our egges, and shared them amongst vs; and presently, the sun being south south-west, we fell to worke to make all things ready to bring the scutes to the water, which were to be drawen at least 270[2] paces

[1] *Ende dat ons voort aen tselvige niet meer gemoeten soude*—and that thenceforth the same would not happen to us again.
[2] "200."—*Ph.*

ouer the ice, which we did with a good¹ courage because we were in good hope that it would be the last time. And getting to the water, we put to sea, with Gods [merciful] helpe [in his mercy], with an east and east north-east wind and a good gale,² so that with the west sun we past by the Crosse Island, which is distant from Cape de Nassawes 10 [40] miles. And presently after that the ice left vs, and we got cleere out of it; yet we saw some in the sea, but it troubled vs not; and so we held our course west and by south, with a good gale of wind³ out of the east and east north-east, so that we gest that betweene euery mealetide⁴ we sailed eighteene [72] miles, wherewith we were exceedingly comforted [and full of joy], giuing God thanks that he had deliuered [and saued] vs out of so great and many difficulties (wherein it seemed that we should haue bin ouerwhelmed), hoping in his mercie that from thence foorth he would [still mercifully) ayde vs.⁵

The 20 of July, hauing still a good gale,⁶ about the southeast sunne we past along by the Black Point,⁷ which is twelue [48] miles distant from the Crosse Island, and sailed west south-west; and about the euening with the west sunne we saw the Admirable Island,⁸ and about the north sunne past along by it, which is distant from the Black Point eight [32] miles. And passing along by it, we saw about two hundred sea horses lying upon a flake of ice, and we sayled close by them

¹ *Grooter*—greater.
² *Recht voort laecken met een goeden voortgangh*—right before the wind, at a good rate.
³ *Een doorgaende coelte*—a steady breeze.
⁴ *In elck eetmael*—in every four-and-twenty hours. See page 88, note 5.
⁵ Phillip here adds, " to bring our voyage to an end".
⁶ *Hebbende noch die heerlijcke voortgang*—making still the same good speed.
⁷ *Den Swarten Hoeck*—Cape Negro. See page 13.
⁸ *Het Admiraliteyts Eylandt*—Admiralty Island. See page 13.

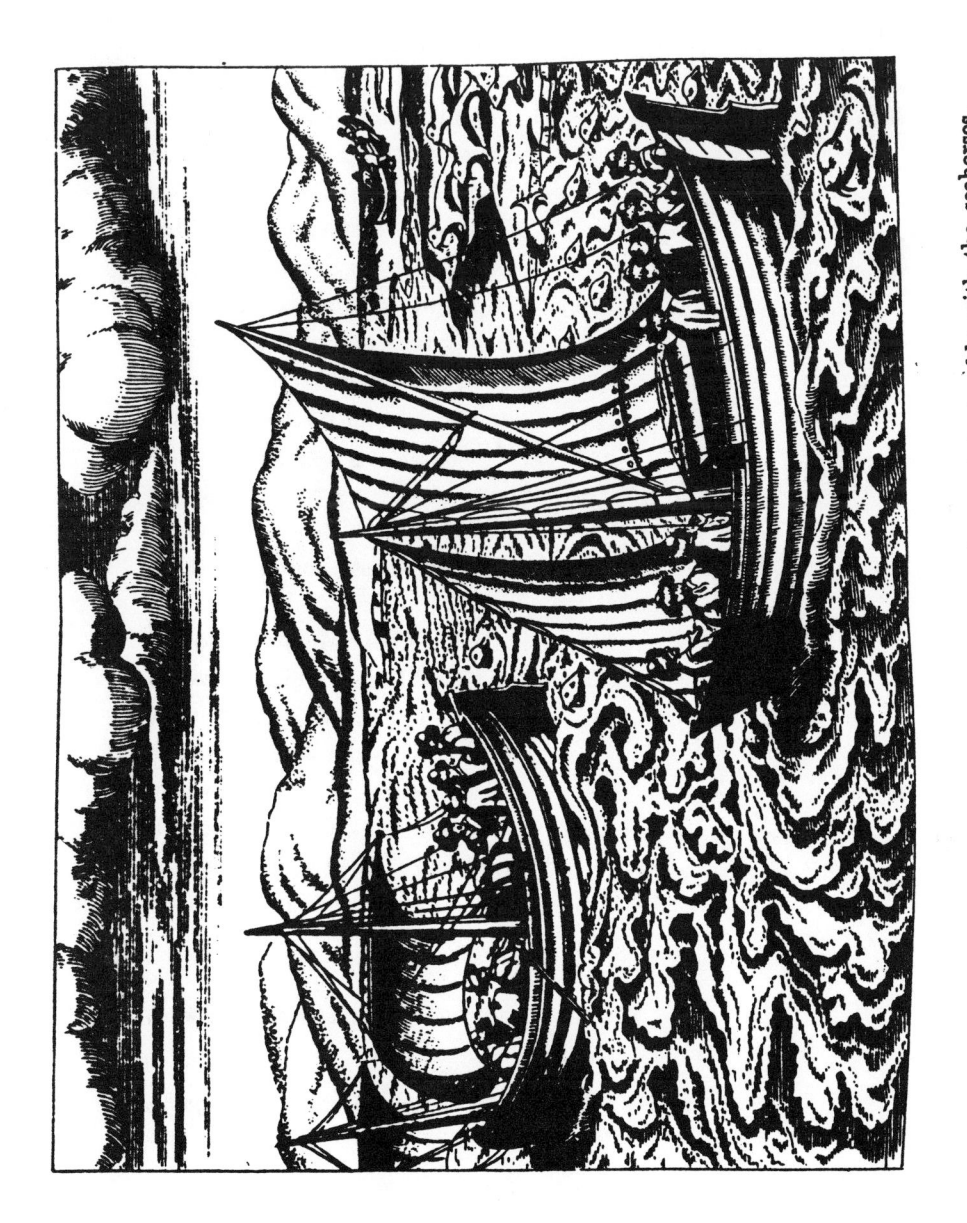

True portraiture of our boats, and how we nearly got into trouble with the seahorses.

and draue them from thence, which had almost cost vs deere;[1] for they, being mighty strong fishes[2] and of great force, swam towards vs (as if they would be reuenged on us for the dispight that we had don them) round about our scuts[3] with a great noyse, as if they would haue deuoured vs; but we escaped from them by reason that we had a good gale of wind, yet it was not wisely done of vs to wake sleeping wolues.

The 21 of July we past by Cape Pluncio[4] about the east north-east sunne, which lyeth west south-west eight [32] miles from y⁰ Admirable Island;[5] and with the good gale yᵗ we had, about y⁰ south-west sun we sailed by Langenes, 9 [36] miles from Cape Pluncio; there the land reacheth most south-west, and we had a good[6] north-east winde.

The 22 of July, we hauing so good a gale of wind,[7] when we came to Cape de Cant,[8] there we went on land to seeke for some birds and egs, but we found none; so we sayled forwards. But after yᵗ, about y⁰ south sun, we saw a clift[9] yᵗ was ful of birds; thither we sailed, and casting stones at them, we killed 22 birds and got fifteene egges, which one of our men fetcht from the clift, and if we would haue stayed there any longer we might haue taken a hundred or two hundred birds at least; but because the maister was somewhat further into sea-ward then we and stayed for vs, and for that we would not loose that faire fore-wind,[10] we [speedily] sailed forwards [close] a long by the land; and about the south-west sunne we came to another point,

[1] Dear.
[2] *Zee-monsters*. De Veer knew better than to call the walrus *a fish*.
[3] Boats.
[4] *Capo Plancio* — Cape Plancius. This headland is not anywhere named in the account of the first voyage, though it appears in the chart of Lomsbay.
[5] Admiralty Island.   [6] *Heerlijck*—splendid.
[7] *Aldus noch een goeden voortgangh hebbende* — making still rapid progress.
[8] *Capo de Cant*.   [9] *Clip*—cliff.
[10] *Die moy deurgaende wint*—that fine steady breeze.

where we got [about] a hundred [and] twenty fiue birds, which we tooke with our hands out of their neasts, and some we killed with stones and made them fal downe into the water; for it is a thing certaine y[t] those birds neuer vsed to see men, and that no man had euer sought or vsed to take them, for else they would haue flowne away,[1] and that they feared no body but the foxes and other wilde beastes, that could not clime up the high clifts,[2] and that therefore they had made their nests thereon, where they were out of feare of any beastes comming vnto them; for we were in no small daunger of breaking of our legges and armes, especially as we came downe aguine, because the clift was so high and so stepe. Those birds had euery one but one egge in their neasts, and that lay vpon the bare clift without any straw or other [soft] thing vnder them, which is to be wondred at to thinke how they could breed[3] their young ones in so great cold; but it is to be thought and beleeued that they therfore sit but vpon one egge, that so the heat which they giue in breeding so many, [having so much more power,] may be wholy giuen vnto one egge, and by that meanes it hath all the heat of the birde vnto it selfe, [and is not divided among many eggs at the same time]. And there also we found many egges, but most of them were foule and bad. And when we left them,[4] the wind fell flat against vs and blew [a strong breeze from the] north-west, and there also we had much ice, and we tooke great paines to get from the ice, but we could not get aboue it.[5] And at last by lauering[6] we fell into the ice; and being there we saw much open water[7] towards the land, whereunto we made as well as we could. But our maister, (that was [with his boat] more to

---

[1] The habits of these birds are not much altered by the presence of men, or else they would not be called *foolish* Guillemots. See page 12, note 3.
[2] Cliffs.
[3] Hatch.
[4] *Van daer af staecken*—put off from thence.
[5] Weather it.
[6] Laveering.
[7] *Mey openinge*—a fine opening.

sea ward,) perceiuing vs to be in the ice, thought we had gotten some hurt, and lauered to and againe along by the ice; but at last seeing that we sailed therein,[1] he was of opinion that we saw some open water,[2] and that we made towards it (as it was true), and therefore he wound also towards vs and came to land by us, where we found a good hauen and lay safe almost from all winds, and he came thither about two houres after vs. There we went on land, and got some eggs and [picked up] some wood to make a fire, wherewith we made ready[3] the birds that we had taken; at which time we had a north-west wind with close[4] weather.

The 23 of July it was darke and mistie weather, with a north wind, whereby we were forced to lye still in that creeke or hauen: meanetime some of our men went on land,[5] to seeke for some egges and [perchance also for] stones,[6] but found not many, but a reasonable number of good stones.

The 24 of July it was faire weather, but the wind still northerly, whereby we were forced to lye still; and about noone we tooke the higth of ye sun with our astrolabium, and found it to be eleuated aboue the horizon 37 degrees and 20 min., his declination 20 degrees and 10 minutes, which substracted from ye higth aforesaid rested 17 degrees and 10 minutes, which taken from 90 degrees, the higth of the Pole was 73 degrees and 10 minutes.[7] And for y^t we lay stil there, some of our men went often times on land to seeke stones, and found some that were as good as euer any that we found.

The 25 of July it was darke misty weather, the wind north, but we were forced to ly still because it blew so hard.

The 26 of July it began to be faire weather, which we had

---

[1] *Daer in seylden*—sailed in that direction.
[2] *Openinge*—opening.
[3] *Coockten*—boiled.
[4] *Mottich*—dirty.
[5] *Te landtwaerts in*—towards the land.
[6] *Steentgiens*—pebbles.
[7] This calculation is altogether erroneous. The sun's declination on July 24th, 1598, was + 19° 47',1; so that, with the observed height (corrected for refraction), the elevation of the Pole was only 72° 28',3.

not had for certaine¹ daies together, the wind still north; and about the south sunne we put to sea, but it was so great a creeke that we were forced to put foure [16] miles into the sea,² before wee could get about³ the point thereof; and it was most in⁴ the wind, so that it was midnight before wee got aboue it, sometimes sayling and sometimes rowing; and hauing past it, we stroke⁵ our sailes and rowed along by the land.

The 27 of July it was faire cleare weather, so that we rowed all that day through the broken ice along by the land, the wind being north-west; and at evening, about the west sunne, we came to a place where there ran a great streame,⁶ whereby we thought that we were about Constinsarke;⁷ for we saw a great creeke, and we were of opinion yᵗ it went through to the Tartarian Sea.⁸ Our course was most south-west: about the north sunne we past along by the Crosse Point,⁹ and sailed between the firme land and an island, and then went south south-east with a north-west wind, and made good speed, the maister with yᵉ scute being a good way before us; but when he had gotten about yᵉ point of the island he staied for vs, and there we lay [some time] by yᵉ clifts,¹⁰ hoping to take some birds, but got none; at which time we had sailed from Cape de Cant along by Constinsarke to the Crosse Point 20 [80] miles, our course south south-east, the wind north-west.

The 28 of July it was faire weather, with a north-east

¹ Several. ² *T'zeewaert in*—to seawards. ³ Round.
⁴ Against. ⁵ Struck, lowered.
⁶ *Een gheweldigen stroom*—a powerful current. ⁷ *Constinsarck.*
⁸ That is to say, the Sea of Kara. If it be an ascertained fact, that there is not here any passage eastward through Novaya Zemlya, this current must come from around the back of the Meyduscharski Island. But its existence, and the inference which was not unreasonably drawn from it, sufficiently explain why this passage has been called a *schar*, and not a *salma*. See page 30, note 4.
⁹ *De Cruijs-hoeck.* See page 31. ¹⁰ Cliffs.

wind; then we sailed along by the land, and with the south-west sunne got before S. Laurence Bay, or Sconce Point,[1] and sayled south south-east 6 [24] miles; and being there, we found two Russians lodgies[2] or ships beyond the Point, wherewith we were [on the one hand] not a little comforted to thinke that we were come to the place where we found men, but were [on the other hand] in some doubt of them because they were so many, for at that time wee sawe at least 30 men, and knew not what [sort of persons] they were [whether savages or other foreigners[3]]. There with much paine and labour we got to the land, which they perceiuing, left off their worke and came towards vs, but without any armes; and wee also went on shore, as many as were well,[4] for diuers of vs were very ill at ease and weake by reason of a great scouring in their bodies.[5] And when wee met together wee saluted each other in friendly wise, they after theirs, and we after our manner. And when we were met, both they and we lookt each other stedfastly [and pitifully] in the face, for that some of them knew vs, and we them to bee the same men which the yeare before, when we past through the Weigats, had been in our ship;[6] at which time we perceiued y[t] they were abasht and wondered at vs,[7] to remember that at that time we were so well furnished with a [splendid] great ship, that was exceedingly prouided of all things necessary, and then to see vs so leane and bare,[8] and with so small [open] scutes into that country. And amongst them there were two that in friendly manner clapt y[e] master and me upon the shoulder, as knowing vs since y[e] [former] voiage: for there was none of all our men that was as then in

[1] *S. Laurens Bay, ofte Schans hoeck.* See page 32.
[2] See page 33, note 6.   [3] *On duytsche*—un-Dutch.
[4] *So veel alsser onser mochten van de sieckte*—as many of us as were able on account of our illness.
[5] *De scheurbuijck*—the scurvy.   [6] See page 56.
[7] *Over ons ontset oft becommert waren*—confused or concerned about us.
[8] *Ontstelt*—miserable.

that voiage[1] but we two onley; and [they] asked vs for our crable,[2] meaning our ship, and we shewed them by signes as well as we could (for we had no interpreter) that we had lost our ship in the ice; wherewith they sayd *Crable pro pal*,[3] which we vnderstood to be, Haue you lost your ship? and we made answere, *Crable pro pal*, which was as much as to say, that we had lost our ship. And many more words we could not vse, because we vnderstood not each other. Then they made shew[4] to be sorry for our losse and to be grieued that we the yeare before had beene there with so many ships, and then to see vs in so simple manner,[5] and made vs signes that then they had drunke wine in our ship, and asked vs what drinke we had now; wherewith one of our men went into the scute[6] and drew some water, and let them taste thereof; but they shakt their heads, and said *No dobbre*,[7] that is, it is not good. Then our master went neerer vnto them and shewed them his mouth, to giue them to vnderstand that we were troubled with a loosnesse in our bellies,[8] and to know if they could giue vs any councel to help it; but they thought we made shew that we had great hunger, wherewith one of them went unto their lodging[9] and fetcht a round rie loafe weighing about 8 pounds, with some smored[10] foules, which we accepted thankfully, and gaue them in ex-

[1] *In de Weygats*—in the Weygats. See page 27, note 4.
[2] *Crabble*: intended for the Russian *korabl*, a ship.
[3] *Crabble pro pal*. The correct question and answer in Russian would be: *Propal korabl?*—is the ship lost? *Korabl propal*—the ship is lost.
[4] Made signs. [5] *In soo soberen staet*—in so poor a condition.
[6] Boat.
[7] *No dobbre*. The correct Russian is *nyet dobre*—not good. These Russian seamen appear to have made use of a sort of *lingua franca*, half Russian, half English, which is still common among the persons of their class, having been acquired from their converse with English traders to the White Sea.
[8] *Van den schuerbuijck*—with the scurvy. See page 152, note 3.
[9] *Lodgien*: intended for the Russian word, *lodyi*—boats.
[10] "Smored."—*Ph.* A misprint.

change halfe a dozen of muschuyt.[1] Then our master led two of the chiefe of them with him into his scute, and gaue them some of the wine that we had, being almost a gallon,[2] for it was so neere out. And while we staied there we were very familiar with them, and went to the place where they lay, and sod some of our mischuyt[3] with water by their fire, that we might eate some warme thing downe into our bodies. And we were much comforted to see the Russians, for that in thirteene moneths time [since] that we departed from John Cornelison[4] we had not seene any man, but onely monsterous and cruell[5] wild beares; for that[6] as then we were in some comfort, to see that we had liued so long to come in company of men againe, and therewith we said vnto each other, now we hope that it will fall out better with vs, seeing we haue found men againe, thanking God with all our hearts, that he had beene so gracious and mercifull vnto vs, to giue vs life vntill that time.

The 29 of July it was reasonable faire weather, and that morning the Russians began to make preparation to be gone and to set saile; at which time they digd certaine barrels with traine oile out of the sieges,[7] which they had buried there, and put it into their ships; and we not knowing whither they would go, saw them saile towards ye Weigats: at which time also we set saile and followed after them. But they sayling before vs, and we following them along by the land, the weather being close and misty, we lost the sight of them, and knew not whether they put into any creeke or sayled forward; but we held on our course south south-east, with a north-west wind, and then southeast, betweene [the] two islands, vntill we were inclosed

[1] *Muschuijt* (for *bischuyt*)—biscuits.
[2] *Een minghelen*—about the third part of a gallon.
[3] Boiled some of our biscuit.
[4] Namely, at Bear Island, on the 1st of July, 1596. See page 85.
[5] *Verscheurende*—ravenous.   [6] *Alsoo dat*—so that.
[7] *Cinghel*—shingle; beach.

with ice againe and saw no open water, whereby we supposed that they were about the Weigats, and that the north-west wind had driuen the ice into that creeke. And being so inclosed w^t ice, and saw no open water before vs, but with great labour and paines we went back againe to the two islands aforesaid, and there about the north-east sunne we made our scutes fast at one of the islands, for as then it began to blowe hard[er and harder].

The 30 of July lying at anchor,[1] the wind still blew [just as stiff from the] north-west, with great store of raine and a sore storme, so that although we had couered our scutes with our sailes, yet we could not lye dry, which was an vnaccustomed thing vnto vs: for we had had no raine in long time before, and yet we were forced to stay there all that day.

The 31 of July, in the morning, about the north-east sunne, we rowed from that island to another island, whereon there stood two crosses, whereby we thought that some men had laine there about trade of merchandise, as the other Russians that we saw before had done, but we found no man there; the wind as then being north-west, whereby the ice draue still towards the Weigats.[2] There, to our great good, we went on land, for in that island we found great store of leple leaues,[3] which serued vs exceeding well; and it seemed that God had purposely sent vs thither, for as then we had many sicke men, and most of vs were so troubled with a scouring in our bodies, and were thereby become so weake, that we could hardly row, but by meanes of those leaues we were healed thereof: for that as soone as we had eaten them we were presently eased and healed, whereat we could not choose but wonder,[4] and therefore we gave God

---

[1] *Aldus aent eylandt ligghende*—lying thus by the island.

[2] The Strait of Nassau. See page 27, note 4.

[3] *Lepel-bladeren*—spoon-wort or scurvy grass (*Cochlearia officinalis*), once in great repute as an antiscorbutic.

[4] *Jae meest al van de scheurbuijck alsoo gheplaecht waren, dat wy naulijch voorts mochten, ende deur dese lepelbladeren vry wat bequaem, want het kielp ons so merckelijcken ende haestich, dat wy ons selfs verwon-*

great thanks for that and for many other his mercies shewed vnto vs, by his great and vnexpected ayd lent vs in that our dangerous voyage. And so, as I sayd before, we eate them by whole handfuls together, because in Holland wee had heard much spoken of their great force, and as then found it to be much more than we expected.

The 1 of August the wind blew hard north-west, and the ice, that for a while had driuen towards the entry of the Weigats, stayed and draue no more, but the sea went very hollow,[1] whereby we were forced to remoue our scutes on the other side of the island; to defend them from the waues of the sea. And lying there, we went on land againe to fetch more leple leaues,[2] whereby wee had bin so wel holpen, and stil more and more recouered our healths, and in so short time that we could not choose but wonder thereat; so that as then some of vs could eate bisket againe, which not long before they could not do.[3]

The 2 of August it was dark misty weather, the wind stil blowing stiffe north-west; at which time our victuals began to decrease, for as then we had nothing but a little bread and water, and some of vs a little cheese, which made vs long sore to be gone from thence, specially in regard of our hunger, whereby our weake members began to be much weaker, and yet we were forced to labour sore, which were two great contraries; for it behoued vs rather to haue our bellies full, that so we might be the stronger to endure our labour; but patience was our point of trust.[4]

derden—yea, most of us were so afflicted with the scurvy that we could scarcely move, and by means of this spoon-wort we were much recovered; for it helped us so remarkably and so speedily, that we ourselves were astonished.

[1] Ran very high.   [2] See note 3 in the preceding page.

[3] The almost instantaneous effect of a change of diet, and particularly of the use of fresh vegetables, in the cure of scurvy, has been noticed on numerous occasions.

[4] *Patientie was ons voorlandt*—lit. patience was our *fore-land*, that is to say, what we had constantly before us.

The 3 of August, about the north sun, the weather being somewhat better, we agreed amongst our selues to leaue Noua Zembla and to crosse ouer to Russia; and so committing our selues to God, we set saile with a north-west wind, and sailed south south-west till the sun was east, and then we entred into ice againe, which put vs in great feare, for we had crost ouer and left the ice vpon Noua Zembla,[1] and were in good hope y^t we should not meet with any ice againe in so short space. At which time, being [thus] in the ice, with calme weather, whereby our sailes could doe vs no great good, we stroke[2] our sailes and began to row againe, and at last we rowed clean through the ice,[3] not without great and sore labour, and about the south-west sunne got cleere thereof and entred into the large sea,[4] where we saw no ice; and then, what with sailing and rowing, we had made 20 [80] miles. And so sailing forwards we thought to aproch neere vnto the Russian coast, but about the north-west sunne we entred into the ice againe, and then it was very cold, wherewith our hearts became very heauy, fearing that it would alwaies continew in that sort, and that we should neuer be freed thereof. And for that our boate[5] could not make so good way nor was not able to saile aboue[6] the point of ice, we were compelled to enter into the ice, for that being in it we perceiued open sea beyond it; but the hardest matter was to get into it, for it was very close, but at last we found a meanes to enter, and got in. And being entred, it was somewhat better, and in the end with great paine and labour we got into the open water. Our maister, that was in the scute,[7] which sailed better than our boate,[8] got aboue[9]

[1] *Want wy haddent al overgheset ende adieu gheseyt*—for we had quite crossed over *and bidden it adieu.*

[2] Struck, lowered.

[3] *Ende royden also deurt ys heen*—and thus rowed forward through the ice.

[4] *De ruyme zee*—the open sea.   [5] *Bock*—Yawl.   [6] To weather.
[7] Boat.   [8] Yawl.   [9] Weathered.

the point of the ice, and was in some feare that we were inclosed with yͤ ice; but God sent vs the meanes to get out from it as soone as he could saile about the point thereof,[1] and so we met together againe.

The 4 of August, about the south-east sunne, being gotten out of the ice, we sailed forward with a north-west wind, and held our course [mostly] southerly; and when the sunne was [about] south, at noone time, we saw the coast of Russia lying before vs, whereat we were exceeding glad; and going neerer vnto it, we stroke[2] our sailes and rowed on land, and found it to be very low land, like a bare strand that might be flowed ouer with the water.[3] There we lay till the sunne was south-west; but perceiuing that there we could not much further our selues, hauing as then sailed from the point of Noua Zembla (from whence we put off) thither ful 30 [120] miles, we sailed forward along by the coast of Russia with an indifferent gale of wind, and when the sunne was north we saw another Russian iolle or ship,[4] which we sailed vnto to speake with them; and being hard by them, they came al aboue hatches,[5] and we cried vnto them, *Candinaes, Candinaes*,[6] whereby we asked them if we were about Candinaes, but they cryed againe and sayd, *Pitzora, Pitzora*,[7] to shew vs that we were thereabouts. And for yᵗ we sailed along by the coast, where it was very drie,[8] supposing that we held our course west

---

[1] *Als hyt van buyten om seylde*—while he was rounding it on the outside.

[2] Struck, lowered.

[3] The point where they thus reached the Russian coast would seem to be in about 55 E. long., on the eastern side of the mouth of the Petchora.

[4] *Een Russche jolle*—a Russian yawl.

[5] *Boven op haer jolle*—on the deck of their yawl.

[6] *Candinaes*—Kanin Nos; the cape at the eastern side of the entrance to the White Sea. See page 38, note 3.

[7] *Pitzora*—the river Petchora. See page 55, note 3.

[8] *Daert seer droogh was*—where it was very shallow.

and by north, that so we might get beyond the point of Candinaes, we were wholy deceiued by our compas, that stood vpon a chest bound with yron bands, which made vs vary at least 2 points, whereby we were much more southerly then we thought our course had bin, and also farre more easterly, for we thought verily that we had not bin farre from Candinaes, and we were three daies sailing from it, as after we perceiued ;[1] and for that we found our selues to be so much out of our way, we stayed there all night til day appeared.

The 5 of August, lying there, one of our men went on shore, and found the land further in to be greene and ful of trees,[2] and from thence called to vs to bid vs bring our peeces on shore, saying that there was wild deere to be killed,[3] which made vs exceeding glad, for then our victuales were almost spent, and we had nothing but some broken bread,[4] whereby we were wholy out of comfort, and[5] some of vs were of opinion that we should leaue the scutes and goe further into the land, or else (they said) we should all die with hunger, for that many daies before we were forced to fast, and hunger was a sharpe sword which we could hardly endure any longer.

The 6 of August the weather began to be somewhat better; at which time we determined to row forward, because the wind was [dead] against vs, [so] that we might get out of the creeke,[6] the wind being east south-east, which was our

[1] We have here a convincing proof that they were no longer under the able guidance of William Barentsz. For this reason it has, since the time of his death, been deemed unnecessary to attempt to fix the hour of the day by the recorded bearing of the sun, as had been done previously.

[2] *Ende bevondt datter groente was, met sommighe cleyne boomkens*—and found verdure there with a few small trees.

[3] *Wilt te schieten*—game (for us) to shoot.

[4] *Wat schummelt broodt*—a little mouldy bread.

[5] *Also dat*—so that.

[6] *Den inham*—the bay or inlet; namely, the estuary of the river Petchora.

course as then. And so, hauing rowed about three [12] miles, we could get no further because it was so full in the wind, and we al together heartlesse and faint, the land streatching further north-east then we made account it had done,[1] whereupon we beheld each other in pittifull manner, for we had great want of victuals, and knew not how farre we had to saile before we should get any releefe, for al our victuals was almost consumed.

The 7 of August, the wind being west north-west, it serued vs well to get out of that creeke, and so we sailed forward east and by north till we got out of the creeke, to the place and the point of land where we first had bin, and there made our scutes fast again; for the north-west wind was right against vs, whereby our mens hearts and courages were wholy abated, to see no issue how we should get from thence; for as then sicknesses, hunger, and no meanes to be found how to get from thence, consumed both our flesh and our bloud; but if we had found any releefe,[2] it would haue bin better with vs.

The 8 of August there was no better weather, but still the wind was [dead] against vs, and we lay a good way one from the other, as we found best place for vs; at which time there was most dislike[3] in our boate, in regard that some of vs were exceeding hungrie and could not endure it any longer, but were wholy out of heart still[4] wishing to die.

The 9 of August it was all one weather, so that the wind blowing contrary we were forced to lye still and could goe no further, our greefe still increasing more and more. At last, two of our men went out of the scute wherein the maister was, which we perceiuing two of our men also landed, and went altogether about a mile [4 miles] into the countrie,[5] and at last saw a banke, by the which there issued

[1] This was the promontory on the western side of the Petchora estuary.
[2] *Hadde deerlijck sien moghen helpen*—if looking deplorable could have helped us.
[3] *Verdriet*—sorrow.
[4] *Ende*—and.
[5] *'t laghe landt henen*—along the low land.

a great streame of water,[1] which we thought to be the way from whence the Russians came betweene Candinaes and the firme land of Russia.[2] And as our men came backe againe, in the way as they went along they found a dead sea-horse[3] that stanke exceedingly, which they drew with them to our scute,[4] thinking that they should haue a dainty morsell[5] out of it, because they endured so great hunger; but we [dissuaded them from it, and] told them that without doubt it would kil us, and that it were better for vs to endure pouerty and hunger for a time, then to venture vpon it; saying, that seeing God, who[6] in so many great extremitys had sent vs a happy issue, stil liued and was exceeding powerfull, we hoped and nothing doubting that he would not altogether forsake vs, but rather helpe vs when we were most in dispaire.[7]

The 10 of August it was stil a north-west wind, with mistie and darke[8] weather, so that we were driuen[9] to lie still; at which time it was no need for vs to aske one another how we fared, for we could well gesse it by our countenances.

The 11 of August, in the morning, it was faire calme weather; so that, the sunne being about north-east, the master sent one of his men to vs to bid vs prepare our selues to set saile, but we had made our selues ready thereunto before he came, and [had] began to rowe towards

[1] *Een baeck staen daer een stroom by uyt liep*—a beacon standing, by which there ran a current.
[2] *Daer deur wy vermoeden datter de cours was daer de Russen heenen quamen, tusschen Candinas ende 'tvaste landt van Ruslandt*—whence we concluded that it was the course taken by the Russians between Kanin-Nos and the main-land of Russia.
[3] *Zee-robbe*—seal.   [4] *De schuyten*—the boats.
[5] *Een goedt wiltbraedt*—lit. a good venison.
[6] *Dat wy ons noch liever lyden souden, want Godt de Heere die*—that we should rather make shift without it; for the Lord God, who . . .
[7] *Maer opt onversienste helpen*—but help us when least foreseen.
[8] *Mottich*—dirty.   [9] Forced.

him. At which time, for that I was very weake and no longer able to rowe, as also for that our boate[1] was harder to rowe then the scute,[2] I was set in the scute to guide the helme, and one that was stronger was sent out of the scute into the boate to rowe in my place, that we might keepe company together; and so we rowed till yᵉ sunne was south, and then we had a good gale of wind out of the south, which made vs take in our oares, and then we hoised vp our sailes, wherewith we made good way; but in the euening the wind began to blowe hard, whereby we were forced to take in our sailes and to rowe towards the land, where we laid our scutes vpon the strand,[3] and went on land to seeke for fresh water, but found none. And because we could goe no further, we laid our sailes ouer the boates to couer vs from the weather; at which time it began to raine very hard, and at midnight it thundred and lightned, with more store of raine, where with our company were much disquieted to see that they found no meanes of releefe, but still entred into further trouble and danger.

The 12 of August it was faire weather; at which time, the sunne being east, we saw a Russia lodgie[4] come towards vs with al his sailes vp, wherewith we were not a little comforted, which we perceauing from the strand, where we laie with our scutes, we desired the master that we might goe[5] vnto him to speake with him, and to get some victuales of them; and to that end we made as much haste as we could to launche out our scutes,[6] and sailed toward them. And when we got to them, the master went into the lodgie to aske them how farre we had to Candinaes, which we could not well learne of them because we understood them not. They held vp their fiue fingers vnto vs, but we knew not

---

[1] *Bock*—yawl.
[2] *Schuijt*—boat.
[3] *Dicht aent strandt*—close to the shore.
[4] *Lodja* or boat.
[5] *Seylen*—sail.
[6] *Om de schuyten inde diepte te cryghen*—to get the boats into deep water.

what they ment thereby, but after we perceaued that thereby they would show us that there stood fiue crosses upon it; and they brought their compas out and shewed vs that it lay north-west from us, which our compas also shewed vs, which reckning also we had made; but when we saw we could haue no better intelligence from them, the master went further into their ship, and pointed to a barrell of fish y[t] he saw therein, making signes to know whether they would sel it vnto vs, showing them a peece of 8 royles;[1] which they vnderstanding, gaue vs 102 fishes, with some cakes which they had made of meale when they sod[2] their fishe. And about the south sunne we left them, being glad that we had gotten some victuales, for long before we had had but two[3] ounces of bread a day with a little water, and nothing else, and with that we were forced to comfort our selues as well as we could. The fishes we shared amongst vs equally, to one as much as another,[4] without any difference. And when we had left them, we held our course west and by north, with a south and a south and by east wind; and when the sunne was west south west it began to thunder and raine, but it continued not long, for shortly after the weather began to cleare vp againe; and passing forward in that sort, we saw the sunne in our common compas go downe north and by west.[5]

The 13 of August we [again] had the wind against vs, being west south-west, and our course was west and by north, whereby we were forced to put to the shore againe,

[1] A Spanish dollar, of eight reals. [2] Boiled. [3] *Vier*—four.
[4] *Soo wel de minste als de meest*—the lowest as well as the highest.
[5] There must be some mistake here. When the sun set on the 12th of August, in latitude 68° N., his azimuth was 46° 37′,7 W., which would give a variation of 35° 22′,3, or more than 3 points W. Perhaps N.N.W. should be read, instead of N. by W.; which would make the variation to have been about 2 points W. It is, however, to be feared that but little dependance can be placed on the observations made during the return voyage, after the death of Willem Barentsz.

where two of our men went on the land to see how it laie, and whether the point of Candinaes reacht not out from thence into the sea, for we gest that we were not farre from it. Our men comming againe, showed vs that they had seene a house vpon the land, but no man in it, and said further that they could not perceaue but that it was the point of Candinaes that we had seene, wherewith we were somewhat comforted, and went into our scutes againe, and rowed along by the land; at which time hope made vs to be of good comfort, and procured vs to doe more then we could well haue done, for our liues and maintenance consisted therein. And in that sort rowing along by the land, we saw an other Russian iollie[1] lying vpon the shore, which was broken in peeces; but we past by it, and a little after that we saw a house at the water-side, whereunto some of our men went, wherein also they found no man, but only an ouen. And when they came againe to the scute, they brought some leple leaues[2] with them, which they had found[3] as they went. And as we rowed along by the point, we had [again] a good gale of winde[4] out of the east, at which time we hoised vp our sailes and sailed foreward. And after noone, about the south-west sunne, we perceaued that the point which we had seene laie south-ward, whereby we were fully perswaded that it was the point of Candinaes, from whence we ment[5] to saile ouer the mouth of the White Sea;[6] and to that end we borded each other and deuided our candles and all other things that we should need amongst vs,[7] to helpe our seules therewith, and so put of from the land, thinking to

[1] *Jolle*—yawl.   [2] *Lepelbladeren*—spoon-wort. See page 226, note 3.
[3] *Opghebluckt*—plucked.   [4] *Een moy coeltgen*—a nice breeze.
[5] Meant; intended. Misprinted "went".
[6] This point, which they mistook for "Candinaes", or Kanin Nos, was apparently Cape Barmin, on the east side of Tcheskaya Bay, over which they now proceeded to cross, under the impression that it was the White Sea.
[7] *Wat wy malcanderen mochten mede deelen* — that we could divide between us.

passe ouer the White Sea to the coast of Russia.[1] And sailing in that sort with a good winde, about midnight there rose a great storme out of the north, wherewith we stroke saile and made it shorter;[2] but our other boate, that was harder vnder saile,[3] (knowing not that we had lessened our sailes,) sailed foreward, whereby we straied one from the other, for then it was very darke.

The 14 of August in the morning, it being indifferent good weather with a south-west wind, we sailed west north-west, and then it began to cleare vp, so that we [just] saw our [other] boate, and did what we could to get vnto her, but we could not, because it began to be mistie weather againe; and therefore we said vnto each other, let vs hold on our course, we shal finde them wel enough on the north coast, when we are past the White Sea.[4] Our course was west north-west, the wind being south-west and by west, and about the south-west sunne, we could get no further, because the wind fel contrary, whereby we were forced to strike our sailes and to row forward; and in that sort, rowing till the sunne was west, there blew an indifferent gale of wind[5] out of the east, and therewith we set saile (and yet we rowed with two oares) till the sunne was north north-west, and then the wind began to blow somewhat stronger east and east south-east, at which time we tooke in our oares and sailed forward west north-west.

The 15 of August wee saw the sunne rise east north-east, wherevpon we thought that our compasse varied somewhat;[6]

[1] *Nae Ruslandt toe.* This is a mistake in the original. The coast of Norway or Lapland is meant.

[2] *Wy ons seijl streecken, ende namen een riff oft twee in*—we lowered our sail and took in a reef or two.

[3] *Onse maets die wat styrer onder seijl waren*—our comrades, who stood somewhat better under sail.

[4] *Aendt Noordtsche cust over de Witte Zee*—on the coast *of Norway*, on the other side of the White Sea.

[5] *Koelte*—breeze.

[6] *Vry wat*—a good deal. As the sun's azimuth at his rising was

and when the sunne was east it was calme weather againe, wherewith we were forced to take in our sailes and to row againe, but it was not long before wee had a gale of winde[1] out of the south-east, and then we hoysed vp our sailes againe, and went forward west and by south. And sayling in that manner with a good forewind,[2] when the sunne was south we saw land,[3] thinking that as then we had beene on the west side of the White Sea beyond Cardinaes; and being close vnder the land, we saw sixe Russian lodgies[4] lying there, to whom we sailed and spake with them, asking them how far wee were from Kilduin;[5] but although they vnderstood vs not well, yet they made vs such signes that we vnderstood by them that we were still farre from thence, and that we were yet on the east side of Candinaes. And with that they stroke their hands together,[6] thereby signifying y[t] we must first passe ouer the White Sea, and that our scutes were too little to doe it, and that it would be ouer great daunger for vs to passe ouer it with so small scutes, and that Candinaes was still north-west from vs. Then wee asked them for some bread, and they gaue vs a loafe, which [dry as it was] wee eate hungerly vp as wee were rowing, but wee would not beleeue them that we were still on the east side of Cardinaes, for we thought verily that wee had past ouer the White Sea. And when we left them, we rowed along by the land, the wind beeing north; and about the north-west sunne we had a good wind againe from the south-east, and therewith we sayled along by the shore, and saw a great Russian lodgie lying on the starreboord from vs, which we thought came out of the White Sea.

49° 56',5 W., the variation would be 17° 33',5 or about 1½ points W. This, as compared with the observation of the 12th August, *as recorded*, shows a considerable difference. But, as is remarked in the note on that observation, the error is more likely to be on that than on the present occasion.

[1] *Koelte*—breeze.   [2] *Een moye coelte*—a nice breeze.
[3] They had here reached the western side of Tcheskaya Bay.
[4] Boats.   [5] *Kilduijn*. See page 7, note 1.
[6] *Zy smeten haer handen van een*—they spread their hands out.

The 16 of August in the morning, sayling forward northwest, wee perceiued that we were in a creeke,[1] and so made towards yͤ Russian lodgie which we had seene on our starreboord, which at last with great labour and much paine we got vnto; and comming to them about the southeast sunne, with a hard wind, we asked them how farre we were from Sembla de Cool[2] or Kilduin; but they shooke their heads, and shewed us that we were on the east side of Zembla de Candinaes[3] but we would not beleeue them. And then we asked them [for] some victuals, wherewith they gaue vs certaine plaice, for the which the maister gaue them a peece of money, and [we] sailed from them againe, to get out of that hole where wee were,[4] as it reacht into the sea; but they perceiuing that we tooke a wrong course and that the flood was almost past, sent two men vnto vs, in a small boate, with a great loafe of bread, which they gaue vs, and made signes vnto vs to come aboord of their ship againe,[5] for that they intended to haue further speech with vs and to help[6] vs, which we seemed not to refuse and desiring not to be vnthankfull, gaue them a peece of money and a peece of linnen cloth, but they stayed still by vs, and they that were in the great lodgie held vp bacon and butter vnto vs, to mooue vs to come aboord of them againe, and so we did. And being with them, they showed vs that we were stil on the east side of the point of Candinaes; then we

[1] *Gantsch in een inham beset*—quite inclosed in a bay or creek. They would seem to have here been at the north-western corner of Tcheskaya Bay.

[2] *Vraeghen wy haer nae Sembla de Cool*—we asked them after *Sembla de Cool*. By this jargon, which is here a compound of Russian and *Spanish*, the Dutch seamen desired to obtain information respecting "the country of Kola", in Lapland.

[3] *Dattet Sembla de Candinas was*—that it was Sembla de Candinas; i.e., Kanineskaya Zemlya.

[4] *Om deur dat gat te comen daer zy voor lagen*—to get through the passage, before which they lay.

[5] *Weder aen haer schip*—back to their ship.

[6] *Onderrechten*—to instruct; to give information.

fetcht our card¹ and let them see it, by the which they shewed vs that we were still on the east side of the White Sea and of Candinaes; which we vnderstanding, were in some doubt with our selues² because we had so great a voiage to make ouer the White Sea, and were in more feare for our companions that were in the boate,³ as also yᵗ hauing sailed 22 [88] miles along by the Russian coast,⁴ we had gotten no further, but were then to saile ouer the mouth of the White Sea with so small prouision; for which cause the master bought of yᵉ Russians three sacks wᵗ meale, two flitches and a halfe of bacon, a pot of Russia butter, and a runlet of honny, for prouision for vs and our boate⁵ when we should meet with it againe. And for yᵗ in the meane time the flood was past, we sailed with the [beginning of the] ebbe out of the aforesaid creeke⁶ where the Russians boate⁷ came to vs, and entred into the sea with a good south-east wind, holding our course north north-west; and there we saw a point that reacht out into the sea, which we thought to be Candinaes, but we sailed still forward, and the land reached north-west.⁸ In the euening, the sunne being north-west, when we saw that we did not much good with rowing, and that the streame⁹ was almost past, we lay still, and sod¹⁰ a pot full of water and meale, which tasted exceeding well, because we had put some bacon fat and honny into it, so that we thought it to be a feastiuall day¹¹ with vs, but still our minds ran vpon our boate,¹² because we knew not where it was.

¹ *Caerte*—chart. ² *Waren beducht*—were alarmed. ³ *Bock*—yawl.
⁴ *Nu wy 22 mylen al over de zee waren geseylt*—now that we had sailed 22 miles right across the sea.
⁵ *Onse mackers*—our companions. ⁶ *Gat*—passage.
⁷ *Het cleyne lodtgien*—the little lodja or boat.
⁸ *Onviel hem n. w.*—turned to the N.W. This must have been Cape Mikalkin, the S.E. cape of Kanineskaya Zemlya.
⁹ *Stroom*—tide. ¹⁰ Boiled.
¹¹ *Datter kersmis was*—that it was *Christmas*. It is *kermis*, which means a festival or fair-day. See page 39, note 2.
¹² *Onse ander maets*—our other companions.

The 17 of August, lying at anchor, in the morning at breake of day we saw a Russian lodgie that came sayling out of the White Sea, to whom we rowed, that we might haue some instruction[1] from him; and when we boorded him, without asking or speaking vnto him, he gaue vs a loafe of bread, and by signes shewed vs as well as he could that he had seene our companions, and that there was seuen men in the boate; but we not knowing well what they sayd, neither yet beleeuing them, they made other signes vnto vs,[2] and held vp their seuen fingers and pointed to our scute, thereby shewing that there were so many men in the boate,[3] and that they had sold them bread, flesh, fish, and other victualls. And while we staid in their lodgie, we saw a small compasse therein, which we knew that they had bought[4] of our chiefe boatson,[5] which they likewise acknowledged. Then we vnderstanding them well, askt them how long it was since they saw our boate[6] and whereabouts it was, [and] they made signes vnto vs that it was the day before. And to conclude, they showed vs great friendship, for the which we thanked them; and so, being glad of the good newes wee had heard we tooke our leaues of them, much reioycing that wee heard of our companions welfare, and specially because they had gotten victuals from the Russians, which was the thing that wee most doubted of, in regard that we knew what small prouision they had with them. Which done, we rowed as hard as we could, to try if we might ouertake them, as being still in doubt that they had not prouision inough, wishing that we had had part of ours: and hauing rowed al that day with great labour along by the land, about mid-

[1] *Bescheyt*—information.
[2] *Soo beduyden zijt ons noch bet*—they explained it better to us.
[3] *Dattet mede sodanighen open schuijt was*—that it was a similar open boat.
[4] *Hadden*—had; obtained.
[5] *Hooghbootsman*—the chief-boatswain, or first mate.
[6] *Volck*—people.

night we found a fall of fresh water, and then we went on land to fetch some [water], and there also we got some leple leaues.[1] And as we thought to row forward, we were forced to saile, because the flood was past,[2] and still wee lookt earnestly out for the point of Candinaes, and the fiue crosses, whereof we had beene instructed by the Russians, but we could not see it.

The 18 of August in the morning, the sunne being east, [in order to gain time] wee puled vp our stone (which we vsed in steed of an anchor,[3]) and rowed along by the land till the sunne was south, then wee saw a point of land reaching into the sea, and on it certaine signes of crosses,[4] which as we went neerer vnto wee saw perfectly; and when the sunne was west, wee perceiued that the land reached west and south-west, so that thereby we knew it certainly to be the point of Candinaes, lying at the mouth of the White Sea, which we were to crosse, and had long desired to see it. This point is easily to be knowne, hauing fiue crosses standing vpon it, which are perfectly to be decerned, one the east side in the south-east, and one the other side in the south-west.[5] And when we thought to saile from thence to the west side of the White Sea towards the coast of Norway, we found that one of our runlets of fresh water was almost leakt out; and for that we had about 40 Dutch [160] miles to saile ouer the sea before we should get any fresh water, we

---

[1] See page 226, note 3.

[2] *Ende als wy meenden voort te varen, so moesten wy daer blyven liggen, want den stroom verloopen was*—and when we intended to proceed on our voyage, we were forced to remain lying there, because the tide had run out.

[3] *Werp-ancker*—kedge.

[4] *Schemeringe van eenige cruycen*—the faint images of some crosses.

[5] *Desen hoeck is een kenlijcken hoeck met 5 cruycen daer op, ende dat men perfect can sien hoese aen beyden syden omvalt, aen de eene zyde int z. o. ende d'ander zyde int z. w.*—this point is a conspicuous one, having on it five crosses, and the direction of it on either side is perfectly discernible; it being on the one side towards the S.E., and on the other side towards the S.W.

sought meanes first to row on land to get some, but because the waues went so high we durst not do it; and so hauing a good north-east wind (which was not for vs too slack[1]) we set forward in the name of God, and when the sunne was north-west we past the point,[2] and all that night and the next day sailed with a good wind, and [in] all that time rowed but while three glasses were run out;[3] and the next night after ensuing hauing still a good wind, in the morning about the east north-east sunne we saw land one the west side of the White Sea, which we found by the rushing of the sea vpon the land before we saw it. And perceiuing it to be ful of clifts,[4] and not low sandy ground with same hills[5] as it is on the east side of the White Sea, we assured our selues[6] that we were on ye west side of the White Sea, vpon the coast of Lapeland, for the which we thanked God that he had helped vs to saile over the White Sea in thirty houres, it being forty Dutch [160] miles at the least, our course being west with a [nice] north-east wind.

The 20 of August, being not farre from the land, the north-east wind left vs, and then it began to blow stiffe north-west; at which time, seeing we could not make much way by sailing forward, we determined to put in betweene certaine clifts, and when we got close to the land we espied certaine crosses with warders[7] vpon them, whereby we vnderstood that it was a good way,[8] and so put into it. And

---

[1] *Die wy niet dienden te versuymen*—which it would not do for us to neglect.

[2] *Ende maeckten een afsteecker ontrent de son n. w.*— we took our departure when the sun was about N.W.

[3] An hour and a half.

[4] *Dat dit een ander clippich lant was* — that it was another rocky shore.

[5] *Met weynich geberchte*—with few mountains.   [6] Made sure.

[7] *Waerders*—cautions; directions.

[8] *Dat daer een goede reede was*— that there was a good *roadstead* there.

being entred a litle way within it, we saw a great Russian lodgie[1] lying at an anchor, whereunto we rowed as fast as we could, and there also we saw certaine houses wherein men dwelt. And when we got to the lodgie, we made our selues fast vnto it,[2] and cast our tent ouer the scute, for as then it began to raine. Then we went on land into the houses that stood vpon the shore, where they showed vs great friendship, leading vs into their stoawes,[3] and there dried our wet clothes, and then seething some fish, bade vs sit downe and eate somewhat with them.[4] In those little houses we found thirteene Russians, who euery morning went out [in two boats] to fish in the sea; whereof two of them had charge ouer the rest. They liued very poorely, and ordinarily eate nothing but fish and bread.[5] At euening, when we prepared our selues to go to our scute againe, they prayed the maister and me to stay with them in their houses, which the maister thanked them for, would not do [and went into the boat], but I stayed with them al that night. Besides those thirteene men, there was two Laplanders more and three women with a child, that liued very poorely of the ouerplus[6] which the Russians gaue them, as a peece of fish and some fishes heades, which the Russians threw away and they with great thankfulnesse tooke them vp, so that in respect of their pouertie [and ill condition] we thought our selues to bee well furnished,[7] and yet we had little inough, but as it seemed their ordinary liuing was in that manner. And we were forced to

---

[1] *Lodja* or boat.

[2] *So maeckten wy ons daer vast*—we anchored there.

[3] *Zy leyden ons in haer stoven*—they led us into their rooms. In Dutch, as in German, a room heated by a stove or oven is called by the name of the latter, *stove* or *stube*.

[4] *Coocten ons een sode visch, ende nooden ons seer hertelijck*—cooked us a dish of fish, and made us right welcome.

[5] *Visch tot visch*—lit. fish with fish; *i.e.*, nothing but fish.

[6] *Overschot*—remains.

[7] *Wy . . . ons heel ontsetteden*—we were quite astonished.

stay there for that the wind being north-west, it was against vs.

The 21 of August it rained most part of the day, but not so much after dinner as before. Then our master brought[1] good store of fresh fish, which we sod,[2] and eate our bellies full, which in long time we had not done, and therewith sod some meale and water in steed of bread, whereby we were well comforted. After noone, when the raine began to lessen, we went [at times a little] further into the land and sought for some leple leaues,[3] and then we saw two men vpon yᵉ hilles, whereupon we said one to the other, hereabouts there must more people dwel, for there came two men towards vs, but we, regarding them not, went back againe to our scute and towards the houses. The two men that were vpon the hilles (being some of our men that were in the [other] boate,) perceauing [also] the Russian lodgie, came downe the hill towards her to buy[4] some victuales of them; who being come thither vnawares[5] and hauing no mony about them, they agreed betweene them to put off one of their paire of breeches, (for that as then we ware two or three paire one ouer the other,) to sel them for some victuals.[6] But when they came downe the hill and were somewhat neerer vnto vs, they espied our scute lying by the lodgie, and we as then beheld them better and knew them; wherewith we reioyced [much on both sides], and shewed each other of our proceedings and how we had sailed to and fro in great necessity and hunger and yet they had been in greater necessitie and danger then we, and gaue God thankes that he had preserued vs aliue and brought vs together againe. And then we eate something together, and

---

[1] *Cocht*—bought.
[2] *Coockten*—cooked.
[3] *Lepel bladeren*—spoon-wort or scurvy-grass. See page 226, note 3.
[4] *Te becomen*—to procure; to obtain.
[5] *Onversiens*—unprepared.
[6] *Om daer eten voor te coopen*—to buy victuals therewith.

dranke of the cleare water, such as runneth along by Collen through the Rein,[1] and then we agreed that they should come vnto vs, that we might saile together.

The 22 of August the rest of our men[2] with the boate came unto vs about the east south-east sunne, whereat we much reioyced, and then we prayed the Russians cooke to bake a sacke of meale for vs and to make it bread, paying him for it, which he did. And in the meane time, when the fishermen came with their fishe out of the sea, our maister bought foure cods of them, which we sod and eate. And while we were at meat, the chiefe of the Russians came vnto vs, and perceiuing that we had not much bread, he fetcht a loaf and gave it vs, and although we desired them to sit downe and eate some meat with vs, yet we could by no means get them to graunt thereunto, because it was their fasting day and for y*t* we had poured butter and fat into our fish; nor we could not get them once to drinke with us, because our cup was somewhat greasie, they were so superstitious touching their fasting and religion. Neither would they lend vs any of their cups to drinke in, least they should likewise be greased. At that time the wind was [constantly] north-west.

The 23 of August the cooke began to knead our meale, and made vs bread thereof; which being don, and the wind and the weather beginning to be somewhat better, we made our selues ready to depart from thence; at which time, when the Russians came from fishing, our maister gaue their chiefe commander a good peece of mony[3] in regard of the

[1] *Ende gedroncken van den claren, als in den Rhijn voorby Colen loopt*—and drank of the *pure article*, such as flows past Cologne in the Rhine. There is here a play on the word *clar*, which signifies "clear", "pure", but is applied to spirits as well as to water. In common life, *een glaasje klare* means "glass of neat Hollands gin".

[2] *Ons ander maets*—our other comrades.

[3] *Een goeden drincpennick*—a handsome present: *lit.* a good drinkpenny.

frendship that he had shewed vs, and gaue some what also to the cooke,¹ for the which they yielded vs great thankes. At which time, the chiefe of the Russians [having before] desired our maister to giue him some gunpowder, which he did, [and he also thanked him much.] And when we were ready to saile from thence, we put a sacke of meale [out of our boat] into the boate,² least we should chance to stray one from the other againe, that they might help themselues therewith. And so about euening, when the sunne was west, we set saile and departed from thence when it began to be high water, and with a north-east wind held our course north-west along by the land.

The 24 of August the wind blew east, and then, the sunne being east, we got to the Seuen Islands,³ where we found many fishermen, of whom we enquired after Cool and Kilduin, and they made signes that they lay west from vs, (which we likewise gest to be so.) And withall they shewed vs great frendship, and cast a cod into our scute, but for that we had a good gale of wind⁴ we could not stay to pay them for it, but gaue them great thanks, much wondering at their great courtesy. And so, with a good gale of wind, we arriued before the Seven Islands when the sun was southwest, and past between them and the land, and there found certaine fishermen, that rowed to vs,⁵ and asked vs where our crable (meaning our ship) was, whereunto wee made answer with as much Russian language as we had learned, and said, *Crable pro pal*⁶ (y^t is, our ship is lost), which they

---

¹ *Den cock mede betaelt*—also paid the cook.
² *Den bock*—the yawl.   ³ See page 203, note 4.
⁴ *Also wy goeden voortgang hadden*—as we were making good way.
⁵ *Met goeden voortgangh seylende, quamen wy outrent de z. w. son verby de selvige eylanden langs de wal henen, onder eenighe visschers die na ons toe royden*—making good speed, we passed the said islands about southwest sun, and sailed along the coast among some fishermen, who rowed towards us.
⁶ *Crabble propal*. See page 224.

vnderstanding said vnto vs, *Cool Brabouse crable*,¹ whereby we vnderstood that at Cool there was certaine Neatherland ships, but we made no great account thereof, because our intent was to saile to Ware-house,² fearing least the Russians or great prince of the country would stay vs there.³

The 25 of August, sailing along by the land with a southeast wind, about the south sun we had a sight of Kilduin, at which time we held our course west north-west. And sailing in that manner between Kilduin and the firme land, about the south south-west sunne we got to the west end of Kilduin. And being there [we] lookt [out sharp] if we could see any houses or people therein, and at last we saw certaine Russian lodgies⁴ that lay [hauled up] upon the strand, and there finding a conuenient place for vs to anchor with our scutes while we went to know if any people were to be found, our maister put in with the land,⁵ and there found five or six small houses, wherein the Laplanders dwelt, of whom he⁶ asked if that were Kilduin, whereunto they made answere and shewed vs that it was Kilduin, and said y^t at Coola there lay three Brabants crables or ships, whereof two were that day to set saile; which we hearing determined to saile to Ware-house, and about the west south-west sunne put off from thence with a southeast wind. But as we were vnder saile, the wind blew

---

¹ *Tot Cool Brabanse crable.* A mixture of Dutch and Russian, meaning "at Kola there are Brabant ships". The correct Russian is *v'Kolye Brabantskyie korabli.* Before the independence of the northern provinces, the entire Netherlands were under the rule of the Dukes of Brabant; and as the Dutch vessels trading to the northern coasts of Europe had first come there under the Brabant flag, the Russians not unnaturally continued to attach the name of Brabant to them in common with other Netherlandish vessels.

² *Waerhuysen.* See page 39, note 1.

³ *Dat de Russen oft Grootvorst ep haer grensen ons eenich verlet soude doen*—that the Russians or (their) Grand Prince might do us some injury on their frontiers.

⁴ Boats.

⁵ *Wat te lantwaerts ingegaen*—going a little way on shore.

⁶ "We."—*Ph.*

so stiffe [from the south-east] that we durst not keepe
the sea in the night time, for that the waues of the
sea went so hollow, that we were still in doubt that
they would smite the scutes to the ground,[1] and so tooke
our course behind two clifts[2] towards our land. And
when we came there, we found a small house vpon the
shore, wherein there was three men and a great dogge,
which receiued vs very friendly, asking vs of our affaires
and how we got thither; whereunto we made answere and
shewed them that we had lost our ship, and that we
were come thither to see if we could get a ship that
would bring vs into Holland; whereunto they made vs
answere, as the other Russians had done, that there was
three ships at Coola, whereof two were to set saile from
thence that day. Then we asked them if they would goe
with one of our men by land to Coola, to looke for a ship
wherewith we might get into Holland, and said we would
reward them well for their paines; but they excused themselues,
and said that they could not go from thence, but they
sayd that they would bring vs ouer the hill, where we should
finde certaine Laplanders whom they thought would goe
with vs, as they did; for the maister and one of our men
going with them ouer the hill, found certaine Laplanders
there, whereof they got one to go with our man, promising
him two royals of eight[3] for his pains. And so the Laplander
going with him, tooke a peece on his necke,[4] and our
man a boate hooke, and about euening they set forward,[5] the
wind as then being east and east north-east.

[1] *Wy meenden dat se telckemael de schuyten in den gront gesmeten souden hebben*—we thought that each wave would have swamped the boats.
[2] *Twee clippen*—two cliffs or rocks.
[3] *Twee realen van achten.* This, though incorrect, was an usual expression in Dutch. It means, properly, two Spanish dollars *of eight reals.*
[4] *Nam een roer mede*—took a musket with him.
[5] *Ende trocken noch teghen den nae nacht op ter loop*—and set off before break of day – *lit.* towards the after-night.

The 26 of August it was faire weather, the wind southeast, at which time we drew vp both our scutes vpon the land, and tooke all the goods out of them, to make them the lighter.[1] Which done, we went to the Russians and warmed vs, and there dressed such meates[2] as we had; and then againe wee began to make two meales a day, when we perceiued that we should euery day find more people, and we drank of their drink which they call *quas*,[3] which was made of broken peeces of [mouldy] bread, and it tasted well, for in long time we had drunke nothing else but water. Some of our men went [somewhat] further into the land, and there found blew berries and bramble berries,[4] which they plucked and eate, and they did us much good, for we found that they [perfectly] healed vs of our loosenesse.[5] The wind still blew south-east.

The 27 of August it was foule weather with a great storm [out of the] north and north north-west, so that in regard that the strand was low,[6] and as also for that the spring tide was ready to come on, we drew our scutes a great way vp vpon the land. [And when we had thus drawn them much higher up than we had done before, on account of the high water[7]], we went [still further upwards] to the Russians, to warme vs by their fire and to dress our meate. Mean time the maister

[1] *Om dat wat te verluchten*—to air them a little.   [2] *Spyse*—food.
[3] *Quas.* The well-known Russian drink. Dr. Giles Fletcher, ambassador from Queen Elizabeth to the Emperor Fedor in 1588, describes it as "a thin drinke called Quasse, which is nothing else (as we say) but *water turned out of his wits*, with a little bran meashed with it."—*Purchas*, vol. iii, p. 459.
[4] *Blauwe-besyen met Braem-besyen*—bilberries and blackberries The latter are probably the *Moroschka* —cloudberries, or fruit of the mountain-bramble (*Rubus chamæmorus*),—the gathering and preparation of which by the females of Kola are described by Lütke, in page 223 of his oft-cited work.
[5] *Scheurbuyck*—scurvy. See page 152, note 2.
[6] *Wy daer een lager wal hadden*—we there had a lee shore.
[7] Phillip substitutes for this the words "this having done".

sent one of our men to the sea side to our scutes, to make a
fire for vs vpon the strand, that when we came we might
finde it ready, and that in the meane time the smoake might
be gone. And while [the] one of our men was there, and the
other was going thither,[1] the water drauo so high that both
our scutes were smitten into the water and in great danger
to be cast away; for in the scute there was but two men and
three in the boate, who with much labour and paine could
hardly keep the scutes from being broken vpon the strand.[2]
Which we seeing, were in great doubt,[3] and yet could not
help them, yet God be thanked he had then brought vs so
farre that neuerthelesse we could haue gotten home, although we should have lost our scutes, as after it was
seene. That day and all night it rained sore, whereby we
indured great trouble and miserie, being throughly wet, and
could neither couer nor defend our selues from it; and yet
they [who were] in the scutes indured much more, being
forced to bee in that weather, and still in daunger to bee
cast vpon the shore.[4]

The 28 of August it was indifferent good weather, and
then we drew the scutes vpon the land againe, that we
might take the rest of the goods out of them, [in order to
avoid the like danger in which the boats had been,] because the wind still blew hard north and north north-west.
And hauing drawne the scutes vp, we spread our sailes
vpon them to shelter vs vnder them, for it was still mistie
and rainie weather, much desiring to heare some newes of
our man that was gone to Coola with the Lapelander, to

[1] *D'ander vast aenquamen*—the others were fast approaching.

[2] *De schuyten qualijck van den wal conden houden, dat se met in stucken ghesmeten werden*—could scarcely keep the boats from going on shore, and thereby being dashed to pieces.

[3] *Seer beducht*—much alarmed.

[4] *Datse in sulcken weer ende reghen aende legher wal verblyven moesten*—that in such wind and rain they should have had to lie under a lee shore.

know if there were any shipping at Coola to bring vs into Holland. And while we laie there we went [daily] into the land and fetcht some blew berries and bramble berries[1] to eate, which did vs much good.

The 29 of August it was indifferent faire weather, and we were still in good hope[2] to heare some good newes from Coola, and alwaies looked vp towards the hill to see if our man and the Lapelander came; but seeing they came not[3] we went to the Russians againe, and there drest our meate [at their fire], and then ment[4] to goe to our scutes to lodge in them all night. In the meane time we spied the Laplander [upon the hill] comming alone without our man, whereat we wondred and were some what in doubt;[5] but when he came vnto vs, he shewed vs a letter that was written vnto our maister, which he opened before vs, the contents thereof being that he that had written the letter wondred much at our arriuall in that place, and that long since he verily thought that we had beene all cast away,[6] being exceeding glad of our happy fortune,[7] and how that he would presently come vnto vs with victuales and all other necessaries to succour vs withall. We being in no small admiration who it might be that shewed vs so great fauour and friendship, could not imagine what he was, for it appeared by the letter that he knew vs well. And although the letter was subscribed "by me John Cornelison Rip,"[8] yet we could not be perswaded that it was the same John Cornelison, who the yeere before had beene set out in the other ship [at the same

[1] See page 249, note 4.
[2] *Met lijtsaemheyt verhopende*—hoping with resignation.
[3] *Ende de saecke dien dach opgherende*—and giving the matter up for that day.
[4] Meant.   [5] *In beducht*—in fear.
[6] *Dat wy al lange om den hals gecomen waren*—that we had lost our lives long ago.
[7] *Over onse comste*—of our arrival.
[8] *Jan Cornelisz. Rijp.* See page 71.

time] with vs, and left vs about the Beare Iland.[1] For those goode newes we paid the Lapelander his hier,[2] and beside that gaue him hoase, breeches and other furniture,[3] so that he was apparelled like a Hollander; for as then we thought our selues to be wholy out of danger,[4] and so being of good comfort, we laid vs downe to rest. Here I cannot chuse but shew you how fast the Lapelander went: for when hee went to Coola, as our companion told vs, they were two dayes and two nights on the way, and yet went a pace, and when he came backe againe he was but a day and a night comming to vs, which was wonderful, it being but halfe ye time, so that we said, and verily thought, that he was halfe a coniurer;[5] and he brought vs a partridge, which he had killed by the way as he went.

The 30 of August it was indifferent faire weather, we still wondering who that John Cornelison might be that had written vnto vs; and while we sat musing thereon, some of vs were of opinion that it might be the same John Cornelison that had sayled out of Holland in company with vs, which we could not be perswaded to beleeue, because we were in as little hope of his life as hee of ours, supposing that he had sped worse then we, and long before that had [perished or] beene caste away. At last the master said, I will looke amongst my letters, for there I haue his name written,[6] and that will put us out of doubt. And so, looking amongst them, we found that it was the same John Cornelison, wherewith we were as glad of his safety and welfare as he was of ours. And while we were speaking thereof, and that some

[1] See page 85.
[2] *Zijn beloofde penningen*—his promised reward: *lit*. pence.
[3] Clothes.
[4] *Ghenoech in behouden haren*—sufficiently in a safe port.
[5] *Dat wy tot malcanderen seyde, hy moet kunsyens kunnen*—so that we said to one another, he must know some (conjuring) tricks.
[6] *Daer heb ick zijn hant noch wel*—there I certainly still have his handwriting.

of vs would not beleeue that it was the same John Cornelison, we saw a Russian joll[1] come rowing, with John Cornelison and our companion that we had sent to Coola; who being landed, we receiued and welcomed each other w*t* great joy and exceeding gladnesse, as if either of vs on both sides had seene each other rise from death to life again; for we esteemed him, and he vs, to be dead long since. He brought vs a barrell of Roswicke beere,[2] wine, aqua uite,[3] bread, flesh, bacon, salmon, suger, and other things, which comforted and releeued vs much. And wee rejoyced together for our so vnexpected [safety and] meeting, at that time giuing God great thankes for his mercy shewed vnto vs.

The 31 of August it was indifferent faire weather, the wind easterly, but in the evening it began to blow hard from the land; and then we made preparation to saile from thence to Coola, first taking our leaues of the Russians, and heartily thanking them for their curtesie showed vnto vs, and gaue them a peece of money[4] for their good wils, and at night about the north sunne we sailed from thence with a high water.[5]

The 1 of September in the morning, with the east sunne, we got to y*e* west side of the river of Coola,[6] and entered into it, where we [sailed and] rowed till the flood was past, and then we cast the stones that serued vs for anchors vpon the ground, at a point of land, till the flood came in againe. And when the sunne was south, wee set saile againe with the flood, and so sailed and rowed till midnight, and then we cast anchor againe till morning.

[1] *Een jol*—a yawl.
[2] *Rostwijcker-bier.* A strong beer brewed at Roswick, a town of Sweden, in West Bothnia.
[3] *Brandewijn*—spirits distilled from malt; common Hollands gin.
[4] *Een stuck ghelts*—some money.
[5] *Mettet hoochste water*—at high water; at the top of the tide.
[6] "The entrance to Kola, which by some is most incorrectly called a river, is one of those bays to which the English apply the designation of Inlet or Frith."—*Lütke*, p. 225.

The 2 of September in the morning we rowed vp the riuer, and as we past along we saw some trees on the riuer side, which comforted vs and made vs as glad as if we had then come into a new world, for in all the time y^t we had beene out we had not seene any trees; and when we were by the salt kettles,[1] which is about three [12] miles from Coola, we stayed there awhile and made merry, and then went forward againé, and with the west north-west sun got to John Cornelisons ship, wherein we entred and drunke.[2] There wee began to make merry againe with the sailers that were therein and that had beene in the voiage with John Cornelison the yeare before and bad each other welcome. Then we rowed forward, and late in the euening got to Coola, where some of vs went on land, and some stayed in the scutes to looke to the goods, to whom we sent milke and other things to comfort and refresh them; and we were all exceeding glad that God of his mercy had deliuered vs out of so many dangers and troubles, and had brought vs thither in safety: for as then wee esteemed our selues to be safe, although y$_e$ place in times past, lying so far from vs, was as much vnknowne vnto vs as if it had beene out of the world, and at that time, being there, we thought y^t we were almost at home.

The 3 of September we vnladed all our goods, and there refreshed our selues after our toylesome and weary iourney and the great hunger that we had indured, thereby to recouer our healthes and strengthes againe.

The 11 of September,[3] by leaue and consent of the

[1] *De soutketen*—the salt-works. The buildings in which the manufacture of salt is carried on are called in Dutch *keten*.

[2] *Daer wy eens overclommen ende droncken daer eens*—into which we clambered up, and there had something to drink.

[3] *Den elfden dag*—on the eleventh day. This would seem to have been the eleventh day *after their arrival*, or after the 3rd of September, rather than the 11th of the month. Reckoned exclusively of that day, it would have been the 14th of September; and it is reasonable to suppose that they would not have parted with their boats till they had found a Russian *lodja* to receive them.

bayart,[1] gouernour for the Great Prince of Muscouia, we brought our scute and our boate into the merchants house,[2] and there let them stand[3] for a remembrance of our long, farre, and neuer before sailed way, and that we had sailed in those open scutes almost 400 Dutch [1600] miles, through and along by the sea coasts to the towne of Coola, whereat the inhabitants thereof could not sufficiently wonder.

The 15 of Sep[tember] we went into a lodgie [and sailed down the river] w^t all our goods and our men to John Cornelisons ship, which lay about half a mile [2 miles] from the towne, and that day [at noon] sailed in the ship [further] downe the riuer til we were beyond the narrowest part therof, which was about half the riuer, and there staied for John Cornelison and our maister, that said they would come to vs the next day.

The 17 of September [in the evening] John Cornelison and our maister being come abord, the next day about the east sunne we set saile out of the riuer [of] Coola, and with Gods grace put to sea to saile hom-wards; and being out of the riuer we sailed along by the land north-west and by north, the wind being south.

The 19 of September, about the south sunne, we got to Ware-house, and there ankored and went on land, because John Cornelison was there to take in more goods, and staid there til the sixt of October, in the which time we had a[4] hard wind out of the north and north-west. And while we stayed there we refreshed our selues somewhat better, to recouer [from] our sicknesse and weaknesse againe, that we

[1] *Den Baynert*—the boyard; a Russian title, signifying a nobleman, great man, or chief.

[2] *Int coopmans huys*. This is a literal translation of the Russian *gostinuy dvor'*, which is a collection of shops, corresponding to the *bazar* of the Persians. It is usually, but not invariably, situated in or near the market-place.

[3] *Lieten die daer staen*—left them there.

[4] *Veel*—much.

256   THE NAVIGATION

might grow stronger, which asked sometime,[1] for we were much spent and exceeding weake.

The 6 of October, about euening, the sunne being southwest, we set saile, and with Gods grace, from Ware-house for Holland; but for that it is a common and well knowne way, I will speak nothing thereof, only that vpon the 29 October we ariued in the Mase[2] with an east north-east wind, and the next morning got to Maseland sluce,[3] and there going on land, from thence rowed to Delfe, and then to the Hage, and from thence to Harlem;[4] and vpon the first of Nouember about noone got to Amsterdam, in the same clothes that we ware in Noua Zembla, with our caps furd with white foxes skins,[5] and went to the house of Peter Hasselaer, that was one of the marchants that set out the two ships,[6] which were conducted by John Cornelison and our maister. And being there, where many men woundred to see vs, as hauing estemed vs long before that to haue bin dead and rotten, the newes thereof being spread abroad in the towne, it was also caried to the Princes Courte in the Hage,[7] at which time the Lord Chancelor of Denmark, ambassador for the said king, was then at dinner with Prince Maurice.[8] For the which cause we were presently fetcht

---

[1] *Dat metter tijt gheschieden moeste*—which required some time.
[2] *De Maes*—the river Maas or Meuse.
[3] *Maeslantsluys*. A town on the river Maas, opposite the Briel.
[4] *Reysde also deur Delft, den Haech ende Haerlem*—thence travelled through Delft, the Hague, and Haerlem.
[5] *Bonte mutsen van witte vossen*—white fox-skin caps.
[6] *Een van de bewinthebbers der stadt van Amstelredam ghewcest was, tot uytrustinge van de twee schepen*—who had been one of the managers, on behalf of the town of Amsterdam, for fitting out the two ships.
[7] *Int Princen Hof*. This was formerly the Court of Admiralty at Amsterdam. But when the Town-House was given as a palace to Louis Napoleon, then King of Holland, the Prinzen Hof was converted into the Town-House, which it still is.
[8] *Aldaer op die tijdt mijn E. Heeren den Cancelier ende Ambassadeur van den Allerdoorluchtichsten Coninck van Dennemarcken, Noorweghen,*

thither by the scout and two of the burgers of the towne,¹ and there in the presence of those ambassadors² and the burger masters we made rehearsall of our journey both forwards and backewards.³ And after that, euery man that dwelt thereabouts went home, but such as dwelt not neere to that place were placed in good lodgings for certaine daies, vntill we had receiued our pay, and then euery one of vs departed and went to the place of his aboad.

*The Names of those that came home againe from this*⁴ *Voiage were*⁵:—

Jacob Hemskeck, Maister and Factor.
Peter Peterson Vos.

Gotten ende Wenden over tafel sadt—where the noble lords, the chancellor and the ambassador from the most illustrious King of Denmark, Norway, Goths and Vandals, were then at table. In the original there is not a word about Prince Maurice and the Hague.

¹ *Mijn Heer de Schout ende twee Heeren van der stadt*—master sheriff and two gentlemen of the town (*i.e.*, town-councillors).
² *Den voornoemde Heere Ambassadeur*—the said lord ambassador.
³ *Onse reysen ende wedervaren*—our voyages and adventures.
⁴ Phillip here inserts the word "dangerous".
⁵ The names will be here repeated, for the purpose of giving them correctly, and also showing those who died during the voyage:—

Iacob Heemskerck, *Supercargo and Skipper.*
† WILLEM BARENTSZ., *Pilot* (died June 20th, 1597).
Pieter Pietersz. Vos.
Gerrit de Veer.
M. Hans Vos, *Barber-surgeon.*
† Name unknown, *Carpenter* (died September 23rd, 1596).
Iacob Iansz. Sterrenburgh.
Lenaert Heyndricksz.
Laurens Willemsz.
Ian Hillebrantsz.
Iacob Iansz. Hooghwout.
Pieter Cornelisz.
Ian van Buysen Reyniersz.
Iacob Evertsz.
† Name unknown (died January 27th, 1597).
† Claes Andriesz. (died June 20th, 1597).
† Ian Fransz. (died July 5th, 1597).

Geret de Veer.
Maister Hans Vos, Surgion.
Jacob Johnson, Sterenburg.
Lenard Hendrickson.
Laurence Williamson.
John Hillbrantson.
Jacob Johnson Hooghwont.
Peter Cornelison.
John Vous Buysen.
and Jacob Euartson.

FINIS.

These make up the ship's company, which originally consisted of seventeen persons in all. The seeming discrepancy with regard to two of the names, as they appear in the list in page 193, is easily explained away. Iacob Ianszoon Hooghwout, of Schiedam, and Ian van Buysen Reynierszoon, have here their family names given in addition to their patronymics, which latter alone they had signed in the former list.